Website Automation Toolkit

Paul Helinski

WILEY COMPUTER PUBLISHING

John Wiley & Sons, Inc.
New York • Chichester • Weinheim • Brisbane • Singapore • Toronto

Publisher: Robert Ipsen
Editor: Robert M. Elliott
Managing Editor: Marnie Wielage
Electronic Products, Associate Editor: Mike Sosa
Text Design & Composition: Benchmark Productions, Boston, MA

Library of Congress Cataloging-in-Publication Data:
Helinski, Paul, 1966–
        Website automation toolkit / Paul Helinski.
              p. cm
        Includes index.
        ISBN 0-471-19785-8 (paper/CD-ROM)
        1. Web sites--Design.   2. Utilities (Computer programs)
        I. Title.
        TK5105.888.H44   1998   97-31687
        005.3'78--dc21   CIP

Printed in the United States of America

10 9 8 7 6 5 4 3 2 1

Contents

The Webmaster
Bottleneck

Has your website imploded yet? My company's did, and so did that of most of our clients. We found that keeping the sites fresh was too time consuming a task to be affordable. Regular updates were time consuming, and HTML jockeys were too expensive to justify the work. Our problem was never lack of hits. It wasn't lack of exposure. It wasn't even that the sites didn't produce. Our problem was getting the new content onto the site. Though several people were writing articles, updating FAQ files, and creating images, only a few designated webmasters could compose and upload new pages. HTML isn't hard; many programs do it for you. But editing the old files with new hotlinks to the new documents takes time, and often we'd have to make global changes to the whole site at one time. The process log-jammed and the sites got stale. I call it the *webmaster bottleneck*.

Imagine a website that administrates itself. Add a new document, and the old ones automatically include a new hotlink to it. Need a color change for the whole site? Hit a web form with your browser, choose the colors and click Submit. The whole site changes. Notify visitors of updates, track statistics, connect a database, run a shopping cart, whatever the bottleneck, we had to find a way to automate it. So in the fall of 1995 my company stopped marketing for new clients and set down to make a set of utilities that would solve our problems. What follows in this book is the result. Whether your site is small, medium, or large, you'll eventually discover the webmaster bottleneck, and in these pages you'll find an answer. These utilities range from a simple wrapper that keeps all your header, footer, and other changing information in one place, to an automail utility that notifies visitors of changes, to a remote authoring tool that allows novices to add pages into the site without a learning curve.

"Oh, this is like FrontPage," you may be saying. No, it's not. FrontPage, Fusion, and other commercial tools have three major problems. First, any changes to the site are made on a local copy of the files, then "published" to the server, so if several webmasters work on the site from different workstations, they will overwrite each other's work. Second, the server component is weak. It allows for little more than the standard server side includes known to most novice webmasters. There are other minor tricks, but none offer the freedom of customization with a long established programming language like the utilities here.

And third, proprietary systems are just that, proprietary. You have no sourcecode to modify, no universal operating system to run the code. Move the website from one server to another and your site could be rendered useless. If your ISP goes out of business, which is a frequent occurrence, you're stuck. The World Wide Web is about cross-platform portability and access. Proprietary systems like FrontPage don't offer that. With the exception of a few, the programs here are written in Perl and portable to any flavor of Unix and NT. I'm not bashing FrontPage; Chapter 3 shows its utility. We'll also install its bulletin board. I'm actually a Microsoft proponent.

But overall, that's what you should expect. My company, World Media Services, developed most of the utilities here and modified others from direct experience with real World Wide Web sites. Each chapter will address a specific issue and provide a way for you to reduce your administrative overhead. Each will make your site more alive, with more ease of use than your static site has now.

Who Needs This Book?

At first glance this might look like a beginner's CGI book but it's not. Granted, I don't assume you know a programming language, but that's only to make the how-to sections accessible to all. I didn't know anything when I began this process and I don't expect my readers to either. If you're a novice, with only a good understanding of HTML, don't be intimidated by the raw code. If you're a Perl guru and see that you potentially could write these utilities yourself, let us save you some work. Developing these took many months of trial and error to determine what our clients needed. Debugging has been an ongoing process that now seems complete. Experienced programmers should just skip the chapters that don't apply.

The target audience of this book is any webmaster who has had enough of wasting time on repetitive, menial tasks. Beginners will find utility here, gurus will find utility here, anyone with an understanding of the web's production problems and an inquiring mind will find utility here. You don't have to reinvent the wheel. This stuff is very easy to install and customize, with flexibility beyond the capabilities of any proprietary system.

For beginners, intermediates, and nontechnical information specialists, take the ideas here and implement them from the front-end backwards. You've learned how to make a pretty site, an interesting site, and, hopefully, a usable site. The bottleneck is waiting. Leapfrog your contemporaries and competitors by automating from the start. You'll be glad you did.

Corporate Webmasters

"You have until Friday to construct a new section containing every press release we've ever sent to the media. Fred from the PR department will fax them to you on Thursday."

Sound familiar? This type of thing happens to corporate webmasters every day. Lots of content, in several formats, coming from people who know nothing about the cumbersome process of hand coding pages. You have to deal with what the industry has termed *shovelware*, existing documents repurposed for the web. In Chapter 11, you'll install an automation system that makes inserting new documents a no-brainer. The people producing the content will post it to the web interactively. They'll do it from a webform. Hit Submit and it's on the web, hotlinked in and live.

Don't worry, you won't be putting yourself out of a job. The utilities here will free you of mundane, repetitive tasks and allow you to learn more about, and how to tackle, the fun stuff. If you're tired of changing the legal disclaimer at the bottom of every page after the seventh time, fear not. Those days are over.

You'll be challenged by the utilities I offer. To install them is easy, but to gain a real advantage you'll learn the little bit of Perl I'll show you and will transform your static corporate web into a vital center of activity for you and your customers.

Small Web Companies

To maintain a competitive advantage, the small enterprise web company has to stay on top of the web's latest and greatest capabilities. This doesn't, however, mean chasing Java applets through several phases of development. It's all about capabilities. What can you provide to your customers that will make the most of every hit to their website? That can mean reducing their maintenance costs by automating some simple tasks. It can mean installing a discussion area, like we'll do in Chapter 15, that will allow your clients to remove offensive messages interactively, with a password in real-time. Throughout this book I'll outline utilities to optimize interactivity and results from all webs, small, medium, and large.

If you've built even one static site you've seen the limitations of HTML, JavaScript, and other client-based interactive systems. You've also seen how much time it takes between the time a customer generates a page of content and when it ends up on the site. If your company is successful and has received a bunch of work orders at once, chances are you've gotten behind on some sites, disappointed customers, and maybe even lost a few customers to firms that could better handle the workload. As you know, it's often the little repetitive things, 10 percent of the overall work, that take 90 percent of the time.

If you follow the instructions for SiteWrapper, SiteColors, and the other utilities of this book, those irritating little problems will dissolve, leaving you free to attack the technology and squeeze it for all it's worth. Mine is a small web company; we think on our feet, solving problems for our clients as they arise. These utilities will give you that same freedom.

Freelancers

The last thing you need is to reinvent the wheel when a client needs an interactive web project. Chances are you work another job, or at least have several distributed customers, and don't have time to conceive and build utilities like these from the ground up.

But if you don't offer interactivity, your customers will disappear. There are too many people who know how to code HTML and sell it. Eventually one will find your customers and snatch them away. What I'll show you here translates as a "Yes" when a potential customer asks you what interactivity you can bring to their website:

Customer: "Can we do [a shopping cart, a discussion area, a connection to my database]?"

You: *"Yes."*

A resounding "Yes" can be the difference between another HTML jockey and you, who are both brighter and more resourceful (I could tell, you bought my book). Now you'll not only be able to say Yes, but offer suggestions as to how they can keep their site fresher, easier than they ever imagined, and without a full-time webmaster.

Do-It-Yourselfers

The stuff in this book will be a bit heavy for most small business owners who "just need a website." But don't be fooled; those days of just being out there are over. Users want something when they hit your site. Be it today's price, today's inventory, or today's special, fresh is what sells on the web.

You, however, don't have time to keep a normal website fresh. It's boring, cumbersome work that should be automated. With a little effort beyond simple HTML, you will learn in this book how to compete with the big guys in terms of interactivity and fresh content. I'll show you how to do it right the first time. Chapters 2 and 3 are meant as options to webmasters, but more importantly to you. NetObjects Fusion and FrontPage are incredible tools for very little money in comparison to what they'll save you. As additions, the Perl utilities aren't as complicated as they might look at first. Adding a simple database, a discussion board, chat room, or even shopping cart can mean only a two-hour learning curve with usable instructions. I've worked at keeping this book simple. The intimidation factor, as with most computer tasks, is more formidable than the actual work.

Specific Departments and Industries

Most big companies will create their website from the inside—using employees. But hiring a webmaster is a challenge these days. Anyone can write HTML, and many who once had the titles Graphic Designer, Marketing Manager, and System Administrator have renamed themselves Webmaster. Unfortunately, once you hire a lot of these "experts," they disappoint you with little knowledge of interactivity on the web. It's not difficult material, they just haven't been exposed to it yet. This book will help them, with quick and informative instruction, and will add the interactivity you and your team need to be successful on the web and from within your intranet.

MIS Departments

Your department is perhaps the most bashed of the web community. Somehow, they say, you people are hopelessly linked to "the old way" and refuse to learn distributed computing in a web environment. I question this, because in my experience, MIS has brought something to the web that it was lacking: reality.

You can't afford to run out and buy new workstations for everyone. Even the new network computer is a stretch. For you, collaborating on the web can't be a Java-enhanced machine for everyone. It's more likely a 486/33 with 4 megabytes of RAM that you bought three years ago with an expected life span of five years. You may be able to produce a server or two, but the content on it must be reachable by all, even those on the 3270s in the shipping department. Do you have webmasters? If so, they've probably experimented with Perl for submitting forms to e-mail. That's all they need. You'll be using WebPost, in Chapter 11, as a groupware application before you can say Altavista. Do an end-run around the bottomless pit of web technology and try these utilities. Everything in the following pages is server-based and runs on any flavor of Unix and NT 4.0. All of your interactivity will be through either a web-master's manual editing of small configuration files or a webform, capable of being used by any web browser, not just the new fat ones. Lynx, the text-only browser, will even work in most instances. Leave those 3270s on the floor! We're going to save you some money while expanding your capabilities. Don't think I expect you to install these yourself. Just read the beginning of each chapter with the description and screen shots, then give the book and CD to your webmaster. Many of these utilities will fit the needs of your company like a glove with little if any modification.

HR Departments

Like MIS, you won't be reading this to install code, but I mention HR because one of the first uses of WebPost, which we'll install in Chapter 11, was to post jobs to the web. In an afternoon I instructed six recruiters on how to use the system and ever since it has worked like a charm for them. What would have required at least one full-time webmaster was reduced to ten minutes here and there, from the people producing the job descriptions, with almost no learning curve.

And besides jobs, HR departments, like very few others, produce lots of rapidly changing content. Employee manuals, insurance guidelines, and help desk functions are perfect for a dynamic, automated web. Where once everything was print, and out of date as soon as it was printed, these new documents will easily be updated. Where once you may have had several versions of a document throughout the company, each that had been printed and distributed at different times, you will now have one version, updated automatically for everyone. Website automation should cut your HR overhead in half.

Publications

Most printed publications face a unique dilemma in web publishing. You have tons of content, but no distribution system to get it to the web in real-time. Sure, you could hire a few full-time webmasters, but at 30–80k, you can't afford it. You also question how it will affect your current print advertisers. Will they pay extra for web advertising? You may even question what the world needs with an online addition when the printed one works fine, and is portable. I can't answer whether your advertisers will bite or not, but I can help with distribution and that last question: "Why a web addition?"

We invented the way WebPost (Chapter 11) inserts new pages for publication distribution on the web. It was for a law firm who had to keep their site fresh with a new article every week. Since then the capabilities of WebPost have grown, but the core features are still the same. To produce a real-time publication, you need only cut and paste content into a webform, then hit Submit. All the back-end coding is done for you. Even a temp can use it.

Why do you need an electronic version at all? Everyone else is doing it. No, really, it's because the web can bring a facet to your print publication that print cannot address. If your headline is "Aldermen to Vote on Plan Proposal," what good would asking people their opinion do for a print publication? A few might respond, but before you could print it, the vote is gone. On the web, and using our discussion.web system in Chapter 15, comments will be real-time, before the vote.

What about advertising? It has come beyond the banner ads that many of you are considering as your only option. We're going to open the possibility of *sponsored areas*. An investing forum by the big CPA firm in town, an insurance how-to area, tips for buying a new car—the possibilities are endless with a little imagination and a lot of automation. On the old model of web publishing, hand-coding HTML and hotlinks, the risk wasn't worth it. With the automation in this book, your risk factor will decrease exponentially as it relates to your paid-out costs. You'll be free to try new things without committing to a larger web staff.

You will, of course, have to install these utilities, but it should be a one-time cost. Once they're in, they're in and almost never break. Just find a reliable ISP and competent web company and go from there. After this book, every corner should sport a web company who can install this stuff (yes, I'm an optimist).

Cars, Real Estate, Retail, Catalog

I class this category as *catalog* sales. You have product set up in a given structure (2 door, 4 door, 2 bedroom, 3 bedroom, drapes, shoes) and need to put it on the web, today. Many sites have tried this and collapsed under the strain of keeping the site fresh. Either you can't get the new stuff out or you can't remove the stuff you already have. Don't worry, it's not your fault if this has happened to you already. Nobody said in those "Learn HTML in 20 Minutes" books and "Web Pages without Coding" ads for software that there would be so much manual labor involved in keeping a site fresh. HTML, as I'll say in several places in this book, is a simple language. It's not really a language at all. The difficulty isn't in the coding, it's in linking everything up and making sure they all work and look the same. We'll be automating this shortly.

Whether you already keep your inventory in a database or not, the utilities in this book will enable you to go on the web live. You'll see a real estate agency, a car dealer, a retail catalog, and other sites that are keeping their data fresh. Keeping inventory up to date is easy with a good automation system, and that's what I'll provide you.

Like several of these categories, you'll need someone to put this in for you. I can't stress enough how easy we've made it for any developer you might find. Even if they are unfamiliar, instruct them to use the utilities in this book. Otherwise your online effort will implode as you try to keep static documents fresh. For anyone with changing inventory, website automation is crucial.

Why Do You Need This Book?

The commercial web as we know it will soon be extinct. Flat, promotional websites that resemble a throwaway brochure don't work. Users want more. Content must be fresh and changing, interactive and productive. What have you done for me lately? That's the new web.

But as you probably know, keeping a site fresh and interactive is difficult. HTML is a *kludge*, something that is inefficient but basically gets the job done. Editing files, even with WYSIWYG, auto document coding, and drag and drop hotlinking, is a time-consuming process prone to mistakes. That is where this book picks up. I'll address specific problems in Chapter 1, "Why Automate," but for now, just understand that there is life beyond static HTML, and that life, taken literally, is the future of the web. Unless you improve your capabilities into this new arena of website production, you will be left behind.

The utilities here aren't about cutting edge technology. That's the space I'll leave for Java, ActiveX, and Shockwave. I used the word "capabilities" in the previous paragraph for a reason. Capabilities are what these things I'll show you are about. I won't show you how you *might* do automatic e-mail ticklers from your website. I'll show you how to do it *today*, before lunch, with a few easy steps that even a complete novice could handle (Chapter 7). A book about Java might not address your core needs. Everything here you should find of use.

How to Use This Book

Some of you reading this are beginners and some are experts, with varying abilities in the world of programming. I suggest the newcomer to website automation and Perl programming start from here and progress forward until Chapter 6, where we install SiteWrapper and its companion, SiteColors. There you'll learn the basics of a central configuration file. But before that, I'll offer an overview of the different types of automation with a fantastic client-based system from NetObjects and an equally impressive offering from Microsoft. After that, pick and choose what you need from the following chapters. Most of the book will drag and drop into any project you create on any server.

As for the guts of this book, the stuff we wrote in Perl, start with SiteWrapper. Whether the first site you plan to automate is less than twenty pages of mostly static information or potentially hundreds of leaf pages of several categories of information, start with SiteWrapper. It will connect to all the other utilities in the book. Then move on to its plug-ins and WebPost.

One note I'll make here is that no matter what your programming or web experience, make sure you have the project direction focused before constructing graphics for navigation. You'll find so many ideas here that it will be tough for you to keep up at first. And don't worry if at first the site seems dead, whether you're starting with Fusion, FrontPage, or SiteWrapper. In the beginning, we'll be setting up infrastructure to save you time in the long run, not installing interactive gadgets. SiteWrapper, without customization, is meant to save you ongoing maintenance more than to provide interactivity. With an automated back-end as your foundation, you'll be able to expand the site later with more static pages or WebPost in a separate directory as part of the site.

I caution experts to review the following chapter outlines before installing any utilities. I've written them so you can take what you like and leave the rest. Each solves a problem, either administrational or interactive. But most of them take a basic understanding of SiteWrapper, or at least of SiteWrapper's central configuration file.

Unix Only, NT Only, All Platforms

We've made most of these utilities completely cross platform. They can be dragged and dropped from a Unix server, any flavor, to an NT 4.0 server with no modification. But installing them is different. Unix involves a permissions structure absent in NT. NT has a few quirks in Perl that you must accommodate for in your modifications. That's why you'll see several separated install sections and options. I've tried to keep the duplicative material to a minimum, but there is some. If you're on Unix, completely ignore the NT sections; if you're on NT, ignore the Unix. Most chapters will pick up early on in the Quick Start as the setup for the two platforms comes together.

Quick Starts

What about those numbered steps at the beginning of each chapter? The idea came from a former editor's comments at *Webtechniques* magazine. He explained that you can't dawdle with the audience for this material. We all have too many trade rags and how-to books thrown at us. You and I don't have time for me to stand on the soapbox of website automation each chapter waiting to get going. This book is about getting the job done. The Quick Starts will get you in and going so you can evaluate each utility on its merits, not my musings. If I've been too brief on what something does, feel free to e-mail with questions before you try the Quick Start. Knowing the web community as well as I do, I won't hold my breath waiting, though. We're a bunch of really smart people.

Line Numbers

If you flip through the chapters you'll see that I look a bit unstable when it comes to numbering lines of code. This is intentional, because Perl will break if you type them in yourself. I've used numbers in places where I want you to look at a place that you might want to customize. If line numbers are absent, usually it's a piece of code that I've customized in advance. No numbers means you can type that code in exactly like it is and it will work. Most examples are on the CD as well.

The CD

Every utility in the book, with the exception of a few commercial programs, is on the CD-ROM. In the chapters I'll provide instructions on how to find and extract them. Perl programs, otherwise known as scripts, can be read and understood as plain text. You'll have to make minor modifications, but for the most part everything you need is included. There are also several examples from which I'll provide the entire directory of modified files.

I'll also include some examples on the CD of some custom sites we've done for our clients. Most I've just downloaded without modification, so the Perl location and path information will be invalid for your system. You'll find both the demo examples and client sites in the "On the CD" sections.

The stuff we didn't write is all in the /software directory. Mostly it's shareware and freeware in beta or early release. And in most cases, I'll instruct you to check the website for a more updated copy or patch. Though the book will be published only two months after I write this, many shareware companies writing in visual basic update their software regularly. Other utilities, Unix-based in tar files, should be checked as well. Regular updates come along as well as extras that might bring more utility.

The Websites

Escaping the bonds of static HTML has one drawback when you write a book about it. No demos can be run from a CD. A CGI program has to be run on a web-server, as does ISAPI. For that reason I've included examples from our clients' sites as well as a few examples made specifically for the book. In addition, check out www.world-media.com/webtoolkit for a discussion area and bug reports. You'll usually see an "On the Web" sign before I reference specific code examples from our clients, and the extras on the site will offer sample code.

Code License

Everything from our company is officially released as CareWare, meaning that the utilities are officially free, but we suggest a donation to a charity if you find they save you money. This is not a requirement, just a suggestion. Most people won't send anything, so don't feel guilty if it's just not your thing. We coined the term because we thought freeware a waste. Many hard hours of thought and coding went into these, and they are worth far more than the price of this book. The Appendix lists a few suggested charities.

You may not redistribute these utilities without permission. They are for your use only, but you may use them as many times and for as many clients, companies, or departments as you wish.

The other programs in Perl will carry some sort of GNU public license that can be found in the README with the sourcecode. Binary distributions of commercial demos are the property of their respective owners. More information can be found on their websites.

Who Am I?

Me? In early 1995 I learned HTML and started to build websites like everyone else. Quickly I recognized HTML for the kludge it was (we were still using UL to indent), and its weaknesses for administrating refreshed content. There had to be a better way, and that way was automation. My first reference, a John Wiley & Sons publication (no coincidence), *The HTML Sourcebook,* had a section on the communication between the client (Netscape .9 at the time) and the server (NCSA, of course). I learned that there was a way to go beyond the standard HTTP request and actually pass information back and forth. I wanted interactive databases, shopping systems, and discussion boards. HTML couldn't do that, but this other thing, CGI, could.

The smart people, I saw, were doing it with CGI programs written in Perl, an easy to use scripting language. With a little creativity, the gurus of Internet technology were automating all sorts of web content. So, though I had never taken a computer or programming course in my life, I set out to learn what they knew and to come up with some creativity of my own. With the help of these gurus (who mostly hang out at comp.lang.perl.misc), and a couple of the same books you'll find on the shelf with this one, I constructed my first all CGI website, a shopping cart at www.racefan.com, which is now defunct, but able to be viewed.

In the following year I hired better programmers than I to do the coding and together we came up with and implemented all the solutions in this book. Then in September of 1996 I began to write. In my previous life I was a fledgling freelance writer so I guess I followed a natural path. *Webtechniques* magazine picked up my series of articles and my life as an automation expert began. Now I speak at conferences world-wide and, as you know, have written a book on the subject.

What You Should Know to Install These Utilities

As I've already mentioned, this book is for the guru as much as the newcomer. Every web technologist will face issues regarding interactivity with customers and between employees. The gurus among my readers will skip along; that's why we numbered the Quick Starts. And newcomers will pick up more and more as they go, in the worlds of both Unix and NT. But starting out, you should know a few things about the basics of the web and how things talk to one another, including humans.

HTML

This book is not an HTML primer. The how-to portion is for experienced webmasters who have written HTML for some time and have experienced the problems of administrating a website made up of static pages. If you don't know HTML, check out *The HTML Sourcebook, Third Edition,* by Ian Graham (John Wiley & Sons, Inc.). It's what I learned on, and will give you the basics of HTTP and CGI, our next prerequisite.

HTTP and CGI Communication

The messages sent between your HTML browser (Netscape, Explorer, et al.) and the server (the website) are very simple. The browser asks for a page and the server sends it. But mixed in there are a whole bunch of extra attributes, both of the browser and server, that we will rely upon for most of the CGI programs in this book. When I refer to "HTTP Referrer" or "User Agent," you should know what they are and how the CGI program listens for these variable pieces of information. Knowing this isn't a strict rule, it will just make the learning curve easier.

The Common Gateway Interface (CGI), if you are unfamiliar, is a server extension that allows your browser to execute programs on the server. If you've ever submitted a form on a website, you've used CGI. They, like the browser and server, have their own methods within the confines of HTTP to speak to each other, to the server, and to your browser.

NT Only: Is ISAPI on Your NT Server?

Most NT servers can utilize a faster alternative to CGI. It's the Internet Server Application Programming Interface (ISAPI). These filters run as .dll files on the server and wait for HTTP requests. With Perl, ISAPI functions as an open mouth, saving the system drain of starting up a new instance of Perl every time someone clicks a Submit button or hotlink. Don't worry about installing ISAPI or the PerlIIS.dll. We'll do that in Chapter 4. All you need to know is that ISAPI exists and that your server supports it. Here is a brief list of some that do:

- Microsoft Internet Information Server
- O'Reilly Website
- Commerce Builder

Unix Only: Permission to Execute Programs

As I'll note later, you don't need server administration skills or root permission to install or run most of the programs in this book, but make sure you are allowed to invoke CGI programs in any directory on the site. Our first utility, SiteWrapper, in Chapter 6, runs as index.cgi instead of index.html in your mail directory. If your ISP denies you this, switch ISPs. Some will cite security risks, but running CGI in any directory is no more dangerous than CGI in the CGI-bin directory. If your administrator is unsure as to how to allow this, I'll cover the necessary configuration edits in Chapter 4.

Usability Conventions

The topic of website usability is for a whole other book (stay tuned), but I've assumed that readers of this book will know the basics of what makes an effective website. Take a look around and see what sites you enjoy browsing. Chances are they have a repeated navigation structure, consisting of a *jumplist* or repeated button bar. I'll repeat those terms several times throughout the book.

Another major concern is the presence of standard headers and footers. If you've ever printed a page then forgot where you got it, that footer of URL and contact information on the bottom saved you, right? Oh, the site didn't have that? Then it was made by a novice. Your footer will contain not only contact information, but your copyright notice and any other information people might need on every page. If you include standard headers and footers, bravo. You've harnessed the most important word-of-mouth marketing feature a website can have. If you haven't, start.

If none of this is making sense to you, take a while and browse around the web. See what sites you enjoy and what sites you do not. Most likely these standards will stick out as core components of your favorite sites.

What You Don't Need to Know

The biggest worry I had going into this book was that newcomers to the web would pick it up and put it back on the shelf because they're afraid of the code. But that's why I wrote it! Just so you could have some fun on your site without having to get a programming degree. Trust me. If you can learn HTML, you can learn this.

Programming

Chapter 5 is a brief overview of the programming language Perl. If you've never seen programming, as I hadn't when I undertook my first CGI project (at www.racefan.com in September of 1995), you may want to pick up a beginner's book or find a basic tutorial on the web. But in general, you don't need programming skills. In the overview I'll cover the basic concepts you need to install most of the utilities contained in this book. Extensive customization will be for the more experienced, but everyone should be able to install and use the basics.

Server Administration

Not many people know the ins and outs of Unix and NT server maintenance. If Perl 5 on Unix and PerlIS.dll (both in Chapter 4) are installed correctly, only a few minor edits to config files and basic FTP commands will get you rolling. I'll explain everything you need in Chapters 4 and 5. I strongly suggest, however, that you learn at least the basics of administration. It will save you time down the road if something goes wrong. Knowing what question to ask is often the difference between a short server outage and a lengthy one.

Root Permission

On Unix you must have special *superuser* access to install certain utilities. The comp.infosystems.authoring.www.cgi newsgroup is full of "Why can't I install *this program*" from people without root permission. None of the stuff here requires that, but as before, you will need some CGI access concessions to run most of what's here.

Shell/Telnet Access

Most webmasters host their sites on an external Internet Service Provider (ISP). Some, the ones we use most, don't allow outside developers Telnet access to a shell account on the server. As we'll show you, this is a foolish security concern, because with a Perl script we can do most of what can be done from a shell. Nonetheless, it's a situation we have to deal with. I'll show you ways around the restriction in a safe and secure manner.

Security

Some of the practices in this book are dangerous for mission critical applications. Without getting unnecessarily technical, most webservers on Unix systems run as the user "nobody." WebPost, SiteColors, the discussion board, and chat room all write to the server. Conceivably, someone could overwrite your files if you're on an ISP with several others running the same server daemon under the same "nobody" user. If you are on your own server, or have complete control over all the CGI programs, there is no danger of this.

In Chapter 6, I'll introduce you to our Encrypt program. It takes a word like toolkit and turns it into garble like to65rcsBnxIuI. You'll place that garble into configuration files that can be read from any web browser, so be careful with what you encrypt. Use a mix of upper- and lowercase letters and numbers, rather than a word you can find in a dictionary. The string of garble cannot be unencrypted, but it can be compared against encrypted dictionary words for a match. Use Uie89rT rather than a word like toolkit, which can be easily matched.

Can someone kerflooey the whole system by sending a nasty HTTP POST request? Yes, they probably can. We've not included any of the standard security flaws of some

CGI programs, but a determined hacker can break anything. Rename your configuration files, as I'll explain, and be careful to whom that information leaks. The most successful hacks break in using inside information, not random POST requests.

Credits

Most of the code in this book was written by Barrett Nuzum, my chief programmer and co-inventor. He's not a writer and wanted no credit for the work he's done, but is getting it anyway. I'm a dreamer. "Can we do *this*?" I'll ask him, and his answer is usually yes. Without Barrett's work these things would never have happened. I have neither the patience nor the ability for complex data structures. Barrett has done a great service for me, for our clients, and now, hopefully, for you.

Of late I also have to thank Rob Holak who has worked for me for only a couple of months. He wrote the Whereami? program in the search engine chapter his first week here, the same time he learned Perl. At present he's working on new and even neater stuff, probably destined for a website chapter and/or the second edition of this book. He's also instructed me on the finer arts of NetObjects Fusion and FrontPage, without which this book would not have been complete.

Chapter Summaries

Chapter 1: Why Automate? By now you've probably seen my biggest sticking points on why every website needs an automation system incorporated somewhere in the back end. In this chapter I'll take this one more step. I'll discuss topics ranging from central design control to security, pointing out the weaknesses of automation as well as its strengths.

Chapter 2: Client-Based Automation Systems Originally I had intended that this chapter be an overview of what client automation might be like, including brief overviews of several products. Then I did my homework and tested NetObjects Fusion. Though it could be its own book, my step-by-step demo will take you through most of its functionality and use. If you can get past the limitations of a client system, this program might be for you. It's expensive, about four hundred dollars, but worth it. An overview for this chapter wouldn't have given client automation its due space as a viable option. Fusion is a viable option.

Chapter 3: The Page Model Server Side Includes (SSI) and Microsoft FrontPage both use the same basic functionality to provide basic automation tasks for your site. You can include a file, print the current or file-modified time and date, and even execute a CGI program from within an SSI document. FrontPage is more extensive, offering an on-site search and other "bots" that run from a set of proprietary extensions to the server. I don't know that absolutely everyone needs to learn a little Perl and extend their capabilities beyond the realm of simple automation. If you lack the time or interest, this chapter could be your ticket to an easy and very useful solution.

Chapter 4: Why Perl for Unix and Perl for NT? Besides an overview of why Perl has become the language that automates the Internet, we'll install it on Windows NT and 95, and briefly address Unix, which usually comes with Perl installed. Recently, the world of programming has changed. Java, JavaScript, and even Visual Basic have become popular for web programming and many programmers are wondering which way to go. In general, all ways is best, as we have done in our shop, but Perl is the most useful place to start. Almost every popular automated website in the world is coded in Perl. Now it's possible on NT as well as Unix.

Chapter 5: Using Perl This is by no means a comprehensive overview of the Perl language. But I thought it important that we start somewhere. With this brief explanation of the most common objects in Perl, you should be comfortable with all the customizations we'll go over here, even if, like when I started, you have never even seen a programming language in the past. Perl intermediates and gurus can skip this chapter.

Chapter 6: SiteWrapper Here is where we begin with the utilities that could change the way you think about the web. SiteWrapper, the first, treats every page of your site as a dynamic document, much like SSIs and FrontPage (Chapter 3), and Microsoft's Active Server Pages. But with these you don't have to code every page with the same code, or learn a proprietary language that you might never use elsewhere. We start by automating header and footer for the site, then move to more rapidly changing content and user customization. Once your site is wrapped the possibilities are endless. If you read only one chapter in this book, read about SiteWrapper.

Chapter 7: E-Mail Push Utilities You've gotten automatic e-mail before and probably wondered how to bring it to your customers. Do you sign up for a push channel? Do you install a special server? Not for this. In this Tickler chapter I'll show you two utilities that send two types of messages, one an e-mail with the URL of a page on your site that has changed, the other an e-mail with the full text of your event. The latter even rewrites a new HTML page at the same time. This chapter is also your first introduction to forms-based input of web content. There is no upload or compiling of lists required. You just plug in one of these simple utilities and bring up a webform in your browser. Hit Submit and it's done.

Chapter 8: Mailing List Software Though it's a bit off the topic of website automation, most web designers are screaming for an effective way to manage collaborative e-mail groups. I've put this chapter after the Tickler chapter because these two utilities are different than broadcast e-mail. The first, Majordomo, is the web's standard for a low-cost answer to Listserv and other server systems. The second is a Windows NT/95 based application that sits on your desktop. Both are incredibly useful, but one note: Majordomo is one of the few places in the book where you'll need some root access.

Chapter 9: Tracking Visitors I've promised in several places that most of the utilities here won't depend upon each other to run. The one exception is Trakkit. It reads the log files of SiteWrapper and decodes them for you. Trakkit shows you hits, referrer, browser software, IP address, DNS Lookup, and some useful search engine keyword analysis. I've also included a non-SiteWrapper utility called Analog, which works with the standard log files of Apache, Microsoft Internet Information Server, and other servers, decoding the cryptic results into a vast array of data.

Chapter 10: Shopping Carts: Saving State HTTP has one specific problem when you're trying to keep track of what someone has ordered. The server forgets who you are after you hit a page. HTTP is a stateless protocol, but yet sites do track orders. Most do it with *cookies*, little text files that sit on the visitor's hard drive, which we'll address in the second half of the chapter. Unfortunately, though, cookies have a few problems of their own. One is that 30 percent of users who know what cookies are dislike them. They consider it a privacy invasion. The other problem is that America Online doesn't support them. WebTV does support cookies, but has had problems keeping track of them in their caching system. The first part of this chapter offers an alternative based on the SiteWrapper pitch and catch system. If you're already running SiteWrapper it will be plug-and-play, or else you'll have to install this version of the wrapper, plus the subtotal and total programs. I should also mention that we have a novel answer for handling image maps with carts. I've never seen it before.

Chapter 11: Unlimited Growth with WebPost Most sites reach a point where the cost of adding new pages is not worth the increasing costs of indexing the old material. It's why so many sites are scrapped periodically and started fresh with a new structure. WebPost allows you to grow your site without the penalty of increasing costs with every page you put on the site. Not only are the new pages submitted and coded through a webform; the entire site re-indexes with each new or edited entry to the site. Included is a simple coding system for such things as [[hotlink]http://] strings of text and [[subheaders]H], as well as a complete file upload system for images and multimedia. Security, archiving, and even version control are all automatic.

Chapter 12: Searching Your Website Whether you stick to a Fusion-type client system or reach into WebPost and databases for truly dynamic content, you'll want to offer visitors a quick and easy way to find material. I'll start this chapter with a simple search that scans static HTML pages, then add in support for SiteWrapper and WebPost.

Chapter 13: Adding a Directory of Hotlinks Classic marketing says that you should never give people a reason to leave, but on the Internet, this thinking has backfired as the number of bad sites outnumbers the good. The most popular and profitable sites on the web are those that screen the wheat from the chaff and offer a comprehensive list of regularly freshened hotlinks. Knowing the amount of research that must go into a list like this, we've at least eliminated the hassle of putting them on the site. These are set up in a directory structure like many of the search engines with a built-in search utility.

Chapter 14: A Free Web Database You may already have a database installed, but if you don't, the first utility here is an easy answer to index your inventory on hand into an easy structure for your website. I will scale only to several thousand entries, the table is kept in text, but I will accommodate for most business needs. The second half of the chapter is for those who have databases, but not the budget for the big guns of database publishing. We'll look at a solution, separately, for both NT and Unix.

Chapter 15: Discussions, Forums, Bulletin Boards Before the web came USENET, a system of online, threaded discussion areas where communities met to discuss topics ranging from computer viruses to the fine arts. Of late, they've been crowded with promotional "spammers" offering get rich quick scams and other annoying distractors to intelligent conversation. It's too public for most. Your site needs a private forum, sometimes called collaborative groupware. The first utility in this chapter we adapted from an old creation called WWWBoard By Matt Wright. We improved its layout and usability, and added an e-mail option for those replying to threads. Before spending a bunch on a commercial application, check this out. In the second part of the chapter we return to FrontPage and its built-in discussion board. For simple plug-and-play you can't beat it, though it includes no remote management.

Chapter 16: Live Web Chat Rooms Sometimes discussion is too boring. You invite a personality to your site, the site is busy enough to support an ongoing interaction, a happening demands quick and immediate interaction; whatever driving the need, chat rooms serve that niche of web content. Most use a chat server requiring either a proprietary client or Java applet. Your chat can be pure HTML with the two utilities we'll cover here. Multiple rooms are easy, and the programs are small. Your server resources should hold up under all but the most intensive use.

Chapter 17: Search Engine Agents This is perhaps the most fun chapter of the book. To start, I'll show you a piece of shareware that submits you to three hundred search engines at one time. It even cheats. The second utility runs on Unix (and maybe NT in the future) and checks your site for where you score on the engines, sending you an e-mail as to whether you made the first twenty pages with your chosen keywords. The last utility in this chapter is similar, but for Windows 95/NT. It's more fancy than the Unix, spitting out several HTML pages of reports verifying your search engine scoring. It also compares this run to the last run and warns you of what you're doing wrong.

Chapter 18: Tracking Banner Ads Some of you old-timers might wince at the ads clouding most websites these days, but for those of us managing these ads, and having to charge for them, we've developed a version of Trakkit that counts and verifies both image downloads and click throughs, tracking the to and from of referrer URLs.

Appendix: CareWare Causes As I promised, this is where you'll find my preferred organizations for CareWare contributions. If you find any of the utilities in the book as infinitely useful as we have, think about sending them, or any non-profit organization of your choice, a special donation. And let us know. This stuff makes it easy to get up for work in the morning.

Why
Automate?

I don't know if this is a strange question to you so I might as well ask it. Automation is a bit of a buzzword these days. I was almost embarrassed to put it in the title of this book. But I'm afraid its use as a word drastically outnumbers its use in practice. Automation is the thing nobody has time for until the website is about to go bust. This book is about preventing that and doing it right the first time, and this chapter is about justifying the initial expense and effort.

What do I mean by my statement that automation is not as used as it is quoted? Take a look around the web. Automated sites are easy to spot. Pick up a copy of *WebWeek* magazine, or *IWorld*, or *ZDInternet*. In them you'll find stories of supposed cutting-edge websites. Check out the sites. Most will have a great look, maybe even some great information, but very few capabilities and almost no automation. Chances are that if you look at the URLs you will see .html at the end, signifying that the page you are viewing is a static HTML document. There will be no question mark (?) in the URL signifying an automation system on the back-end of the website, which means that the pages are hand coded or generated from a template. Some might be on a simple, client-based HTML automation system like we'll look at in Chapter 2, but with that .html extension, you can be sure they're working too hard and spending too much money to keep the site's content formatted.

In six months some of those sites will go away. My bet is that they've either imploded or shut down. By imploded I mean that the content has gotten behind; old content isn't where it used to be; there is no search; dead links outnumber the live ones. We've all seen these sites. Eventually they just sit there, dead in the water.

And then there are the sites that don't shut down, that continue to throw money at a money-losing effort. If such a site appears to be kept fresh, call the site management team and ask whether the operation has been profitable. If they say yes, they're lying. Webmasters, even those who don't know HTML and can use only a WYSIWYG, are going at 30K-plus as I write this book. Five are needed for a small to midsize news or retail operation. Making $150,000 in a year on a website doesn't add up, just to break even. Without an automation system taking the place of four out of five of those webmasters, the site will never be profitable. If you're one of those fortunates who are saying "No, that's not us, we're doing OK," just wait. As the site grows and old content is archived, it will get out of hand.

There are trade-offs when you automate a website. I'll discuss those next and address them as we go with the utilities in each chapter of this book. The easy answer to "Why Automate?" is that you can't afford not to.

Learning Curve

A static website, one based on flat HTML pages with no automation characteristics, requires that everyone inserting content learn some sort of HTML authoring package. Although many would say "Sure, but PageMill makes it simple," learning PageMill, with all its complexities, is more than a day's project. Some people spend an entire semester learning it, because, like Microsoft Word, the basics are easy, but to use its power is difficult. If one of your webmasters has a gall-bladder attack this week, and this week happens to be primary week at politics-usa.com, a new hire or temp can't learn your system fast enough.

I've walked into a major public corporation whose MIS manager was hand-coding HTML. His department heads generate press releases, product updates, help sheets, and other web content, but he is forced to insert it all himself because nobody else knows the system. A simple, automated back-end would solve this. He would release a password to the content generators, who then in turn would update the website with a simple set of directions through a web form in real-time on the server. What? you ask. Check out WebPost in Chapter 11.

T **I P**   We have such a hard time explaining to potential users of WebPost what it actually does. For them, and for you, I suggest the demo on our site. If you're confounded by the choices in web-site automation, try it out. Growing your site, page after page after cate-gory after category is a snap with WebPost, and after the demo most likely you'll go to Chapter 11 and give it a go.

The other situation I've encountered is the company who would settle for less rather than automate. They post an online brochure, vague and general, to a media that thrives on real-time, specific information. The example I'm speaking of (can't say the name as they are still a client), writes at least one commentary a week that would be of value to a large number of their clients. The web is an ideal media to do this, but when we first encountered them their prospects of such a thing were nil. They couldn't afford an in-house person, and paying us by the hour (at $125/hr.) was out of the question. Without automation the content for the site would have gone unused. With automation, what would have been an unimpressive brochure became a vital information dispersal system.

In both cases the problem boils down to a learning curve. In the first, the MIS manager took on the task and became the webmaster bottleneck I mentioned in the introduction. In the second, the company shunted the learning curve altogether and stuck their head in the sand. As much as I'd like to say that the web has pro-gressed beyond that, it hasn't at present. And the way development tools are com-ing out, it won't for quite some time. The web is a new and exciting media, but it can't be learned in a day. By installing a back-end automation system, your site will leap-frog this era of technology and progress to the next, which should be more dynamic and interactive. You will neither experience the bottleneck nor the online brochure syndrome.

But doesn't installing and maintaining an automation system require a learning curve as well? Yes, but it's an occasional thing. We've installed some of these utili-ties for clients, trained them in an afternoon on how to use the webform interface, then not heard from them for several months until they wanted to expand the breadth of what the site could do. If you're a medium-sized company, hiring a web firm or consultant once for a week of programming, it's worth not paying five webmasters for a year. You'll pay only for a small learning curve spread out over several employees whose salaries will not go up with these duties.

If it's your web firm, you are cringing right now. Most of your revenue may be derived from keeping websites fresh with hand-coded HTML pages. Sorry, but this constant bleeding doesn't work for your clients. You may have already seen a drop in how much dedication they put into the project as it passes the six-month or year mark. The problem is that you've assumed the entire learning curve, but then are being paid not for what you know, but for useless hours of monkey work coding HTML. Automation will increase what you know. It will increase your value, and it will increase the price you charge to set up a website. You'll make your money up front, rather than in an annuity stream of monthly maintenance, which is never guaranteed. You will be paid for this increased learning curve, freeing you from countless hours of HTML, freeing you to seek and fulfill more clients, and freeing the client to have a fresher and more interactive website.

Time Savings

Beyond even the learning curve is the time it takes to insert new content onto an old website. I won't restate the idiocy of coding HTML pages here. I'm writing about edits to old pages more than constructing new ones. You have the new page coded, now you have to tell the rest of the site, the pre-existing pages, that it exists. This could mean editing one page, a main directory, by adding one hotlink. But it could also mean changing "Next Listing" and "Previous Listing," two pages on a real estate site, or two plus one more site-map page on a retail store, or every page should you decide to add "Home & Garden" to the major jumplist of topics on your news site.

Nobody considers a site all-inclusive when it's built. Though you should user-test and interview beforehand, you'll never catch everything. The most common approach doesn't address this. "In a year," the project leaders say, "we'll revisit what the site can do and build a new one. By then we'll have a good idea of whether it will be profitable." Heresy! I say. The web community is like the saying on Missouri license plates: "Show Me!" It's a subculture unto itself that expects you to save them time, effort, and money with your web presence. If you're not replacing a call to an 800 number, or an e-mail to support@yourcompany.com, or a price list that will save them waiting a week for your catalog, forget it. The Back button is only a click away, and Yahoo! awaits with a list of your competitors.

Many project leaders skirt the issue that their site cannot be complete on the first pass by planning for holes to be filled. They'll leave open two or more areas with general descriptions of what is to come, testing user interest. Where this idea breaks is that they have to build it into the navigation system for the site. People click it, and—whoops—nothing there, and I'm outta here. Don't promise something you don't intend to deliver on the web. Users won't put up with it, and they won't return.

An automation system, however, plans for expansion as it's built, but without the smoke and mirrors show. With a database, you are indexing by category. Adding a new category is easy, and with a few minor modifications to the program that queries it, the whole site and all its pages can reflect the new category. You may have to tap the graphic designer for a new button, but the jump around lists, the things that would have to be edited manually on the site, are composed dynamically from the database's active categories.

We take this simple example a touch farther by automating other frequently changing items on the site with a central configuration file that every page draws from as it loads. Whether it be page colors, header sizes, or the phone number and address at the bottom of every page, changing every page is a nuisance and a horrible waste of time.

Again, I won't re-expound on the utility of WebPost, but it goes even one better by allowing nontechnical personnel the ability to insert new pages into the site. If you're a webmaster reading this and fear that you'll give up your job, you might. But most webmasters will use WebPost to save time on mundane coding of HTML. If you are coding new pages and updating old ones for 40 percent of your day, WebPost will reduce that to 5 percent, leaving you the freedom to learn and implement more advanced automation systems, Java front-ends, and multimedia enhancements that you would otherwise be too strapped for time to accomplish.

Central Management

All of you MIS people are dripping with saliva at the promise of controlling the look and feel of every page on your website. That's because you know that automation is not for free-spirits who want their corporate sites to resemble the directory of personal homepages at Mindspring. Automation means tight control on design, as well as strict content monitoring. For most companies and organizations, this is desirable.

You may have tried templates to control the look and feel of pages with little success. Because no matter how much instruction you give, it's too easy to mess up a preformatted HTML page while adding new content. Especially when updating old pages with new hotlinks to new pages, it's difficult to guarantee that your team members won't break something, or that they will stick to the design structure and not reinvent a "better" layout.

Server-based automation, which we'll start with SiteWrapper in Chapter 6 and continue with through the rest of the book, draws its page formatting (or at least some of it with the simplest) from a set of configuration variables. Updating the site is either through a webform or from a database which is re-uploaded to the server, so you control the formatting. You control the look and feel. You control what comes and goes.

"Ick," say the webmasters reading this chapter. "That flies in the face of what the web is all about, what's important about the web." Not true. It's a common misconception. The web is really about people interacting with information and each other at the same time. Even purists will admit that the web has improved with all the corporate dollars that have proliferated since 1994. But it's not the dollars that have made the web better. They've only facilitated the change. What's done it is organization.

When you go to a website, you are looking for something. Whether it be virtual flowers for your sweetie, information on why your Cabletron stock skyrocketed last week, or a good discussion on plumbing drainage systems, you don't need someone's creative ambitions getting in the way of your end goal: finishing your task easily so there's still time on your break for checking Nascar.com for this weeks Darlington results. At virtual flowers, that might mean that the various pages of bouquets look all the same. At CNN Financial, it's that every story has the same look, feel, and navigation. At the Plumbing and Drainage Institute, it's a discussion board that posts messages in real time.

If those pages were laid out differently, you wouldn't be able to get your task done. You might not even be sure whether you're at the right site. You might have inadvertently clicked a link and left. No matter what, you'd feel like an amateur, or at the very least, feel someone who cares little for your user-experience designed the site. You'd leave and not return. So where do you stand? Are you the MIS manager whose job it is to make quality websites? Or are you the webmaster whose job it is to make quality websites?

Centralized control does not limit the effectiveness of your site, it heightens it. By enforcing a standard, you are creating an environment on your web that allows people to get what they want and leave satisfied. You are imprinting a loyalty. They'll want to return. I don't care who you are, a web geek (like me), an MIS manager, a marketing person, an outside sales agent, even a customer. What you hope for your website is that visitors find what they're looking for, tell their friends, and return for more. To accomplish this requires control, not as in "control-freak" control, but the control that helps people accomplish their goals.

Efficiency

Nothing is worse than doing the same thing twice. But unless all of your internal documents are written in HTML, that's what's happening every time you update a page on the site. The page was originally written in MSWord, which was then coded into HTML. Now the original Word document is edited and the changes have to be put on the site. You must either reformat the entire Word document into HTML again or go in and make the same changes to the HTML document as you did to the Word document. Confused? Try it in practice.

Reliability

I think of automation as "I quit" insurance. Webmasters are a funny lot (present company included). We get bored fast and have a tendency to want to move on after a year. For a web company like mine it's great. I get a new customer to work on regularly and it keeps my mind focused and excited. If I were on one website, eight hours a day, just updating content and keeping the server alive, I'd get bored and quit after a short time. But I wouldn't feel bad about it because of the automation utilities I'd install from this book.

Many of you reading this chapter are in this situation now. Your site is on FrontPage, PageMill, or another web-editing/site-management program, and you're the only one who knows how to use it. You've been doing all the updating yourself. The rest of your team knows only how to send you blurry faxes and you know that the site will fall drastically behind if you quit.

Your boss knows that too. He's terrified that you'll quit and leave the company high and dry. The whole web structure and control is in your head, even if it's on paper. Only you know how all the pieces come together. What happens if you get sick or leave?

We've made sites from the utilities in this book that allow our customers to add, remove, and edit content every day with nearly one hundred percent reliability. They don't even have a webmaster, so they don't worry about one quitting. In the true spirit of downsizing, we've created systems where existing employees do the site editing, and as I mentioned previously, without a learning curve. So if one of our employment companies has 15 jobs to post, the agents post them; if not the agents, a temp with 10 minutes training. By eliminating the webmaster bottleneck we've guaranteed reliability.

Does the Model Break Down?

I talked about reliability because that can be one of the two gaping holes in any automation system. You hire a programmer, consultant, or developer like my company, and in a year, when you find a major bug or the system crashes, they're nowhere to be found. The system goes down for weeks as you struggle to find the sourcecode and a new developer to figure out what the program did and all of its interworkings. In the end, you'll most likely abandon the old system and start from scratch.

That's why my colleagues and I wrote most of what's in this book in Perl, and it's why I put out a book about it. Perl is not a binary program. The sourcecode is always readable and modifiable by just about any Unix hacker involved in the Internet. The book is, in effect, an instruction manual to your system. There will be customizations, at the places at which the code is modified, but these should be obvious as all the functionality of the system is in the original code. Most customization is in look and feel.

Your data is equally protected with our utilities and the other scripts and applications in the following chapters. By data I mean the actual text meant for the web. I've run into clients who can't extract their data from old proprietary systems. It's been converted to a binary file and is useless to them. We planned for this, knowing that the web outdates itself every year to 18 months or so. So nowhere will your text meant for HTML pages be stored in a proprietary file or database (except for the database chapter). It's all saved in plain text, either all in one directory or split into in a file-structure organizational system.

But even more important, all of the utilities here are modular in nature. The automatic e-mailer never interacts with the discussion board. The chat room never interacts with WebPost. And WebPost's submit, delete, and edit programs never interact with each other, so even if one piece of your site breaks the others won't be affected.

Expandability is the other side of the coin. You're probably asking: What happens when you've written the most comprehensive system for the day, and a year later you need to add new components? Your data is trapped in this automation system (which has now become a four-letter word), and you have to try to add new functionality without losing the old and without having to re-invent the entire wheel.

I hate to sound like a Perl preacher, but as a programming language for the web, you really can't beat it for the basic automation systems needed to keep your website fresh. This is another benefit: your code, I'll repeat, is not trapped in a binary file. Therefore it easily can be manipulated and added to (Perl is also object oriented) so you are never locked into any system. And again, your text data is left in text form, so even if you repurposed the entire project into a new entity, the file structure and variables within the text (I know, a bit too technical) wouldn't change.

Looking at the future of the web, it doesn't appear that much of what HTML is about will change in the next few years. Think of MS Word 3.0 when you used it back then. It hasn't changed much. Pieces of add-on technology have come and gone from it, but a Word document from 1991 will still work today. HTML will be the same way. Bells and whistles will come and go, but the heart will stay the same, and your documents will never go out of date and be unable to be read by modern applications. As long as the information on your site is still viable, its formatting will be.

For expansion, that means that you'll improve your website with new categories of information. Where you might start with company and product information, later you might add a jobs section or an interactive bulletin board. With the automation programs we've designed, you'll capitalize on the modular approach I mentioned previously. And because your files will be in a standard directory structure, it will all make sense as the site grows and changes. You'll just add a new module to the existing structure. Most likely you'll change the look and feel of your site with these new modules, and that's the next section.

Design Changes

According to Jakob Nielsen, the guru of website usability (www.useit.com), every site should be redesigned once a year as HTML standards expand and the user-base gets more adapted to the technology. Most sites look archaic after a year. People get more adapted. The web is about change. But changing your whole site means changing every page on the site, both its content and its look and feel.

Hand-coded HTML pages, or those coded in a page-based editor (and even some site-based editors), can't "all change at once." This is as true for changing the color of all the titles on your product pages as it is to replace your old 800 number with a new one. HTML pages can't "listen" for instructions. They're like keeping every item of your product catalog as separate documents in MSWord. At first, you set it up so the picture is in the left-hand corner, the title on the right, and price under the picture. If, a year later, you decide to swap the title and picture, automation cures all that. Pages listen and change with minor modification to configuration files.

Dramatic redesigns are where true automation shines in this regard. Your text is in a structured system of text only, with only minor formatting. The formatting is done on the fly, as the pages load, and will change all at once, eliminating the need for any modifications by an editor. Automation can't help you with rewriting your content, but changing its design will be a no-brainer.

Remote Authoring

Many of the chapters of this book enable you and your visitors to change pieces of the site without having to log into the system, download the pages or database to be changed, make the changes and re-upload the updated files. You make the changes right on the server, through a webform. Hit Submit and it's done. Whether it's adding an e-mail address to your database of customers or editing an entire section of your website, all interaction is via HTTP and your web browser. There are a number of benefits, which I'll cover later, and included are all I've just covered. If you plan to keep your site fresh with content from several teams from several locations, remote authoring is your solution for site management.

Security

Even the CIA's website got hacked by professional bad guys. Nobody is immune, but minimizing the number of people with login access reduces the chances it will happen to you. Most security breaks, according to the current research, begin with nontechnical leaks. A disgruntled employee uses her or his old password. A hacker tricks a security person into full access; they have a family connection behind the firewall. The fewer people to whom you give FTP and Telnet access to your server the better, but what if you can't control it? What if several people, some of whom you don't know well, must be given access to post material to the site?

Each of the utilities we developed, and some of the others in the book we didn't, have their own password that can changed easily by the one person with FTP or Telnet access. The HTTP updating takes this password as a passed parameter of the webform that transmits the update. The password is encrypted. Changes to the site are made through HTTP, a safer protocol with special permissions much more strict than FTP. The program runs in a "sandbox" with controls that you set for the webserver as a user on the system.

And, as you probably know, the webform transmission can also be encoded with standard Secure Sockets Layer (SSL) encryption. You can't do this with FTP, so there is always the possibility of someone intercepting the login and password as they pass from the client to the server.

Version Control

If you've ever had two webmasters at different locations trying to update one remote copy of a website, you've had someone overwrite the other's changes. Even if you're among the few who haven't, tracking changes and accountability has been almost nonexistent. Keeping track of who did what and when is impossible on a frequently changing website without a comprehensive tracking system, a server-based automation system, or both.

We've addressed most of this problem by basing most of the automation in the book at the server, not the client, so is there is never more than one copy of the site. The only hole in this is when the administration is updated through a webform. HTTP is a *stateless protocol*, meaning that the server doesn't know or care who you are or what documents it has served you. So if two people are editing the same page in their respective browsers, one could hit Submit before the other one does, but after they have grabbed the latest page version to be edited.

So in Chapter 11, where we install WebPost, we've included a version control system that tracks who made changes when, and stores copies of all edited documents. This could save hours of work should the situation I described in the last paragraph happen to you.

T I P As a bonus to this book, you'll find a useful utility called Client Tracker on the website at www.world-media.com/toolkit. Included are full installation and training instructions. Managing multiple sites for multiple clients on multiple servers can be difficult. This web-based system will track it for you. It even comes with a billing system.

But WebPost and the rest of the utilities in this book aren't the be-all, end-all to automation. Even a simple but elegant solution like FrontPage could be used to track changes to documents with its table of contents bot. The web team could have a work guideline that says put the old copy in a special directory. The bot could give you a complete directory listing with time stamp. See Chapters 2 and 3 for more, the basic point being that the issue of accountability is more feasible when there is an automation engine on your back end.

Interactivity

I almost didn't include this benefit here because to me it's redundant that a site that has these components will be interactive, but it's nothing to take for granted. As the web progresses beyond the stage of hype, and media battles over who offers the hippest browser, interactivity will become the measuring stick for the success of your project. What may start as a simple discussion board today will transform into an entire customer service department in the near future. Businesses ranging from giant Cisco Communications to tiny software houses have already seen what moving their support systems to the web can mean. Cost savings, loyalty, customer satisfaction, they're all fringe benefits of an interactive website.

Also included is the issue of community for media sites and online news and information. No longer are people satisfied to simply read *Inc.* magazine. They have to go online and discuss what they've read. *Inc.* has done a great job of supplying online forums for their readers and feeding off the printed magazine without the online effort becoming shovelware. Automation has enabled it.

That's what automation is to interactivity. It's an enabler. Once you learn how to use a few of the utilities in this book, you'll be off inventing stuff that's twice as useful to your visitors. You'll hit the pages of *Wired* as a most innovative site. You'll look back and remember the days when your site was comprised of only static HTML pages. You'll laugh at how short-sighted the majority of websites still are. Without interactivity, you might as well print a brochure.

Customization

Presenting a different page based on a user's preferences or capabilities can be a mess when tried through conventional static means: "Click here for frames, click there for ActiveX, Sorry, you can't view this portion of our site without Netscape Navigator." It's confusing for users. Maybe you've tried offering a "no frames" alternative (even though it's built into the frame tag) and wondered if it was worth it, if people even understood the difference.

If you've tried it, you may have also found that it's nearly impossible to track what version of what ties to what and how (say that ten times fast). Keeping several versions of a site is a workflow nightmare. Many blame the proprietary content, but that's not it. It's trying to keep track of it on several static documents that have some global content and some user-specific content. You can't possibly accommodate all the preferences and capabilities of every user with multiple versions of the same static page.

But at the same time, you've read about firefly.com, my.yahoo and others who customize information based on users' preferences and capabilities without making them click around and without maintaining a huge accumulation of static documents.

You've probably known this was automated but assumed that such a system would cost millions to build. In some cases, that's true, but several of the solutions in this book allow you to customize at length with only a minor learning curve. This chapter isn't about getting technical, so I won't cite code examples, but it's as simple as "if this, do this, else, do that." Customizing your pages for a browser can be as easy as ten lines of code. One example that just went up as I write this is our customer Experts International. The green sidebar to the site goes away if you hit it with Microsoft Internet Explorer 3.0, because it does not format the blockquote tag correctly, causing the text of many of the pages to flow down around the button bar. This makes it unreadable against the dark green, so we had to correct it with an if/then test in the site's back end, which is written in Perl.

In several places you'll see me discuss how a page "listens." This is just another application for it and is how the documents we'll create in this book differ from all of the static page and site generators on the market. Give a page ears, and it can listen for browser-type, time of day, referring page, address of the visitor, cookies, and other customization options to create a unique page for every visitor. We can even listen for form variables as they're passed from one page to another, customizing as we go. Wouldn't it be nice to put a "Welcome America Online Subscriber" at the top of your shopping site? With the automation in this book you'll be able to.

Conclusion: Justifying the Expense

"Do it right the first time" couldn't apply more than to a website. In a world where only 10 percent of visitors ever even scroll down the page, it doesn't pay to promise lots and deliver little. If your website stinks, you will not be given a second chance.

The problem is rarely with the startup content. It's that the content gets stale and is missing the needed interactive component that the web demands. Perfectly good sites implode under the weight of ongoing expense because nobody foresaw how difficult a static site can be to maintain. Technology directors and webmasters design a series of templates through which content will be streamlined, but it's not enough and costs rise as the site gets older with more and more archived content. Even some high-profile sites like PCWeek and CNN seem to be built on a static, page-based template system. If I'm right, they could be saving a bundle by automating the posting of content.

I've priced an automated website for several large companies who have chosen a cheaper option based on static HTML pages. I get angry, thinking that they can't see past their noses, but it's more than that. The web is a misunderstood media, and technology decision-makers range from neophyte to *netizen,* or citizen of the net. Making an intelligent decision isn't going to come entirely from reading this book, and I'm not promising that our Perl programs and other utilities in this book are the absolute answer for you, your company, and your company's needs, but we've designed everything here from the perspective of a sustainable web, one that can expect the changes that will occur and be flexible enough never to become a throw-away. Too many websites are first efforts that are thrown away as the company learns more. Delay your project until you are willing to build it right and sustain it. Compel that 10 percent to scroll down your page.

Client-Based
Automation Systems

I admit that when I sat down to research this chapter my plan was to bash programs like NetObjects. I've seen more bad sites than good come from WYSIWIG editing tools that claim to automate your site, but this one really impressed me. A ton of thought went into its capabilities and interface, and in the right hands NetObjects is a powerful automation tool for a webmaster on a budget who doesn't have access to and/or interest in server CGI/API automation.

Most of this chapter is about NetObjects, but the underlying premise of why this book needed a section on client-based automation is most important as we progress further. As I noted in the introduction, websites that don't implement some sort of automation eventually implode. The content for the site gets bogged in the webmaster bottleneck of coding new pages and re-coding old ones with new hotlinks. If you sell dinosaurs, as we'll try later in Chapter 10, adding a new pterodactyl to the "Flying Creatures" page is too cumbersome to keep a site fresh with new inventory as it comes and goes. Automation, whether through a database connection, a custom server program, or a client system like this one, updates the Flying Creature page automatically when you either update the database or enter a new item into a template. The difference between client and server systems, in this model, is real-time versus publish, in which you take a snapshot of your data, save a copy of your whole site with your data filled into the templates, then upload the whole site. Client systems do this, and when your data changes, the site goes out of date. Periodically, you take a new snapshot and upload the whole site again. With server-based, you either feed the website from your database real-time, or you periodically upload just your data and the site hits that real-time. The latter has little advantage over client systems in this context but is advantageous in others.

The biggest weakness of client automation is that the pages it spits out can't "listen." If I want my customers to log into my website via a password screen, look up their account on the fly, and give them a price based on their buying pattern, I'm dead in the water. If I want to put different keywords into my page's META tag for different search engines that spider the site, listening for their HTTP_USER_AGENT, I can't. Sound like neat stuff? It is, and it's possible very easily with the server-based systems in the later chapters. But you might not need that stuff. You might just need an easy way to put a new dinosaur on your website without having to keep a full-time webmaster on the payroll. You might also be a full-time webmaster who just needs a good site management utility without building an interactive wonder of modern web science. Innovation isn't for everyone, and NetObjects has done enough innovating for a whole generation of webmasters with Fusion.

Before deciding whether Fusion is for you, ask yourself one final question: Does more than one person have to edit the same section of the site at one time? We ran into this at www.mas-jobs.com, an employment firm. They needed to have up to six agents input a job into the Microsoft Technology section at the same time. In Fusion this would be impossible. Even if each one had a copy of the software on her or his desktop, every time one published the site it would erase the others' changes. Fusion accounts for this a bit with a publish option that only uploads changed assets, but for them it wouldn't work. It could help only if each agent posted only to one category of job (e.g., one did Microsoft, one did Unix Sysadmin, one did Webmastering, etc.). Use Fusion only if the qualifiers in the last paragraph apply and you can logistically work out a system whereby different administrators work on completely different sections of the site.

But why did I choose Fusion over the virtual landslide of client-based site management utilities? Even with its recent price decrease it's still two hundred dollars and this is a "for the webmaster on a budget" book. One reason is because I don't think you could do better than the organization interface and code automation that it generates. Another is that it comes with an incredible array of premade graphics, with more available on the NetObjects website. (Fusion actually makes graphics, not only pages, on the fly for you when you preview or publish the site.) And the other big clincher for Fusion is its database options, which as you'll see in our test, didn't work entirely right but are still really well done. Its big database benefit is for those without a database but a large list of products. We've dealt with several clients over the years with a large, organized product line but no database. Usually they've just printed a catalog in the past and kept it on hand for orders. In such cases we've had to create web-based administration systems for those who could afford it (custom database CGI ain't cheap), but others have had to settle for no dynamic product system at all, only informational product category pages. Fusion allows you to create and manage all sorts of data objects, including databases, with almost no learning curve and absolutely no programming ability. You can also connect natively to Access files and through OBDC to just about anything else. To quote a poster on the user USENET group netobjects.fusion20.databases (their newserver is news.netobjects.com), "Actually, the price gives us an advantage over Joe Blow, who would be throwing together pages for a sub-rate cost, bypassing the critical design stages of a professionally developed site. The price is perfect for a corporate design firm." The short answer to "Why Fusion?" is that I couldn't find a client-only system that comes close for twice its price.

Fusion's interface is also fairly easy to use. Although I wouldn't set a temp in front of it and ask him or her to put a new stegosaurus on the site, it's usable enough for a trained beginner to remember how to do basic tasks without having to relearn the system every time. This is my biggest concern with proprietary client-based systems. The user interface can be forgotten easily if you don't update the site regularly. Fusion is fairly intuitive, especially if you've ever used any kind of publishing program.

It also handles complex layout very well. Fusion builds all of its pages as a series of nested tables, so you can drag and drop any text, form field, image, whatever from one place on the page to another without much trouble. Fusion adjusts the table accordingly, even allowing you to resize the entire page. One other note is that it has the best frames generation I've ever seen. For every link you click on the site it generates an entirely new frameset, allowing you to bookmark any page on the site, something devoid of most frames pages. You retain the usability of keeping your menu always on top without losing the bookmark capability.

I've approached the following tutorial from the perspective of "get the job done." Rather than take you through Fusion feature by feature, I've begun constructing an online catalog, demonstrating some of Fusion's usability and capabilities as I go. It's quite a machine, worthy of at least a book this size, but if you follow this exactly, then go in and follow NetObject's online tutorial, you should be a pro in no time. The best news about Fusion is that we've spoken with their development team and a server component is planned for the next major release. Let's hope it's more than just a form CGI. Adding functionality similar to SiteWrapper in Chapter 6 and WebPost in Chapter 11 would make Fusion the killer application the web's been waiting for. But for now, in the field of client-based automation, you won't beat it.

If you follow this tutorial exactly it should last less than an hour, with minimal data-entry (short for "wasted time") and very little throw-away content. I'm using a template to get us started.

TIP We've included version 201 version g07d on the CD in the /software/ directory. It will run only on Windows 95 and NT. The file name is fusion.exe. Copy it to a temporary directory and either Run it from the Start menu in Windows or double-click on it in your Windows Explorer. This will launch the autoinstaller. Before installing g07d, you should check the www.NetObjects.com site to see if there is a patch later than g07d. They periodically upgrade the software. The CD will at least save you the initial 15 megabyte download. If you do find a later patch, download and install it. You should then be ready to go. The trial is only for thirty days, but the copy and patch are fully functional.

Getting Started with Fusion

When you open Fusion, a box pops up that asks you for a Site Name (or the last site you worked on if you've already run it). Type in a real name for the site, not necessarily a www.yourcompany.com address. This is just a formal name.

Next, for the demo I'm going to choose an AutoSite Template. It will give us some fodder to quickly learn the editor. You could also use the Remote Site Import to experiment with an existing site. Any changes you make locally will not affect the online version unless you publish the site to the web. The last option is Save Site To, which is just the location of the files. We left it alone for our test, but if you have an established directory structure you'll want to use that. Click OK. Fusion will then create a template for you. You should have a screen like Figure 2.1.

First, let's take a look at the editor. Click the registration page twice or highlight it and switch views by clicking Page in the top menu bar. You're probably saying "neat-o" at the user interface. I did. It even highlights the button for you that the page is on. Figure 2.2 should be in front of you. I'm going to change the page from a registration page to an Order a Demo page. We'll pretend this is a manufacturer of the prizes you get from the claw-arm machines in arcades.

In the properties menu along the right side of the screen, click the page tab. Change the name to "Send Me a Demo." Then click Custom Names. It gives you a chance to pare down your page name to text that will fit on a button or Banner. In

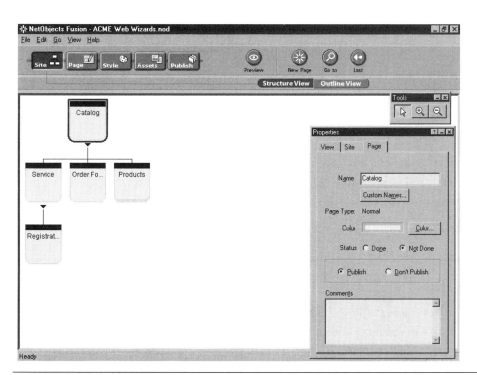

Figure 2.1 Fusion Wizard.

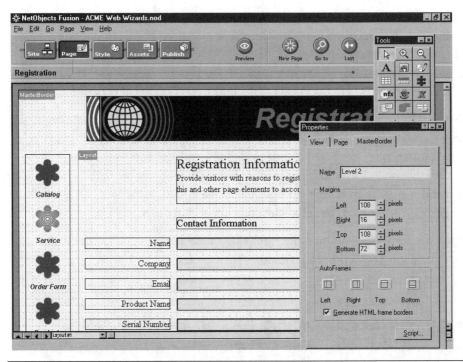

Figure 2.2 The page tab.

the title field, put in a descriptive name for the page that the search engines will like. Then I'll put in Demo for the button and leave the banner as Send Me a Demo. Click OK. You don't have to press Enter or anything else for the changes to take affect in the site, but you have to switch tabs to see it visually. The page name in the left-hand corner will read the old name of the page unless you go back to the site view.

Now I'm going to replace the text in the first box at the top of the screen where it says Registration Information to my own, and make the name, company, and e-mail fields of the form more friendly by adding Your to them. Then I'll add Select a to the product and Please Fill in its Serial Number to the next two fields.

Now let's make the Product Name into a drop-down list of four products. Select the text box in the form and look at the properties for it by clicking the Single Line tab of the Properties menu. Make a note of the name and then delete the form field. After the field is deleted, go into the Tools bar that should be hanging in the upper-right corner. If you don't see a Tools menu, select View/Tool Palette. In the bottom-right corner of the palette is the Forms button. Click it, and the bottom of the button will extend with possible forms input types. The bottom right is a drop-down list (they call it a "forms combo box"). Click it; your cursor turns into a plus sign, and you're ready to draw. Click on the page and drag out the box where you want it. Don't be alarmed if it looks ugly at first, because it will.

Return to the Properties menu again, where you'll see a tab called Combo Box. Click there and set the name to the name you noted previously (contact_product). Then change the Type to Dropdown List.

Next, in the Elements box, add your items. Click the plus sign to add one. For each you'll be asked for a Name and Value pair and whether you want it selected by default when the page loads. If you don't select any default the drop list will be blank as the first value. Click OK for each item. Remove items with the minus sign and change the order of the pages with the arrow buttons. Select one and click up or down. Figure 2.3 shows you the menus.

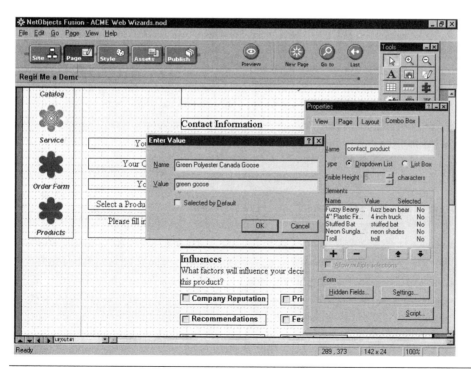

Figure 2.3 Managing elements.

Let's preview what we've done so far. In the top middle of the screen, click the eyeball preview button, and it will launch the default browser, starting from the page which you were last on. Keep in mind that we're still on a local copy of the site.

Changing Styles

At this point you may want to change the look of your buttons. From the page you're on, click the Style button at the top of the page. It will bring up an entirely new screen, light-purple in color. On the left is the list of premade styles, on the right is the preview window to view changes. I'm going to select Rascal. It's really neat and they deliver not only your banners, but three different types of buttons and a bar. All images are created on the fly whenever you preview the site.

Go to the Elements button at the top right of the screen. It brings up a menu of your style properties. I think the text in my Primary Button should be all those different colors, so I'm going to set it as black. Either double-click on Primary Button or click the Edit button next to Set Style. It pops up a box to select the image I want for both highlighted (the page you're on) and regular buttons. I'm going to leave the default images, but click on Text Settings for the Regular button. There I'll change the color to white by clicking the Set button next to color. Figure 2.4 shows the series of menus that I've gone through. Click OK twice, then switch the Highlighted color in your test if you want. I then went back and made the font bold as well. Once you've selected a style and edited it accordingly, click the orange Set Style button in the upper left of the screen below Style. Then click the Page button to view your changes.

Understanding MasterBorders

There are two views from the page layout, each with their own properties. You should see the word MasterBorder in gray in the top left, and Layout diagonally left and down. The Layout, as you can see by the lines extending around it, is a middle to MasterBorder. Click outside the Layout box and you'll see the Properties Menu change to include a MasterBorder tab, which you should now check.

The Name field lets you assign several border styles to different classes of pages. I'm going to name mine "final leaf node" and use it for pages like our current form. Below the Name field is Margins. You can set top, bottom, right, and left margins

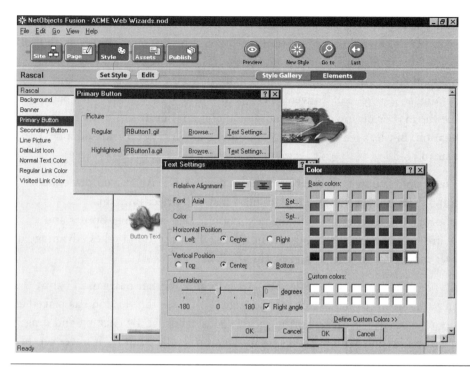

Figure 2.4 Style properties.

by edging the sliders or typing in a value. To kill the border entirely, just set it to zero. You'll see the changes take effect as you make them. Keep in mind that what we're altering is the perimeter, which will remain the same for every page to which I apply the final leaf node MasterBorder. If you have trouble seeing the difference between the MasterBorder and Layout pieces of the screen, go to the View tab under Properties and click None for Grid/Guides.

You can also change MasterBorder by moving or adding the navigational graphics on the page. Click on the header for this page and you'll see the tab Banner added to the Properties menu. It's very easy not to use the Fusion-supplied graphics and to use your own on any given page, diverting from the style you chose before. It's easy to divert to another preselected style for any given page by assigning either Site Style or Other.

If you click on the Side Navigation bar, the Properties menu changes yet again. Under the Nav Bar tab you can first select which links Fusion should include. The set button will let you choose from four options. The First Level is the main navigational node from the homepage. The Parent Level is the level before the documents to which you plan to assign this MasterBorder. It could be the same as the First Level if these are links immediately off the homepage. The next, Current Level, you'd use for horizontal entries in a category of information. So if our sample company sold stuffed animals, plastic cars, souvenir pens, and plastic wristwatches, this page might be the master plastic cars list and would contain buttons to other major areas of navigation. But let's leave this button bar alone as First Level and add a new one later instead.

The next option down on our Nav Bar settings is Style. Again you can either plug in the default site style or a replacement that will affect only this MasterBorder. I'm leaving this and the next choice, Display, alone. Border and Spacing are for the table that holds the buttons. Fill Background takes advantage of the newer table background option of HTML 3.2.

While we're in this MasterBorder I'm going to add another navigation bar at the bottom. Scroll down to the bottom of the page. You'll see that Fusion has placed a text-only navigation bar in the bottom of this MasterBorder. By clicking and dragging one of the middle white squares on its edge I'm going to move it lower on the page and add a graphical bar above it. While you're in the bottom of the MasterBorder, click the Toolbar on the third row down, middle button. Then select the bottom horizontal navigation bar and click and drag a new bar in the bottom border. A bar will appear with the default Top Level buttons. I'm going to change it in the Properties menu by clicking the Nav Bar tab and Current Level, Secondary Buttons. As you'll see in Figure 2.5, I've not made anything substantial for the bar.

The Layout View

Let's move to the Layout. You can change that by clicking its area. The Layout tab automatically appears, allowing you to name the Layout (if you're still confused about the difference, go the main View menu at the top of the page and select Layout Only). Give it a name and select the width and height of this middle layout we're working on. We select the width and height because Fusion sets your site up as a table. Due to differences in monitor type you may want to try your pages at different monitor sizes.

Next in the Layout menu you can select a MasterBorder to apply, then modify the style of the page as before. You also add a background picture and sound or

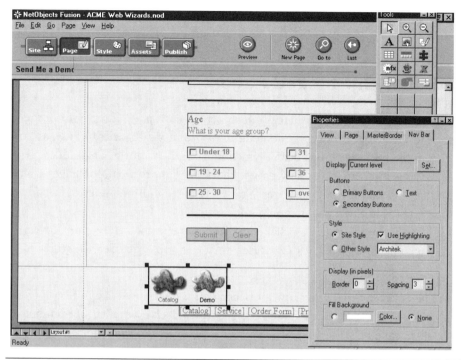

Figure 2.5 MasterBorder controls.

specify an external HTML document to grab the layout's innards from. The last option, Table Structure, lets you choose whether Fusion should prioritize vertical or horizontal alignment when constructing your layout. Columns makes it so your site will line up perfectly from top to bottom, Rows prioritizes horizontal relationships. If this is confusing, search for Structure in the help topics. The last button is Show HTML Table. Hold it down and Fusion will show you exactly how it's going to construct your page.

By clicking Site at the top left of the screen, we'll move out of the page mode and into a whole new area of easy automation. From here I want to turn what Fusion is calling the Catalog page into our homepage, then spider three product category pages, then spider individual product pages below them. First, take a look at the way the products page is stacked with pages. This means that there are several of the same Layout. Change one product page Layout (from the middle section), and you change them all. This is different from what we were doing before. Altering the form Layout section didn't effect any other document. Only altering MasterBorder made changes to documents sharing its format. We're not going to use this page, so rename Products to OldProducts by clicking on the title of the page on the yellow tab and typing the new title.

Working with Stacked Pages

I don't like the way they've got their products set up. You jump directly from the homepage to the actual products, not a choice of product categories, which, as you can see from the homepage, has been divided into three categories of products. To do this, we have to create three new pages. First, highlight the Catalog page (a blue border will be around it), then click the New Page button in the upper-right corner three times. Three untitled pages should appear under the Catalog pages as hotlinks. Then name the pages by clicking on the name in the yellow tab Gloves, Stuffed Arachnids, and Dried Sea Creatures, then click on Dried Sea Creatures to bring it up in the editor.

Fusion has created three pages, one of which you should now have in front of you, with an empty layout and your default MasterBorder. Click on the left-bottom button in the Toolbar, called Data List. It will extend the Toolbar into two choices. Click the left one, Data List, which changes your cursor into a plus sign. Drag a box along the grid within the layout page. This brings up a Data Publishing menu that lets you choose what you want to show the world about your product on your website. Select your Data Object, which should be Products, and sort by Product Name or whatever you prefer. The template came with this little sample database. These are our fields.

The next button, Filter Set, we won't use yet. It's to prevent items from your database from appearing on the site. Our next field is the Name field. Here we'll use Gloves, or Stuffed Arachnids, or possibly even Dried Sea Creatures. I'm choosing Dried Sea Creatures.

Then from our sample database, check off what fields we want to include in the product page overview site. I'm just going to check Product Name and Price. Then I'll select Product Name and click Link/Unlink. That will hotlink only the name to the actual product page, not the price. The word (link) should appear (it actually crashed the program the first time we tried it but worked the second time).

Now check the Display All Fields button and Add Navigation buttons (next/ previous/up). Click OK. That should bounce you back into your Line 1 page as in Figure 2.6.

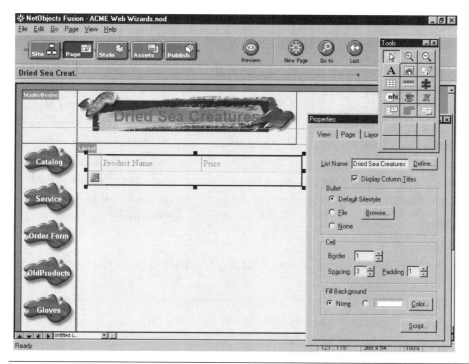

Figure 2.6 Database controls.

Go back to Site view and you'll see the change we just made. Under the page Dried Sea Creatures, there should be a page called Untitled Stacked Page. Rename that Dried Sea Creatures as well, then click Page to change your Layout. The bar at the top is called Dried Sea Creatures. The MasterBorder automatically plugs in the page name for the entire set of stacked pages.

Changing the Look

The default product page is ugly. Looking at the page there are a set of black boxes on the left and red boxes on the right. The black are just text that's printed on the page. The default says Product Name, colon, next line, Product Image, colon, next line. Boring. The red are the actual database fields (remember, it's keeping its own little database here and plugging it into the stacked page layout). I liked the way that they set up their Product page much better than this default so I'm going to go and steal it to replace this. Click the Go To button in the upper-right corner. It will give you a choice of Begins With, Contains, and Ends With. Leave Begins With, check and type Old, and press Enter. You'll be catapulted to the OldProducts page.

Now I'm going to capture the whole layout by clicking in one corner of the Layout and dragging to the opposite corner. Don't go outside the layout into the MasterBorder. It will select all the boxes from the layout. Then go to your Edit menu at the top of the screen and select Copy. Then use the same Go To button we used before to go back to the Dried Sea Creatures page. Select everything within the Layout of that page and press your Delete key. Then select Edit/Paste. Your Sea Creatures pages are now ready to input items. Do the same for Gloves and Stuffed Arachnids. Notice that the two red boxes at the top of the Layout don't say anything next to or above them. You usually wouldn't print Product Name before its name; this layout shows you how a nice screen could look.

The Description and Technical Specifications fields say that within them. When you add an item, you will remove those words in the boxes. To find out what the other fields are, click on the red box. It will turn white and allow you to type within it. Then from the Properties menu, click the Data Field tab. It shows you where you are, and allows you to change it.

I'm going to type Five Inch Urchins into the Product Name text box, then follow up with descriptions for the others. The second box down is SKU Number, then the Description, Technical Specifications, and Price. While you're adding text to the box, experiment with the Text tab in the Properties menu to see how Fusion can format text within a database field entry. To add a picture, browse for it from your Properties menu as well, from under the Picture tab. To add another item, click on the plus sign in orange next to the Stacked Page. It's just simple input screens from here, and you can duplicate this for all of your item categories.

Before we move on, though, I'd like to note that Fusion automatically selected MasterBorder Default. You find this by first clicking inside the MasterBorder. I want a MasterBorder for just my product pages, so I have to make one. Click back in the Layout section. Then under the Layout tab, click New, next to the MasterBorder. It will give you Untitled 6 or something similar. To rename it, click in the MasterBorder area of the screen, which will change the Properties menu, then rename it Products. Now we can modify just the products MasterBorder without touching those on the other parts of the site. This could get a bit unwieldy for a big site with several sections, but the management is about as easy to use as you can get. Note that our modifications to the Products MasterBorder don't affect the Products Layout.

To change that, we can drag and drop, but first I want to save this layout in case I mess up or wish to revert to an old setting. First, I want to rename my layout from the title it gave me, Untitled Layout, to DSC1. Then, at the bottom of the screen, next to the arrows, should be a small white box that just changed to DSC1. Click there and you'll see the option Add..., which will give you a new Layout with nothing in it called Dried Sea Creatures Layout. You can then rename this DSC2. It will put that as a choice on the little menu now. Then do what you did to get the layout for DSC1, Copy it either from OldProducts or DSC1 and Paste it into DSC2. Note that you can switch back and forth between layouts and make edits to each without affecting the page. As you'll see, it keeps your data for the page.

Now I'm just going to drag and drop the price field from the bottom of the page to below the image. Shrink it so it fits nicely, then click in the Technical Specifications box. Then click delete; Dried Sea Creatures don't have technical specifications.

I do need to tell potential buyers two other things that aren't presently data fields. One is how many I have on hand, and the other is a field for an occasional Sale on odd lots. That means we have to add Data Fields. Click on Assets, in the top middle of the screen. Then click the orange Data Objects, then double-click on Products. It's showing you the actual database properties Fusion has created for you. In the screen below are all your Data Fields. Click the plus sign for a new one. Then name it Inventory, and select Formatted Text in case we want to bold it or something. Click OK and then repeat it for a field called Odd Lots. Click OK, then go back to the Page view.

Where it says Technical Specifications, in a little blue box (colored table data), replace the text with Current Inventory, then click the middle bottom-button on the Toolbar. We have plus sign again, so draw a small box the size of the Current Inventory box. Select the Inventory Data Field and click OK.

Next, to the right of the Current Inventory box, I want to put the Odd Lots, so next to it I'm going to put another blue box. Click on the A in the Toolbar, then draw a little box. Type Odd Lots and select Background Color from the Properties/Text tab. OOPS, Fusion used a color not in the master palette, so go to the old blue box that says Current Inventory and click on its Color Properties/Text/Background/Color tab. It will bring you to the palette that blue preselected. Add to Custom Colors and click OK. Then, while you're there, do the same for its Text Color and note that the font size is Arial 8-2. Then go back and alter the colors on the Odd Lots text. Click again on that middle bottom button in the Toolbar and draw in the data field below the blue box you just created. Note that no matter how big you draw it, it will snap back to single height. If you want it bigger as a default, like the Description box, click in it and check Lock Size from the Properties menu. Then manually resize the box with your mouse and its edges will stay put.

Now I'll put some default content in the box about some odd lots on hand at special prices. One thing I noticed is that Fusion puts a <P> tag when you press Enter. If you hold down the Shift key it inserts a <BR>, which I'm using for my Odd Lots. Figure 2.7 shows my finished screen.

Next, I wanted to copy the entire stacked page layout directly to Stuffed Arachnids and Gloves from the Site View, but that didn't work. The only way we could find to do it was to go into the Dried Sea Creatures page and Edit/Copy the middle layout. To do that we go back to site view, double-click on the master Gloves page, add the Data List from the Toolbar, drag a box, then fill in the dialog

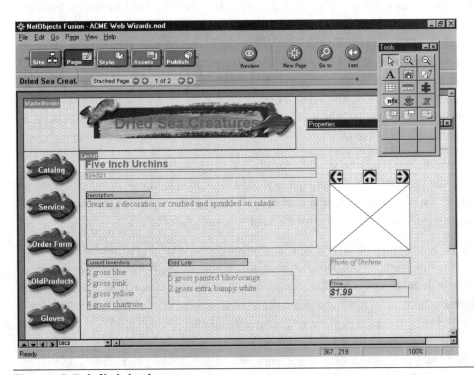

Figure 2.7 A finished page.

box that allows you to select the fields to put in. Don't forget that you also have to assign the Products MasterBorder.

Another breakdown we found in this stage of the automation was in multiple Layouts for your pages. It was convenient to be able to flip back and forth between types of Layouts with that select list at the bottom left of the screen, but nowhere could we find an import Layout to copy one layout of stacked pages to another. If you want multiple Layouts on multiple stacked page sections (Dried Sea Creatures, Stuffed Arachnids, Gloves), you have to copy them manually just like the master one. Double-click on Catalog (the homepage) in the Site View now.

Manipulating Images

Fusion automatically put three graphics on our homepage with Line, Product on them. You'd replace these in our examples with product photos or logos, then replace the text as well. One note is that by clicking on a photo and using the Picture tab on the Properties menu, you can alter all the settings for the image. The first is the actual file and the second is Transparency, which you have to prepare with the Toolbar first. By clicking the middle button in the second row down, you will be offered five choices to alter the image. The right top one is Transparency. Use the dropper to select a color. The button to the left of it is the Picture button; draw a box with it to insert a new picture. The bottom three buttons are all image mapping options. Click on either the rectangle, ellipse, or polygon and draw a hotspot on the image, then select either an Internal, Smart, or External link. Keep in mind, getting back to the original purpose for sidetracking into the Toolbar, that only the .gif format will image map.

The next setting is the Align, Stretch, and Tile. If you make a box around an image bigger than the image in Fusion, it doesn't resize the image to fit automatically. That's what stretch is for. Tile repeats the image within the box. Figure 2.8 shows an image in the bigger box aligned left, stretched, and tiled.

Show Hotspots outlines your image maps—they are just client-side. Text in Element is neat; check the box and click Settings. You can type in your text, set the relative alignment, the font, the color, and the position on the page. The orientation bar rotates the text in any position you wish. One nice feature of this is that you can see the changes in the image as you go.

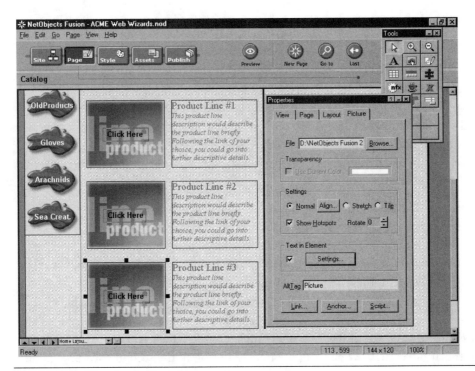

Figure 2.8 Manipulating images.

You should put in the Alt tag, and the next thing (the real reason we came to this page in the first place) is Link. It pops up that same menu you saw on the image map section. Here we're going to choose the Internal Link, which is a bit confusing because as you can see, Dried Sea Creatures has two possible pages. The first one is the link page, showing all the products in that category of our catalog. The second is the first of our Dried Sea Creatures. If I select the top one on this menu (as you can see I am from Figure 2.9), when people click on this image they'll get the whole list. If I select the bottom they'll get the Five Inch Urchin. Click OK and the image is now linked to the main link page.

Database Parsing Features

Now I'm going to divert a bit and pretend that we have a database to connect to our site. I'm going to assume you have Microsoft Access, but not Access 97, which can publish databases the same way as Fusion. With Fusion we're going to "eat" one of the sample databases that comes with Access 97. We wiped out old

Figure 2.9 Linking an image.

Access when they sent the review copy. First, from the Site View, click the New Page button. Then rename Untitled page to Other Products.

Next, double-click on the page to go into Page View, then click that same bottom-left Data List, then the right-bottom button for External Data Source. That changes your cursor into a plus sign. Drag a box, and that will pop up a Data Source Type box. Leave Access selected and find the file /Fusion/db/North-wind.mdb on the CD. Click Open and you'll see a list in the database. It's a relational database, so these are actual tables with values for several entries in them. We're going to select the top one, Products. The plan as we go forward is to create a set of stacked pages of just one category of products, which you'll duplicate for other categories.

As you can see, we only have several fields of information. Start at the top of the page with Sort by ProductName. Then click Set Filter. It gives us three filtering options; the first we'll set at Category "equal to" 1, which is Beverages in the companion table (we looked in Access). Then we'll set "and" at the end of that line, and on the next line, set UnitsInStock to greater than 5. At the end of that line, select "and," then on the next line, select UnitPrice less than 26. What we just did was create a set of stacked pages called Beverages that only grabs items with more than five units in stock, and whose price is less than twenty-six dollars. Click OK.

Next, name the Data List Beverages Below $26 to remember the query we just built. Then we move to selecting the fields to extract onto the page, which highlights Fusion's weakness when compared to full-featured database publishing tools. You can't extract the supplier's name from the SupplierID field. It's their ID number, which will mean nothing to a user. The Access database knows how to link this

Product table to the Supplier table, extracting the name of the supplier. However, Fusion is limited to one table at a time. Our only usable fields for this page are ProductName, which you'll also click the Link/Unlink button for, then UnitPrice and UnitsInStock. These are the field that people will see when they browse to the main Beverages page. Click OK.

In this version of Fusion, the filtering in Figure 2.10 didn't work correctly. The Comparison choice in the Query menu defaulted to the value in the top field. So if we set CategoryID equal to the others below, it would default to equal to. We could change them on the menu, but when we clicked OK twice, returning to the Page View, the stacked list was empty. By double-clicking on the Data List we got back the Data Publishing menu, then we clicked on Set and the filters had all been reset to equals to. I almost went back and deleted this detailed explanation, but figured the bug will be fixed for your patch level. If you are buying NetObjects off the shelf, be sure to get the latest patch and check for the bug. Their bug department knows of the defect.

Now we're going to edit the stacked pages. From the Other Products page view, click the down arrow in the lower-left corner of the screen. Here you'll see the weakness of the ID fields I just mentioned. First, before we really start, I'm going to delete all the ID fields. Then I'll get rid of the Reorder Level and Discontinue.

Then we'll work on the Layout. Our colors are still saved from before, so making these product pages look similar to the others is easy. In Figure 2.11, you'll see the result, along with a great little feature I would never have found without one of their beta tester's (Rob Holak, who also works for me) assistance. It's called Size Layout to Elements, which is under the Edit menu. At any given time, after you placed all of your elements within the page, you can click that and it will snug everything up and reduce the amount of whitespace on the page between elements.

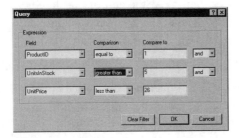

Figure 2.10 The filtering bug.

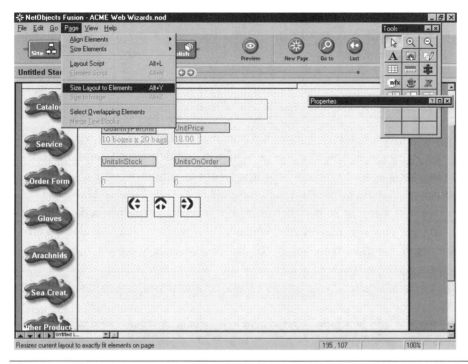

Figure 2.11 The Size Layout function.

Now we have to title our Untitled Stacked Pages by going to the Site View and clicking inside the yellow tab. I'm calling it Beverages; you'd make a link just like it for every Data List you put on Other Products or duplicate the whole process and start a New Page again called Condiments, in which case you would not have called the last New Page Other Products, but Beverages. For this model, which we'll publish later, we're setting up another filtered, stacked list called Condiments.

Just in case we ever need its layout again, I'm going to set OldProducts to stay in our tree, but not publish. Highlight it, then go to the Properties/Page tab and Don't Publish, which puts a red dot in the upper right of the yellow tab folder. Notice the Done and Not Done selections on that same tab. You can set this for any page. It puts a checkmark in the upper left of the yellow tab.

Next, I want to reorder our buttons on the automatically generated navigation bars. The order form should be last on our list so we don't seem pushy. Click and drag it to the end. The yellow tabs will highlight with a red arrow to wherever the page will land when you let the mouse button go. If you don't have the program loaded in front of you, Figure 2.12 should give you a good idea of what it should look like even without the color.

Processing Forms

The one thing I have yet to do is hook up our form to a CGI processing component. From Site View, double-click on Order Form and delete the Submit button. Go into the Tools menu to the nfx item (the fourth down on the left). When you click on it you'll see six options on the bottom. The bottom right is AutoForm (click around on these for some other neat toys as well). Then draw a new Submit button with the plus sign it gives you, which will then bring up a Component tab in your Properties menu. Rename Submit if you like, then the Success and Error URLs. The output file is where your form data will be saved. When you click on Publish, it will offer you a Windows and Unix option. If you can use the Unix

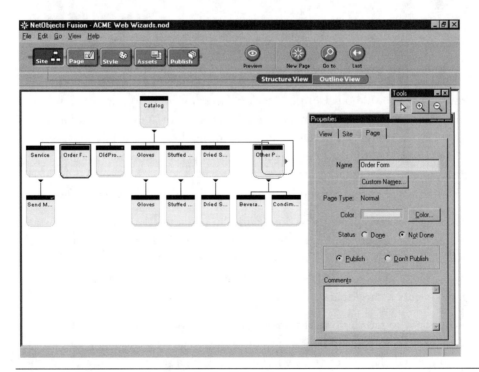

Figure 2.12 Navigation Tools in Site View.

option, do so. The support people at NetObjects have said the Windows option is still buggy.

The last is your Perl path, which you should check with your system administrator. And one final note: you have to go back to all your form fields and change them all from names to numbers. It's in the NetObjects program manual. NetObjects strongly advises that you use your own scripts to handle forms.

That's it for now as far as editing the site. As I said at the beginning of the chapter, Fusion is quite a machine. It deserves a whole book, of which I'm sure there are a few, but you've seen most of the features. All that's left is first to preview our site, then publish it to the server. To preview, click on the eye button at the top. To just preview the highlighted page, hold down CONTROL while clicking the eye.

Time to Publish

Now click the Publish button and the Settings button. You'll see three tabs, Stage, Publish, and Modify. Stage and Publish are actually the same thing, but different. With Stage, you set a previewing location for the site in case you have a boss or client who needs to preview the site live before you upload it to the server. Publish is the site's final resting place. Both have the same options, so we'll go ahead and publish.

I'm selecting Remote and Configuring the settings. Figure 2.13 shows an example configured. The Remote Host should be your server's name. You should leave the Base Directory blank if you're configuring for www.yourcompany.com. The CGI Bin is dependent on your system, Name and Password are yours. The Password field won't light up unless you click Remember Password; click OK.

Under the Files options, you can publish the homepage as index, what's shown, or if you're on an NT server you might want to use default. The extension should be either .htm or .html unless you're running a server component externally. I'd leave the other two as checked; otherwise you'll be generating some possible dead links and re-uploading the whole site every time you make a spelling change.

The Modify tab was a shocker. Its first choice is to publish an optional Text Only site for visitors. The second is a Greyscale site for lower bandwidth graphics and users on LCD monitors, and Low Bandwidth reduces the color depth in images

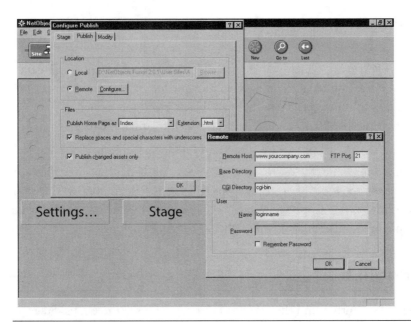

Figure 2.13 Configuring the Remote Server.

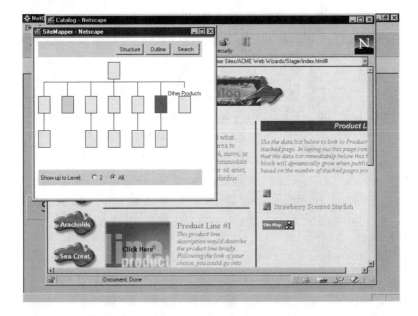

Figure 2.14 Fusion Mapping applet.

for others on 14,400 or below modems. The Site Map options are both only slightly viable. The NetObjects map is a Java applet, and the HotSauce is a plug-in. HTML Generation can be with Comments, and you can skip High ASCII character set conversion, which converts to ampersand characters. We checked them all and clicked OK. Then click Publish (or Stage), and Fusion munges for quite a while.

You'll link to index_greyscale.html, index_text_only.html, and index.low_band-width.html from your homepage manually. And to put the site maps, go to your homepage and click the nfx button in the Toolbar. Then click the bottom-left SiteMapper button. When you get the plus sign, draw a box and you're good to go. You'll now have a little SiteMap logo on your homepage. The applet in Figure 2.14 is the result. Hover over a page and it highlights; click on one, and your browser goes there.

3

The Page Model

The most basic type of website automation might be all you need; this chapter discusses two types that are very useful. The first is called Server Side Includes (SSIs) and is a type of server-parsed HTML. You generate dynamic content in your HTML pages by inserting little pieces of code that the server "sees" and knows to substitute with the correct value or file. You've seen these files called on the web. Usually they will display the current time, your identity, or a hit counter. But SSIs go much farther than that, and we'll explore the possibilities on both Unix and NT systems. One note is that the commands available are different for every server. I'm basing this part of the chapter on Apache and Internet Information server. They are both free.

On the Web There is a server for NT called WebQuest that supports a proposal for SSI+ 2.0, which does some great form handling and eliminates the need for quite a bit of CGI. It's at **webquest.questar.com/reference/ssi/ssi+20ref.sht.**

The second part of the chapter is a bit proprietary but far too useful not to mention. It's Microsoft's FrontPage software, which we looked at in the last chapter. Here we extend it with its *bots* interface, which is similar to SSI but far more useful. If you're not a programming type but need a quick way to automate a few basic features, it's worth a look.

Configuring Server Side Includes: Unix

Make sure SSI is enabled on your system by checking with the system administrator. In the server's access.conf (on Apache, in /var/lib/httpd/conf) file should be the Options Includes, or at best, Options IncludesNoExec. It's common to disable them, especially the exec option, due to security risks and system load. SSIs can access files on the system, and the server parsing takes a toll on the overhead of the HTTP transaction.

While you're asking about access.conf, ask the administrator about srm.conf. It should have the line AddType text/x-server-parsed-html .shtml in it so the server knows what to send as a mime type when someone calls yourpage.shtml. You may also need AddHandler server-parsed .shtml. You don't need to understand the why of either of these steps, just confirm that they've been done. Otherwise you'll beat your head against the wall trying to get this stuff to work to no avail. It's a common mistake in the newsgroups.

Make a little file in your server's main directory with one line that reads <!--#include file="index.html"--> (or whatever your index file is), with no spaces in between anything at all. Name it test.shtml and hit it with your browser. If it works, SSIs are up and running on your server.

Configuring Server Side Includes: NT

Unlike Unix servers, Microsoft's Internet Information Server enables SSIs by default. You shouldn't have to edit any registry options to start, but ask your sysadmin. From what I could gather, only a few SSIs were supported with version 2.0. Version 3.0 adds mostly full support. You do, however, have to set a mime type for the .shtml server, which means editing a registry file. Open the registry editor (Regedt32.exe) and find the file hkey_local_machine\system\ CurrentControlSet\Services\InetInfo\Parameters\MimeMap. Add the line text/html,shtml,,1 with two commas before the 1. That translates as mime type, document extension, and gopher type. Also note that there is no period before the shtml. If you are unfamiliar with registry files, ask your system administrator to do this. It can be dangerous stuff.

Now make a little file in your server's main directory with one line that reads <!--#include file="index.html"--> (or whatever your index file is), with no spaces in between anything at all. Name it test.shtml and hit it with your browser. If it works, SSIs are up and running on your server.

Using SSI

If this is confusing to you, don't worry, this is confusing stuff. Server side includes are parsed by the server, which means that the server looks at the page for comments of the right <--# format. Then, before it spits the HTML at the browser it plugs in the requisite values. Sometimes these are simple, like time of day, this documentís name, or what server the visitor is coming from, but server side includes can include a whole text or HTML file, execute a CGI program, and on some servers can even send different results depending on variable conditions.

All server side includes use that same format you started with previously. It's like an HTML comment, but with the # mark before a word that does something, like "include" in our Quick Start example. One type takes the format <!--#config type="value" -->. In practice it's more like <!--config sizefmt="abbrev"-->, which sets the way the server displays the file's size. We'll get to the configuration options, but first here are some simple echo SSIs.

ECHO

You've probably seen "This Document Last Modified," or "You've just come from" on pages that appeared to be static HTML. Chances are you were viewing SSIs calling the echo command. The format is <!--#echo var="variable_name"-->, in practice <!--#echo var="last_modified"-->. Here are your different options and a brief description.

> **document_name.** Just what you think it is. Useful as part of your footer if you only want to print the document name.

> **document_uri.** The Universal Document Identifier. You'd use it on the page in your footer as "This document is located at www.yourcompany.com<!--#echo var="document_uri"-->." It includes a preceding slash, so don't put one at the end of your base URL. Why put this in? So if someone prints the page and

gives it to a friend the full URL is there should they want information from some of the relative links on the page.

last_modified. Just as it says. This is one way to get the date and time that the current file was last modified. The format is controlled by the config option timefmt, which we'll get to in the next section. An example output is: 4:17 PM EST June 17, 1997.

http_user_agent. We'll reference this several places in the book. It's the name of the browser you are using. Netscape's old name was Mozilla in this variable, and it has stuck through the versions. Microsoft Internet Explorer includes it in its user agent as well as for sites who test for it. Example output from Netscape is Mozilla/3.0Gold (Win95 I).

date_gmt. Displays Greenwich Mean Time, a standard on all Unix servers that ignores time zones. Its format, as with last_modified, is dependent on the timefmt config setting.

date_local. This one doesn't ignore time zone. It's meant to deliver the time of day at the server locations. You'd use it like "Welcome to Beijing, the current time is <!--#echo var="date_local"-->" and you'd get back output similar to last_modified, also dependent on timefmt.

remote_addr. Gives back the IP address of the person accessing the system. It's not as reliable these days because of dynamic IP addressing, used by most ISPs to conserve the number of addresses they've been allocated. You may not know it, but you are most likely on a different IP address every time you log on.

remote_host. If your server is configured to resolve host names, your guests will get the name of the server they're dialing out from, like monadnock.world-media.com. If not, this is exactly the same as remote_addr. It returns the IP address.

server_admin. I had never seen this one before. It might just work on Apache. From what I can tell, it returns webmaster@server.com, whatever the server might be. If your administration is from other than webmaster, or if the mail doesn't go through your domain name, don't use it.

server_name. Like remote_host, this will return only the IP address unless you have the server configured to resolve IP addressing. It can be useful on an intranet with several webservers.

server_software. Do you or your visitors care? If so, this is the variable to show the world what server your website is running on.

CONFIG

As I began to explain, the format for this one is <--#config type="value"-->. There are three types: the first formats all time stamps, the second does file size, and the third controls the error message that is displayed if an SSI on the page goes ker-flooey (yes, that's a word) on you. Config identifiers are about the only SSIs that can take multiples within one set of <--# --> tags. A common config might be <--#config timefmt= "%c" sizefmt="bytes" errmsg="Sorry, try again later"-->. You may set them separately, as I'll explain later, and they may be reset several times on one page.

> timefmt. Controls the way the time is formatted in all of the preceding echo variables. The following sidebar lists all the possible values. You'll format it as <--#config timefmt="%A, %B %d, %Y"--> which will deliver Thursday, June 18, 1997.

> sizefmt. Sets the format that file size is displayed in. The two choices are bytes, which returns the actual number of bytes, and abbrev, which rounds to the nearest thousand and returns output like 5k. The syntax is <--#config sizefmt=abbrev-->. We'll get to the command it controls, fsize, in the miscellaneous commands at the end.

> errmsg. Displayed when an SSI encounters an error while loading. The default is [an error occurred while processing this directive], so you'll want to change it to something else, like <--#config errmsg="This spot was to be something really great and dynamically generated, but it broke. Could you please < a href =mailto:yourname@yourserver.com>email</a> me and let me know. Thanks."-->.

INCLUDE

This is one of the most useful SSIs as we delve into the topic of website automation. Just about every chapter in this book will have some way for you to use a standard header and footer for every page on your site. This is the simplest. Just put a <--#include file="header.txt"--> at the top and a <--#include file="footer.txt"--> at the bottom and you're good to go. The server will paste the HTML together and serve it to the browser.

---

timefmt options

%a—Abbreviated day of week (Mon., Tue., etc.)
%A—Full name of day (Monday, Tuesday, etc.)
%b—Abbreviated month (Jan., Feb., etc.)
%B—Full month (January, February, etc.)
%c—Full local date and time (Wed Jun 18 17:43:58 1997)
%d—Day of month (1–31)
%H—24-hour clock hour (0–23)
%I—12-hour clock hour (1–12)
%j—Day of the year (1–366 including leapyear)
%m—Month number (1–12)
%M—Minute (0–59)
%p—Local AM or PM
%S—Second (0–59)
%U—Week number of the year (0–52)
%w—Weekday number (0–6)
%x—Full date in numbers (06/18/97)
%y—Two-number year (0–99)
%Y—Four-number year (1997)
%Z—Time Zone (EDT, PDT, etc.)
%%—The only way to print a % sign with your output; useless

The only modification you'll want to make is if you plan to call include documents from directories that are parents to the one from which you are calling the HTML page. In that case you'll use the syntax <--#include virtual="../header.txt"-->. The file option cannot look in preceding directories, shown in this example by the ../ before the file name. If we did the opposite and looked in the directory <--#include file="new/headers/header.txt"--> we'd be fine. Children of our current directory are included with the file option.

Note also that on Apache and some other servers, including a CGI program is the same as executing it.

EXEC

If, back in the beginning, you checked with your sysadmin and the IncludesNoExec option was selected, you will not be able to do this command. But for those of us who can, it's a great little tool, especially if you've looked at SiteWrapper in a subsequent chapter and it looks like overkill to you (it shouldn't). As far as I can tell, IIS shouldn't need any special administration.

Exec allows you to embed the output of a shell (Unix or DOS) command or CGI file in your page. It takes one of two arguments, cmd or cgi. Either will run a shell script, Perl script, or compiled binary, but cmd will also deliver the output of one shell command. For instance <!--#exec cmd="echo Hello World"--> will show up as Hello World in your browser. And <pre><!--#exec cmd="ls -al"--></pre> (dir instead of ls for NT) will deliver a complete file list in the middle of your HTML page (perfect for an upload directory with an index.shtml page of instructions followed by a file list).

The cmd and cgi can both execute a program, with cgi called by <!--#exec cgi="hits.cgi"-->, or whatever your filename is. We prefer, as you'll see from the rest of the book, to format the entire HTML pages on the fly, but for a simple database query this works fine without having to commit to an involved automation system. You could embed an SSI with the script name very easily and wherever in the HTML you put it the results would be inserted.

The most common task for SSI on the web is in counting page hits to a website. You include an <!--#exec cgi tag, and it runs a small CGI program that increments a log file. I wrote something a little more involved, shown next, that prints environment variables to both the screen and to a little database file for you to run queries on called logfile.txt. Note that on Unix you must CHMOD the file to 755 and on NT the .cgi extension must be associated with Perl on your system.

```
1: #!/usr/bin/perl

2:

3: open(HITS, ">>logfile.txt");

4: print HITS "$ENV{'DATE_LOCAL'}\t$ENV{'DOCUMENT_URI'}\t$ENV{'REMOTE_HOST'}
$ENV{'HTTP_REFERER'}\t$ENV{'HTTP_USER_AGENT'}\n";

5: close(HITS);

6: select(STDOUT);

7: print<<END;

8: Content-type: text/html

9:
```

```
10: <pre>

11: $ENV{'DATE_LOCAL'}\n$ENV{'DOCUMENT_URI'}\n$ENV{'REMOTE_HOST' $ENV{'HTTP_REF-

ERER'}\n$ENV{'HTTP_USER_AGENT'}

12: </pre>

13: END
```

 On the CD Look for the NT sourcecode in the \sourcecode\NT\SSI directory and the Unix stuff in /sourcecode/UNIX/SSI for the two versions of two programs. One is the code shown here called hits.cgi and the other is linenumbers.pl. The former I'll explain in the main text, but linenumbers.pl is an extra. It's a great tool if you're stuck working with Perl without an editor that can count line numbers for you. Errors in Perl are given in line numbers, but that's useless if you can't find your place, so I wrote this little script that takes a file name as its single argument and spits every line of a file with its line numbers appended to standard output (the screen). We'll use it here to count the lines in the logfile.txt database and spit both the numbers and the full text of the hits into our browser. To use it make a single file called hits.shtml with the following lines:

```
<!--#include file="header.txt"<p>
<pre><!--#exec cgi="linenumbers.pl logfile.txt"--></pre>
<!--#include file="footer.txt"-->
```

This will give you a page of all the hits for your system, line numbered so you can scroll down to the total. It's a nice public access should you want to show everyone your hit totals and user statistics outside of a full database analysis.

You'll call hits.cgi from within your .shtml page as <!--#exec cgi="hits.cgi"-->. What that does is write one line of user information to the file logfile.txt and print to the screen the user's environment, as I just explained. To log separate files for different pages you will have to modify hits.cgi at line 3 to write a different file per page, so you'd have thispagelog.txt, nextpagelog.txt, etc., and rename each version of hits.cgi to thispagehits.cgi. On Unix only you could then compile the results all on one .shtml page with a series of SSIs calling each thispagelog.txt set up as

<!--#exec cmd="wc -l logfile.txt"-->. This returns the number of lines in the file followed by the file's name, so you could conceivably make one page with an <!--#exec for each file to assess your entire hit statistics. I don't know how to get this on NT, but we'll get to a better system later with SiteWrapper and Tickler anyway. This is a simple answer for now.

Exec also can be called as a virtual like include for executing programs. If the program you're executing is in a parent directory you'll call it as <!--#exec virtual ="../../programs/myprogram.cgi"-->.

FSIZE

Just as you think it would be, <!--#fsize file=thisfile.jpg--> is another way to report a file's size. It's particularly useful with live video, audio, or regularly changing images that always keep the same filename, or as just a simple addition to hotlinks you put in your pages to big files. You'd use it as <a href="www.yourserver.com/ yourvideo.mov">Download the Movie, <!--#fsize file="yourvideo.mov"--></a>. You may substitute virtual for file as with include and exec.

FLASTMOD

Again, this duplicates the echo variable and is meant to list multiple files on one page. If, on your site, you'd like a page of the modification dates of every file on your system, you'd fill a .stml page with <!--#flastmod file="yourpage.html"-->
 lines. When you call the page, the modification date will load accordingly. This is another page that can be called as <!--#flastmod virtual="../../pages /yourpage.shtml"-->.

SET and CONDITIONALS (Apache Only, 1.2 and Above)

Though this feature is a bit proprietary (can't get it to work anywhere else), it's too neat to pass up because so many of you are running Apache. What set does is let you preset a variable before using the echo function to print it to the screen. Conditionals work just as they do in Perl or any other programming language. If this, do that, else, do something else.

The set function is pretty simple and is configured as <!--#set var="menu" value="$server_name/menu.html"-->. You'd use this example in a set of HTML pages that are distributed to several different networks. As the page loads, the server will plug in the correct $server_name, just in case someone saves the file to their local PC. On the page you'll put a "This document's Main Menu is located at

<!--#echo var="menu"-->" in various locations on the page. This is just one idea I came up with writing, so don't take it as revelational.

Conditionals can include variables you have set above them, but more likely will be those that come from your environment. The following code tests for browser type and puts in the appropriate code.

```
<!--#if expr="$HTTP_USER_AGENT = /MSIE/" -->

<HTML TAGS>That are Microsoft proprietary.</HTML TAGS>

<!--#elsif expr="$HTTP_USER_AGENT = /Mozilla/" -->

<NETSCAPE>'s little doodads of standards-breaking nonsense.</NETSCAPE>

<!--#else -->

<REAL HTML TAGS> that all browsers understand.</REAL HTML TAGS>

<!--#endif -->
```

You must include the <!#endif --> statement to let the server know that the set is done. The words to be matched in this example are in backslashes as an exact match, but the full set of regular expressions from the Unix egrep program may be used to test for conditionals. You can also match a conditional to a variable you've <!--#set. In addition, there is a whole set of standard statement-type things to extend your capabilities like there are in Perl (I think it's a bit ridiculous when you can use Perl). When something is true, you're testing <!--#if expr="variable"--> whether the variable exists, or <!--#if expr="$remote_host = /aol.com/"--> whether something in the environment variables matches a given value. This could get quite complicated so start simply and work your way to more complicated examples. In our second example, we could output customized messages for people visiting from America Online.

```
string of text - true if string exists

string1 = string2 - true if the two strings are identical.

string1 = /string2/ -true if string1 contains the text in string2

string1 != string2 - true if string1 is not exactly identical to string2

string1 != /string2/ - true if string1 does not contain the regex in string2

( expression ) - one example might be <!--#if expr="$http_referer"-->
```

```
! expression   - true if expression is false

expression1 && expression2 - true if both are true

espressione1 || espressione2 -true if either or both are true
```

FrontPage Bots

My priorities for this book were that all the utilities I offer, whether we wrote them or not, must be compatible with both NT and many flavors of Unix. Java isn't quite there yet, so most of the book is in Perl. As you'll see in the following chapters, only basic Perl knowledge will get you on your way to automating a large amount of your site. But what if something breaks? You might try the Perl and decide it's not for you. If you're in an MIS department that demands 100 percent reliability, not knowing much about the underlying code will make you queasy; FrontPage isn't a bad little engine. It's hard to use for beginners, and the customization of bots requires that you know Visual Basic, but I'm including it. They've ported to most flavors of Unix, and of course it runs cleanly on Windows NT. Many of you Unix junkies are cringing at calling FrontPage cross-platform, but technically, you don't even have to use the FrontPage editor. XEmacs in HTML mode will work just as well for your editor, and I'll explain this as we go along. I'm not, however, going to specify Unix /NT only sections. Some of you might be wondering why I'm using such a high-profile Microsoft product to begin with, instead of a shareware/freeware program you can download from the web. One reason is that I don't recommend this chapter for anyone who is willing to learn a little bit of Perl. The rest of this book will give you far more leverage as your needs change than any bundled, proprietary product. The other reason is that I couldn't find anything this functional and useful to download for free. If you've got a suggestion, e-mail me and I'll include it in version 2. Until then, FrontPage is only a hundred and forty nine bucks, and, from what I can tell, you technically could use its bots on a Unix server without even buying the software, but I don't recommend it. If you don't want to learn any Perl, FrontPage is a no-brainer.

What differentiates FrontPage from other shareware programs is that there is a server component. It offers you a series of bots that you insert into your web pages like server side includes. You do have to install the server component for both NT and Unix, but the process and administration are very easy, and that's our Quick Start for this chapter. It's mostly verbatim from www.microsoft.com/frontpage/wpp/kit/unixinstall.htm but I've clarified some areas that confused me at first.

Quick Start: Unix

1. You must be at root to install these on Unix, so ask your system administrator to do this if you don't have access. If you can't get your ISP to do it, Microsoft offers a whole list of some who do.

2. Make the directory /usr/local/frontpage as root, then change its ownership and group to the webserver's user and group ID (in the server's httpd.conf file).

3. CHMOD the directory to 775, then super user yourself out of root and into the webserver's user name, which is probably www with su www.

4. Go to www.microsoft.com/frontpage/softlib/UNIXdownload.htm and download the WPP kit (web presence provider) and the other file called vt20.yoursystem.tar. They may download with a .Z extension, and if so you'll have to use the uncompress filename command on each of them to get them into a plain tar file.

5. Go to the readme file at www.microsoft.com/frontpage/wpp/bullet /readme.htm and check for new developments you might need to know about before installing.

6. Go to /usr/local and type the command tar -xvf/path/to/vt20yoursystem .tar to open up into the correct directory structure.

7. From /usr/local/, change directory (cd) to frontpage/version2.0.

8. Create a directory called extensions/.

9. Rename the executables/ directory with the command mv executables _vti_bin.

10. There should be a file fpsrvadm.suid.exe in your current directory. Move it to the bin/ directory with mv fpsrvadm.suid.exe bin.

11. In Step 8 of the /unixinstall.htm, the directory listing was a bit different from what we ended up with. Check it and the readme for an update before you install it if you like, but we just followed the preceding instructions and it worked out fine (we even forgot to su out of root).

12. Step 9 in the Microsoft version of the installation instructions is a bit confusing—it doesn't tell you that "We're about to run the install program so here's the things you need to check." It just starts listing them with no particular rhyme or reason. Well that's what we're about to do, and the first thing you need to do is confirm where your server's configuration file is. For Apache it's in

/usr/local/httpd/conf, for Netscape /usr/ns-home/https-443/config. Next it gives you the Netscape server-type, which is netscape-enterprise.

13. Next, you must know who owns the directory where the website will be located. This would be your login name if someone is installing it for you. Use your login name if you're doing it for yourself. If you want people only to be able to update their site with the FrontPage explorer client and not have any standard FTP access, set this to root. This will, of course, preclude you from manually FTPing files in there, but it will not prevent you from using an external editor.

14. FrontPage has three levels of access: administrator, author, and browser. The next piece of information you must decide in advance is the user name of the administrator and the password. As I explained previously, there is a difference between FTP access and FrontPage access, and this gives you the extra login name to separate the two. If you want them to have both FTP and FrontPage access, you might just want to just give the same login and password, if you know the password, but keep in mind that they're two different password systems and if one changes the other must as well.

15. Now you have to go back to being root for a bit. Otherwise the install won't be able to set the proper user IDs. You have to run fp_install once for each web.

16. Type fp_install -user paulh -group 100.

17. It should give you a directory listing something like that in Figure 3.1 of all the possible servers, both virtual and individual, for the server.

18. If you have virtual hosts, pick which one you want to use and give FrontPage the number. It will then give you the configurations it reads in, then it will ask you for an administrator's name. If you're installing in a ~yourname or other directory, type 1 for root, and give FrontPage a web name, which is the final name in the URL where all the user homepages are kept. So if you are a sysadmin and the eventual account will be www.yourname.net/users/frontpagesite, use the name that will appear in frontpagesite.

19. Whether you picked a virtual host or a root web, you should now be at Administrator's user name. Put in the name you just selected, then enter the password once, and then again to confirm.

20. Now it goes through a lot of screens that scroll in front of you as you wait. There might be some error messages, but as long as you get to Installation Complete you should be fine.

21. If you have a Windows 32-bit PC, install FrontPage from the CD.

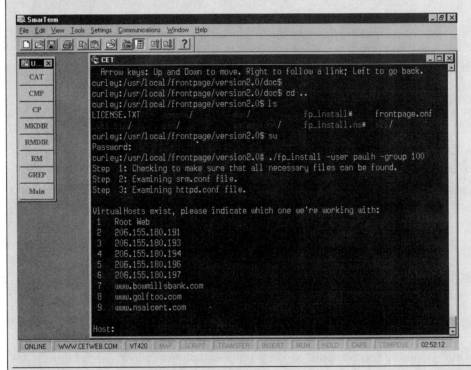

Figure 3.1 A correct directory listing.

Quick Start: NT

1. If you've installed FrontPage from the CD, you've already seen that it gives you the option to install the server extension bots automatically. I won't go over the standard install here. One note is that it might be confusing for a newcomer to web technology to differentiate between the concept of an HTML page that is like a Microsoft Word document and one that has dynamic components that are dependent upon the server. Most likely you understand that the copy of your website that people hit is different from the one on your hard drive. You upload it to the webserver, where it is accessed.

2. In FrontPage, the copy of your website on your hard drive is different from a Word document because it has dynamic pieces that aren't HTML coded in advanced, but are coded instead as the page loads into the visitor's browser. That's why you must have your Internet service provider install these extensions for you, which means that they must own a copy of the software and agree to set it up for you.

3. If you're on a local intranet it's the same. The webserver, not just your local machine, needs to have FrontPage installed. The bots are an addition to the webserver software that delivers the pages. It tells the server to look at documents as they load, inserting the appropriate things.

Using FrontPage

I see three possible scenarios for buying this book and looking at FrontPage as one of the automation options within it. The first is that you are about the begin a new web project and this is your first one. From what you've read elsewhere, the only way to guarantee the ability to grow is to install an automation system. The second reason is that you're an established web person looking for a better way. You may have created some sites that imploded and were scrapped as they tried to grow but could not. And the third is that you have an existing site that is starting to get out of hand and you see the need to install an organizational system that will automate tiresome functions and free you to learn and create. FrontPage has an option for all three, with the first two grouped into what I would call "Create a New Web." The third would be "Automate an Existing Web" and is as it says. You'll be importing your site into a new FrontPage site.

When you open the FrontPage editor it greets you with the screen shown in Figure 3.2. The first radio button enables you to quick-open the last web you worked on. The next button lets you open another previously worked-on web, then the bottom three buttons are options to Create a New FrontPage Web. We were confused here because FrontPage, as it seems to be set up, does not let you work on the base directory of where FrontPage sits on the server at www .yourcompany.com. It considers that directory already made, so it would not be new. The New options are for only a subdirectory off the main, at www.yourcompany .com/user or /directory. I've set up four scenarios in the following table and

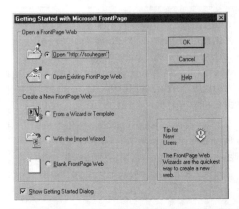

Figure 3.2 The FrontPage welcome screen.

in this introductory text. We're either going to create a new or automate an old, and do it in either the main or a subdirectory off the main. I don't suggest that you dive into your real site and use FrontPage's automation until you get a good feel for the editor, the server bots, and the rest of this book, so I'm only going to brush on the Import Wizard in Table 3.1.

Table 3.1 FrontPage Start Options

If You Are	Steps
Creating a new www.yourcompany.com site	Open Existing FrontPage Web from main menu. Input your www address, list webs, <Root Web>. File, New, FrontPage Web, Customer Support, Check Add to the Current Web.
Automating an old www.yourcompany.com site	Open Existing FrontPage Web from main menu. Input your www address, list webs, <Root Web>. File, New, FrontPage Web, Import Web Wizard, Check Add to the Current Web. Browse your disk and find the directory where index.htm of the old site exists. If you're updating the same site as the old one, on the same server, you must store a copy of the site first. Click Next. Select files to Exclude, holding down your Control button to select multiples. Click Next, then Finish. FrontPage will upload and index your whole site. Then use the same stuff I'm covering for the Customer Support demo.

Table 3.1 *Continued*

If You Are	Steps
Adding a new www.yourcompany directory	From a Wizard or Template on the main menu. Select Customer Support, fill in the .com/user web server's name or IP, fill in the user that you just created.
Automating an old www.yourcompany.com/user directory	With the Import Wizard on the main menu. Fill in the server name or IP. It asks you for a user name and password. Wait until it asks you to find the files, browse your file system and find the directory, click Next, Exclude the files that shouldn't be uploaded, Next, Finish. FrontPage will upload your existing site to the /directory/ you selected.

To create a new site at www.yourcompany.com we have to edit the root site, as I'd expect most people reading this book will do, so check the second button on the main menu and click OK. You'll get a box that asks for your company's server name. The IP address will also work. Fill it in and click on List Webs.

It should fill in the box with only one <Root Web>. Select it and click OK. You should then get a screen like Figure 3.3. Then open File, New, FrontPage Web. Then select Customer Support, and make sure to check the box that says Add to the Current Web, which is grayed out in Figure 3.4. That's the trick you have to play on FrontPage to edit your main directory.

If this new site is to be a directory off the main, go from the main FrontPage menu to From a Wizard or Template and you'll get Figure 3.4. The checkbox that says Add to the Current Web is grayed out unless you have a web open. For this test, we're going to use the customer support web for the new web, just to show you what FrontPage can do.

You should now have either a Customer Support FrontPage web that looks like Figure 3.5 or a version of your existing site. It's located at either www.yourcompany .com or www.yourcompany.com/. It has no colors or other variable elements. Setting the colors for the site is our first task.

FrontPage Colors

Double-click on index.html (or default.htm depending upon your server) in the FrontPage Explorer. This will bring it up in the editor, where you can choose your

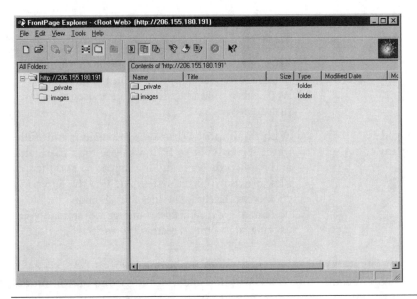

Figure 3.3 Root Web screen.

colors. Leave Specify Background and Colors checked, then set the colors and/or background image as you wish. Then Click OK.

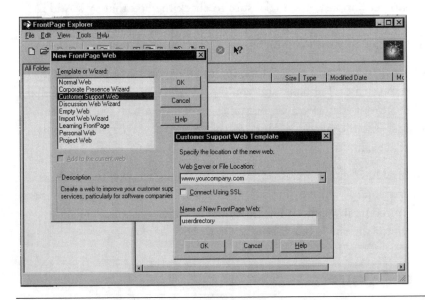

Figure 3.4 From a Wizard or Template.

Figure 3.5 The sample web.

Your index.html should have changed colors, but that's not all. Now we're going to go into another page. Go back and open whatsnew.htm or another page of your site in the editor. Right click somewhere within the page and go to Page Properties. It will bring up a four-tabbed list of options. In the Background tag you'll find Set Background Colors from Page. Check that button and Browse your FrontPage web for index.html (or default.htm) and select it with OK. Click OK again and that page will now get its color information from the main index. Change the main index and every page you have so modified will change.

Screen Options

After you created/imported the site, FrontPage should have shown you the files listed in a Windows Explorer-type interface, where you can click on the file and it will load into the browser. This is one of two screen types. If you click on the fifth icon (shown in Figure 3.6), you'll get a site view, which can give you a flow-chart diagram of which pages link to each other. I'm going to spend a little time explaining this because I didn't get it at first. Until light dawned on marble head, it seemed that the whole system duplicated itself.

On the site-view screen there is a middle document. Several pages spider out from the left and the right of it. The left are pages that link to the middle, and the right are pages that the middle links to. That means that for several of your HTML pages, the included header and footer will be on both sides of index.html if that is your middle document.

I should mention the concept of headers and footers. Right now, your HTML pages are not whole files. They are middles, not to be confused with the middle document on the site-view screen. This middle doesn't have any <HTML> <HEAD><TITLE><BODY> at the front or </BODY></HTML> at the back. The server tacks the front and back on the middle as the page loads for the browser, so at any time you can change the header and footer, changing every page on the site. That will be our next task, but first I'd like to continue with the site-view layout.

When you start, index.html should be in the middle. On the right and left you can see that Included Page Header both links to it and from it, but don't confuse a link with an include. An include link means that the document is part of the page in the middle. You find this not by the name of the page, like Included Page Header, but by positioning the cursor over the page. It will say Internal Hyperlink: document name, as shown in Figure 3.6.

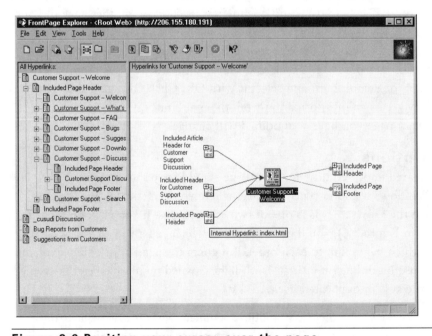

Figure 3.6 Position your cursor over the page.

If a page has links in it, the upper-left corner will have a plus sign in it. By clicking on it you can open the page links to another level in the flow chart. In Figure 3.7, I've opened up the header, which led me to all the pages of the site. One of those is the default Customer Support Download. I then clicked on its plus sign, and it opened up into the pieces that it's made from. As you can see, we again see the header. We know what that contains. And you also see the footer, which has no plus sign, and therefore no links. The middle contains several FTP hyperlinks, which FrontPage details for us. I could click on the plus sign in the header and it would open up again to the pages listed in the footer. That's why it seems confusing and circular. You just came from the header and there it is again. The chart on the right is what the clicked document is made of, for hotlinks. This works only for internal site documents. An external website that your pages lead to will not have a plus sign.

To make another document the middle, right-click on it. This will spider out all the links to and from it without having to scroll. This feature is particularly useful for big sites with several depths of drill down. One other note is that there can be several headers and footers for different parts of the site.

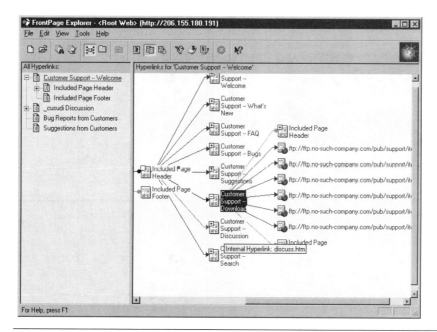

Figure 3.7 Click to open a page.

Using the Editor

Bring up the header in the FrontPage editor by double-clicking it in either the site or explorer view. It's a WYSIWYG editor that resembles the top of the HTML page. I'm first going to kick the hotlinks down, one on top of each other, put a box around them with a <TABLE>, and right-align them, adding images here and there.

Kicking the links down into a vertical list is just deleting the [and | symbols and pressing Return after each link. Then drag the table menu down (15 from the left as shown in Figure 3.8) and select an eight-high by two-wide table. It will insert it above your hotlink list. Then drag each hotlink into the right side of the table, leaving the left side for an image bullet.

To get a bullet, put your cursor in the top-left table data, then either bring down the Insert, Image menu or click on the sixteenth icon in the button bar. It will give you a menu with three tabs: Current FrontPage Web, to bring it in from elsewhere on the site; Other Location, which can bring it in from either a disk or URL location (being careful of copyrights); and Clip Art, which will let you select from the few lines, icons, and bullets that come with FrontPage. I'm grabbing blue arrow. Then hold down your Control button while dragging the image to the remaining table data. Now right-click on the table, go to Table Properties (Figure 3.9), and

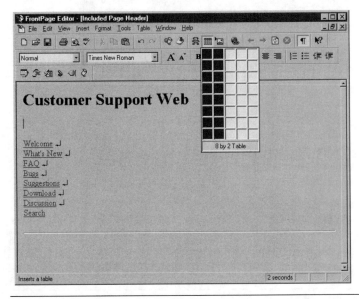

Figure 3.8 Accessing the table menu.

change the alignment to right. Save it by clicking on the third icon (you're saving it to the FrontPage web with its own name), renaming it appropriately.

Aha! You (well, I helped) found a weakness of FrontPage. Sometimes its HTML is not quite what you'd think. I right-aligned the table, which should be coded as <TABLE ALIGN=RIGHT>, but FrontPage put a <DIV ALIGN=RIGHT>, which doesn't like to have text snugged up next to it. When you're faced with this type of situation, when the HTML just won't do what you think you're telling it to, go to either the explorer mode or site-view mode and right-click on the file. A menu will pop up that lets you open the file with one of a list of editors. If your preferred editor is not there (I like Webber), go to Tools, Options, Configure Editors, and Add yours in.

Aha again! You've found another weakness along the same lines. If you edit a file in an external program, then bring it up in FrontPage, it changes your code back to its screwy version. We solved this by using its include feature for our navigation bar. It's not as confusing as it sounds. The header that we're editing in FrontPage is just another small HTML file that other files include at the top. It too can include other files, so I'm going to make a tiny file navbar.htm and include it in the header. First I bring up header.htm in my external editor, then I cut the table out and paste it into a new file I'll name navbar.htm, changing the <DIV> to a right-aligned

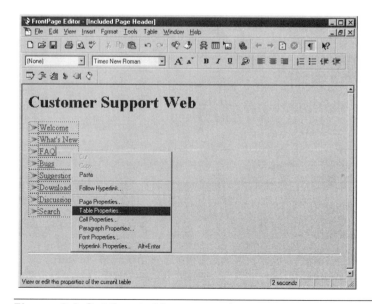

Figure 3.9 Setting table properties.

table. Then I save both and exit the external editor. Now you have to upload it with the FrontPage Explorer. Go to File/Import and find the navbar.htm we just made. Click Add File and OK.

Now, bring up header.htm again in the FrontPage editor. The table is gone. To put it back we have to use a WebBot Component or bot. This one is called the Include bot. It allows you to use the contents of one file pasted into another, much like the include we just saw with server side includes. To use it, you go to either the Insert WebBot Component menu or click on the little robot icon in FrontPage, four-teenth on the toolbar. It brings up a window like that in Figure 3.10, from which you choose Include and OK. Then click Browse and find the file where you saved it on your FrontPage web. Click OK and it's included.

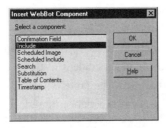

Figure 3.10 Inserting a WebBot component.

Inside the Bot

As I explained before, you can insert a bot into an HTML file manually with an external editor, even a Unix-based text editor, without ever utiliz-ing the power of the FrontPage editor. Bots look like server side includes. The one we just inserted is:

```
<!--webbot bot="Include" u-include="navbar.htm" tag="BODY"

startspan -->
```

All the bots have a similar syntax. They are objects that take parameters like u-include and startspan. Outside the space of this book you could disect the existing list of bots, shown in Table 3.2, and manually insert them into your HTML pages.

Now we have a fully functional header that will be peeled as every page on the side that calls it loads. As header.htm loads, it in turn loads navbar.htm to itself to complete the page. When you change either header.htm or navbar.htm, everything changes, but be sure to save after all changes. All the pages that include the header will change to that layout. Table 3.2 lists some other features and how to use them.

Table 3.2 WebBot Components and Specifications

WebBot Component	What It Does	How To Use It
Confirmation Field	When users fill out a form on your site, it bounces back some of the values they filled out to confirm their identity.	This will probably be a separate confirm.htm page on your site. Create the basic page then click the robot. You'll have to click the Confirmation Field for every form field you bounce back. It's like a mail merge in MS Word. You'll have Dear... on your page, click the robot, Confirmation Field, and enter first-name into the box. Click OK and you're all set, then go back and do that for your entire thanks or confirmation page, plugging in the appropriate variables.
Scheduled Image	Puts a different image on the page at given intervals. Useful for advertisements, time-limited sales, and New buttons.	Click the robot, browse for image, select start date and time, select end date and time, browse for optional image before and after.
Scheduled Include	Puts a whole different HTML file into the text of your page, so if you have a time-limited event with its own page about the event you'd make a little HTML document of, just	Create the file by clicking the first icon New Page. Save it with a file name. Click the robot, browse for the file you just created, set the start and stop date and time, then the before and after file should you want one (maybe the You Missed It file).

Continued

Table 3.2 *Continued*

WebBot Component	What It Does	How To Use It
	<A HREF="eventpage.htm"> Check out our Event This Weekend</A> in it, then schedule an include to end Sunday at 4 PM.	
Search	Allows you to insert a search box into any page on the site. Users type in keywords and go.	You can insert a search box into any page, or create one, so if you want a separate page, make one. Then, where you want the search bot, place the cursor and click the robot. Label for Input is the text before the input field. Width is the physical width of the input box; Start Search is the Submit button; Clear is the Reset button. Under World List to Search For, you can either make it All, which searches only the pages on the site, not the discussion boards, or a discussion board directory, which should be an underscore in your file list (_custudi comes with this template). We tried to get it to do both in the same search but couldn't. You either would have to have two search boxes on one page, each with their own Word List, or put the different ones on the actual discussion pages.
Substitution	You can put a variable into the text, like page URL, one of four included, or one of your own, like your 800 number, which could change for the whole site. The bot acts as a placeholder, this bot automatically substituting the correct value.	To insert one of the four included bots, click the robot, Substitution, click the arrow in the box, select Page URL, then OK. To make your own bot, go to the Explorer, select Tools, Web Settings, check the Parameters tab, Add. Fill in the name (e.g., 800#), whatever value you select, then OK (or Apply if you're

Table 3.2 *Continued*

WebBot Component	What It Does	How To Use It
		adding multiples). Now if you change your 800 number it changes for the whole site.
Table of Contents	Generates a table of contents and inserts it in any page, wherever you like.	If you want a separate contents page, create a blank HTML page and insert the bot into it. Click the robot, Table of Contents, select the start page, which could be index.html for the whole site, but note that you could make separate tables of contents for main directory pages. No one bot is dependent upon another for its list. There is no global table of contents. Every bot has to be inserted manually. You could, of course, make a small TOC.html file and include it everywhere, then when you change that, everything changes. Heading size controls how big the Table of Contents appears. Showing each page only once addresses the problem I ran into with the site-view confusion. If pages link back and forth to each other it could get confusing. Showing pages with no incoming hyperlinks is tough to understand. Why not just link to it? This might be used for reading a directory that people are uploading into without editing a link page. I suggest you Recompile Table of Contents when any of the other pages is edited to avoid dead links and give people a fresh view of your whole site. Click OK.

Continued

Table 3.2 *Continued*

WebBot Component	What It Does	How To Use It
Time Stamp	Inserts the correct time.	Click the robot, Time Stamp, choose whether to show the last edit date or the last auto-update date, which could be a table of contents modification, variable modification, or modification of an include document, then choose your date and time format and click OK.

Parsing Forms

The Customer Support site we created from the template came with two forms. We'll use suggest.htm, which gives you three options. Load it into the editor and right-click on it anywhere in the form part of the document. Select Form Properties. It will give you a box of options. Leave the WebBot Save Results Component selected (unless you've written your own CGI/NSAPI/ISAPI parser, in which case you'd use that tab) and click Settings. On the file for Results page, name the file with whatever extension that makes sense for the file format you select below it. The results can be saved as a long HTML page in various formats or as a database. FrontPage can't e-mail forms. Then select what you'd like to include beyond the form variables. The next tab, Confirm, is the page visitors will get after filling in the form (the one on which the Confirmation Bot would reside). The Advanced tab isn't really advanced. It's just a second file in which to save the results. Then click OK, which brings you back to the main Form Properties box. The Form Name and Target Frame are for your use in JavaScript and frames. One note here is that you can't put hidden fields into a WYSIWYG document, so here is where you do it. Plug in a name/value pair for each. Click OK and you're all set to submit the form on the site and have it parsed correctly.

Permissions

You can't use this feature on an NT system that was installed over an old MSDOX/Windows 3.x FAT file system. But for fresh installations of NT and all Unix flavors, it works great. One thing is that you have to make a New FrontPage Web if you want to protect only a small part of your site. A web is either on or off for Browse access, but individual users can be allowed to author and/or administrate. Go to Tools/Permissions and select Only registered users have browse access, then Add a user. When the menu pops up, set the name and password, confirm the password, then check off which permissions the user has. Remember when we were asked for our user name and password? This is where it's administrated from. This is where you add authorized people to the opened FrontPage Web. The second tab is to limit from which computers authorized users can use to get in to edit the site. It should be set by IP address and will accept the same three-tiered access restrictions. If you check Everyone has browse access, the browse check button on the users and computer permissions will be disabled as everyone can get in anyway.

Discussion

As you saw, FrontPage automatically set up a discussion board as part of this Customer Support Web. But rather than cover it here, I'm saving it for Chapter 15 where I'll show you the various formats and administration features, some undocumented, that this FrontPage tool can build.

JavaScript/VBScript Extras

FrontPage supplies a few of the most common tricks on the web, plus an entire code-free library of most of JavaScript's and VBScript's functionality. We tried to test this with a simple mouseover on an image but couldn't get FrontPage to understand that we were selecting the image to apply the script to. So rather than run through all the steps to implement an applet, I'll just suggest that you take a look at the script wizard, which looks like Figure 3.11. On the left is the thing you have available to edit (a Submit button in this instance), on the right are the things you can make it do.

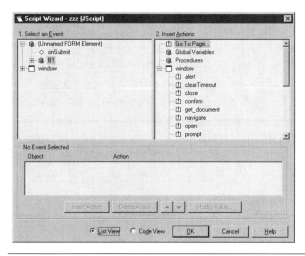

Figure 3.11 The JavaScript wizard.

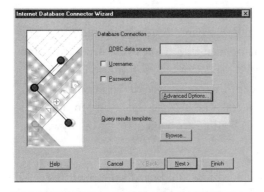

Figure 3.12 The database wizard.

Database Connectivity

The 1997 version of FrontPage added a database connector wizard that makes bots for you in the Microsoft IDC format. The wizard (Figure 3.12) is fairly intuitive, and again, covering it in full is beyond our scope here, but I'd like to add a reminder that we are just exploring possibilities in this chapter. I'm not telling you to stay away from FrontPage; it's the most incredible one-stop tool I've seen. It's that there are other options (some even from Microsoft) that we'll cover later that might be more expandable.

Java/ActiveX et al.

Under the insert menu is the Other Components option. There you can add an applet tag for just about any file type or plug-in available on the web. I mention it here not because it's a vital component, but because many of you are cringing at using a WYSIWIG editor. I prefer hacking the code myself, but they've really covered the bases here. Overall FrontPage is an incredible machine. Reviewing it we were hard-pressed to find a reason not to use it on sites less than twenty pages. Its only drawback is the mistaken code, which is easily worked around. Read through the following chapters, but if you're a true beginner and don't want any Perl knowledge, give FrontPage a hard look.

Why Perl for Unix
and Perl for NT?

You're probably asking why I broke here in the chapters into a discussion about Perl. It's because at this point the book changes from a general overview of how you might want to automate into a nuts-and-bolts how-to of utilities for the most common of web tasks. In most cases, unless I've found a Windows-based program that was too good to pass by, the language of choice is Perl.

But why Perl? Why not C or C++ or even Java? Isn't Perl a hacker language that the web is getting away from in favor of rapid development environments and compiled binaries? No, and I'll explain why, but first I'd like to review the weaknesses of Perl for those of you who don't even know what a compiled binary is.

Perl is an *interpreted language*, meaning that it is compiled, or transformed into binary machine language when the program is run, not beforehand. Imagine if you could open the code that makes up Microsoft Word and edit it in Notepad whenever you needed to add a function. You'd see things like "if, open the File Menu, drop down a list with the words Open, Close, Save, Save As," and so on. That's how a programming language works. Programmers write in human-readable code and then compile that code into programs like those you know as Word and Excel. That's why you can't add Send To

Trashcan into the preceding quasi-code. When you compile a program, it becomes a black box. Perl isn't like that. You can edit a Perl program, also called a Perl *script,* at any time. And the next time you run it, your changes will take effect automatically.

This is one reason why Perl has become so popular on the web. Websites have to change all the time, and the back-end automation system drives that change. If you had to recompile a whole program every time your boss or client wanted "that font a little smaller" you'd go nuts. The interpreted nature of Perl lets you make edits— small ones, big ones, bug fixes, layout tweaks—on the fly. Make a change to a program and the next visitor to the site will get the newly enhanced or fixed page.

There's a dark side to the interpreted nature as well, and that's the primary reason Perl is bashed by IS departments and the Internet press. Compiled programs, those black boxes, are all ready to run when you activate them. Perl programs aren't. You run the program, it starts Perl, then Perl interprets and compiles the program, then runs it. This is a big hit to efficiency on a webserver because with CGI, whatever automation program you're using is called every time a visitor hits an automated page. If the program is written in Perl, an instance of Perl (a program of over a megabyte in size) has to be run for every CGI, regardless of the CGI's size, so it's like running MS Word when all you need is Notepad. On NT, it's not as bad, but I'll get to that later.

In case you didn't notice, the argument against Perl is the same as that against Java. It too is a language that's compiled at run-time, but with Java you precompile it first for the Java virtual machine, which in practice isn't much different than the way we do Perl. This is a good time to talk about Java because it's touted as the programming language of future, a revolution in computing, etc. Java may be all those things, but it's not that today and won't be in the near future. As I write this in the second half of 1997, Java is used for little more than animation on the web. At present, only two webservers can even call a server-based Java component as a CGI without requiring a client applet. As I'll state in several places in this book, until the America Online browser (Microsoft Internet Explorer for Windows 3.x) and Netscape for Windows 3.x running on a 486/100 can run Java, it's not an option for the public web. Java may be a cross-platform wonder horse, but at the current stage of computing and at the state of computing in which we will remain until the turn of the century, it's not a replacement for Perl.

And what about cross-platform? That's another reason why Perl has dominated the Internet and why we and others wrote the utilities offered in this book in it. With no modifications at all, you can drag any Perl program to any flavor of Unix, and it will run cleanly. Until recently that's where the line ended, at Unix. Perl was the science of sysadmin geek types and not accessible to the likes of Microsoft NT. There has been an NT port for some time, but it was never stable, and most people implemented CGI programs with gaping, dangerous security holes. But now that's changed. With only one simple modification (improved from the last release as you'll read later), Perl programs can be run from Windows NT 4.0. We've made the modification to everything we wrote for the book.

This is a crucial feature for the web, because every website is "The Great Experiment." User acceptance will determine how much computer has to go on the back end. Your site could start on a 486/33 machine running Linux and Apache and end up on an eight-processor Hewlett Packard running NT 4.0. With Perl, if the design was sound, you could drag and drop the whole site. In practice this means that www.halloween.com could switch from a shared space at the local mom-and-pop ISP to a server array on a NAP on September 15th with no noticeable downtime or modification of the site's code.

The reason Perl is cross-platform is its greatest strength over C and C++. Perl is public domain software, distributed under the GNU public license. Though Perl was invented and developed by Larry Wall and has been extended and championed by Tom Christiansen, Randal Schwartz, and all the others at comp.lang.perl.*, nobody owns it, so nobody has to license it to get it to run on their operating system. Nowhere was this more evident than when we were first designing a site running on an Alpha Server from Digital Equipment Corp. Though Digital makes its own flavor of Unix, they have an entire team to support Linux and Perl, both public domain. Free, for some reason that no one can put their finger on, works on the Internet.

And yes folks, there's more! This one's about Rapid Application Development (RAD) environment, which has become not only a buzz phrase for the entire realm of software development, but a must-have for internal IS departments everywhere. I translate RAD as a graphical user interface (GUI) that both insulates you from some code-writing with predeveloped objects of reusable code while optimizing the ease with which you write the code that ties the objects together, packaged with a compiler that optimizes better than the other products on the market. Wow, those were two long sentences—symbolic of the need most web programmers have in relation to the capabilities of a RAD environment.

The web isn't that complicated or that difficult. HTTP is simple, and though HTTP can be extended with Java and ActiveX, in most cases you don't need to. Perl is and has been for many years an object-oriented language, even before it caught on. And through the years, as server administration, Internet, and web problems have come and gone, an entire library of free modules has accumulated at the Perl archive site.

So where are the RADs in this? Perl is itself a compiler, and the second feature of a RAD, predeveloped modules, is covered at CPAN. What's left is the graphical interface, which, as I'll suggest in the next chapter, is easily duplicated with the shareware program Multi-Edit. RADs are great if you are developing only one type of server, on one operating system in a controlled environment, provided you have the budget. Chances are this will occur only on an internal web server (intranet), and it's why all the most popular RADs call themselves intranet tools.

News Flash: Perl for NT a Reality Now!

As I previously mentioned, the Perl picture for NT has changed only recently. Before Perl 5, NT 4.0, and Internet Information Server, Perl was called directly from the web as perl.exe. There were .bat file workarounds, but most NT system administrators considered Perl a dangerous place to play for mission-critical applications on the web. Porting programs was a nightmare, too. You lose some standard Unix commands running Perl on NT; that's accepted. But worse was that you had to escape backslashes in HTML. Between security and the nuisance factor, Perl for NT just wasn't worth it.

Then along came Bill Gates and crew, who invented Internet Server Application Protocol Interface (ISAPI). It provides a revolving pool of processes running CGI-like programs on the server that wait for HTTP requests. Perl runs as an "open mouth" in these processes as a .dll program, safe and fully functional for the Perl 5.0 standard. Two companies, HIP Software and now ActiveWear, have picked up the Perl for Win32 ball and delivered a PerlIS.dll that runs as an ISAPI filter, interpreting Perl programs on the fly. We're going to install it later in the chapter.

So now we've established that Perl is flexible, cross-platform, and has an entire library of predeveloped free objects. The only other thing I'll note is that Perl seems as though it was created for the World Wide Web. Without getting too technical in this informational part of the chapter, Perl has a system of regular expressions, similar but more extended than traditional Unix shell programs, used for parsing text and extracting useful information. It also offers another function that connects to sockets, which reach out and grab things over TCP-IP. Together, these two functions mean that I could enable my homepage, as it loads, to hit the NASDAQ homepage, suck in its contents, follow its links to a search for my company stock, parse the results of that page into a little table with my stock in it, then insert it into the finished homepage. All a visitor to the site would get is the homepage with my up-to-the-minute stock price. They'd never know of the back-end process that's behind it. In practice we'd probably do it differently for speed, but that's how useful Perl is for the web. HTML is only text, and Perl is unparalleled for parsing text.

Figure 4.1 is from the GVU Internet survey taken in October of 1996. Perl outnumbers other languages from two to three to one for Internet programming languages. This book will go to press before the next survey, but I doubt that number will change very much in this survey or any in the near future. For the corporate IS manager, this means that writing your back-end web applications in Perl virtually guarantees that your applications will have support into the next century. For the

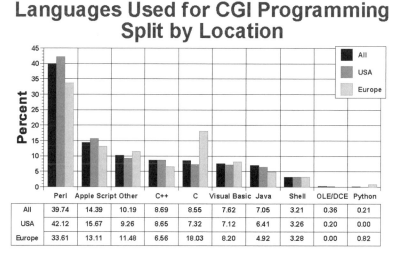

Languages Used for CGI Programming Split by Location

	Perl	Apple Script	Other	C++	C	Visual Basic	Java	Shell	OLE/DCE	Python
All	39.74	14.39	10.19	8.69	8.55	7.62	7.05	3.21	0.36	0.21
USA	42.12	15.67	9.26	8.65	7.32	7.12	6.41	3.26	0.20	0.00
Europe	33.61	13.11	11.48	6.56	18.03	8.20	4.92	3.28	0.00	0.82

Source: GVU's Sixth WWW User Survey[tm] (Conducted October 1996)
<URL:http://www.cc.gatech.edu/gvu/user_surveys>
Copyright 1996 GTRC - ALL RIGHTS RESERVED
Contact. www-survey@cc.gatech.edu

Figure 4.1 Perl is everywhere!

webmaster, it guarantees that you'll have a job at those IS departments. From the chart you'll see that 47 percent of webmasters don't know any language. You might even be one of them now. If you're going to learn one language, make it Perl.

Is Perl on Your Unix Machine?

You shouldn't have to install Perl on your Unix machine, but you may have an old copy, most likely version 4.036, which lingered for years as we awaited version 5. You do need version 5 for most of the stuff in this book and it should be at least build 5.003. Test what version is running by typing perl -v at the command shell. If it sends back a message like the one in lines 3–9 of Figure 4.2, type perl5 -v as I did in the figure or ask your system administrator which command runs Perl version 5.

Unix Only: Testing without Shell Access

We've put several clients on an Internet provider called tiac.net in Bedford, Massachusetts, and though they are fantastic at hardware, connectivity, and support, they don't allow shell access to the webservers (screaming SGIs). We found that the webserver does have access to a shell and can run standard shell commands like perl -v, perl-c (that tests for syntax), and even perl -d, the complete Perl debugger. To do this we made a CGI script that calls the shell and echoes a content type and the results of a shell command back to the browsers:

```
#!/bin/sh

echo Content-type: text/plain

echo

perl -v 2>&1
```

This will give you the version of Perl on your system. Please note that this is a dangerous activity if you don't know your way around Unix commands, as the line after the second echo line is capable of any shell command. You can also stack several of them on top of each other. If you are testing a program, not simply executing a "cat" or "ls," you'll want to put the 2>&1 after the command with a space in between. This little program will not work on NT.

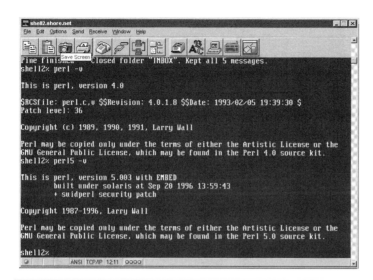

Figure 4.2 Checking your Perl version number.

Updating Perl to a new copy should be done by a system administrator with experience. You have to compile the source, which is readily available at www.perl.org/CPAN/CPAN.html, but which requires root permission. Here is one of the few places in the book where I won't walk you through a procedure. Most of you will have Perl installed, and we've got other ground to cover. A complete help file for install is at www.perl.org/CPAN/doc/relinfo/INSTALL.html. Perl comes with a Configure script that should work fine, provided you download the current source at www.perl.org/CPAN/src/. It will be in the file latest.realease.tar.gz and is about two and a half megabytes.

Installing Perl for NT

NT (and Win95, Mac, DOS) is different from Unix in that you install a binary file from the get go. There is no compiling of sourcecode. You download a binary and double-click it just as if you were installing the latest version of Netscape. There are a few other steps to get Perl programs to execute from a webserver, but I'll show you how to configure those for Internet Information Server.

First, download the source from www.Activestate.com. Version 3.10 into a temp directory on your hard drive. Select Pw32i310.exe from the Run menu or double-click on it in the Windows Explorer. It will pop up a little OK box identifying ActiveWear as the author. Click OK, which will then pop up a WinZip window setting C:\Perl as the install directory. Click Unzip. The files will be unzipped into that directory, then you'll get a "251 files unzipped successfully" message. Click OK. This will bring up a DOS window with the first line as shown in Figure 4.3. Press "y" and your Enter key four times. You'll scroll through all of the text in Figure 4.2. After DOS has finished scrolling, the release file will pop up, which is mostly useless to the non-techie, but look through it for new features. Close the Notepad window, then press any key to continue from the DOS window, which will close it. Do the same Run/double click on PIISi310.exe. The OK box pops up again; click it. Again you should be at WinZip. Click unzip, which will give you the four files successfully unzipped box. Click OK, and again you'll get a DOS window that will ask you to press any key to continue. Press any key.

You'll then be asked to associate a filename extension with Perl. Don't use the .pl for our purposes here. Type in cgi, without the dot before it and press Enter. That will pop up the release text, which you should browse and close. One note about this build we're including on the CD is that most FAQs on the web will tell you that you have to put HTTP/1.0 200 OK\n in your Perl programs. This build has fixed that, so any Perl program may now be dragged and dropped from a Unix server into an NT server with no modifications if you write it without Unix system calls from the start.

Now go back to the DOS window and press any key when it asks, which will close the window. Figure 4.4 is the complete session as you enter your input.

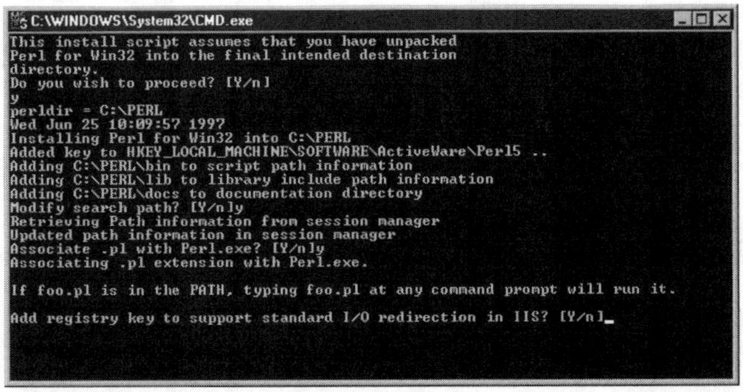

Figure 4.3 Installing Perl.

Figure 4.4 The DOS window session results.

You now have Perl and PerlIIS.dll set up in the same directory, which is required. Now I'm going to shift from standard NT to the modifications required for Microsoft Internet Information Server, the most common NT webserver. Without these modifications you'll have a devil of a time with Perl and ISAPI. On other servers you should consult their install instructions or contact customer support. You won't be the first person to call about installing Perl for ISAPI, so there should be a FAQ.

From your start menu, go to Programs, Microsoft Internet Server, Internet Server manager. That will bring up a window with a list of computers on your system. Choose the one with WWW service and double-click on it. That will bring up a menu of WWW Server Properties for your computer name (Figure 4.5). Click the Directories tab. Then, in the Default document space, put index.cgi, index.html, index.htm, before default.htm, with commas between.

What you've just done is enable someone to hit your site at www.yourcompany .com/ without them having to put index.html or default.htm at the end of the URL. That's what the default document is for, and includes a www.yourcompany.com/ thisdirectory/. You won't have to put index.html there either. By enabling index.cgi, you've opened this default serving of documents to automated pages created by a Perl program, which is what the remaining chapters of this book will show you how to do.

Now reboot your computer. Internet Information Server will run a Perl program through its native ISAPI interface.

Figure 4.5 Server Properties.

 On the CD In the /examples/ISAPI directory you'll find two files, one called test.cgi and one called test2.cgi. The first, test.cgi, merely prints Hello World to your web browser. Install it in your web directory and hit it. If you get an error that says "File type not recognized by NT," you forgot to restart your system. If you get "Document contains no data" you probably have an old version of PerlIS.dll that didn't print an OK status automatically before the content-type line. The other, test2.cgi, is a print Location: test that adds in the 302 status that this version of PerlIS.dll does not fix.

Perl for Windows 95

Yes, you can download the same Perl file we used on NT for your local Windows 95 machine. I've found this helpful for finding bugs and typos in files I modify, especially config files. I always seem to have a typo.

The installer will default your Perl location to C:\Perl\Bin. To use it from the command line, use your Programs/MSDOS utility to open up a DOS session. It will default to C:\Windows, from which you'll change directories to the document location where the files you're working on are kept. One note about this is that changing directories on long directory names can be a bit of a challenge. If you do a dir \p (directory listing one screen at a time), you'll see that a directory called Modem Utilities in Windows 95, which can handle more than just the old eight/three naming convention, is called MODEMU~1 in the DOS shell. That's exactly how you'll change directory to it. Type cd modemu~1 and you'll go there; then Windows 95 steps in and shows you the real directory name.

Once you're in the directory where your files are, type path = \perl\bin. That will activate Perl as if you were in a Unix shell. I couldn't get the debugger to work right, but take a look at many of the other utilities. Some are very helpful, and of course there's the old command-line search and replace.

Using
Perl

As I explained in the opening, most of the utilities in this book are written in Perl. Using Perl, as we do here, is easy, but you should know some of the basic concepts and syntax. Don't be intimidated. I started learning Perl about a year and half before writing this book. So even if this is your first look at it, I've only got a bit of a jump on you. I expect that you'll be caught up to my level in no time and if you so choose, running circles around me within a couple of months. This overview is just a primer on how to think in Perl, not how to use it effectively. Keep in mind that the most common Perl joke is "How do you do *this* in Perl?" The answer is "Well, that depends." There are other ways to use almost everything in the examples I offer here.

To install the utilities in this book, you must know the overview of Perl variables provided in this chapter. Most of what we'll do in the following chapters is to modify existing quantities that are previously defined. Almost all of these quantities are variable definitions.

Perl in Practice

Because we're working on all platforms, Perl has some quirks you should know about for different systems. Luckily, most Unix flavors behave the same, so coding for them involves only one standard of operations. But NT is different. It's based on the DOS file naming, structure, and format, so it has to be worked around at times.

T I P If you're on a Unix system you'll have to check and possibly change the Perl location for every utility in this book. At the beginning of every Perl program is a line that looks like this:

```
#! usr/bin/perl
```

With the correct path information to your system's location of Perl 5. This points the current program to the Perl compiler. Make sure it's Perl 5 and not 4, as many of these utilities require the added security and functionality of the fifth version.

Windows NT doesn't require a Perl location, though it won't hurt to leave it in there. In Chapter 4 we set all files with the .cgi extension to know automatically where Perl is on the system.

 On the Web Check out www.tucows.com for the nearest mirror of the latest and greatest web applications. My personal favorite Telnet program is NetTerm, located at

starbase.neosoft.com/~zkrr01/.

Editors

Unix for Unix and Windows for Windows is the most convenient way to edit Perl programs, but as I just reviewed, most of us are stuck working on Unix servers from PCs. This is fine for most of Perl, but with one quirk. Many Windows editors (including Hotdog) insert a ^M character at the end of every line of text. It's invisible to the eye but can be viewed with the Unix text editor. In Figure 5.1 you'll see the extra line-ending ^M characters in a plain HTML document from one of our oldest client sites at www.newcemcorp.org. Many of the new Windows 95 editors have solved this with a "save as Unix" option, but not all. Check yours by uploading a saved file to the shell account (in NetTerm you can do this with zmodem directly) and opening it in Emacs, VI, or Jove.

 On the CD I've included my favorite Perl editor for Windows in the \binaries directory of the CD. There you'll find multiedit.zip, 1.388 meg. It's a fully functional demo of the licensed product that includes Perl high-lighting, multifile search and replace, and other time-saving functions you'll really enjoy. You'll need to set some parameters for it to recognize our files in Perl mode:

1. Click Tools.
2. Click Customize.
3. Click Filename Extensions.
4. Click PL.
5. In the Extension(s) box type PL cgi wms cfg (with spaces in between).
6. Click OK.
7. If you get a box that says Reset in Current Files, click Yes.
8. Click Close, Close.

Yes, you noticed the nagging screen that popped up? That's the annoyance of the unregistered version.

```
<HTML>^M
<HEAD><TITLE>Choices To Make Now for the Future</TITLE>^M
</HEAD>^M
<BODY BGCOLOR="#FFFFFF" LINK="#0000FF" VLINK="#8000FF" ALINK="#FF0000">^M
^M
<H1 align=center>Choices</H1>^M
<H2 align=center>To Make Now for the Future</H2>^M
^M
<P align=center>This page is part of a series from the Cremation Association of\
 North America.  Please also take a look at <A HREF="http://www.NewCemCorp.org/\
cmopt.htm"> <STRONG>Cremation Memorials -- Options for Those Who Care</STRONG> \
</A>and <A HREF="http://www.NewCemCorp.org/cqa.htm"><STRONG>"Cremation Explaine\
d -- Answers to Questions Most Frequently Asked"</STRONG></A>.  You may also re\
turn to the <A HREF="http://www.NewCemCorp.org/">Main Index</A> from which this\
 site is  linked in its entirety. </P>^M
^M
^M
<HR WIDTH=20% ALIGN=left SIZE=3 NOSHADE>^M
<H3>Plan Now for Tomorrow</H3>^M
^M
Just as you have made your own decisions on important^M
matters up to now, you will want to continue to do so^M
---**-Emacs: choices.htm        (Fundamental)--Top-------------
Auto-saving...done
```

Figure 5.1 Control-M characters on DOS/Windows.

> ## Working on Unix Perl from Windows Computers
>
> When I first started writing in Perl I was faced with the same quandary that many developers encounter. How do I test Perl programs for Unix from a PC running Windows 3.1? Perl has been ported to 16-bit Windows, but not well—it's very unstable. These days, the 32-bit Windows version is more stable but is always behind the Unix build in new features and bug fixes.
>
> The answer is Telnet. First I got a shell account at my ISP. It's different from PPP in that it's more than just a hard connection to the Internet. A shell gives you a command line prompt, like a DOS prompt, from which you can edit programs in real-time and execute Perl for testing.
>
> You actually need two accounts, a shell and a standard PPP. The shell you *could* dial directly into, but don't bother. It's kludgy, slow, and you can't run a browser over it at the same time (except Slipknot, which I won't even mention—oops). I keep the shell with the ISP and purchase a second PPP. Then I run a Telnet application over the PPP and access the shell. It sounds like a hack but actually is quite efficient. I've even given lectures from California demonstrating applications on servers in Massachusetts without any noticeable latency. It's all ASCII text traveling back and forth.

Perl Coding in Review

As I just explained, please don't take this overview as comprehensive. I include it only because I needed a simple idea of what Perl was before really setting down to learn it. I found it on the web, as you could, but this should give a good idea of what the language is like and how you'll be modifying it in the near future.

Move into intro and replace with traditional; now we'll be looking at coding...roadmap.

Variables

What's a variable? Don't laugh. I didn't even get it back in algebra class. For a non-programmer, it can be a tough question. My best definition is that a variable is what you say it is. Without you, it's a placeholder identified by either a $, @, or % before it. You add a value, which depends upon a condition or a set of conditions. A variable holds something you'll need later. Perl has three types of variables, all of which we will use in the following chapters. Figure 5.2 is a visual representation of the differences.

Scalars hold a single value, which can be a string of text, a number, or anything that you need to define in one piece of information:

```
$cost = .1;

$text = "We the People, in order to form a more perfect union ...";

$sport = "golf";

$header = "<H1> Welcome to XYZ Corporation</H1>";
```

A regular array, named with an @ sign, holds a list of single values, separated by commas and placed between parenthesis:

```
@days = ("Monday","Tuesday","Wednesday","Thursday","Friday","Saturday","Sunday");

@fish = ("Grouper","Hogfish","Barracuda","Char","Bass");
```

An associative array, which is also called a *hash*, looks like a normal array when you write it, but associates the first value with the second, the third with the fourth, fifth with sixth, and so on. Name it with a percent (%) sign:

Scalar is a single value

$sport = " "; $cost = " "; $text = " ";

Array is a list

@fish = " ";

Associative array is a list of associations

%states = " ";

Figure 5.2 The differences in Perl variables.

```
%states = ("mo.gif","moflag.gif","nh.gif","nhflag.gif","ny.gif","nyflag.gif");

%hexcolors =

("black","#000000","white","#FFFFFF","blue","0000FF","red","#FF0000");
```

Scalars

If you see a dollar sign in front of a Perl variable, it's a *scalar*, which can hold only one value. It can be a long or short value, consisting of either an integer, a floating point value, or double and single quoted character strings.

All of these constructs are legal variable names and values:

```
$variablename = "Variable Value";

$number_of_states = 50;

$state = "New Hampshire";

$pauls_license_plate = "CJP199";

$nh_motto = "Live Free or Die";

$state_meals_tax = .07;
```

Notice that the 50 and .07 don't need quotes, but that the text strings, including the text with numbers in the license plate variable, do. If the value of your variable contains only numbers, just print the number. If it contains letters, letters with numbers, or letters with special characters, wrap it in quotes. I used double quotes on all of the above, but you can also use single quotes. Doubles interpolate variables within them identified with either $ or a @. Next I've defined the variable $today, then included it in $intro.

```
$today = "Wednesday";

$intro = "Hi, today is $today.";
```

would result in:

```
$intro = "Hi, today is Wednesday."
```

Sometimes you'll need to include a $ or @ sign in the value of the variable. One way to handle this is with single quotes. In the following example, I need to reference the price of milk in a web page:

```
$price_of_milk = '$1.50';

$milk_headline = "<H2>Wow! Milk to your door for only $price_of_milk.</H2>"
```

This produces:

```
$milk_headline = "<H2>Wow! Milk to your door for only $1.50.</H2>"
```

But what if you have to print both a $ and a real variable within the same reference? The backslash character (\) disables variable interpolation as well. The following example will interpret the dollar sign as a dollar sign and $today and $month as variables, identified elsewhere in the program.

```
$price_today = "Eggs are \$2.50 today, $today, $month $monthday.";
```

Assuming you identified the day and date variables elsewhere, this would interpolate as:

```
$price_today = "Eggs are $2.50 today, Wednesday, March 26.";
```

T I P All variable names must be composed of only letters, numbers, and underscores. Special characters in Perl have specific meanings, so never use them. This is true for all types of variables, not just scalars.

```
$variable-with-a-dash = "no can do";

$expensive$$$variable = "this either";

$isn'tthisclever = "it will break";
```

Standard Arrays

A standard array, as I explained previously, is a list of values. The values in the list can be single words, numbers, or a combination thereof. They need not have anything to do with each other as no two items in the list are connected:

```
@golfscores = (72,95,53,"Too bad to list","Even Worse");

@randomstuff = ("shoes","Henry Kissinger","squash","Nice Teeth");
```

An array can also include scalar variables or other arrays. In the following example, I need a list of all relevant phone numbers that will be updated automatically for the footer on our website. The first two elements in the list are our toll-free number and main number, which always stay the same. The third element is the phone number for sales, which will vary depending upon the location of the user hitting the page. This variable, $sales, will be determined somewhere else in the program, probably from webform input. The last item in the array is another array, or list, and is composed of help lines drawn from another yet another area in the program. I've placed them in one array for convenience:

```
@our_phone_numbers = ("800.555.1212","603.594.9321","$sales","@helpdesks");
```

TIP A scalar variable can hold the same name as an array but have no association to it. For example, although these two variables have the same number, they have nothing to do with each other.

```
$jobs = "There are currently $numjobs jobs in our database right now!";

@jobs = ("Programmer","Systems Analyst","Copy Editor");
```

An Array Slice

Usually you will not need every element of an array all at once. But once you set a standard array you can extract all of its contents, as previously shown, or just specific items as you need them. Next, the array @chrysler would be composed of the Viper and Voyager, which is referenced from the original @cars array:

```
@cars = ("Explorer","Viper","Continental","Monte Carlo","Voyager");

@chrysler = @cars[1,4];
```

But "No," you say. Viper is the second item in the array @cars. That's a quirk of Perl. The first item of an array is indexed as zero, not one. This also works backwards:

```
@cars[5,6] = ("Escort", "Town & Country");
```

With these I've expanded the @cars array to include two more items in the list. It will automatically grow in size to accommodate. All of these use an array slice as a smaller array, but using an array slice as a scalar is also common. I would extract Town and Country as follows:

```
$new_car_on_lot = "Take a look at today's arrival, a late model $cars[6]";
```

would produce:

```
$new_car_on_lot = "Take a look at today's arrival, a late model Town & Country";
```

Within the context of a website, you probably wouldn't put that text string into a variable like that. You'd plug it right into the page directly. SiteWrapper, in Chapter 6, translates variables like that dynamically.

 On the Web You'll find an example of this at www.AndoverInn.com. Click the Meeting Rooms link on the jumplist. It will bring you to the ?rentrate.htm page. Now take away the question mark, hitting rentrate.htm without the variable interpolation of SiteWrapper. You should get a page that has a gray background and the variables $HEADER and $TEXTLIST at the top of the page. Figure 5.3 shows you what to expect.

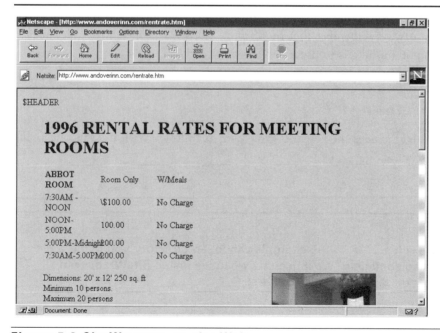

Figure 5.3 SiteWrapper on the Web.

Associative Arrays (Hashes)

Often you will need to keep a list of related things. An associative array does just that. It holds pairs of values that should be kept together. The following example differs from an array like @fish because list item one, Toupee, is connected to list item two, Bald Guy. Bat is connected to Ball, Frame to Picture.

```
%pairs = ("Toupee","Bald Guy","Bat","Ball","Frame","Picture");
```

The pairs of list items in an associative array not only have a relationship with one another, they have names. The firsts, like Toupee, Bat, and Frame, are called *keys*. The seconds, Bald Guy, Ball, and Picture, are called *values*. Unlike a standard array where the items have @index[0] numbers, these keys and values are how we add and extract pieces of hashes.

Manipulating Associative Arrays

If we need to extract Ball from the previous array, Bat is our access point. It is the key for Ball:

```
$catching_a = $pairs{"Bat"};
```

As you can see, we reference the associative array %pairs by calling our scalar from it. Many of our configuration files in the following chapters will reference values like this. Always remember that the variable is a scalar, called with a dollar sign. A common mistake is to use a percent sign.

```
You can add to an array much the same way:
```

```
$pairs{"Lox"} = "Bagels";
```

Now %pairs includes the key and value pair, as follows. We'll use this one again in the next section.

```
%pairs = ("Toupee","Bald","Bat","Ball","Frame","Picture","Lox","Bagels");
```

 On the CD In the examples/andover/ directory you'll find a file called config.cfg. We'll use this when we install SiteWrapper in Chapter 6. The first 12 lines are:

```
1: #!/usr/bin/perl
   .
   .
```

```
27: $server = "http://www.AndoverInn.com";
 .
 .
 .
42: @logs = ("homepage.htm", "breakfst.htm");
 .
 .
 .
63: %jumpnames = ("index.htm", "Andover Inn Home",
64:              "chronicl.htm","The Chronicle",
65:              "breakfst.htm","Dining Menus",
66:              "rijsttaf.htm", "Indonesian Rijsttafel",
67:              "tea.htm","High Tea",
68:              "function.htm","Function and Wedding Menu",
69:              "confmen.htm","Conference Menu/Rates",
70:              "horsdovr.htm","Hors d' Oeuvres",
71:              "rentrate.htm", "Meeting Rooms",
72:              "stations.htm","Station Reception",
73:              "regform.htm", "Reservation Request",
74:              "directn.htm", "Directions/Maps",
75:              "mail.cgi", "Events");
```

As you can see, all three types of variables are represented here. Line 27 is a standard scalar. Notice that the @ sign is escaped with a backslash character. Without the backslash, this file would break the www.AndoverInn .com website. You would receive a server error upon hitting the homepage. We also could have wrapped the e-mail address in single quotes.

The array, @logs, lists the pages to be logged as people hit the site. There are only two, and as with any standard array in Perl, they have no relationship to each other.

At line 63 is the hash %jumpnames, a variable you'll know very well by the end of this book. It's the way we automate the jumplist at the top or bottom of every page on the site. Figure 5.4 shows the Andover Inn homepage showing most of the choices (they don't quite all fit). As you can see, a hash need not always be on one line. Perl 5 recognized several of the preceding formats, as well as another that we'll visit later with => between the associated list items.

When you click a link on Andover Inn it grabs the HTML page you clicked and sends it through a Perl program called index.cgi. This in turn grabs the config from above, a header and footer. Below is the header. You can see the scalar variables $thispagetitle and $bodytag in includes:

Figure 5.4 An associative array you'll see again.

```
<!DOCTYPE HTML PUBLIC "-//W3C//DTD HTML 3.2//EN">

<HTML>

<HEAD>

<TITLE>

$thispagetitle

</TITLE>

</HEAD>

$bodytag


<!--end header.txt-->
```

And where does $thispagetitle come from? Line 50 of index.cgi references it like this:

```
1: #!/usr/bin/perl
```

```
50: $thispagetitle = $titlenames{"$document_filename"};
```

You guessed it. The %titlenames variable is set in the config.cfg as:

```
88: %titlenames = %jumpnames;
```

which you saw previously as a hash of all the page HTML files and their associated titles. If this is confusing, chances are you've never seen programming. Just think of arrays as lists. The @ arrays are lists of things that don't have anything to do with each other, the % arrays are pairs listed one after the other.

So You've Noticed the Semicolon?

Yes, as you can see from all the preceding examples, every Perl statement ends with a semicolon. Forget one and your Perl program will break. It's the most common mistake for programmers, new and old. Luckily, finding these errors is easy. Perl's built-in warning messages will tell you where to look.

And the # Marks?

Any lines beginning with a # are ignored by Perl—they are called *comments*. Comments are most commonly at the start of a line, usually to explain the use or syntax of a variable that follows, but (except on "here documents," as I'll explain later) they can be inserted anywhere:

```
# this can be a comment

@variable = "content";  # as can this
```

Operating on Variables

In our travels through this book I'll show you several ways we've manipulated our utilities for custom projects. To take full advantage, you'll need a good understanding of the Perl language, but not the status of guru. These are some of more basic ways to manipulate variables in Perl. I mean it only as a taste of what you'll learn with a comprehensive Perl book. If you have some programming experience but are unfamiliar with Perl, check out www.ncsa.uiuc.edu/General/Training/PerlIntro/ for a more comprehensive overview.

Arithmetic Operators

On log files and shopping carts we'll be adding and multiplying variables to and by each other with regular math. All the arithmetic operators work like this:

```
$apples = 5;

$oranges = 2;

$fruit = $apples + $oranges;
```

The scalar variable $fruit now holds the value 7. This syntax is the same for –, *, /, and **, applied as minus, times, divided by, and exponent, respectively.

```
$todays_apples = 100;

$yesterdays_apples = 250;

# then

$todays_sales = $yesterdays_apples - $todays_apples;   #$todays_sales = 150

$projected_year_sales = $todays_sales * 365;

$monthly_sales_average = $projected_year_sales / 12;

$three_year_estimate = $projected_year_sales ** 3;   #sales will double every year
```

For strings of characters, like pieces of HTML encoded text (I'll refer to them as *strings* from here forth), you can't use arithmetic. Those are only for numbers. Perl provides a different way to add additional material to text strings called *concatenate,* and uses a dot:

```
$fontcolor = "<FONT COLOR=\"white\">";

$text = "See our new selection of Widgets";

$fontcolorend = "</FONT>";

$concatenatedtext = $fontcolor . $text . $fontcolorend;
```

This would be useful in place of style sheets. You could reference $concatenated-text from anywhere in your site and it would contain the entire HTML string made up of $fontcolor, $text, and $fontcolorend. In reality like we'd most likely set the $text variable on the fly from some sort of data source. You'll see this again.

TIP I bet you noticed that the HTML in the preceding example looked a little funny. The quotes around the word "white" have been escaped with that same backslash character I used earlier for dollar signs and @ signs. This is to tell Perl that those quotes don't end the text to be included in the variable. I also could have composed the statement with single quotes around the string and left out the back-slashes:

```
$fontcolor = '<FONT COLOR = "white">';
```

Comparisons

Later we'll look at conditionals like if *this*, then *do this*. In them, we'll need to compare things. For these, Perl provides logical operators. No surprises here. Just like the arithmetic operators, most follow from your high school algebra book. All of these are considered true. We'll test on true in future chapters:

```
$noses < 2       # the value of $noses is less than 2, considered
                 # "true" for most

$iq > 150        # well for me it's true ;*)

$states == 50    # numerical equivalent

$shoes <= 2      # you get the point?

$computers >= 5

$customers != 0  # the value of customers does not equal 0
```

For strings, as you just saw with simple operators, Perl supplies a different set of comparison operators from those meant for numbers. You won't use these much but you should at least understand them:

```
$string eq "Show Me the Money";    #for this to be true, $string must be exact.

$string ne "Use the Force Luke";   #true if Obi Wan forgot to show up.
```

There are also lt, gt, le, and ge for less than, greater than, less than or equal to, and greater than or equal to, but we won't use them here.

Other operators you'll use are "or," represented as ||, and "and," represented as &&. Both test two separate arguments, and in both, the argument on the left is tested first. If it's true, the right side is never addressed. If it's false, Perl looks to the right and tests that:

```
$home_by < 10 || up_by < 5
```

In other words, if you aren't in by ten, Perl doesn't need to check whether you were up by five. It proceeds with the next operation. The "and" operator, implemented as &&, works the same:

```
$home_by < 5 && $roses == 12
```

In this case, if you're not home for dinner, don't even bother with the roses. If you are home, Perl checks for $roses to see if your sweetie will be truly happy. We'll see all of these operators in the following chapters, but remember, to install the utilities in this book you only need to understand and use the different types of variables.

Matching a Pattern

Here we test whether a variable contains a certain string of text. Like the simple comparisons earlier, we will use these in an "if *this* contains *pattern*, then *do this*" construct. The operator is =~, literally translated as "contains":

```
$the_future =~ /internet/;                  # this is of course true

$ENV{"HTTP_USER_AGENT"} =~ /Mozilla/;     # and this is usually true
```

For the first line to be true, $the_future would have to contain the text string "internet," as in "The Future is Here, Harness the Internet" or some such foolishness. The second line you'll see again. It tests whether you are using a Netscape or compatible browser. The variable %ENV is an associative array of pairs, each corresponding to some aspect of your environment. The %ENV variable contains time of day, referring URL, and other information, including what browser you are using to access the site. We can extract those values in any Perl program for our use. The

HTTP_USER_AGENT value, (browser software) we extract with a scalar, as we do with all associative array keys and values, and test to see if it contains "Mozilla," the working name of Netscape Navigator. In this case, the statement is true, because Microsoft Internet Explorer 3.01 is the value referenced, and it contains the word Mozilla. Following is what MSIE sends and what Perl reads in from the HTTP_USER_AGENT:

```
Mozilla/2.0 (compatible; MSIE 3.01; Windows 95)
```

Most of the time, pattern matching isn't that simple: we have to match parts of words, or the match has to be at the beginning of a line, or the match might be spelled one of many ways. For situations like these, Perl provides a set of matching operators called *regular expressions*. They use special characters to signify specific aspects to the match you seek. They can get pretty complicated, so if you use them start simple and test your work as you go. If this is confusing, don't worry. We've supplied them for all the programs in the book. This is just so you'll understand what we're giving you.

The * character matches zero or more of the characters it comes after:

```
$string =~ /abc*d/;
```

matches abd, abcd, abccd, abcccd, etc.

The ? character matches only zero or one incident of the character preceding it:

```
$string =~ /abc?d/;
```

matches only abd and abcd.

The + character matches at least one or more of the preceding character:

```
$string =~ /abc+d/;
```

matches abcd, abccd, abcccd, but not abd as with the asterisk.

The . character matches any character but a newline:

```
$string =~ /abc.d/;
```

matches abc, anything but a newline, then d. So ab Have a nice day d would match, because the whitespace characters are all included in the . catch-all.

To match one of a set of characters, use square brackets:

```
$string =~ /abcd[eE]fg/;
```

which will match either one.

For a set of consecutive letters or numbers, you can substitute a dash:

```
$string =~ /a[b-y]z/;
```

```
$string =~ /1[2-98]99/;
```

Specify that the matched pattern must come at the beginning or end of a line with the ^ and $ characters:

```
$string =~ /^<HTML>/;
```

```
$string =~ /<\/HTML>$/;
```

In the first example, the line of text in $string must start with <HTML>. In the second, it must end with </HTML>.

Aha! You noticed that the / in </HTML> was escaped with a backslash character. As you can see, it's needed because otherwise Perl might think that the pattern had ended. You also will need to use the backslash for escaping *, ?, +, ., and \, another backslash, if you want to match them literally.

Some conveniences are built in with the backslash character as well. They match common character sets and behaviors:

```
\w        # matches any letter or number, including underscores

\W        # any non-letter, number, or underscore

\d        # matches any numeric digit

\D        # any non-numeric digit

\s        # any whitespace, space, \t (tab), \n (newline)

\S        # any non-whitespace

\b        # match must be at a word boundary

\B        # at a non-word boundary
```

For example:

```
$holiday =~ /\bc?han+uk?ah*\b/i;
```

matches any version of the word [C]han[n]uka[h] that occurs within a word boundary. The \b is a word boundary, zero or one c, han, with one or more n's, uk, with one or more k's, and ah, with zero or more of the letter h. This covers hannukah, hanuka, chanuka, chanukka, and Channukah, because I added an i at the end after the last slash. That renders the match case insensitive.

If you have a group of characters to match, you can wrap them in parenthesis to apply a single condition. Because some URLs these days include a www and some do not, I wrapped the letters with an escaped dot in parenthesis and followed them with an asterisk, signifying zero or more of the preceding character, or in this case, group of characters in parenthesis:

```
$hotlink =~ /<A HREF\s*=\s*"http:\/\/(www\.)*cnn\.com"*>/i; # what?
```

Don't get scared by the complex look of this example. Break it down piece by piece. It begins with a normal <A HREF, adds optional space between the = and quotes, then groups the www with its following dot into a group of characters that may be in the URL or not, signified by the third asterisk. Then cnn.com must follow, and the closing parenthesis is optional as many people forget it when writing HTML. Still look confusing? You're probably being thrown by the escaped periods and slashes. This is what it looks like without them:

```
$hotlink =~ /<A HREF\s*=\s*"http://(www.)*cnn.com"*>/i
```

This would not work in practice because Perl sees the slashes in the URL as closing the statement. Add the escape characters back in and you'll arrive at the preceding example. There are other ways to do this, but this is most common.

Functions

OK, what do I mean by functions? That was my question when I saw the word for the first time, too. We use functions in Perl to manipulate variables, strings of text, and input/output. A function can be as simple as:

```
open(INPUTFILE, "file.txt");
```

which simply opens a file so that we can read from it, to:

```
chop(@array);
```

TIP Something you might not expect, and a frequent mistake, is the use of the . character to catch any and every character between HTML tags, as in "catch everything between the <H2> tags." The following example is how you'd think to write it. But the unexpected comes when there are more than one <H2> on the page. This would grab everything between the first <H2> tag and the last </H2> on the page. That's fine if there is only one <H2> on the page, but with multiples of the same tag set, it grabs them all. The . character matches everything, including angle brackets.

```
$subhead =~ /<H2>.*<\/H2>/i;

$subhead =~ /<H2>([^<>].)*<\/H2>/i;
```

I fixed the second one with something you haven't seen yet. The ^ character (a carat) negates the class of characters in the brackets. So that translates as "anything within <H2> tags except angle brackets." This would work unless you had nested HTML tags within the headers.

This is really an abomination of regular expressions in Perl. They are complex and require lots of trial, error, and careful study of existing examples. A good Perl book will help you more, and the web is rich with information as well. Start at www.perl.org and use their search engine to get to the exact page.

---

which chops the last character off the end of every item in the list of things in @array, to

```
keys(%states);
```

which returns the first associated items in %states into a list we could store in a normal array.

Following are the most common functions we'll use for customization of the programs here. Usually you'll be altering only existing functions or duplicated ones that already exist. A complete overview is at the Perl online manual.

open(), close(), select(), and FILEHANDLES

There will always be input and output in everything we do. Input acquires information, output disburses information. In Perl, all input and output comes from a FILEHANDLE, usually written in all uppercase as I have here. To read input with a FILEHANDLE we either will be opening a text file on the local machine or accepting data from a webform. From a file, the syntax is:

```
open(FILEHANDLE, "filename.txt");
```

which reads in all the lines of filename.txt and puts it in <FILEHANDLE>, which we can then access. This is an example from parser.cgi, found in WebPost, Chapter 11:

```
open (RAWFILE, $file_to_conv) || &error;

@data = <RAWFILE>;
```

This first puts all the lines of the file held in $file_to_conv (which is a scalar variable we will assume holds the value thisfile.txt) into the FILEHANDLE RAWFILE, then assigns the individual lines of the file to the array @data. Each element in the list @data now has a line of thisfile.txt. If thisfile.txt were a standard HTML file that looked like this at the top:

```
<HTML>

<HEAD>

<TITLE>

Welcome to the Show!

<TITLE>
```

and were we to write out @data in a parenthetic form to show its elements, it would look something like this:

```
@data = ("<HTML>\n","<HEAD>\n","<TITLE>\n","Welcome to the
Show!\n","<TITLE>\n");
```

Line 1 is in $data[0], the first element, line 2 is in $data[1], and so on. Also, you probably notice that every element in the array includes the newline character, represented by \n. This is an invisible character, like a space or tab, that tells the program rendering the file to move down a line.

You can also open a file to write to it or append to it. This is done the same way, but with a greater-than symbol, for completely overwriting or two of them for appending:

```
open(DATAFILE, ">thisfile.txt");      #opens thisfile.txt for us to overwrite

open(DATAFILE, ">>thisfile.txt");     #opens for us to append
```

The other thing we read from and write to is the screen, sucking form data after someone clicks Submit and spitting HTML results back at the browser. These two FILEHANDLES are known as standard in and standard out, which we access in Perl as <STDIN> and <STDOUT>. Down the road you'll see more of these and how we access them.

In most programs, you'll be opening several files as well as STDIN and STDOUT. That's where the select function comes in. It tells Perl that the next print statement goes there.

```
select(STDOUT);

print "content type: text/html\n\n";
```

This would send the browser the first part of an HTML header. All CGIs send this line, including the two blank lines, so the browser knows what's coming.

Closing a file is as you would expect. It's not crucial to close every file you open but is suggested practice and makes for clean code. This is the way you do it:

```
close(FILEHANDLE);
```

The print() Function and Here Documents

When you hit a link on any dynamically generated site, you are clicking on a program, usually signified by a ? mark somewhere in the URL. That means that there is no static HTML document to access on the server. The page is created for you on the fly and the program prints HTML to the screen. Likewise, when you place an order on a commerce site, sign a guestbook, or participate in an online discussion, a program prints your form input to a file. We do this with the Perl print() function. Both of the following examples demonstrate this by printing a line of HTML to the screen. As you can see, the FILEHANDLE is not needed if you use select() before the statement. The parenthesis are optional for one line of text:

```
select(STDOUT);

print "<H1>Our Website Title</H1>";        # prints that HTML to the browser

                                            # via STDOUT


print (STDOUT, "<H1>Our Website Title</H1>");  # does the same
```

"Ugh," you say? "Do I have to do that for every line of HTML in a document?" No. That's a common time waster among programmers who migrate to Perl. For multiple lines we use something called a *here document*, which says "print everything between this END tag and the next."

```
print<<END;

Content-type: text/html


<HTML>

<HEAD>

<TITLE>

Welcome to the Show!

<TITLE>

<BODY BACKGROUND="bacground.jpg" TEXT="red" LINK="blue" VLINK="green">

<H1>Hey, Order Some Tickets</H1>

END
```

 On the CD Open the file wmsstorer.cgi in the examples/mas directory of the CD. It's one of the programs you'll learn with WebPost in Chapter 11. At line 267 is an example of a here document on a screen you'll see a lot in the future.

```
267:           print<<END;

268: <CENTER>

269: <HR><h1>$tbar_title</h1><HR>

270: <FONT SIZE=4><STRONG>

271: You may now<BR>

272: <A HREF="$server/parser.cgi?FILE=$output_filename">Go to your

     Posting</A><BR>

273: or<BR>

274: <A HREF="$server/">Go Back To $name_of_org Home Page</A>

275: </STRONG><BR>

276: </CENTER>

277: END
```

Notice that there are variables within the here text that the program will interpolate. If the statement at line 267 had contained single quotes, as follows, those variables would render as plain dollar signs, without interpolation.

```
267:           print<<'END';      # this stops interpolation within the here
                                  # text
```

What if you have to print a dollar or @ sign manually, but need interpolation in other parts of the document? Escape them, as you would with variable assignments:

```
print<<ENDPOTATO;

<H1> Potatoes are only \$5.00 today</H1>

<H3>Email our sales department at

<A HREF="mailto:sales\@couchpotato.com">sales\@couchpotato.com</a>

ENDPOTATO
```

Note that there is one easy pitfall with here documents, one that took me a week to solve before Larry Wall, the inventor of Perl, personally mailed me the answer. The line that contains the END word, which can be anything, in caps or not, has to contain only that word and nothing else. There cannot be a comment after it, nor a semicolon, nor what broke me, a space. Press Enter on your keyboard right after it and don't go back.

eval()

This function has a whole bunch of uses in Perl that I won't explain here. I don't even understand some of them. What I will explain is how we use it and why.

We use eval() to "eat" a file, extrapolate variables within it, then spit the evaluated contents back to the screen or to a file. Usually this is some sort of HTML document that contains dynamic elements, like today's date, this week's press release, or the newest job in our database. We eat a file with a $variable in it. The variable extrapolates in the program, and a finished page is sent to the browser.

 O n   t h e   W e b Take a look at the front page of www.andoverinn.com—it's the page shown in Figure 5.4. What you're seeing is an evaluated page called homepage.htm, just like rentrate .htm, earlier. Now hit homepage.htm and view it alone, without the eval(). What you should see looks like Figure 5.5. The variables $bodytag and $TEXTLIST are evaluated as the page loads, serving you a completed HTML page.

We use eval() specifically because it traps errors. That means that if, somewhere in the HTML being evaluated, there is something that would break Perl, the program calling eval() won't break. If you've ever hit a site and got a SERVER ERROR 500 message, you should appreciate this. A simple mistake, like escaping an @ sign, can kill an entire Perl-generated website. By using eval(), we trap the error. It kills only the line on which the @ sign resides. We'll see the functionality of eval() in Chapter 6, on the uses of SiteWrapper.

Unix Only: CHMOD

The Unix file structure has a system of *permissions*. You have permission to read *this* file, you have permission to write to *this* directory, you have permission to execute *this* program.

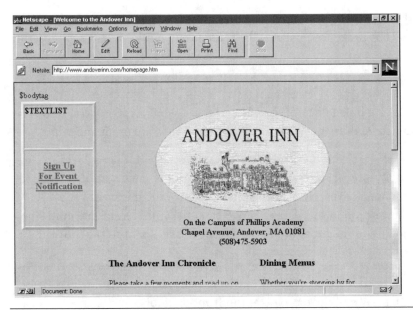

Figure 5.5 $bodytag and $TEXTLIST evaluated.

"You" are not necessarily "You." Unix splits identities into three categories. The first is you, yourself, the owner of the file, directory, or program. Second, you belong to a group, and then the third permission identity extends to everyone, regardless of ownership or group. This fits into a simple numbering system, like 644. The first number is what you have permission to do (6, I have permission to read and write), the second number is what the group has permission to do (4, the group I belong to can only read), and the third is what everyone has permission to do (anyone can read it, 4 again). You add to the three numbers with either 4, 2, or 1.

- 4 is read

- 2 is write

- 1 is execute

So for a file that's 755, the owner can read, write, and execute (7 = 4 + 2 + 1) , and the group and everyone can both read and execute (5 = 4 + 1). This is the most common change of permissions we will do. Using the CHMOD function in Perl is the same as from the command line, except that it is followed by a semicolon:

```
chmod 755 index.cgi;
```

opendir(), readdir(), closedir()

I'm including these three functions because you'll see them often. In several places we'll have to open a directory, read all the file names in it, then extract ones that match our needs. For functionality, opendir() and closedir() work like open() and close(), but are for directories, not files. You open and close FILEHANDLES that are actually directory handles. The readdir() function takes that FILEHANDLE and places its contents in an array.

```
opendir(DIR, ".");

@files = readdir(DIR);

closedir(DIR);
```

sort() {and grep()}

As we go I'll explain how to modify these two functions. For now though, it's important that you just recognize them and understand what they're for. The sort() function does just what it says, for a @list variable. If the contents are numeric it sorts them in order; if they are words or multiple words, it sorts them alphabetically. You can also reverse the order with a reverse modifier.

```
@sortedstates = sort(@states);
```

The variable @sortedstates now lists Alabama first. If the list @states contained abbreviations, AK would be first.

The grep() function grabs at a list of text resources, be they strings of text or complete files, for a pattern match of letters. It uses the regular expressions from before:

```
open(FILE, "news.txt");

@newstext =(<FILE>);

@tired = grep(/Simpson/, @newstext);
```

This first line opens the news.txt file, puts each of its lines in the variable @newstext, then extracts only those lines containing Simpson into the variable @tired.

Conditionals—if, else, elsif

A few pages back I mentioned the construct "if *this*, do *this*." We use it in almost every utility in this book. You won't have to modify many, but there are a few.

On the CD I grouped these two functions together and placed them after the directory operators to show you this piece of code from the examples/tps directory on the CD. Look in the file wmsdb.cgi.

```
49:            opendir(DIR, "$dbdir/$groupnum");
50:            @file_list = sort grep(/$dbfname\.(.*)/, readdir(DIR));
51:            closedir(DIR);
```

Line 49 opens the directory in the variable we've saved as $dbdir/$groupnum, which will look like jobs/4 when it extrapolates (referencing a category of information on the site like Manufacturing Engineers). In line 50, we sort all the files grep'd from reading that directory that contained another variable's value, $dbfname, which is a dynamic filename. Sound confusing? It isn't, and remember, you won't have to touch this type of code except for extra customization.

Figure 5.6 is a screen shot of the Multi-Edit editor with a piece of our Trakkit code. It tests for the most common search engines from which the visitor jumped. This example doesn't contain else, which is the last conditional in a series, or the second when there are only two choices. At its most basic, the code looks like this:

```
if ($variable =~ /^Please/)   {

    open(STDOUT);

print "<H1>We'll send you a free gift right away!</H1>";

close(STDOUT);


} else {

    open(FILE, ">rudepeople.txt");

    print "$date,$time\n";

    close(FILE);

    }
```

What I did was test if the $variable began with the word "Please." If so, I bounced a message back to the browser; else, I copied the date and time to a file of

Figure 5.6 Conditionals.

rude people. This would require much more, but you get the idea. The most important thing to understand is that a statement can be true or false. After the if, the expression in the parenthesis is tested for this. A true expression can include the contains operator, as before, or it may simply say:

```
if ($variable) {°
```

which translates as "if $variable exists, do…". This is useful when reading in form data. If *a field exists* do *this action*. Again, I'll explain specific uses of this in later chapters.

The elsif (that's right, no e) conditional is just an intermediary as you can see from the preceding figure. It allows you to add additional choices between the if and else.

Repeating and Looping—while, until, for, foreach

Now that you know how list and associative array variables work, it should be easy to picture testing for or looping through their individual items. The first two in this heading test for a property within an item. While *this* is true, do *this*. Until *this* is true, do *this*. The bracket construct is the same as the if sequence:

```
select(DATAFILE);

while($in{"items"}) {
```

```
    print "$in{items}";

    }
```

While the %in array has items in it, print the items to a data file. This same construct would work for until. This won't print to DATAFILE until someone orders a coconut:

```
select(DATAFILE);

until($in{"items"} =~ /coconut/) {

    print "$in{items}";

    }
```

Looping through a list variable is done with for and foreach. They are mostly the same, with a slight syntax difference. This is foreach:

```
foreach $step (@stairs) {

    print "$step";

    }
```

This would iterate through all the values in the list @stairs and print each one to whatever FILEHANDLE was last opened. Most commonly, for is used to do something a specific number of times:

```
for ($repetitions = 1; $repetitions <= 5; $repetitions +=1);
```

This translates as "$repetitions equals one; while $repetitions is less than or equal to five, increment it by one." If I lost you, don't worry. You'll get specific instructions when one of these can be modified.

Other Stuff

I may have missed a few along the way, so again, please don't take this as a comprehensive guide. Perl has hundreds of pieces to learn, and even experienced hackers use a desk reference. Expect, however, a very easy process as you learn the utilities in this book. In a few hours you'll be modifying variables. In a few weeks, perhaps you'll add some unique customizations. In a few months you'll be answering questions on comp.lang.perl.misc.

```
sunspot:/disk3/home/paulh$ perl -c test.cgi
Scalar found where operator expected at test.cgi line 11, near "$thisdomain"
        (Missing semicolon on previous line?)
syntax error at test.cgi line 11, near "$thisdomain "
test.cgi had compilation errors.
```

Figure 5.7 Using the perl-c function to find errors.

Checking Your Work Unix/NT/95

At the end of the previous chapter, I mentioned that Perl can be configured for command-line operations from all three operating systems. This is most helpful for catching spelling and typo errors in your Perl programs, because as I've noted in several places, Perl is an exacting language. One dropped semicolon or parenthesis and you're dead in the water. Catching these visually is difficult, so Larry Wall, the program's creator and maintainer has provided a library of error messages for each of Perl's most frequent mistakes. Figure 5.7 is a simple one I generated by deleting a semicolon from a working program. On the first line you'll see that I typed perl -c test.cgi, which is the program's name. Perl delivered back the error and what it thought I did. It was right.

The most important thing to understand about perl -c is that it's not a cure-all for every error you encounter on a webserver. You might get "programname.cgi syntax OK" from Perl but still encounter errors on your Unix or NT server. Other simple errors can be incorrect header, wrong permissions (even on NT), and forgetting to install an included file, but perl -c at least will eliminate the chance that you missed a closing quote or something.

If you type perl -c and an entire screen of stuff spatters in front of you, take heart. Most of it you can ignore. Perl forgets every error it finds as it reports it and pretends that everything is fine up to the point just after the error, even though it knows there is an error. Go to the first error, fix it, then go back and do a perl -c again.

If you get a "Can't find string terminator "END" anywhere before EOF at test.cgi line 3" message, where the word "END" is replaced with one from a here document within the file, you've inadvertently put some whitespace or something on the line with your END word. That one took me a week to figure out.

6

SiteWrapper

In these days of Active Server Pages, it's not as difficult as it once was to explain SiteWrapper. It's a server-based automation system based upon the premise that every good website is made from a series of consistent elements. You define strategies with designers. You brainstorm your identity and create your look and usability to the standards of your corporate or organizational image. When it's ready, you have a template that can be deployed throughout the whole site with various elements; for example, all page headers (in <H1>) are blue, the background image is always positioned with the left table data, your 800 number and URL are at the bottom of every page, and you've provided a jumplist to every section of the site in text only, and it's always at the bottom.

Oops, I meant burgundy page headers. And put them in <H2> tags, the smaller looks better, please, and please have it done by noon. We have a staff meeting, and I need to demo the site. Hey, that's not the right 800 number. That's sales. You want the main number. Change that too...

Even if your website consists of only ten pages, you've encountered such problems. Flat, static HTML pages can't "all change at once," so you're stuck as the human search and replace program (because we all know how well those supposed programs work).

Earlier in the book we looked at NetObjects Fusion and FrontPage. Both answer this problem to some degree, but only from their proprietary client. Again I'll stress that both programs are wonders of modern programming and perfectly suitable for most webmasters, but will not work if you have multiple webmasters (preferably, not really webmasters, as this book suggests) editing the same areas of the site from different machines at the same time. This chapter offers alternatives. Some we've developed, some others have. We invented SiteWrapper to save our clients costs as their site grew. It draws all the potentially changing elements of your site, from its colors to the webmaster's e-mail, from a central configuration file. Windows programs do this with .ini files, and in this context our "config" works the same way.

Your site, rather than being a compendium of static documents much like Microsoft Word files, are programs with SiteWrapper. As they load, they listen to the config and plug in variable elements. So if you add a page to your site and it has to be in the jumplist at the bottom of every page, you merely change the one config file. This can be done from anywhere through any standard FTP program. SiteWrapper is for sites of less than 25 pages, but you can still install it if your site is a monster, if only to get your brain thinking in terms of automation based on the server.

What SiteWrapper won't give you is a drag-and-drop GUI like the programs I just referenced. It has nothing to do with HTML. If they don't meet your needs, give SiteWrapper a look. It has no proprietary GUI; all of its administration is by editing Perl variables in a configuration file.

But more important than simple changes, HTML pages can't listen. If you upload a new page to the site, the old pages don't know it exists. We're all willing to change a main directory page, but every page? SiteWrapper changes every page, automatically, by altering one file. There's lots more, but first let's get started.

Quick Start: Unix

1. Select the directory for your installation of SiteWrapper. It runs as index.cgi and will come up as the default if your server is configured correctly. If you want it to load as your homepage, at www.yourcompany .com, make sure it's in the base directory at that IP address location.

2. If you have a shell on the web server, from the CD, upload the file in the sourcecode/UNIX/sitewrapper directory called sitewrapper.zip directly to the directory you just chose. If you don't have a shell, or would prefer to work from a local machine with Multi-Edit (see

Chapter 5), look in the sourcecode/UNIX/sitewrapper directory for the individual files. Upload them all.

3. Find the Perl location on your system. If it's different from /usr/bin/perl you'll have to change it in all the .cgi files and in config.cfg. Open each in your text editor and change the first line of each file so that it matches Perl on your system. We will edit config.cfg and index.cgi again later, so you may want to leave them in the editor. If you are uploading, upload the fixed files.

4. Then go to your Telnet or FTP program and set all the CGI programs to CHMOD 755 to make them executable. If you're in a shell, type chmod 755 *.cgi. If you have no Telnet access to the server but are using a shell FTP program, the command is the same, but you may have to use the syntax SITE CHMOD 755 index.cgi, and repeat it for every program. The standard FTP on my shell does the SITE for you. The program ncftp also does, as well as expanding *.cgi for every file.

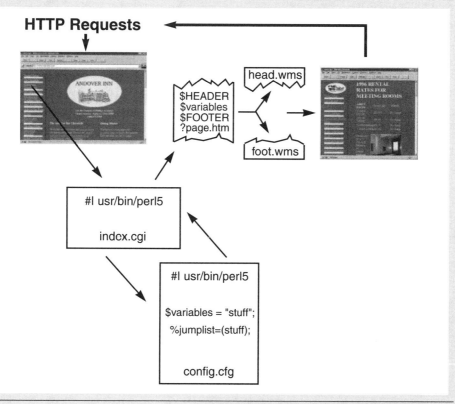

Figure 6.1 SiteWrapper tacks page elements together on the fly.

120

Chapter 6

5. Now we need some HTML files, but not whole ones. In Figure 6.1 you'll see a representation of the SiteWrapper system. The torn page in the middle is what we want here. Make some middles without header or footer information like <HTML><HEAD><BODY> and </BODY></HTML>. This should include your homepage, called homepage.htm, and a few others, like the rentrate.htm example from this chapter.

6. Next we'll edit config.cfg. Scroll down in your editor until you come to the variable $serveradmin. Replace the value with your e-mail or the e-mail of whomever you'd like to send errors. Notice that before you wipe out the existing value, the @ sign is escaped with a back-slash character. Make sure you do this to your e-mail as well. And don't forget the semicolon on all of these.

7. Right under that is $server. It's important that here you plug in the exact directory where SiteWrapper will run as index.cgi. If it's at your main directory, plug in http://www.yourserver.com. If it's in a subdirectory, plug in http://www.yourserver.com/subdirectory. Don't follow the URL with a slash, but do include the http://.

8. The next variable is $password. Don't put a normal word into the value between the quotes. What goes there is garble generated by

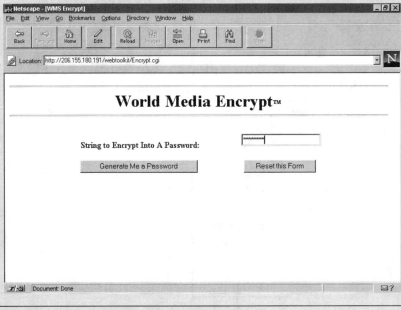

Figure 6.2 Screen capture of Encrypt.

Encrpt.cgi, which you should have uploaded and set executable previously. Hit that file now with your browser. It should look like Figure 6.2. Plug in your password and click "Generate me a password." It will spit out garble that looks like IuTDemOTOK09k, which is the word "password" encrypted on my system. Don't worry if yours is different for encrypting the same word. That's why we gave you the program, so your system's encryption will match.

9. Ignore the next variable, @logs. We'll get to that in a later chapter.

10. The following variables, $headerfile and $footerfile, can be left as they are. We'll edit the files they reference in this chapter and show you ways to send a different header or footer depending upon the browser.

11. Figure 6.3 shows how the next variable should be edited. I've set up the Andover Inn pages (well, most of them, but we'll get to that) in the associative array %jumpnames. As you can see, the left item is the file name of the page, the right is how you would want it to appear in the jumplist. The => functions the same as a comma but is more intuitive—use either. Make sure to enclose the individual items, both filenames and titles, in quotes.

12. Earlier I asked you to make some middles. I bet you wondered how these files got their titles to appear in the title bar. The %titlenames

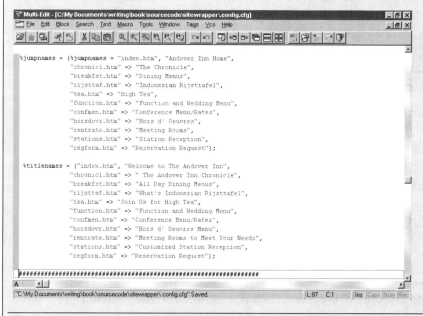

Figure 6.3 The %jumpnames associative array.

variable, next on our list, is much like %jumpnames and does just that. As you can see from Figure 6.3, I've elaborated a bit for the titles to show you the difference between the two associative arrays (different from the actual website). The tea.htm page will link as "High Tea" from the jumplist but have the title "Join Us for High Tea" in its title bar. For screen real estate, sometimes it's best to shorten your jump-names and use both variables.

13. Now hit the base directory where SiteWrapper sits with your web browser. The homepage should load with the default colors of white background, black text, blue links, and purple visited links. If you don't like the colors, don't worry, we're about to change them.

14. Without realizing it, you've enabled SiteColors, a CGI program that controls the colors on your website. Hit the sitecolr.cgi URL from your browser. You should be greeted with Figure 6.4. Plug in your password, then play with the colors. One note is that you must click the "Would you like to add or remove background image" button to switch to a colored background from an image. Both image and color can exist (and should) in the same tag. Your background color shows through your table borders.

15. A security note: If you don't want people to read this book and then check out your config.cgi file, rename it either .config.cfg or

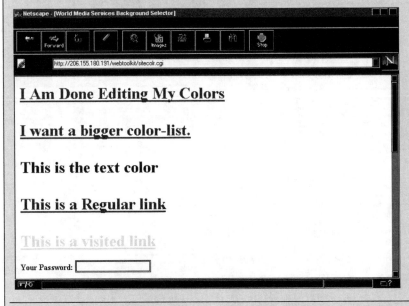

Figure 6.4 SiteColors.

myname.cfg, then edit the line in index.cgi at line 18 that says require config.cfg to read the correct file name.

16. Now read the rest of the chapter, after the NT Quick Start, of course. From here you should have a fully functional copy of your website up and running. Don't worry if it's not how you want it yet. By the end of the chapter you'll have all the customization tools you need.

17. If, after you followed the preceding steps, you were brave enough to hit the directory where site wrapper sits (index.cgi should be served automatically if your server is configured properly), the results are apparent. If you haven't, try hitting the URL now. The homepage.htm file should load automatically. If $bodytag is in place of the <BODY> tag, the colors you chose with SiteColors should be active. If you view source, the footer should be attached, replete with a text and <OPTION> list of all the pages in the %jumpnames variable. In the jumplist you'll notice that all the pages are preceded by a question mark. Following is an example of the Hors d' Oeuvres page shown in Figure 6.5. You'll see the difference SiteWrapper makes. A live version is at 206.155.180.191/andover/?horsdovr.htm.

18. Try hitting the horsdovr.htm page without the question mark, as we did in the second half of Figure 6.5. As you can see, it's the middle, without standard header and footer. With SiteWrapper, all the URLs on the site must be called with a ? before them.

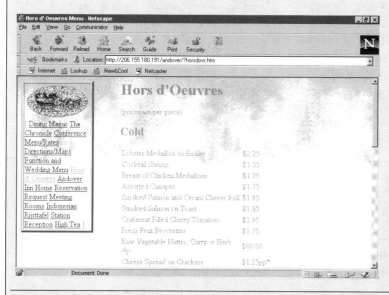

Figure 6.5 Hors d'Oeurvres page. (Continued on following page.)

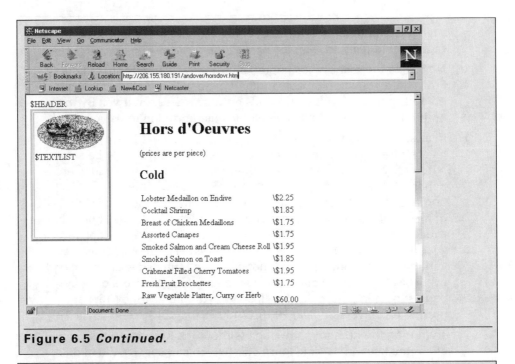

Figure 6.5 *Continued.*

QuickStart: NT

1. Select the directory for your installation of SiteWrapper. It runs as index.cgi, so it will come up as the default if your server is configured correctly. If you want it to load as your homepage, at www.yourcompany.com, make sure it's in the base directory at that IP address location.

2. Chances are you'll be working from an editor like Multi-Edit (Chapter 5) in a Windows-based environment either real-time on the server or uploading via FTP. Look in the sourcecode/NT/sitewrapper directory for the individual files. Upload or save them all to the webserver.

3. We need some HTML files, but not whole ones. In Figure 6.1 you'll see a representation of the SiteWrapper system. The torn page in the middle is what we want here. Make some middles, without header or footer information like <HTML><HEAD><BODY> and </BODY></HTML>. This should include your homepage, called homepage.htm, and a few others, like the rentrate.htm example from this Chapter. At the top of each, put the variable $HEADER and at the bottom put $FOOTER. Upload them to the server.

4. To edit config.cfg, scroll down in your editor until you come to the variable $serveradmin. Replace the value with your e-mail or the e-mail

of whomever you'd like to send errors. Notice, before you wipe out the existing value, that the @ sign is escaped with a backslash character. Make sure you do this to your e-mail as well. And don't forget the semicolon on all of these.

5. Right under that is $server. It's important that here you plug in the exact directory where SiteWrapper will run as index.cgi. If it's at your main directory, plug in http://www.yourserver.com. If it's in a subdirectory, plug in http://www.yourserver.com/subdirectory. Don't follow the URL with a slash, but do include the http://.

6. The next variable is $password. Don't put a normal word into the value between the quotes. What goes there is garble generated by Encrpt.cgi, which you should have previously uploaded and set executable. Hit that file now with your browser. It should look like Figure 6.2. Plug in your password and click Generate me a password. It will spit you out garble that looks like luTDemOTOK09k, which is the word password encrypted on my system. Don't worry if yours is different for encrypting the same word. That's why we gave you the program, so your system's encryption will match.

7. Ignore the next variable, @logs. We'll get to that in a later chapter. You do have to make a directory called logs, but just leave it for now. SiteWrapper just needs it to exist for this chapter.

8. The next variables, $headerfile and $footerfile, can be left as they are. We'll edit the files they reference in this chapter and show you ways to send a different header or footer, depending upon browser.

9. Figure 6.3 shows how the next variable should be edited. I've set up the Andover Inn pages (well, most of them, but we'll get to that) in the associative array $jumpnames. As you can see, the left item is the file name of the page, the right is how you would want it to appear in the jumplist. The => functions the same as a comma but is more intuitive—use either. Make sure to enclose the individual items, both filenames and titles, in quotes.

10. Earlier I asked you to make some middles. I bet you wondered how these files got their titles to appear in the title bar. The %titlenames variable, next on our list, is much like %jumpnames and does just that. As you can see from Figure 6.3, I've elaborated a bit for the titles to show you the difference between the two associative arrays (different from the actual website). The tea.htm page will link as High Tea from the jumplist but have the title Join Us for High Tea in its title bar. For screen real estate, sometimes it's best to shorten your jumpnames and use both variables.

11. Now hit the base directory where SiteWrapper sits with your web browser. The webserver should serve you index.cgi automatically. The homepage should load with default colors of white background, black text, blue links, and purple visited links. If you don't like the colors, don't worry, we're about to change them.

12. Without realizing it, you've enabled a helper program to SiteWrapper called SiteColors, a CGI program that can control the colors on your website. Hit the sitecolr.cgi URL from your browser. You should be greeted with Figure 6.4. Plug in your password, then play with the colors. One note is that you must click the "Would you like to add or remove background image" button to switch to a colored background from an image. Both image and color can exist (and should) in the same tag. Your background color shows through your table borders.

13. A security note: If you don't want people to read this book and then check out your config.cgi file, rename it either .config.cfg or *myname*.cfg, then edit the line in index.cgi at line 18 that says require config.cfg to read the correct file name.

14. That's it for now. In a bit we'll examine the actual code of index.cgi to customize the look and feel of the site. If you're at the 206.155.180.148/andover/ page, notice that the jumplist at the side of the page looks different from the one at www.andoverinn.com. By the end of the chapter you'll have this and other customization options to work with.

15. OK, it's set up. Now what do I do? If, after you followed the preceding lists, you were brave enough to hit the directory where site wrapper sits (index.cgi should be served automatically if your server is configured properly), the results are apparent. If you haven't, try hitting the URL now. The homepage.htm file should load automatically. If $bodytag is in place of the <BODY> tag, the colors you chose with SiteColors should be active. If you view source, the footer should be attached, replete with a text and <OPTION> list of all the pages in the %jumpnames variable.

16. In the jumplist you'll notice that all the pages are preceded by a question mark. Figure 6.5 is an example of the Hors d' Oeuvres page with SiteWrapper turned on and off, at 206.155.180.148/andover/ ?horsdovr.htm.

17. Try hitting the horsdovr.htm page without the question mark, as we did. As you can see, it's the middle, without standard header and footer. With SiteWrapper, all the URLs on the site must be called with a ? before them.

Using SiteWrapper's Automation

As I said in the introduction to the book, the site probably seems pretty dead right now. But now that we're past the Quick Start, it's important that you understand what those variables we set actually do. What we've just built isn't exciting, it's infrastructure that we'll use to go forward, customizing and expanding through the rest of this and the following chapters. At present we've automated these parts of our site:

Headers and Footers. You set a header and footer file in the config. You'll use these to simplify the edit process should your logo change from long and thin to short and fat or should your sales number change for a new phone system. Sure, it's a simple benefit, but don't discount it. We're actually evaluating the text of the header and footer, which means that you can expand it to include anything, interactively, from any data source. As we examine the dynamic nature of SiteWrapper, the possibilities will open up to you.

Jumplist Navigation. When you set the %jumplist variable in the config you probably imagined how we use this to save you time. Now, at the top, bottom, or anywhere else in your pages, you can include an active jumplist of every page on the site, both in plain text and through a drop list. Later I'll show you how to add a page and alter the appearance of the jumplist.

Global Variables. When I instructed you to set the $adminemail variable, we introduced a variable element that could change at any time. In the past you would have had to search every occurrence of your 800 number if it changed. Now you'll set it as a configuration variable and change it once.

if, then, else: Testing on Environment. The following section on customization will show you how to use SiteWrapper to serve different variables and even pages depending on the users capabilities, time of day, or other dynamic event. Once you understand the basic functionality, your limitations are those within Perl. You can customize pages with input from form variables, from the user's environment, or even from what URL they originated. Later we'll expand this with a shopping cart and other customization options. For now it's good to think about this configuration file we're dealing with as the home for all the customized material of the site. You'll make middles of pages with interactive elements. SiteWrapper will listen for your code as the page loads, executing for individual or groups of users.

Standard Error Document. All but the tiniest sites have dead links from time to time. Though SiteWrapper's jumplist and textlist help you avoid them, nobody's perfect. The most frequent cause is a dead link coming from Altavista; with SiteWrapper, a standard error document, ERROR 400, File Not Found.

 On the Web You'll see the error document at www.andoverinn.com. Go there now and request a document that doesn't exist, but do it with a question mark before it, like ?gone.htm or ?nothing.htm. You'll get back the standard error file, which you'll also find in the /examples/andover directory on the CD. Another example is in Figure 6.10 at the end of this chapter.

Customizing the Code: All Platforms

As I just explained, what we've done so far is to install a basic, generic copy of SiteWrapper. First we'll alter the look and feel of the site, then progress into more elaborate customizations. As we go, don't think these are limitations. Because the pages are listening, any element can be drawn from the config—an external document, even, for those Perl gurus out there, a socket connecting to a server across the world.

Edit the Header and Footer

Now that you've got the basics set up, I'll help you dissect two important elements in the design of your site. Back in the Quick Start, you set header.txt and footer.txt as your standard header and footer. I explained that your middles will include these by putting $HEADER and $FOOTER at the top and bottom of the page.

The following HTML code is the sample header.txt contained in the SiteWrapper zipfile. Compare it to the code following it, which is the header.txt from the Andover Inn.

```
<!DOCTYPE HTML PUBLIC "-//W3C//DTD HTML 3.2//EN">

<HTML>

<HEAD>

<TITLE>
```

```
$thispagetitle

</TITLE>

</HEAD>

$bodytag



<!--end header.txt-->



<!DOCTYPE HTML PUBLIC "-//W3C//DTD HTML 3.2//EN">

<HTML>

<HEAD>

<TITLE>

$thispagetitle

</TITLE>

</HEAD>

$bodytag

<TABLE ALIGN=left BORDER=4 WIDTH=150 height=250><TR><TD valign=top><IMG

SRC="small/coach.gif" ALT="stage coach graphic" ALIGN="Left" HEIGHT="73"

WIDTH="134"><BR clear=left>$TEXTLIST</TD></TR></TABLE>



<!--end header.txt-->
```

As you can see, the Andover Inn header contains the table jumplist found on their homepage, so when we call $HEADER at the top of our middles, the jumplist is inserted automatically.

Note the variable $bodytag. You'll find it here and on homepage.htm, which doesn't call the $HEADER variable. It contains the standard HTML <BODY BACKGROUND=... > tag that follows the <HEAD> section of the document.

We've kept it as a separate, detachable part of header.txt so it could be used in places where all the header information doesn't necessarily apply. Take a look at homepage.htm in Figure 6.6. You'll see that the table is inserted manually, with $TEXTLIST and $bodytag inserted manually in the HTML text. In this case we could have used $HEADER, but didn't, to stress a point.

If part of the Andover Inn header was an text graphic, say <IMG SRC= "andoverinn.gif">, I would want it at the top of all my secondary leaf pages but not the homepage. The $bodytag variable, because it's independently called, could be used to control the colors on the homepage without utilizing the entire $HEADER information. If you view source on homepage.htm (without them in the URL), you'll notice that it includes the standard header information, including TITLE, but uses $bodytag for its colors, then is followed by the table, which draws $TEXTLIST from the config.

```
<!DOCTYPE HTML PUBLIC "-//W3C//DTD HTML 3.2//EN">

<HTML>

<HEAD>

<TITLE>Welcome to the Andover Inn</TITLE>
```

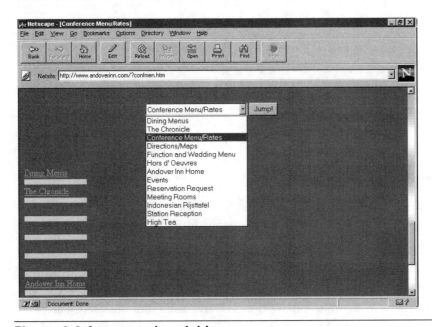

Figure 6.6 Automated variables.

```
$bodytag


<TABLE BORDER = 0 width=100%><TR><td valign=top><TABLE ALIGN=left BORDER=4

WIDTH=150 height=250><TR><TD valign=top><STRONG>$TEXTLIST</STRONG><p>

<EMBED

SRC="http://www.midifarm.com/files/midifiles/General_MIDI/CLASSICAL/BWV10201.MID"

HEIGHT=0 WIDTH=0 LOOP="false" AUTOSTART="true">

</TD></TR><TR><th valign=top><BR><A HREF="mail.cgi"><H3 align=center>Sign Up<BR>

For Event

<BR>Notification</H3></A></th></TR></TABLE>
```

The standard footer that comes in sitewrapper.zip and the Andover Inn footer
follows. They both call two variables, $TEXTLIST and $JUMPLIST. The
$TEXTLIST rendering you just saw. It's the text version of the jump list in the left-
hand table. The $JUMPLIST variable is that same list, but set up as a GET form
request with an OPTION menu of all the pages. SiteWrapper automatically sets
OPTION SELECT for the page you are on. Figure 6.6 shows this in Netscape with
$TEXTLIST repeated below the OPTION list, as you can see in second footer.

```
<!--this alternating keeps the whitespace from collapsing in most browsers-->

<BR><P><BR><P><BR><P><BR><P>

$TEXTLIST<P>

$JUMPLIST

</BODY>

</HTML>




<!--this alternating keeps the whitespace from collapsing in most browsers-->

<P ALIGN="Center"><EM>Food and lodging prices do not include tax</EM></P>
```

```
On the Campus of Phillips Academy<BR>

Chapel Avenue<BR>

Andover, MA  01080<BR>

(508)475-5903<BR>

info\@andoverinn.com<BR>

http://www.AndoverInn.com<BR>

<FONT color=#97694F>&copy; 1996 The Andover Inn</FONT>

<P><BR></P>

<P ALIGN="Center">$JUMPLIST</P>

<BR><P><BR><P><BR><P><BR><P>

$TEXTLIST

</BODY>

</HTML>
```

TIP How perceptive of you to notice the info\@andoverinn.com in the preceding code. That backslash character is the escape operator I told you about in Chapter 5. Use it for all @ and $ signs you wish to print to the screen, as in e-mail addresses in this example, and prices in the screen capture in Figure 6.4. Do this for not only headers and footers, but also for your middles.

Add a Page

If you hit the 206.155.180.148/andover/ example, you'll notice that not only is the jumplist a little odd looking, but also that I intentionally left off two pages from the real Andover Inn site. We'll get to the looks in a bit, but for now let's add one of those missing links, the Directions/Maps page. In the next chapter we'll add the events link, so hang on. The altered list of jump and title pages from the Andover Inn config follows. In the /andover/ directory, it's in config2.cfg.

```
%jumpnames = ("index.htm", "Andover Inn Home",

            "chronicl.htm" => "The Chronicle",

            "breakfst.htm" => "Dining Menus",

            "rijsttaf.htm" => "Indonesian Rijsttafel",

            "tea.htm" => "High Tea",

            "function.htm" => "Function and Wedding Menu",

            "confmen.htm" => "Conference Menu/Rates",

            "horsdovr.htm" => "Hors d' Oeuvres",

            "rentrate.htm" => "Meeting Rooms",

            "stations.htm" => "Station Reception",

            "regform.htm" => "Reservation Request",

            "directn.htm", "Directions/Maps");




%titlenames = ("index.htm", "Welcome to The Andover Inn",

            "chronicl.htm" => " The Andover Inn Chronicle",

            "breakfst.htm" => "All Day Dining Menus",

            "rijsttaf.htm" => "What's Indonesian Rijsttafel",

            "tea.htm" => "Join Us for High Tea",

            "function.htm" => "Function and Wedding Menu",

            "confmen.htm" => "Conference Menu/Rates",

            "horsdovr.htm" => "Hors d' Oeuvres Menu",

            "rentrate.htm" => "Meeting Rooms to Meet Your Needs",

            "stations.htm" => "Customized Station Reception",

            "regform.htm" => "Reservation Request",

            "directn.htm", "Directions and Maps");
```

As you can see, I simply added the pages HTML file and name to the jumplist and titlenames. Now, not only will that page be included in the site-wide jumplist, SiteWrapper will automatically plug in its title when the page loads with a ?directn.htm URL request.

Modifying the Look of $TEXTLIST and $JUMPLIST

Now we'll take a turn at editing the main SiteWrapper program that will run as index.cgi. Line 71 is a subroutine called JumpGate whose virgin configuration looks like this:

```
71: sub JumpGate {

72:      ################################################################

73:      ## This vital function takes a filename as its sole parameter, and

74:      ## returns a string. It makes a small table/HTML form to allow your

75:      ## visitors to jump to any page on the site with a simple press of a

76:      ## button. It uses the hash %jumpnames from the configuration

77:      ## file, which you will need to set before using $JUMPLIST or
$TEXTLIST.

78:

79:      local($fname) = $_[0];

80:      $TEXTLIST = "[ ";

81:      $JUMPLIST =<<END;

82: <BR><CENTER>

83: <FORM METHOD=POST ACTION=index.cgi>

84: <TABLE BORDER=0 CELLSPACING=0 CELLPADDING=0>\n<TR>

85: END

86:      $JUMPLIST .= "<TH><SELECT NAME=redirect>";

87:      foreach $item (sort keys(%jumpnames)) {

88:          if ($fname eq $item) {
```

```
89:              $JUMPLIST .= "<OPTION SELECTED VALUE=$file_number{$item}>";

90:              $JUMPLIST .= "$jumpnames{$item}\n";

91:          } else {

92:              $JUMPLIST .="<OPTION

VALUE=$file_number{$item}>$jumpnames{$item}\n";

93:          }

94:          $TEXTLIST .= "<A HREF=\"?$item\">$jumpnames{$item}</A> ";

95:      }

96:      $JUMPLIST .= "</SELECT>\n<BR>";

97:      $JUMPLIST .= "<TH><INPUT TYPE=SUBMIT

VALUE=\"Jump!\">\n<BR></TABLE><BR>\n";

98:      $JUMPLIST .= "</FORM></CENTER>";

99:      $TEXTLIST .= "]<BR>";

100: }
```

Picking up at line 79, we first identify a local variable called $fname, which is given the page name of the page just called by clicking on a ?hotlink.htm. At line 80, we begin the look of $TEXTLIST with a bracket. You can see this on the current /andover/ site by calling either index.cgi or index2.cgi. The $JUMPLIST variable begins at line 81, but with a bit more HTML. Through line 85 is a here document that starts a form and a table for the visual rendering of the <OPTION> list. Then, at line 86, we start the <SELECT> list of options; its name is redirect. Then, at line 87, the code says "for each item in the jumpnames associative array, if the filename of this page matches that item, put an <OPTION SELECTED> tag with its value and title, followed by a new line, else, if the filename does not match, just put it in normal <OPTION> tag." That ends at line 93's right brace.

At line 94, $TEXTLIST is a bit simpler. It says "print a plain hotlink with each item's HTML file and its title from the %jumpnames array." The code then returns to $JUMPLIST at line 96, closing the select list, adding the Jump! button (type = submit>, then closing the table and form. At line 99 $TEXTLIST then closes, followed by a bracket.

Whew! Did you get all that? Follow the code as it jumps back and forth between the two variables and it will make sense. It, like the HTML files on the site, consists of a beginning, a middle, and an end. The middle is the confusing part. For each value in %jumpnames, it prints one <OPTION> in the $JUMPLIST and one hotlink in $TEXTLIST. Now we'll change $TEXTLIST as it appears on the Andover Inn site. We begin at line 80, the start of $TEXTLIST:

```
$TEXTLIST = " ";
```

I got rid of the bracket. We don't need it and I've added nothing new. Note, however, that I could have entered the entire <TABLE> enclosing the $TEXTLIST on Andover as it appears, but, because it's in the header, I elected to keep it simple here in the code and mark up the header.txt page with the HTML.

Now we'll add Andover's look to the individual values of $TEXTLIST as they appear on the site. At line 94, after the </A> for each item in %jumpnames, I'll add a <BR> and an image of a tan colored line with vertical spacing of three pixels. Note that this code would normally appear on one line, but we're constrained by page width here. This could break if the line wrapped in Perl, so turn line wrap off in your text editor.

```
$TEXTLIST .= "<A HREF=\"?$item\">$jumpnames{$item}</A> <BR><IMG
SRC=line.gif ALT="-----------" HEIGHT=10 WIDTH=120 VSPACE=3>";
```

Then, on line 99, I eliminate the right bracket set as the $TEXLIST default. I will, however, leave the <BR>. It just kicks the next line down by default:

```
$TEXTLIST .= "<BR>";
```

Hit in the /andover/ directory the file index3.cgi. This will show you what we get. It should look just like the left-hand table contents at the Andover Inn site.

In this next exercise, I'll modify $JUMPLIST to show radio buttons instead of a <SELECT><OPTION> list. Below is the modified code. Note that the line numbers would not appear in your normal index.cgi. I've added them due to the line wrapping limitations of this printed book. In real life, lines like 90 would extend off to the right without breaking.

```
79:     local($fname) = $_[0];

80:     $TEXTLIST = " ";

81:     $JUMPLIST =<<END;
```

```
82: <BR><CENTER>

83: <FORM METHOD=POST ACTION=index4.cgi>

84: <BR> <FONT SIZE=3>

85:

86: END

87:

88:        foreach $item (sort keys(%jumpnames)) {

89:          if ($fname eq $item) {

90:              $JUMPLIST .= "[<INPUT TYPE=\"RADIO\" NAME=\"redirect\"

VALUE=\"$file_number{$item}\" CHECKED>]";

91:              $JUMPLIST .= "$jumpnames{$item}\n";

92:          } else {

93:              $JUMPLIST .="[<INPUT TYPE=\"RADIO\" NAME=\"redirect\"

VALUE=\"$file_number{$item}\"> $jumpnames{$item} ]\n";

94:          }

95:                 $TEXTLIST .= "<A

HREF=\"index4.cgi?$item\">$jumpnames{$item}</A> <BR><IMG SRC=line.gif ALT=\"-----

-------\" HEIGHT=10 WIDTH=120 VSPACE=3><BR>";      }

96:      $JUMPLIST .= "\n<BR>";

97:      $JUMPLIST .= "<INPUT TYPE=SUBMIT VALUE=\"Jump!\">\n<BR></FONT><BR>\n";

98:      $JUMPLIST .= "</FONT></FORM></CENTER>";

99:      $TEXTLIST .= "<BR>";

100: }
```

As you can see, I've left $TEXTLIST like it was for the last example and modified $JUMPLIST with radio buttons. Figure 6.7 shows what you'll get by hitting the 206.155.180.148/andover/index4.cgi URL (also note that I've modified the FORM

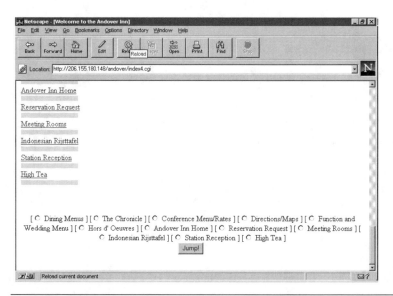

Figure 6.7 A modified jumplist.

and $TEXTLIST jump to point here). Each value in %jumpnames from the config is listed as a button with the same Submit button. The current page is checked, just like the <OPTION> was selected.

AOL and WebTV: Alternate Homepages

Though I don't advocate that you construct a separate homepage for each brand of browser, certain browsers are an exception. This used to be the case with America Online. They had, at that time (late 1996), over 7 million subscribers and their browser didn't support <TABLE>. You can't ignore those numbers, no matter what business you're in, and not just newbies use their service, so your interface should be clean. With the release and adoption of AOL 3.0 this is no longer a concern. It supports <TABLE> and even <FRAMESET>, but it still has a quirk of not rendering <TABLE><TR><TD BGCOLOR=blue> table data correctly. This affects page layout only when you use specially colored text within a colored table data. Rather than show you this at the Andover Inn site, I'm going to depart from that location for now and move to another of our clients. The first box in Figure 6.8 is the Corcoran Management Company homepage at www.CorcoranApts.com rendered in Netscape 3.0 for Windows 95. As you can see, the left and right columns are table data with the color #000099, a dark blue. The <BODY> tag, if you view source, will look like Figure 6.8. This is true only if you are using something besides America Online or WebTV.

```
<BODY BGCOLOR=#FFFFFF LINK=#EAEAAE VLINK=#00FFe2>
```

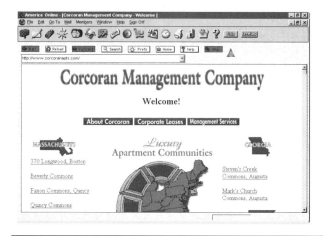

Figure 6.8 Multiple homepages.

The second and third boxes in Figure 6.8 are the same page in the AOL 3.0 browser. In both, you'll see that the colored table data are gone. As I explained, AOL can't do that. But what AOL can do is render text color that we, for our links, have set to a light #EAEAAE in contrast to the heavy blue against which it normally lays. The first AOL screen shows what you'd normally get from the AOL browser without modifications to SiteWrapper. The second AOL screen is what you actually get at the site. We've made some minor modifications to the program. Here's the basic code we've added to config.cfg.

```
$fontcolor = "#FFFFFF";

$tablebgcolor = "#000099";
```

And we added this to index.cgi:

```
## Server is requesting a document.

    if ( $ENV{'HTTP_USER_AGENT'} =~ /AOL/i ) {

        $fontcolor = "#000000";

        $tablebgcolor = "#000000";

        $bodytag = "<BODY TEXT=#000000 LINK=#0000FF VLINK=#00FF00>";

    } elsif ($ENV{'HTTP_USER_AGENT'} =~ /WebTV/) {

        $bodytag = "<BODY BGCOLOR=#000099 TEXT=#FFFFFF LINK=#EAEAEA

VLINK=#00FFE2>";

        if ($document_filename eq "homepage.htm" ) {

            $document_filename = "webtv.htm";

        }
```

In the config, we've identified two variables to be called from the HTML middles at CorcoranApts.com. The first is $fontcolor, which is the color of the text within tables, and the second is $tablebgcolor, the background color of the tables. With the LINK color in the normal <BODY> tag, this covers every application of the contrasted page elements.

In index.cgi, we first test for AOL and WebTV, then override the colors if either of those browsers are present. SiteWrapper detects the browser through the $ENV{'HTTP_USER_AGENT'} variable and switches colors to the appropriate values—white background with black text.

But how does it end up on the page? With variables in the HTML. Instead of hard setting your table data font colors, you use the same syntax but with the variable names you set in the config. If you go to www.corcoranapts.com/stevenscreek.htm, without the leading question mark, the viewed source will show you examples of these two code snippets:

```
<border=0 cellpadding=10 cellspacing=0  BGCOLOR=$tablebgcolor>

<FONT COLOR=$fontcolor>
```

The page you find should look like Figure 6.10 in the next section.

Moving along to the elsif option in our modification to index.cgi, we test for WebTV. As I write this book, it was just purchased by Microsoft and looks to be a contender for consumer Internet access. To leave out its subscribers would be foolish, but unfortunately like AOL, its interface has special design considerations. For one, the screen shouldn't be more than 550 pixels wide—the browser can't scroll horizontally. The other major concern is contrast. Dark backgrounds with light text work best on the TV screen.

Figure 6.9 is the replacement homepage the modification sends when someone hits the site with a WebTV browser (rendered in Netscape because I couldn't screen-capture WebTV). It removes the image with the big C in the middle and gives only the list of properties. Chances are that's what they came for, and now, even if the browser pads with borders, we are way under the 550 pixel wide limitation. Also, the background, set dynamically with index.cgi, is set to blue with white links and white table text.

The Backup Plan for Direct ?Hits

Earlier, I asked you to hit the stevenscreek.htm page at CorcoranApts.com. It's the first box in Figure 6.10.What's different about it and the second box, the same page loaded with ?stevenscreek.htm? The first box has a "Please click here for the right page" sign emblazoned on the front. We developed this specifically for Corcoran because they were going to advertise specific properties on the site in print ads. We were worried that someone jotting down a quick URL would forget the question mark and call the wrapped page without the wrapper.

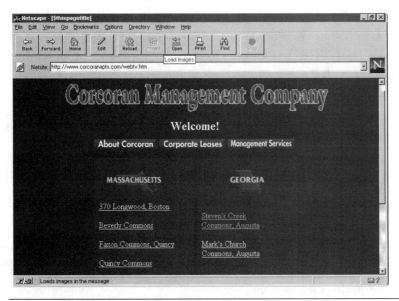

Figure 6.9 The WebTV altered page.

 On the CD The entire Corcoran site is on in the /examples/corcoran directory on the CD. There are even some utilities not covered in this book, so look around. It's a great template from which to build your first SiteWrapper project.

By adding a little code to the config and this default HTML addition to every page on the site, you can eliminate this risk. In the config add the lines:

```
$begincomment = "<!-- ";
```

```
$endcomment = " -->";
```

Then, in your HTML documents, place the lines:

```
$begincomment
```

```
<A HREF=?stevenscreek.htm><h1> Please click here for the right page </h1></A>
```

```
$endcomment
```

with the correct page name in the HREF.

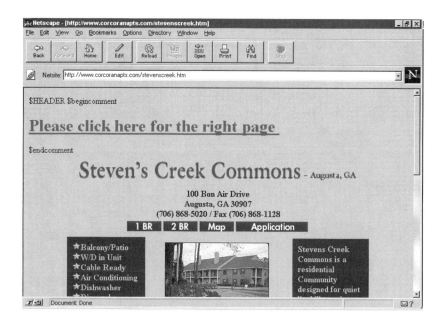

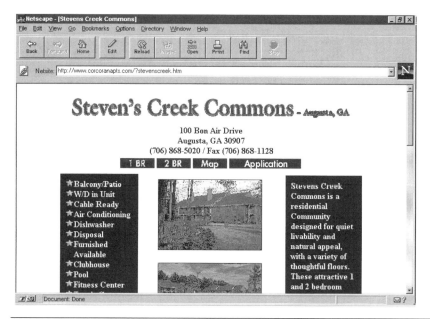

Figure 6.10 Hidden code protects from misunderstandings and misprints.

Other Variables

As I've explained before, these are merely examples to show you the breadth of SiteWrapper's ability to save you administrative work on the most rudimentary elements of your site. Here are a few more scenarios, just to whet your appetite.

You are a small business with only one sales person. When she or he is on the road, which is every afternoon, the cell phone is the best way to get a quick answer. Otherwise, the main office number is appropriate. Try adding this code into the config:

```
if ($hour > 12){

    $officephone = "800-555-5555";

    }

else {

$officephone = "800-555-9999";

}
```

which sends them the cell number after noontime. You'd call it in the footer with the $officephone variable.

Do you have an e-mail reply form on your site? When someone fills it out, SiteWrapper can tell you from which page on the site they jumped to the form. Just add the following variable:

```
<INPUT TYPE=HIDDEN NAME=jump_page VALUE="$ENV{'HTTP_REFERRER'}">
```

Parse the $in{jump_page} variable as normal.

We can take this one step further, as you'll notice on the Corcoran Management site, and send a specific e-mail for different properties and rental offices. This could work for ordering products, sending "more information" or "Contact an Office Near You." Just tack a variable onto the URLs of the links within the site:

```
<A HREF="?thispage.htm&send_to=8005559999>More Information</A>
```

or, in the case of the $JUMPLIST or any other form:

```
<INPUT TYPE=HIDDEN NAME=send_to VALUE=80055559999>
```

Some Final Code

Because we're dealing with Perl, every line of SiteWrapper is modifiable. Here are the sections we haven't dealt with yet, and some ideas for customizing them.

In this first section at line 133 (note again that the line numbers will not and should not appear in your usable code), SiteWrapper evaluates in the header and footer files:

```
133:     # These Statements load our header and footer as defined in the config
file

134:     if (-e "$headerfile") {

135:         $HEADER = &file_to_string("$headerfile");

136:     }

137:     if (-e "$footerfile") {

138:         $FOOTER = &file_to_string("$footerfile");

139:     }
```

which says that if the header and footer files exist, scrunch them into the variables $HEADER and $FOOTER. This, as you can imagine, does not limit you to only one header and footer. If you are Nashua Corporation, which has several divisions that have nothing to do with one another, one footer won't apply to your entire site. Just duplicate the code of line 134–139 for several headers and footers that will be kept in the config:

```
134:     if (-e "$div2headerfile") {

135:         $div2HEADER = &file_to_string("$headerfile");

136:     }

137:     if (-e "$div2footerfile") {

138:         $div2FOOTER = &file_to_string("$footerfile");

139:     }
```

Now you would add to the config a $div2headerfile and $div2footerfile, and call them from you middles with $div2HEADER and $div2FOOTER.

In this next section, we test whether the document being called from a ?hotlink is an HTML file or a CGI program elsewhere on the server. If, as you can see, the document contains htm (which includes html), we test for server type and print the proper header information. An NT server requires the extra HTTP/1.0 200 OK line, so it sends that if it detects PerlIS.dll as the Perl translator, then it prints the standard content type that all CGI programs should.

Then, if the requested HTML document exists, the server evaluates it in and prints it to the screen. If not, it sends the error file I explained earlier in this chapter. As I did in the previous example, you could send different error screens for different areas of the site by assigning a separate variable. Figure 6.11 is the default error file for Corcoran Management. As you can see, it's easily customizable.

```
141:    if ($document_filename =~ /htm/) {

142:        ## if file requested is an html file, print it.

143:        if ($ENV{'PERLXS'} eq "PerlIS" ) {

144:            print("HTTP/1.0 200 OK\n");

145:        }
```

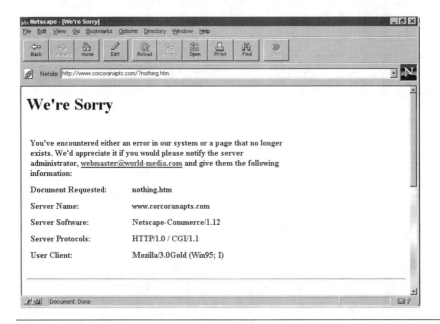

Figure 6.11 Make sure to customize your error file.

```
146:          print("Content-type: text/html\n\n");

147:          if (-e "$document_filename") {

148:                &print_file("$document_filename");

149:          } else {

150:                &print_file("error.htm");

151:          }
```

At the next line, SiteWrapper picks back-up for requested documents that are CGI programs. Just in case, it prints the same HTTP header information, then redirects to it with the HTTP Location: function. As with HTML documents, at line 172, if it can't find the CGI program, it sends the error file.

```
152:      } elsif ($document_filename =~ /\.cgi/) {

153:          ## if file requested is a CGI script, redirect to it.

154:          if (-e "$document_filename") {

155:                if ($ENV{'PERLXS'} eq "PerlIS" ) {

156:                   print("HTTP/1.0 302 OK\n");

157:                }

158:                print("Location: $server/$document_filename\n\n");

159:          } else {

160:                if ($ENV{'PERLXS'} eq "PerlIS" ) {

161:                   print("HTTP/1.0 200 OK\n");

162:                }

163:                print("Content-type: text/html\n\n");

164:                &print_file("error.htm");

165:          }

166:      } else {

167:          if ($ENV{'PERLXS'} eq "PerlIS" ) {
```

```
168:                print("HTTP/1.0 200 OK\n");

169:            }

170:

171:            print("Content-type: text/html\n\n");

172:            &print_file("error.htm");

173:        }

174: }    ##send_document
```

This next section, a subroutine, does the same as the preceding routine, but is for Post requests coming in from the form created by $JUMPLIST:

```
181: sub redirect {

182:    # if we were called by FORM submit in $jumpstring, try

183:    if ($in{'redirect'} ne "") {                          # to redirect the
user

184:        if ($ENV{'PERLXS'} eq "PerlIS" ) {

185:            print("HTTP/1.0 302 OK\n");

186:        }

187:

188:        print("Location: $server/?$number_file{$in{redirect}}\n\n");

189:    } else {

190:        if ($ENV{'PERLXS'} eq "PerlIS" ) {

191:            print("HTTP/1.0 200 OK\n");

192:        }

193:

194:        print("Content-type: text/html\n\n");

195:        &print_file("error.htm");
```

```
196:       }

197: }
```

This is how SiteWrapper ends—it simply tests for how a document comes in and invokes the correct subroutine:

```
203: if ($ENV{'REQUEST_METHOD'} eq "GET") {

204:     &send_document;

205: } elsif ($ENV{'REQUEST_METHOD'} eq "POST") {

206:     &redirect;207: }
```

In the next chapter, we'll move from simple automation to user interaction. I'll refer back to several examples in the chapter as we go. SiteWrapper is the main engine from which the rest of these utilities have grown. Its config file will be the basis for the rest of the site.

E-Mail Push
Utilities

Do you ever get the feeling that you've set up a tent in the desert? Your site is whiz-bang, with up-to-the-day information and quality content. But, from the analysis of your log files, most visitors come once and never return, if they find you at all. There are so many websites and so little time for your busy customers to remember all of the great stuff going on at your site. Every day they are inundated with the Wall Street Journal's hotlist of paid advertisers, ESPN's scores, the local paper's article on local sites of interest, the investing section at the Women's Wire Guide (www.women.com/guide/), etc. The web is too busy, and without a compelling reason to return to your site, most people won't.

In the past, you've most likely received e-mail from sites like the New York Times, Information Week, and other big sites with *tickler* information reminding you to return. Once you filled out a membership form, they captured your e-mail address and automated periodic responses to lure you back. This chapter gives you that same ability, but in a less intrusive, more *netiquette-friendly* manner. People sign up for only what they want and need without the requirement of personal information or demographics.

How does this differ from Push Technology? Most Push systems are really pull. Your web browser, or a custom client (PointCast), dials the server at given intervals. It requires a special setup, usually with a download that many users frown on due to virus worries. Targeted, user requested e-mail is simpler—and that's why it works.

This chapter offers you two ways to solicit e-mail addresses on your site. Both are based on our Tickler system. The first is for sites that change their content regularly and want people to return again and again. The second is Tickler for events, which is intended to save people the time of hitting the site when you have a new event or other time-sensitive announcement to get them as quickly as possible.

Use Standard Tickler For Repeat Visitors

As I just explained, this version of Tickler is meant for sites that want as many hits as possible and don't care that visitors have to fire up a browser to receive new content (you insensitive money chasing scum). It fires an e-mail message with the URL of changed pages when you launch it from a password-protected administration menu.

Quick Start: Unix

1. Tickler may be installed in the main directory at www.yoursite.com; you don't need to make a tickler directory. If you do, however, edit the "require" line in tickler.cgi that points to the config to say ../config.cfg, or whatever you named the config. Also, CHMOD the tickler directory to 777.

2. On the CD, find the directory /sourcecode/UNIX/tickler and upload tickler.zip to the webserver or unzip it into a local directory and upload the individual files.

3. CHMOD tickler.cgi to 755.

4. Test it by hitting the tickler.cgi program. You should get a screen like Figure 7.1, with All Registered Pages as the only option in the <OPTION> list. Don't enter your e-mail just yet. It will produce an error message as we have not added Tickler's variables to the config yet.

5. If you changed config.cfg to another name in the last chapter, edit the line in tickler.cgi that says "require ../config.cfg;".

6. Bring up config.cfg (or whatever you changed its name to) and add the first of our Tickler variables. It's called $sendmail_location and should be set to wherever sendmail is located on your system. The

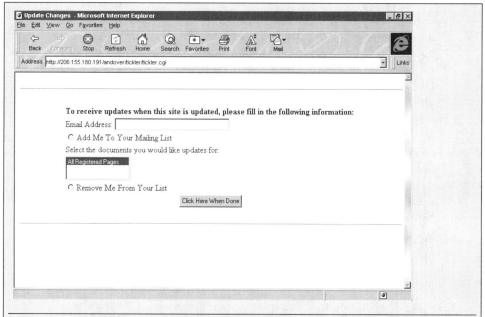

Figure 7.1 The default Tickler screen before you change the look.

first method, next, is the way to do it if you are worried that the location of sendmail might change and you have "which" installed on your system. The second method manually sets the location and is preferred:

$sendmail_location = 'which sendmail';
$sendmail_location = "/usr/sbin/sendmail";

7. Tickler allows you to add a second administrative e-mail to the config called $adminemail. You already should have $serveradmin in the config, so if you want, just set $adminemail = $serveradmin;. Otherwise set it manually with $adminemail="yourname\ @yourserver.com";.

8. The next variable is the response page the visitor will bounce to after plugging in the e-mail address and checking preferences. It should look like this:

$response = "http://www.yourserver.com/?thanks.html";

9. The e-mails you collect will be stored in a little text database file. In this next variable, you name it. The default we use is emails.db, but you'll probably want to change it so other readers of this book can't snag it on you. Its syntax is standard:

$emaildbfile = "email.db";.

10. You can also set a separate password for Tickler. It's called $mailpassword. Most sites will set it to $mailpassword=$password;, but it's up to you. We kept it separate so that a different person could be assigned to administer Tickler other than the one who administers all the other functions of utilities in the book. To generate a Tickler password, go back to the Encrypt.cgi program. In the sample for this example, I'll encrypt the word tickler and plug it in as: $mail_password = "luTIBL92Jhrro";

11. Have you ever tried to submit a form on a site and had it hang? It's not always as it appears. Though it may not appear so, in most cases the form data is processed, but because of Internet lag, the browser times out. You then resubmit the form, in effect entering the same data twice.

12. Tickler protects against this with the next variable to the config, $already_sub. Set it to an HTML middle (meaning that it need not have <HTML> and other tags) that you create. It should read something like, "Sorry, you're already subscribed to that group."

13. The final variable is much like %jumpnames and %titlenames in the last chapter. It's an associative array of the pages you think people will find interesting, called %ticklerpages. You can, of course, set it equal to either %jumpnames or %titlenames to save yourself some admin time as you add new sections. We could have just read in either of them as the default but kept it separate and definable for sites with lots of boring sections. Most sites will set it as follows: %ticklerpages = %titlenames;

14. One last variable goes in the config. It's what the page subscribers see when they've already subscribed to a group and they click Submit again. This is a huge problem with newbies. They just won't get it that HTTP is sometimes slow. They click and click and click, then complain when ten tickle messages show up in their inbox. This feature prevents this from happening. Set the variable as $already_sub = "path to /already.htm";.

15. You should now have a complete rack of variables in your config that looks like Figure 7.2. Notice that the thanks page is a demo we were running with the dummy Andover Inn site. Before moving on to testing now, make sure your tickler.cgi is pointing to both the correct Perl location and config file (as you can see, the example is ../config2.cfg, which means the parent directory of where tickler.cgi is installed, in an alternate config).

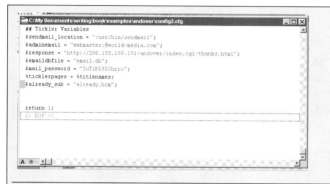

```
## Tickler Variables
$sendmail_location = "/usr/bin/sendmail";
$adminemail = "webmaster\@world-media.com";
$response = "http://206.155.180.191/andover/index.cgi?thanks.html";
$emaildbfile = "email.db";
$mail_password = "InTiBL923hrro";
%ticklerpages = %titlenames;
$already_sub = "already.htm";


return 1;
>> EOF <<
```

Figure 7.2 New Tickler variables.

16. If you rehit tickler.cgi with your browser, you should now get the same page as Figure 7.1, but with a full list of whatever you put in %ticklerpages. Plug in your e-mail and subscribe to a few groups, then plug in your friend's e-mail and plug in a few more. Pretty soon you both should have a full mailbox of Thank you! messages.

17. It's time to send updates. Launch the admin menu by typing ?admin after tickler.cgi. It automatically will bring you the screen in Figure 7.3. To launch a Tickler message, highlight the pages, plug in your admin password (set in $mail_password), and click Send Update Notification.

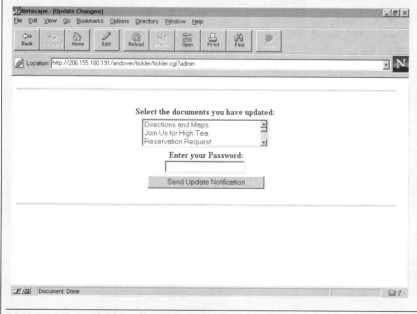

Figure 7.3 Tickler's administration menu.

Quick Start: NT

The installation of Tickler and Events Tickler should work by the time you read this, but as of this writing Activeware, the company in charge of Perl for NT, has not yet fixed a bug in the sockets function that prevents sendmail.pl from sending its messages. Check the website for this book at www.World-Media.com/webtoolkit for an update before installing. We'll probably have a new version of Perl for you.

1. On the CD, find the directory sourcecode/NT/tickler. Upload either the tickler.zip file or each individual file in the directory.

2. Tickler may be installed in the main directory at www.yoursite.com. You do not need to make a tickler directory, but if you do, edit the "require" line in tickler.cgi that points to the config to say ../config.cfg, or whatever you named the config.

3. Test it by hitting the tickler.cgi program. You should get a screen like Figure 7.1, with only All Registered Pages as the only option in the <OPTION> list. Don't enter your e-mail just yet. It will produce an error message as we have not added Tickler's variables to the config.

4. If you changed config.cfg to another name in the last chapter, edit the line in tickler.cgi that says "require ../config.cfg;".

5. Bring up config.cfg (or whatever you changed its name to) in your editor and add the first of our Tickler variables, a second administrative e-mail called $adminemail. You already should have $serveradmin in the config, so if you want, just set $adminemail = $serveradmin;. Otherwise set it manually with $adminemail="your-name\@yourserver.com";.

6. The next variable is the response page the visitor will bounce to after plugging in the e-mail address and checking preferences. It should look like this: response = "http://www.yourserver.com/-?thanks.html";

7. The e-mails you collect will be stored in a little text database file. In this next variable, you name it. The default we use is emails.db, but you'll probably want to change it so other readers of this book can't snag it on you. Its syntax is standard:
$emaildbfile = "email.db";.

8. You can also set a separate password for Tickler, called $mailpassword. Most sites will set it to $mailpassword=$password;, but it's up to you. We kept it separate so a different person could be assigned to administer Tickler other than the one who administers all the other functions of utilities in the book. To generate a Tickler password, go back to the Encrypt.cgi program. In the sample for this example, I'll encrypt the word tickler and plug it in as: $mail_password = "luTIBL92Jhrro";

9. Have you ever tried to submit a form on a site and had it hang? It's not always as it appears. Though it may not appear so, in most cases the form data is processed, but because of Internet lag, the browser times out. You then resubmit the form, in effect entering the same data twice.

10. Tickler protects against this with the next variable to the config, $already_sub. Set it to an HTML middle (meaning that it need not have <HTML> and other tags) that you create. It should read something like, "Sorry, you're already subscribed to that group."

11. Ask your ISP what the mail host for the virtual server is. This next variable, $smtp_host, is required for messages to be sent correctly. Set it in the config as $smtphost = "mail.yoursite.com";.

12. The final variable is much like %jumpnames and %titlenames in the last chapter. It's an associative array of the pages you think people will find interesting called %ticklerpages. You can, of course, set it equal to either %jumpnames or %titlenames to save yourself some admin time as you add new sections. We could have just read in either of them as the default, but kept it separate and definable for sites with lots of boring sections. Most sites will set it as follows: %ticklerpages = %titlenames;

13. One last variable goes in the config. It's the page subscribers see when they've already subscribed to a group and they click Submit again. This is a huge problem with newbies. They just won't get it that HTTP is sometimes slow. They click and click and click, then complain when ten tickle messages show up in their inbox. This feature prevents this from happening. Set the variable as $already_sub = "path to /already.htm";.

14. You should now have a complete rack of variables in your config that looks like Figure 7.2. Notice that the thanks page is a demo we

were running with the dummy Andover Inn site. Before moving on to testing now, make sure your tickler.cgi is pointing to both the correct Perl location and config file (as you can see, the example is ../config2.cfg, which means the parent directory of where tickler.cgi is installed, in an alternate config).

15. If you rehit tickler.cgi with your browser, you should now get the same page as Figure 7.1, but with a full list of whatever you put in %ticklerpages. Plug in your e-mail and subscribe to a few groups, then plug in your friend's e-mail and plug in a few more. Pretty soon you both should have a full mailbox of Thank you! messages.

16. It's time to send updates. Launch the admin menu by typing ?admin after tickler.cgi. It will bring you the screen in Figure 7.3 automatically. To launch a Tickler message, highlight the pages, plug in your admin password (set in $mail_password), and click Send Update Notification.

Requested E-Mail: The Ultimate Push

Now that you've got the basic install down, let's talk about how and why you'd use Tickler. As a hit generating tool, it's cumbersome to cull e-mails from guestbooks, reply-forms, and personal e-mails sent to you from the website. At best, you'll get them all into the addressbook of your e-mail program and send a blanket e-mail when your site is updated. People may have requested that you do, but they may also have not, and at worst, will be upset that you are sending unsolicited e-mail.

Maybe you've had people complete a form on your site that includes a Send Me Updates box, but it still doesn't maximize the potential of what you can garner from the site. "All I want to know is when you added a new doll house to the 'Colonials' page. Why do you need my fax number?" some will ask. Tickler gives people the freedom simply to leave an e-mail address, and more importantly, to tag only the areas of the site they are interested in. Automatically e-mailing people that your site has changed isn't a new idea, but the way Tickler does it is a bit novel.

In the next section, we'll hit the real strength of Tickler's customizable messages. In addition to the dynamic element of "this page has been updated," you can online coupons, specials, newsletters, and other message-specific information that will increase the rate at which your website produces. With Tickler, one random hit can generate thousands of return visits. Sound a little high? People forward interesting e-mail to friends and associates.

Customizing the Thanks Message: Unix

Bring up the file confirm.txt in your editor. It governs the e-mail message visitors are sent when they subscribe to a page initially. As you can see, it's fairly simple:

```
$action

If you feel you have reached this message in error, please

contact $adminemail.
```

That generates a message like the one in the first tile of Figure 7.4 rendered in Netscape's mail client, which automatically hotlinks URL addresses.

Of this file, the only mandatory element is $action, which prints the message "You will receive updates on the following pages:" and the list of links. Above or below that lone variable you can put corporate information, the unsubscribe URL, and any additional information users might need. If you have a burning desire to be different beyond the simple modifications to confirm.txt, you'll find the rest of the e-mailed text in tickler.cgi at line 141:

```
141:     $action = "You will receive updates on the following pages:\n";

142:     foreach $key (@items) {
```

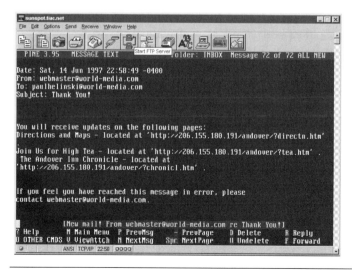

Figure 7.4 A Tickler message before you customize it.

```
143:     if ($ticklerpages{$key} ne "") {
```

```
144:     $action .= "$ticklerpages{$key} - located at \'$server/?$key\' .\n";
```

The modifications to 141 are obvious, but look at lines 143 and 144. They read "if the page key in the %ticklerpages variable exists, append the text of the $action variable with the name of the page followed by the dash, followed by the $server location (which you'll remember is the full path name in the config), and the page's file name.

One final element of this file you might want to edit is the subject line of the e-mail. The default is set to Thank You!, but can be changed in the print statement at line 156:

```
156:     print <<END;
```

```
157: To: $Email
```

```
158: From: $adminemail
```

```
159: Subject: Thank You!
```

```
160: Reply-To: $adminemail
```

```
161: \n\n
```

```
162: END
```

Not only the subject can be changed. Many ISPs require that you set your sendmail priority as bulk. This could be added here as well. Ask them for the proper configuration and add that line, making sure not to put any other character after the word END at line 162. And don't forget, these line numbers are only listed for reference. Don't include them in your file modifications.

Customizing the Thanks Message: NT

Use the directions for Unix until the final section that begins "One final element" where we modify the subject of the message. In the NT version, this is controlled at line 152:

```
150:         if ($ENV{'PERLXS'} eq "PerlIS" )
{
```

```
151:             require "sendmail.pl";
```

```
152:                    $thanks = "Thank You!";

153:                    &sendmail($adminemail, $adminemail, $addr, $smtphost,
$thanks, &file_to_string("confirm.txt"));
```

The code reads "if we're on Perl for NT, use sendmail.pl instead of the Unix sendmail daemon, set the thanks for registering message to say Thank You!, and process the mail request. Alter the thanks message with the $thanks variable.

Customizing the Update File: Unix

This sample file is just as simple and is edited in the same way. The demonstration copy of update.txt has only two lines, and you can edit them as you like.

```
$action
```

```
Thanks again for registering.
```

And again, $action is the only mandatory variable. The rest of the file is modifiable to change the stock look and feel of the message without modifying the Tickler code itself.

But again, if you want, the tickler.cgi file is easily editable. At line 185 you'll find the following (note that the lines are wrapped for print formatting):

```
185:   $action = "As per your request, the following pages have been
updated:\n";

186:   if ($groups =~ /all\*/) {

187:     foreach $key (@groups_form) {

188:     if ($ticklerpages{$key} ne "") {

189:     $action .= "$ticklerpages{$key} - located at \'$server/?$key\' .\n";
```

You'll edit them in the same way. Modify the code at line 189 to whatever you like. The page name and file name are in the variables $ticklerpages{$key} and $key.

The subject line for the update page is at line 212. As before, it's a print statement with a here document:

```
212:           print <<END;
```

```
213: From: $adminemail

214: To: $addr

215: Subject: Update

216: Reply-To: $adminemail

217: Apparently-To:

218: END
```

Modify line 215 to the appropriate value, and keep in mind that you can use any variable in the config, as well as the $ticklerpages{$key} and $key values. This is true for update.txt as well.

Customizing the Update File: NT

Again in this section, we pick up the NT modifications in the last section on modifying the subject line. Until that point, follow the Unix directions. Line 205 begins the NT-specific code, again, using the included file sendmail.pl:

```
205:            if ($ENV{'PERLXS'} eq "PerlIS" ) {

206:                require "sendmail.pl";

207:                $update = "Update";

208:                &sendmail($adminemail, $adminemail, $addr, $smtphost,
$update, &file_to_string("update.txt"));
```

It's just like the previous section. Modify the $update variable and you're all set. Note, as I mentioned in the Unix section, that all the config variables and $ticklerpages{$key} and $key are available, as well as any you might add to the config especially for this message. This is true for update.txt as well.

Customizing the Signup Form: All Platforms

When you hit tickler.cgi, it gave you the very basic form shown in Figure 7.1. There are two ways to alter its appearance: in the file form.htm and from within the tickler code.

If you open the form.htm file, you'll be greeted with a page of one variable: $form. It prints all the code you've seen so far, without, as you can see, a header or footer attached. The background on the page you access with tickler.cgi should have a gray background with black text. Now we start to customize the layout to match your site.

The top and bottom of form.htm are devoid of any front and back HTML code. It's a middle, as you saw with SiteWrapper. Add $HEADER and $FOOTER and it will attach like the rest of site, but only if you made a tickler directory earlier, as opposed to installing tickler.cgi in the main directory. If so, make sure the following two variables are edited to the full path name.

```
$headerfile = "/full/path/to/header.txt";

$footerfile = "/full/path/to/footer.txt";
```

You should now have a header and footer attached, a complete document with no more on the page than what appears in Figure 7.1. Above and below the $form variable on form.htm, you may add whatever content you wish, but to alter the look of $form, we have to edit the tickler.cgi file itself. Line 70 begins a table that houses the form, line 74 is the first instructional text, and line 77 is the second. We are submitting two variables from this form—one is in this text, called Completed. You must include the two radio buttons, add and remove, but the page layout may be altered to fit your design needs.

```
70: <FORM METHOD=POST ACTION="$ENV{'SCRIPT_NAME'}">

71: <INPUT TYPE=HIDDEN NAME="send_update" VALUE="yes">

72: <HR><BR><CENTER>

73: <TABLE BORDER=0>

74: <TR><TH ALIGN=LEFT>Select the documents you have updated:

75: <TR><TH>$updatelist

76: <TR><TH>Enter your Password:<BR><INPUT TYPE="Password" NAME="password"
SIZE=20>

77: <TR><TH><INPUT TYPE="Submit" VALUE="Send Update Notification"><BR>

78: </TABLE><P><HR></FORM>

79: END
```

At line 63 you'll see the variable $updatelist. That's the <SELECT> <OPTION> list you see on the form. The following is the code as it's presented in the stock tickler.cgi:

```
63:     $updatelist = "<SELECT MULTIPLE SIZE=3 NAME=\"groups\">\n";

64:     if ($ENV{'QUERY_STRING'} =~ /admin/) {

65:     foreach $key (keys(%ticklerpages)) {

66:         $updatelist .= "<OPTION VALUE=\"$key\">$ticklerpages{$key}\n";

67:     }

68:     $updatelist .="</SELECT>\n";

69:     $adminform=<<END;

70: <FORM METHOD=POST ACTION="$ENV{'SCRIPT_NAME'}">

71: <INPUT TYPE=HIDDEN NAME="send_update" VALUE="yes">

72: <HR><BR><CENTER>

73: <TABLE BORDER=0>

74: <TR><TH ALIGN=LEFT>Select the documents you have updated:

75: <TR><TH>$updatelist

76: <TR><TH>Enter your Password:<BR><INPUT TYPE="Password" NAME="password"
SIZE=20>

77: <TR><TH><INPUT TYPE="Submit" VALUE="Send Update Notification"><BR>

78: </TABLE><P><HR></FORM>

79: END

80:     &give_menu;

81:     } else {

82:     $updatelist .= "<OPTION VALUE=\"all\">All Registered Pages\n";

83:     foreach $key (keys(%ticklerpages)) {

84:         $updatelist .= "<OPTION VALUE=\"$key\">$ticklerpages{$key}\n";
```

```
85:    }

86:        $updatelist .="</SELECT>\n";

87:      $form=<<END;

88: <FORM METHOD=POST ACTION="$ENV{'SCRIPT_NAME'}">

89: <HR><BR><CENTER>

90: <TABLE BORDER=0>

91: <TR><TH ALIGN=LEFT>To receive updates when this site is updated, please fill
in the following information:

92: <TR><TD>Email Address: <INPUT NAME="Email" SIZE=40><BR>

93: <TR><TD><INPUT TYPE=radio NAME=Completed VALUE="1">Add Me To Your Mailing
List

94: <TR><TD>Select the documents you would like updates for:

95: <TR><TD>$updatelist

96: <TR><TD><INPUT TYPE=radio NAME=Completed VALUE="nuke">Remove Me From Your
List

97: <TR><TH COLSPAN=2><INPUT TYPE="Submit" VALUE="Click Here When Done"><BR>

98: </TABLE><P><HR></FORM>

99: END
```

Line 63 begins a <SELECT> list, which then picks up at either line 66 or line 82. At 66 it begins the iteration over the $keys in %ticklerpages, which we set in the config for the ?admin screen, adding only the individual pages to the $updatelist. Each key gets its <OPTION> in the form. Then line 68 caps $updatelist with the end of the <SELECT> list.

Line 82 picks up differently. It offers first an option to subscribe to all registered pages. The iteration begins at line 83, capped at line 86. Then at line 88, it picks back up with the editable code for the form.

In the following code, I've converted the <SELECT> <OPTION> list to a row of checkboxes for usability (most people don't know to hold down their CONTROL button to select multiples). Figure 7.5 shows this graphically.

```
63:     $updatelist = "<P>\n";

64:     if ($ENV{'QUERY_STRING'} =~ /admin /) {

65:     foreach $key (keys(%ticklerpages)) {

66:         $updatelist .= "<INPUT TYPE=CHECKBOX NAME=\"groups\" VALUE=\"$key\"
MULTIPLE>$ticklerpages{$key}<BR>\n";

67:     }

68:         $updatelist .="</p>\n";

69:     $adminform=<<END;

70: <FORM METHOD=POST ACTION="$ENV{'SCRIPT_NAME'}">

71: <INPUT TYPE=HIDDEN NAME="send_update" VALUE="yes">

72: <HR><BR><CENTER>

73: <TABLE BORDER=0>

74: <TR><TH ALIGN=LEFT>Select the documents you have updated:

75: <TR><TH>$updatelist
```

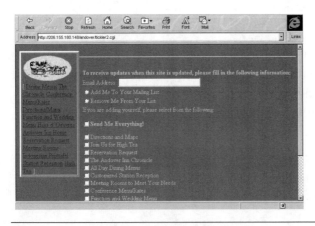

Figure 7.5 Changing the signup page.

```
76: <TR><TH>Enter your Password:<BR><INPUT TYPE="Password" NAME="password"
SIZE=20>

77: <TR><TH><INPUT TYPE="Submit" VALUE="Send Update Notification"><BR>

78: </TABLE><P><HR></FORM>

79: END

80:     &give_menu;

81:     } else {

82:     $updatelist .= "<STRONG><INPUT TYPE=CHECKBOX NAME=\"groups\"
VALUE=\"$key\" MULTIPLE>Send Me Everything!</STRONG><P>\n";

83:     foreach $key (keys(%ticklerpages)) {

84:         $updatelist .= "<INPUT TYPE=CHECKBOX NAME=\"groups\" VALUE=\"$key\"
MULTIPLE>$ticklerpages{$key}<BR>\n";

85:     }               $form=<<END;

86: <FORM METHOD=POST ACTION="$ENV{'SCRIPT_NAME'}">

87: <HR><BR><CENTER>

88: <TABLE BORDER=0>

89: <TR><TH ALIGN=LEFT>To receive updates when this site is updated, please fill
in the following information:

90: <TR><TD>Email Address: <INPUT NAME="Email" SIZE=40><BR>

91: <TR><TD><INPUT TYPE=radio NAME=Completed VALUE="1">Add Me To Your Mailing
List

92: <TR><TD><INPUT TYPE=radio NAME=Completed VALUE="nuke">Remove Me From Your
List

93: <TR><TD>If you are adding yourself, please select from the following:

94: <TR><TD>$updatelist
```

```
95: <TR><TH COLSPAN=2><INPUT TYPE="Submit" VALUE="Click Here When Done"><BR>

96: </TABLE><P><HR></FORM>
```

As you can see, I altered some of the text in the form layout, moved the "remove me" choice to the top and changed the "All Registered Pages" to "Show Me Everything!" But the most important parts are the code attachments of $updatelist and iteration of %ticklerpages. In both the admin and user menus, I've removed the <SELECT> list start and replaced it with a <P>. Then, again for both, I've replaced the <OPTION> iteration with an iteration over $updatelist .= "<INPUT TYPE =CHECKBOX NAME=\"groups\" VALUE=\"$key\" MULTIPLE>$ticklerpages{$key}
\n";, which prints a checkbox followed by a <BR> for each listing. Note that I had to escape all the quotes in the variable because I didn't use single quotes to identify it due to my need to call the variables $key and $ticklerpages{$key}.

Full-Text Tickler for Events and Specials

The standard Tickler program is great when your goal is to get people to your site over and over again. We call this program the *event mailer*; it's for when you'd prefer that people do *something*, whether it be attend a workshop, buy merchandise in a sale, call their state representative, or some other time-specific action. The idea isn't necessarily to publicize the site as much as it is to use the Internet as a way to get them to act. Event Tickler allows you to tag everyone in your e-mail database with full-text information, the simplest form of push technology.

Now I'm going to show you another way to use Tickle messages. These are different from the last variety in that they are full text rather than a list of updated URLs. It's for those times when you have to get a quick word out to a large group of people without the bother of compiling and updating your personal address book in an e-mail program such as Eudora. It's short of a listserv type approach, as we'll cover in the next chapter, but does not allow the capability for people to respond and discuss topics. It's very effective when all you need to do is post a message quickly and cleanly. That's why we call it Event Tickler, because it is specifically for an event, as opposed to a new content item.

This version of Tickler also addresses another website automation need in addition to broadcasting e-mail. It writes an actual page to your website and rewrites it every time you launch a new event, sale, or special notice from the admin form, which is an actual webform into which you paste text. It formats the page in HTML and sends a full text message of e-mail to the list in your e-mail database.

 On the Web Remember the Andover Inn site? Go back there now (www.andoverinn.com) and go to the events link at mail.cgi, shown in Figure 7.6 (the event might be different when you view it). Now edit the link to say mail.cgi?admin. You'll see that the Andover Inn posts new content to that page interactively, without calling us to construct and upload a new page. Notice that their version is a bit different from the one we'll initially set up. That's because Event Tickler is highly customizable, both in functionality and look and feel. The customization directions will explain this later.

Imagine you get in a shipment of porcelain dolls every two weeks or so. Your customers—avid collectors—call you forty times a week to ask whether the new truck has arrived. Plus, to make matters worse, you've opened a homepage on the World

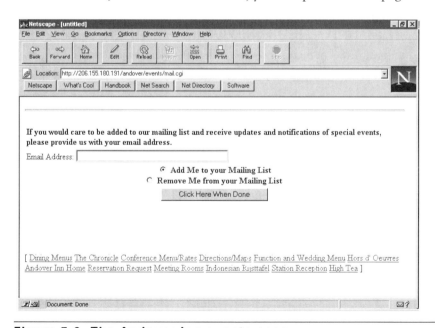

Figure 7.6 The Andover Inn events page.

Wide Web and are hosting your site on an internal server through a 14,400 modem. You've developed some regular customers there too, so to do them justice you better have the website updated in pronto time with the availability of new dolls for your walk-in customers. Between the two, you spend hours of your week saying no and trashing the hopes of eager doll fanatics, and the rest of your time preparing a stock list in HTML.

With Tickler for events, you'll ask your customers, both walk-in and web, to supply you with their e-mail addresses. Then, as soon as the truck arrives, you take inventory and input the information into the webform accessed by mail.cgi?admin. Enter it once, click Submit and the information is fired off to hungry doll collectors the world over. The walk-ins, as well as your web-only customers, need only check their e-mail, then obey the posted speed limits. And remember, you've mailed them the full text. They don't have to return to the site to check the inventory. Only those who wish to order will return.

Installing this version of Tickler is much like the earlier one, but I'll go through it in case you read ahead and did not install the first one. You'll notice that Events Tickler does not ask for categories in the form like the basic version.

Installing Tickler for Unix

Look in the sourcecode/UNIX/event-tickler directory on the CD. There you'll find a zip and the individual files. There are only four files, including a dummy config.cfg. The dummy config is included because you need not have SiteWrapper running to use Event Tickler.

Either unzip the archive in your webserver's main directory or upload the three files—form.htm, adminform.htm, and mail.cgi—into the main directory of your webserver at www.yourcompany.com. If you've already installed plain Tickler you'll want to do it in a separate directory as the form.htm and adminform.htm will overwrite it (you could also edit the code in mail.cgi at line 141 that evaluates adminform.htm and the code at line 177 that evaluates form.htm—just change them to a different file name and rename the files). That way you can run standard and Event Tickler at the same time. You can, of course, make an events/ directory to install it into. If you do, make that directory CHMOD 777. Make sure the Perl !# location line is correct for your system.

Check the require config line in mail.cgi to make sure it's pointing to the correct configuration file. You may have changed the name in the SiteWrapper chapter and it should be reflected in mail.cgi or your jumplist won't be used. If you are installing it somewhere other than the directory where the config is, edit the required line with the full path name (e.g., require "../myconfigfile.cfg";).

TIP If you have kept one config file but put Tickler in another directory (like /events/), make sure your $headerfile and $footerfile are specified as complete path names. Otherwise they won't be found.

Set the permissions on mail.cgi to CHMOD 755. This will make it executable by the webserver. Now go and hit the URL mail.cgi. It should present you with a page like that in Figure 7.7, but with your jumplist at the bottom instead of the Andover Inn's. If you get an error message, chances are your Perl location, config location, or permissions are wrong. If you get a gray background instead of the normal background for your site, the $headerfile and $footerfile files must be converted to full path names.

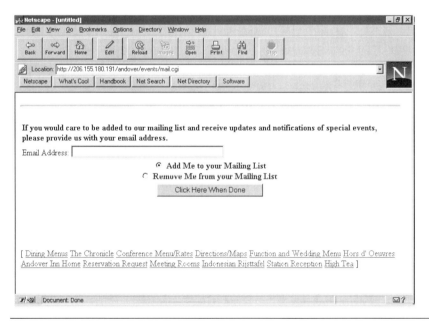

Figure 7.7 Your mail page.

Once that's up and running, if you haven't already done this for the first version of Tickler, add the following variables to the config:

$sendmail_location = "/usr/bin/sendmail";

$adminemail = "webmaster\@world-media.com";

$response = "206.155.180.191/andover/index.cgi?thanks.html";

$emaildbfile = "email.db";

$mail_password = "IuTlBL92Jhrro";

$already_sub = "tickler/already.htm";

These examples are from my tests as I write this. I'm installing everything in the book to check for bugs as we go. These in particular are copies of the Andover Inn, which you're probably sick of by now. All are pretty self-explanatory, but I'll go over them anyway.

The $sendmail_location and $adminemail should be set for whatever is correct for your system. Don't forget to escape the @ sign in the e-mail. The $response variable identifies what page your visitors get after their e-mail is registered. It can be a relative path or a full URL. The $email.db is the file in which your e-mails will be saved. Be sure to re-name it so everyone reading this book doesn't steal your database. In $mailpassword, you can either use Encrypt to create a new one or set it equal to the $password you set earlier. Remember, though, that it has to be the encrypted mishmash, not the real word. And the last variable is $already_sub, which is the page you get when you've already subscribed to the database and try to again.

TIP Event Tickler can be used as an approval system to get you into the next of a series of pages or a download screen. It will collect a database of e-mails for you and allow constant tickling of potential customers. You'd do this by not sending people directly to mail.cgi, but instead to an approval page with a mini form built in. In this form will be one visible e-mail field and two hidden ones. The code you need is <INPUT NAME="Email" SIZE=40>
<INPUT TYPE=hidden NAME=groups VALUE="all"><INPUT TYPE=hidden NAME=Completed VALUE="1">. Then, elsewhere on the site you'll use mail.cgi to post new news and press releases. Great stuff!

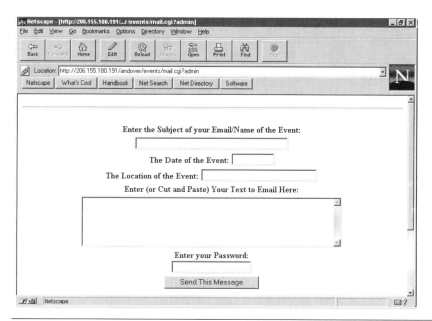

Figure 7.8 Enter a new event.

You are ready to add your e-mail to the database by filling it into the box and hitting Click Here When Done. The Add Me To Your Mailing List is the default. You'll be presented with the thanks page you just added in the config. You need an event, special, or other time-sensitive item to post to the site. Hit the mail.cgi?admin full administration URL and fill in the fields. The form you start with should look like Figure 7.8. When you Submit the form you'll be bounced to the thanks page.

This should have written a new event to the site and e-mailed you the full text of the message. If you didn't get the e-mail, it's possible that your sendmail location is wrong. Manually check the e-mail database file and see if you were logged. Then check mostrec.txt and see if it was written. If neither of those are true, you probably have a permissions problem. Again, the directory where mail.cgi resides must be 777.

Installing Tickler for NT

Your files are in the sourcecode/NT/event-tickler directory on the CD. There you'll find a zip and the individual files. There are only five files, including a dummy config and sendmail.pl which, as I just warned, might not work on your system unless Activeware has fixed the sockets bug. You might try Blat in such a case, but we had little luck from that as well. The dummy config is included because you need not have SiteWrapper running to use Event Tickler.

Either unzip the archive in your webserver's main directory or upload the three files form.htm, adminform.htm, and mail.cgi into the main directory of your webserver at www.yourcompany.com. If you've already installed plain Tickler you'll want to do it in a separate directory as the form.htm and adminform.htm will overwrite it (you can also edit the code in mail.cgi at line 141 that evaluates adminform.htm and the code at line 177 that evaluates form.htm instead if you like). That way you can run standard and Event Tickler at the same time. You can, of course, make an events/ directory to install it into. Make that directory CHMOD 777 if you do.

Check the require config line in mail.cgi to make sure it's pointing to the correct configuration file. You may have changed the name in the SiteWrapper chapter and it should be reflected in mail.cgi or your jumplist won't be used. If you are installing it somewhere other than the directory where the config is, edit the require line with the full path name (e.g., require "../myconfigfile.cfg";).

TIP If you have kept one config file but put Tickler in another directory (like /events/), make sure your $headerfile and $footerfile are specified as complete path names. Otherwise they won't be found.

Now go and hit the URL mail.cgi. It should present you with a page like that shown in Figure 7.7, but with your jumplist at the bottom instead of the Andover Inn's. If you get an error message, it could that your Perl is not configured properly, but more likely it's that the bug in Perl has not been fixed. Upgrade it to the latest version and try again. If you get a gray background instead of the normal background for your site, the $headerfile and $footerfile files must be converted to full path names.

Once that's up and running, if you haven't already done this for the first version of Tickler, add the following variables to the config:

$adminemail = "webmaster\@world-media.com";

$response = "http://206.155.180.148/andover/index.cgi?thanks.html";

$emaildbfile = "email.db";

$mail_password = "IuTlBL92Jhrro";

$already_sub = "tickler/already.htm";

$smtphost = "granite.interwebb.com";

These examples are from my tests as I write this. I'm installing everything in the book to check for bugs as we go. These in particular are copies of the Andover Inn, which you're probably sick of by now. All are pretty self-explanatory, but I'll go over them anyway.

The $adminemail should be set for whatever is correct for your system. Don't forget to escape the @ sign in the e-mail. The $response variable identifies what page your visitors get after their e-mail is registered. It can be a relative path or a full URL. The $email.db is the file in which your e-mails will be saved. Be sure to rename it so everyone reading this book doesn't steal your database. In $mailpassword, you can use either Encrypt to create a new one or set it equal to the $password you set earlier. Remember, though, that it has to be the encrypted mishmash, not the real word. Next is $already_sub, which is the page you get when you've already subscribed to the database and try to again. And the last is the SMTP host for sendmail.pl to use when it sends out confirmation and tickle messages.

TIP This tip is as true for NT as for Unix, so in keeping with the usability of the book I'm repeating it. Events Tickler can be used as an approval system to get you into the next of a series of pages or a download screen. It will collect a database of e-mails for you and allow constant tickling of potential customers. You'd do this by not sending people directly to mail.cgi, but instead to an approval page with a mini form built in. In this form will be one visible e-mail field and two hidden ones. The code you need is <INPUT NAME="Email" SIZE=40>
<INPUT TYPE=hidden NAME=groups VALUE="all"><INPUT TYPE=hidden NAME=Completed VALUE="1">. Then, elsewhere on the site you'll use mail.cgi to post new news and press releases. Great stuff!

You are ready to add your e-mail to the database by filling it into the box and hitting Click Here When Done. The Add Me To Your Mailing List is the default. You'll be presented with the thanks page you just added in the config. Now you need an event, special, or other time-sensitive item to post to the site. Hit the mail.cgi?admin full administration URL and fill in the fields. The form you start with should look like Figure 7.8. When you Submit the form you'll be bounced to the thanks page.

This should have written a new event to the site and e-mailed you the full text of the message. If you didn't get the e-mail, it's possible that your sendmail location is wrong. Manually check the e-mail database file and see if you were logged. Then check mostrec.txt and see if it was written.

Customizing the Look: All Platforms

Like standard Tickler, this version allows the screens we just viewed to be edited for your look and feel. In this section I'm not changing functionality. We're still recording the same fields, but customizing the way the information is presented.

Open form.htm, one of the three core files. In it you'll find four variables and nothing else: $HEADER, $mostrecevent, $form, and $FOOTER. The header and footer, as you know from SiteWrapper, are drawn from the config. The $form and $mostrecevent are in the mail.cgi code and are editable, which I'll cover next. But before that, in between the variables you can add HTML code to customize the way the page lays out. For instance, build in an introduction or explanation above $mostrecevent. It could tell people the scope of your coverage. You could also raise $form (the code that prints the e-mail collector form) to the top of the screen or customize the page for your users from a database (as we'll cover in the database chapter).

To edit the look of $mostrecevent, go to line 107 and the following code:

```
107:        $mostrecevent=<<END;

108:  <HR>

109:  <CENTER>Here is our next special event:<BR>

110:  <TABLE BORDER=0 CELLPADDING=2 CELLSPACING=0 WIDTH=300>

111:  <TR><TH COLSPAN=2><FONT SIZE=4>$name</FONT></TH></TR>

112:  <TR><TD>Date:</TD><TD>$date</TD></TR>

113:  <TR><TD>Location:</TD><TD>$location</TD></TR><TR>
```

114: </TABLE></CENTER>

115: <blockquote><pre>$text</pre></blockquote>

116:

117: END

This is what prints on the form.htm page in the variable $mostrecevent. If you change it, just make sure to keep the END as the only word on its line with not even a whitespace (space, tab, etc.) character after it.

The $form variable is just like with regular Tickler, but has a hidden field "All" for its group names (yes, this is a modified standard Tickler). Its code starts at line 120:

120:     $form=<<END;

121: <FORM METHOD=POST ACTION="mail.cgi">

122: <HR>
<CENTER>

123: <TABLE BORDER=0>

124: <TR><TH ALIGN=LEFT>If you would care to be added to our mailing list and receive updates and notifications of special events, please provide us with your email address.

125: <TR><TD>Email Address: <INPUT NAME="Email" SIZE=40>

126: <INPUT TYPE=hidden NAME=groups VALUE="all">

127: <TR><TH COLSPAN=2><INPUT TYPE=radio NAME=Completed VALUE="1" CHECKED> Add Me to your Mailing List

128: <INPUT TYPE=radio NAME=Completed VALUE="nuke"> Remove Me from your Mailing List

129: </TR></TH>

130: <TR><TH COLSPAN=2><INPUT TYPE="Submit" VALUE="Click Here When Done">

131: </TABLE>

```
132: </FORM>

133: </CENTER>

134: END
```

Make sure in this case that, besides not messing up the END from the here document, you keep the hidden groups variable. Tickler will break without it. Notice also that we've given people the option to remove themselves (or anyone else as there is no security) from the e-mail database. You can comment or remove that radio button if you like, keeping it only on a form accessible to you. This would reserve the delete right to only you, unless someone recognized the code from this book.

More Code Customization

You've probably noticed that the fields in the demo you just created are not all encompassing for most businesses and organizations. More fields, different formatting, other options—I'm going to take you through several different editing options for Event Tickler. If you are a beginner Perl hacker, this might look and sound complicated, but if you follow my steps exactly you probably won't mess it up. I'm figuring it all out as I go, and you're probably smarter than I am.

Let's start simply, by just changing the event to a close-out sale we plan to run every week. Change the title of the page at line 9 from the $thispagetitle = "Send Special Event Notification"; to something to do with "Clearance". Next we'll go to the administration menu from where you post a new event. The following code starts at line 83, where the variable $adminform begins a here document.

```
83:     $adminform=<<END;

84: <FORM METHOD=POST ACTION="mail.cgi">

85: <INPUT TYPE=HIDDEN NAME="send_update" VALUE="yes">

86: <HR><BR><CENTER>

87: <TABLE BORDER=0>

88: <INPUT TYPE=HIDDEN NAME=groups VALUE="All">

89: <TR><TH>Enter the Subject of your Email/Name of the Event:</TH></TR>
```

```
90: <TR><TH><INPUT TYPE=TEXT NAME=Subject SIZE=40></TH></TR>

91: <TR><TH>The Date of the Event: <INPUT TYPE=TEXT NAME=Date SIZE=10></TH></TR>

92: <TR><TH>The Location of the Event: <INPUT TYPE=TEXT NAME=Location
SIZE=30></TH></TR>

93: <TR><TH>Enter (or Cut and Paste) Your Text to Email Here:</TH></TR>

94: <TR><TH><TEXTAREA NAME="Text" WRAP=PHYSICAL COLS=60
ROWS=5>\n</TEXTAREA></TH></TR>

95: <TR><TH>Enter your Password:<BR><INPUT TYPE="Password" NAME="password"
SIZE=20></th></TR>

96: <TR><TH><INPUT TYPE="Submit" VALUE="Send This Message"><BR></TH></TR>

97: </TABLE><P><HR></FORM>

98: </CENTER>

99: END
```

The first thing we have to change is at line 89. Change the text explaining the Subject variable to "Enter name of clearance items" or something that explains what the purpose of the message is to the eventual administrator. You can leave the variable name, Subject, alone. At line 91, change the date of event to "Effective dates of sale." Then change the Location at line 92 in the same manner.

Now we'll alter the page of HTML that advertises the new event. This is what spits when you hit the mail.cgi program:

```
107:        $mostrecevent=<<END;

108: <HR>

109: <CENTER>Here is our next special event:<BR>

110: <TABLE BORDER=0 CELLPADDING=2 CELLSPACING=0 WIDTH=300>

111: <TR><TH COLSPAN=2><FONT SIZE=4>$name</FONT></TH></TR>

112: <TR><TD>Date:</TD><TD>$date</TD></TR>
```

```
113: <TR><TD>Location:</TD><TD>$location</TD></TR><TR>

114: </TABLE></CENTER><BR>

115: <center><B>$text<B></center>

116:

117: END
```

As you can see, at 109 you'll change the event title to information about your sale. Don't think, however, that your options end there. You have the variables $name, $date, $location, and $text to play with. The HTML, titles, and preceding and ending text are your own. You can, of course, also control the header.txt and footer.txt as you wish as well. Most of SiteWrapper's functionality is built in except for $thispagetitle, which we manually changed earlier.

What's left on the page to change is the place where people sign up for automatic e-mail. The code starts at line 120 for the $form variable:

```
120:    $form=<<END;

121: <FORM METHOD=POST ACTION="mail.cgi">

122: <HR><BR><CENTER>

123: <TABLE BORDER=0>

124: <TR><TH ALIGN=LEFT>If you would care to be added to our mailing list and

receive updates and notifications of special events, please provide us with your

email address.

125: <TR><TD>Email Address: <INPUT NAME="Email" SIZE=40><BR>

126: <INPUT TYPE=hidden NAME=groups VALUE="all">

127: <TR><TH COLSPAN=2><INPUT TYPE=radio NAME=Completed VALUE="1" CHECKED> Add

Me to your Mailing List<BR>

128: <INPUT TYPE=radio NAME=Completed VALUE="nuke"> Remove Me from your Mailing

List

129: </TR></TH>
```

```
130: <TR><TH COLSPAN=2><INPUT TYPE="Submit" VALUE="Click Here When Done"><BR>

131: </TABLE>

132: </FORM>

133: </CENTER>

134: END
```

Like the modifications we made to the standard Tickler earlier, this text can be changed as you wish. There are no groups in this version, so that code doesn't need to be modified. It is crucial, however, that you leave the hidden variable groups to All. We reused some code from the standard version.

Now let's alter the way the finished page looks. I'd prefer the e-mail box to be on top and to the right. Open the file form.htm in your browser; it's a little page with the variables $HEADER, $FOOTER, $form, and $mostrecentevent, with no HTML at all. I modified the code to the following and got Figure 7.9.

```
$HEADER

 <table border=3 align=right><Tr><td>$form</td></tr></table>

$mostrecevent

$FOOTER
```

Now let's alter the outgoing message text in the same way. At line 187 is the variable $string = "You have been added to our mailing list,\n and will receive future notification\n of special events.\n"; It's a manually formatted text message that goes out when someone first signs up. Change it to your welcome message. Then go to the line a bit after it at 196 to alter the subject of the message. You'll find an if statement ending at 207 that sends the welcome message according to which type of platform you're running on. NT is the first, then Unix starts at 195:

```
190:    if ($ENV{'PERLXS'} eq "PerlIS" ) {

191:       require "sendmail.pl";

192:       $subject = "Event Notification";

193:         $number = &sendmail($serveradmin, $serveradmin, $Email, $smt-
phost, $subject, $string);
```

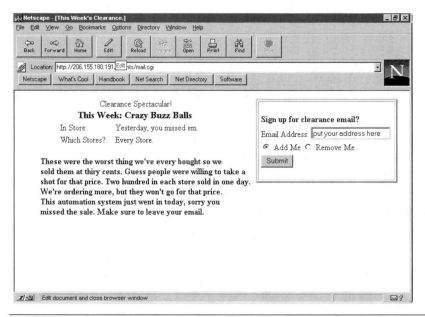

Figure 7.9 A simple example.

```
194:      } else {

195:      open(MAIL, "| $sendmail_location -f \"$serveradmin\" $Email");

196:      select(MAIL);

197:      print <<END;

198: To: $Email

199: From: $serveradmin

200: Subject: Thank You for Registering!

201: Reply-To: $serveradmin

202: \n\n

203: $string

204: END

205:
```

```
206:     close(MAIL);
```

```
207:     }
```

If you're on NT, change 192 to your title. Line 200 is for Unix machines. If you plan to drag and drop this across platforms, change them both. Then try signing up with another e-mail address. You'll get the new message.

It's time for the update message that sends out the full text. It's set up a bit different (some of this was written at different times for different clients) but is just as easy to change. The code starts at line 224:

```
224: $string=<<END;
```

```
225: $in{'Subject'}
```

```
226: Date and Time: $in{'Date'}
```

```
227: Location:      $in{'Location'}
```

```
228:
```

```
229: $tickletext
```

```
230: END
```

```
231:
```

```
232: # send to NT, with string as the body
```

```
233:          if ($ENV{'PERLXS'} eq "PerlIS" ) {
```

```
234:            require "sendmail.pl";
```

```
235:            $number = &sendmail($serveradmin, $serveradmin, $addr,
$smtphost, "Event Notification", $string);
```

```
236:          } else {
```

```
237:            #or unix with string in a here document
```

```
238:            open(MAIL, "| $sendmail_location -f \"$serveradmin\" -t
$addr");
```

```
239:            select(MAIL);
```

```
240:                    print <<END;
241: From: $serveradmin
242: Subject: Event Notification
243: Reply-To: $serveradmin
244: \n
245: $string
246: END
247:                    close(MAIL);
248:                    select(STDOUT);
249:            }
250:        }
```

In the first part, we set up how the body of the message is to look with $string. It's a here document, so format it however you like. If you were to have a sponsor, additional advertisements, or other stuff, this is where you'd add it. The $in{} variables and $tickletext are the only musts and can be inserted anywhere.

The subject lines are at 235 and 242 for NT and Unix, respectively. You can include $in{Subject} in them if you wish. Notice that both use $string as their body text.

Now we'll add another field called Price to the message so that we can include it in the Tickle e-mail and print it to a specific place on the screen every time rather than just include it in the $text we read in from the main text box. First we'll go back to the administration form, with my edits for this clearance example. I've added a Price variable to the here document $adminform:

```
$adminform=<<END;

<FORM METHOD=POST ACTION="mail.cgi">

<INPUT TYPE=HIDDEN NAME="send_update" VALUE="yes">

<BR><CENTER>

<TABLE BORDER=0>
```

```
<INPUT TYPE=HIDDEN NAME=groups VALUE="All">

<TR><TD>Clearance Item(s):</TH></TR>

<TR><TD><INPUT TYPE=TEXT NAME=Subject SIZE=40></TH></TR>

<TR><TD>Price:<INPUT TYPE=TEXT NAME=Price SIZE=40></TH></TR>

<TR><TD>In Store Date: <INPUT TYPE=TEXT NAME=Date SIZE=10></TH></TR>

<TR><TD>Location of Clearance Items: <INPUT TYPE=TEXT NAME=Location

SIZE=30></TH></TR>

<TR><TD>Enter (or Cut and Paste) Your Text to Email Here:</TH></TR>

<TR><TD><TEXTAREA NAME="Text" WRAP=PHYSICAL COLS=60

ROWS=5>\n</TEXTAREA></TH></TR>

<TR><TD>Enter your Password:<BR><INPUT TYPE="Password" NAME="password"

SIZE=20></th></TR>

<TR><TD><INPUT TYPE="Submit" VALUE="Send This Message"><BR></TH></TR>

</TABLE><P></FORM>

</CENTER>

END
```

Now I'll go to where we write the mostrec.txt file:

```
255:        open(MOSTREC, "> $mostrecentfile");

256:        print(MOSTREC

"$in{'Subject'}\r$in{'Date'}\r$in{'Location'}\r$in{'Text'}\n");

257:        close(MOSTREC);
```

We have to read in the variable I just added to the administration form and print it to the database. Modify line 256 to include it like the line below (all on one line in Multi-Edit or another editor capable of not wrapping lines, unlike this book).

```
print(MOSTREC
"$in{'Subject'}\r$in{'Date'}\r$in{'Location'}\r$in{'Text'},\r$in{'Subject'}\n");
```

It's being recorded in the little database now, but we're not yet printing it to the HTML screen or e-mail message. At line 102 we read the file in:

```
102:     if (open(MOSTREC, "$mostrecentfile")) {

103:     $/ = "\r";

104:         ($name, $date, $location, $text, $price) = <MOSTREC>;

105:         close(MOSTREC);
```

You must modify line 104 to include the price field we just tacked on. After $text at line 104, add a comma and $price before the closing parenthesis. Then go back to the $mostrecevent variable at line 109. My modifications look like this:

```
$mostrecevent=<<END;


<H1>Clearance Spectacular!</H1>

<TABLE BORDER=0 CELLPADDING=2 CELLSPACING=0 WIDTH=300>

<TR><TD COLSPAN=2><FONT SIZE=4>This Week:<B> $name</B></FONT></TD></TR>

<TR><TD>Price:</TD><TD>$price</TD></TR>

<TR><TD>In Store:</TD><TD>$date</TD></TR>

<TR><TD>Which Stores?:</TD><TD>$location</TD></TR><TR>

</TABLE></CENTER><BR>

<blockquote><B>$text<B></blockquote>

END
```

Next I moved down to line 225 and included it in the outgoing e-mail message:

```
$mostrecevent=<<END;


<H1>Clearance Spectacular!</H1>

<TABLE BORDER=0 CELLPADDING=2 CELLSPACING=0 WIDTH=300>

<TR><TD COLSPAN=2><FONT SIZE=4>This Week:<B> $name</B></FONT></TD></TR>

<TR><TD>Price:</TD><TD>$price</TD></TR>
```

```
<TR><TD>In Store:</TD><TD>$date</TD></TR>

<TR><TD>Which Stores?:</TD><TD>$location</TD></TR><TR>

</TABLE></CENTER><BR>

<blockquote><B>$text<B></blockquote>

END
```

You could do much more, but this should be an easy start for most of your needs. You can now change the look and feel of the HTML administration and result page as well as the layout of the Welcome and Tickler e-mail messages. You can change the name of fields and add new ones when you need to.

 On the CD Figure 7.10 is the sample e-mail of another clearance sale I posted with this demo version. I've put the modified files in the /sourcecode/UNIX/event-tickler/examples and /NT/event-tickler/examples folders for you to install and try. Compare these to the originals and to my instructions.

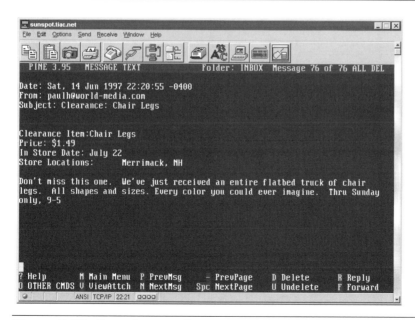

Figure 7.10 Sample e-mail.

Mailing List
Software

I know this isn't officially website stuff, but I've found that most websites have some need for an offline discussion forum outside the space of threaded, web-based bulletin boards and chat. This is different from the previous chapter where the e-mail was strictly broadcast. You can't reply to Tickler messages and have your message forwarded to the whole list. The following three options offer that functionality and a whole lot more. When I first got into the game, Majordomo, our first tool (which is Unix-based), was in its early release stages. Tools like SVList, the NT/95 offering, didn't even exist. Either will suit all your needs to set up an online e-mail discussion. The last section, on how to use Pine, a Unix shell-based e-mail program, is meant for those who only need a basic, small discussion. Its functionality can be duplicated with just about any good e-mail program that has the capability to make lists within an addressbook. If you have access to an NT or Windows 95 machine, can get an extra POP mailbox, and need only one list, I'd use SVList. It's really easy and costs only thirty bucks.

Majordomo: Unix Only

This program was the reason I wrote a list server chapter for the book. Because it's the most recognized mailing list server on the Internet, no automation book should be without it. Majordomo is famous as one of the most powerful list servers in the world. It allows you to create an unlimited number of mailing lists with separate administrators and moderators for each, should you require it. The setup is cryptic, but if you follow my instructions exactly, you should do fine. My test system was a Pentium 200 running Red Hat Linux, and I ran into no errors that weren't my own fault.

Unlike the rest of this book, however, Majordomo requires some root permission. I've minimized it by taking you step-by-step through the process I followed as I relearned the setup process after not having installed it for several years.

I'll mention that Majordomo was created several years ago by Brent Chapman and is the copyright and property of his company, GreatCircle associates. You must keep all the copyright information intact should you download and install it. See the copyright file for more information.

The following steps were derived from my own installation and the INSTALL file included in the Majordomo distribution. Subscribe to the Majordomo-users list at greatcircle.com if you have serious trouble. Later in the chapter I'll set up a mailing list for this book, so feel free to join that as well.

Download the source from www.greatcircle.com/majordomo/ and save a copy of it on your local system (or use lynx from your shell). Make a directory to untar the files into. I put it at /usr/local/majordomo and set it to CHMOD 777 so I would have permission to expand the archive. If you downloaded the gzip'ed version, unzip with gunzip majordomo-1.94.3.tar.Z in that directory. Use the command tar -xvf majordomo-1.94.3.tar to expand the archive. As you can see, it creates a number of directories for you, but it's not yet installed. These are just the raw files.

According to the INSTALL sheet, you now have to decide on a group and user for Majordomo to run as. It has to be a trusted user according to the configuration of sendmail. This sounds really complicated, but I had no trouble with only a smattering of Unix system knowledge. First, I edited the /etc/group file and set up a group called majordomo.daemon, as the INSTALL suggests. There were 15 groups, so I numbered this one 16 and stole the rest of the configuration from the other deamons in the file. The exact line I added is : majordomo.daemon::16:bin,daemon which puts the majordomo.daemon group as a member of the bin and daemon groups.

Next I had to edit the /etc/passwd file a line adding the majordomo user. Again I copied from other deamons and added the line majordomo:*:100:16:majordomo:

/:/bin/bash, which, according to my sysadmin buddies, means that I'm adding user majordomo, with a temporary password * (special), who's in group 16, user 100 in that group, and its home directory is majordomo. The last, /bin/bash, is my login shell. It's important now that you change the Majordomo password to one you know. Use the Unix passwd majordomo command. It will prompt you for a new password.

Now we have to go in and edit the Makefile, which is a simple set of instructions. Go over the lines you don't understand with your sysadmin, but you should be able to handle most of it yourself. The first is Perl location, which we've dealt with before. Then the C compiler should be either cc or gcc. I left it at cc, and it worked fine. There is a symbolic link to it usually from gcc (the GNU C compiler).

You should have created a majordomo directory already, so the next editable line, W_HOME, should be a spur off that. I used W_HOME= /usr/local/majordomo/ bin to signify the binary compilation. Then, I left the MAN directory as the default, and the W_USER = 100 and W_GROUP = 16 should be set as you arranged them earlier.

In the next two sections, I left the file permissions and wrapper modes alone. It worked fine. After that, the posix section should be fine for most systems as well; if not, consult your sysadmin.

The last section is another like the Perl and C locations. It's where Majordomo looks for other programs on the system. Check them to make sure the defaults are correct as W_SHELL = /bin/sh, the Unix shell; W_PATH = /bin:/usr/bin:/usr/ucb, the path to look for other needed programs; W_MAJORDOMO_CF = $(W_HOME)/majordomo.cf, the Majordomo config (you'll edit that in the next step); and TMPDIR = /usr/tmp, your directory for temporary files. Nothing else in the makefile should require editing.

 Now edit the file sample.cf and save it as majordomo.cf wherever you named it in the previous step. For $whoami, it should be the name of the actual machine you are on, not a virtual domain like www.yourcompany.com. It can be done like that but requires some sendmail configuration beyond what I'll cover here. The $whoami is the address of Majordomo, as in "send email to majordomo@yourmachine .com." I created a special account for the $whoami-owner, piping admin menus all to one place. In $digest_work_dir, you should create a directory somewhere in your tree and log it there. For lists you want to digest, you'll make a directory with that name later. For $sendmail_command, find the correct location by typing which sendmail from your shell, then plug in it with correct Perl syntax. I then left the rest of the variables as the defaults. For security, this is best unless you are an experienced system administrator. From your command line, type make wrapper, just to confirm that things are going smoothly. It might return some path information, which is fine.

Now you must change yourself to either root or the Majordomo user to compile the wrapper. It's not complicated, but if you have no sysadmin experience you may want help. From the shell prompt, type make install, which, if successful, will deliver an instruction telling you to type make install-wrapper. If you do that and it is successful, you will then be asked to type wrapper config-test, which will either deliver nicely explained error messages or the screen in Figure 8.1, which invites you to register the software (don't yet). On my first test (so detailed I had to use wrapper config-test |more to read it all), I had forgotten to escape an @ sign in the $whoami-owner. I also had left $TMPDIR as the default, which the wrapper did not recognize. There were other errors below it that didn't make sense, so I fixed the obvious two. Then I ran the config-test again and got a clean bill of health. Again, wait two steps to register it.

Make sure all the directories you've listed in the config are created and set to CHMOD 777. You should have, off of the home directory, a lists directory plus two others called tmp and digest, located wherever you listed them in the config. If

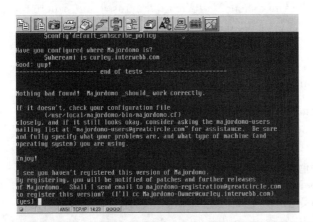

Figure 8.1 If your permissions are correct, you'll get these results from wrapper config-test.

you set the file to Log in the $log variable, make sure the directory (most likely in the home directory) is writeable to the Majordomo user.

Included in the distribution is a sample sendmail aliases file called majordomo .aliases. As the INSTALL file explains, you have several options for adding the needed entries. I chose to add the OA/path/to/majordomo/majordomo.aliases line into the sendmail.cf and to edit the existing file with the correct path information and addresses. You'll notice that there is also a sample list in there called test. Don't worry about it for now. The lines on my system are as follows:

```
majordomo:  "|/usr/local/majordomo/bin/wrapper majordomo"

majordomo-owner: majordomo-owner@world-media.com

owner-majordomo: owner-majordomo@world-media.com
```

Once you've added the line to sendmail.cf and edited majordomo.aliases, you must refreeze the sendmail.cf by executing sendmail -bz, then restart with sendmail -bd -q 15m. That should reload the changes and allow you to move on. Now (with thanks to Gregory Neil Shapiro who found this quirk for me), type newaliases at the command line. It will make a file called majordomo.aliases.db in the same directory (if you correctly made that directory writeable).

Change back to a nonprivileged user (su - yourlogin) and try running the config-test again on the wrapper. If you experience no errors, which I did and easily fixed, you'll get an option to e-mail a registration again automatically. This time I suggest you accept the invitation as it will notify you of bug reports and new version announcements.

Step 10 in the INSTALL file is twofold. First, you are to create an empty lists file by typing the command touch /path/to/majordomo/bin/lists/test, which will make an empty file in the lists directory. Then, send a test message from your shell with echo 'lists' |mail majordomo, which will deliver a status message from the Majordomo program with the lists it serves. The first line creates a dummy test list. If it's working properly, the message you'll get will look like the following code. If not, it will look like a regular mail message. For me, not being advised of the newaliases command prevented a solid install. I had to go out and search for answers. If you are having difficulty, check out the Majordomo FAQ at www.math.psu.edu/barr/majordomo faq.html. If it appears to be a sendmail problem, I was able to get help from the page at www.sendmail.org.

```
>>>> lists

Majordomo@curley.interwebb.com serves the following lists:


   test


Use the 'info <list>' command to get more information

about a specific list.

>>>>

>>>>
```

Creating a List

Now that we've got Majordomo up and running, creating a list should be easy. The documentation comes with a file called NEWLIST, which I'll follow as I did with INSTALL earlier. The steps are laid out cleanly. I'll merely elaborate for those of us to whom Unix-speak is foreign. The examples I'll use will set up a list for discussion on this book and all its utilities, so wish me luck. I say this to take out the intimidation factor. This stuff is cryptic, but a beginner (me) can figure it out with some patience and trial and error.

Names of lists can be only letters, numbers, or the dash or underscore characters, so a list could be Lewis-Clark, but not Lewis&Clark. They are not case sensitive anywhere but in our setup, so keep your alias and config entries in all lowercase. Here we go.

Earlier, you created a sample list called test with the touch command. Now, in the lists directory again, do the same for this list you are about to activate. In my example, it is touch webtoolkit. CHMOD the file you just created to 664 (the default is probably 644). Make sure you are logged in as a user in the Majordomo group for this. Otherwise, set it to 666.

Open your text editor and create a file called *listname*.info (webtoolkit.info for me). It should contain some introductory words welcoming people to the list, along with any and all topics you plan to discuss. CHMOD 664 the info file, unless Majordomo is not in the group you create the file from. In that case, CHMOD it 666.

Next we add more aliases to the majordomo.aliases file. These are in the same
format you saw earlier, an e-mail alias on the system (the name before the @your-
domain.com), followed by a colon and a destination address. The destination, as
you'll see next, can be a user on the system (where we just plug in the name), a program (as in wrapper) and its arguments, another e-mail alias (as in owner-
webtoolkit), or an e-mail address outside the system. The following entries are the
basics that I've derived from the NEWLIST file. Between my examples and their
examples, you should get a good feel for what's needed. To translate a bit, the first
line says "pipe the message sent to webtoolkit to the wrapper program, which will
activate the resend program for the list webtoolkit." It will also send to the second
line, webtoolkit-list, to get its addresses.

```
webtoolkit:"|/usr/local/majordomo/bin/wrapper resend -l webtoolkit webtoolkit-
list

webtoolkit-list:    :include:/usr/local/majordomo/bin/lists/webtoolkit

owner-webtoolkit:    paulh

webtoolkit-owner:    paulh

webtoolkit-request: "|/usr/local/majordomo/bin/wrapper majordomo -l webtoolkit"

webtoolkit-approval: paulh
```

Run the newaliases command again. It should return a message with how many
new aliases are indexed and their size. To clarify a bit from step 4 in the NEWLIST
file, make a directory called yourlist.archive off of the lists directory. For my list, I'll
type cd lists, mkdir webtoolkit.archive, chmod 775 webtoolkit.archive (only if
you're logged in as someone in the Majordomo group; otherwise set it 777). We'll
set this up in the next section. Same thing for digests if you wish to give your participants that option. We haven't included it yet in the alias file but will get to it
soon. In majordomo.cf you listed a $digest_work_dir. Now go to that directory and
create a directory with the name of the digest list. My commands are: cd digests,
mkdir webtoolkit-digest, chmod webtoolkit-digest 775. Your tree is now complete.

Make sure that all your directories are 755 (drwxr-xr-x with an ls -l command)
and all files are 664 (-rw-rw-r— with the same). That's if you're logged in and the
files are owned by someone in the Majordomo group. Otherwise, set them to 777
and 666, but take my warning that this can be dangerous if you are not the only
person on the server as everyone can read, write, and execute your files.

The next and final step in the NEWLISTS file confused me. It directs "Now issue a 'config <listname> <listname>.admin' command to Majordomo." How? After much deliberation I figured out that this means e-mail majordomo@yourserver.com with text in the message body that says :config webtoolkit webtoolkit.admin. It sends you back a configuration file, which you then remail to Majordomo with updated information.

In my mail program (Pine), I had to export the message out to text, then read it back in (control R) rather than send it as a reply. The > symbols broke it. Whatever mail program you are using, make sure your return message is stripped of them. Mail it back to majordomo@yourdomain.com. The following steps are the individual values in the config.

At the top of the message body, type newconfig yourlist yourlist.admin. The yourlist.admin is the temporary password Majordomo automatically sets for you. Then leave a blank line, then import the text of the config. Figure 8.2 shows that I imported it in Pine. (I could have also forwarded the message rather than import to leave out the > marks.) One note before we move on is that there is no $ at the beginning or ; at the end of any config settings as we're accustomed to in Perl. Many of these we'll leave as the defaults.

The beginning of the file contains a whole bunch of commented text. Some of it was confusing the first time I read it, but became more clear as I set the individual values. The comment characters (#), here documents, and regular expressions are the same in Chapter 6's Perl basics. The values are preceded by a basic definition

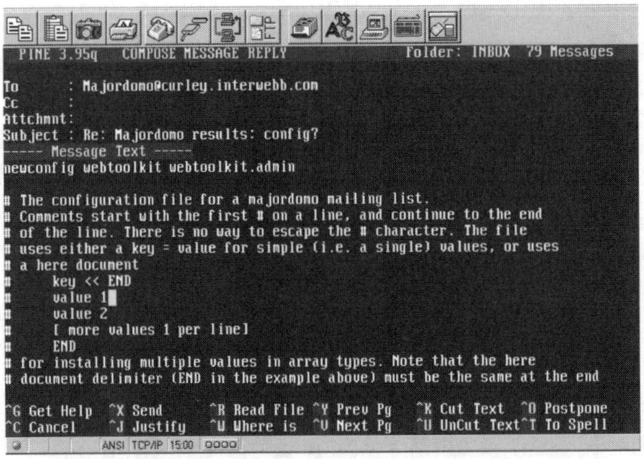

Figure 8.2 The sample list configuration file.

with the [type of input expected], the (default value in case it is missing), and the [program that calls it]. Sometimes the default of a value is undefined. This is shown as (undef) as the default in the explanation, but is left blank in the actual config variable.

Scroll down to the admin_password. As you can see, it's set to yourlist.admin as I explained earlier. Reset it to your password, and write it down as admin in your notes. There is another password, so don't confuse them. Leave administravia as the default yes. It forward all those "How do I unsubscribe" messages to the list owner instead of the whole list.

I set advertise with the regular expression /.*/, which means that anyone sending a lists command to Majordomo will get back a message with this list included. This variable is useful for those of you with a list that targets a special company or community. In that case, set it to /.edu/ if only students participate, or /ibm\.com/ for only employees of IBM.

The approve_passwd variable is the other password I mentioned. You, the list owner, will send this back for any approvals of questionable messages. Replace the yourlist.pass with your own value and record it as the approve password in your notes.

The archive directory does not presently work from the list config. Ignore it. If you have any comments that you wish to keep from config to config, place them here as future comments could be erased. The comments variable is always left in tact.

The date_intro and date_info are both useful for people requesting information about the list from other than e-mail. The default, yes, on both, should be left alone unless they are offensive. Set the next variable, debug, to "no" unless you are just testing and don't want messages sent.

Description is a useful addition that provides up to about 50 characters worth of informational text about the list. It's only sent when someone sends a lists command to Majordomo. Instead of just the blind list name they get this appended.

Ignore the next variable digest_archive because it doesn't yet work. But the digest_issue is very important. If you've had an online discussion before installing Majordomo you might want to set this higher than 1 to reflect that there are old archives. Likewise for digest_maxdays. Depending on the activity on the list, you might want to set this at a low value so people don't get three-week old messages. This relates to the next variable, digest_maxlength. It is the number of lines the digest must grow to before sending an issue. I set 400 as a test (even though we have yet to configure digest). I altered the digest_name variable because the default is all lowercase. Set it how you wish. As with the previous two, digest_rm_ footer and _fronter are not yet working. I don't know why they include them. Digest_volume is again for those who have used previous means to post earlier versions of the list. The help text says not to touch digest_work_dir, so I didn't.

The next four variables were confusing to me at first. They all control who has control to different commands sent via e-mail. The three possibilities are open, closed, and list. Open allows anyone to issue the get (list), index, info, and intro commands. Closed bans the command altogether, and list opens the command to only those listed in the files in restrict_post, which we'll cover later.

The next variable, maxlength, is set to a default of 40,000 characters. This controls how big posts can be and is there more to prevent the attachment of large binaries than anything else. Keep in mind that you, the list owner, will get bounced messages of greater value. Watch for virus-laden software.

The message_footer, _fronter, and _header are up to you. They provide two variables: the actual $SENDER e-mail of the message and the $LIST from which the message came. I set the footer to: "This was generated by $SENDER. As part of an automated email list. If you did not subscribe remove yourself by sending to $LIST the message unsubscribe\@$whoami."

I set the moderator to no because this list doesn't require it. But if you do choose to moderate and that moderator is other than the list owner, the next variable, moderator, allows you to set a full, qualified e-mail address.

If you've ever been on an educational institution's system for e-mail you'll understand the next variable. Most such systems change the domain part of your e-mail address regularly. One week you're youraddress@machine.yourdomain.edu and the next week you're youraddress@othermachine.yourdomain.edu. This can be true in large corporations as well. With mungedomain, everything but the top-level domain is stripped, preventing confusion on incoming mails if your address does not match exactly. Set it to yes if you expect list members to face this difficulty.

The counter to advertise is noadvertise, the next variable. If you've made a private list just for your customers and want to remove this list's name from a competitor's employees, put /competitiondomain.com/ between the END signs. It overrides advertise.

For most systems, leave the mail precedence to bulk. I didn't understand the point of purge_received, so I left it at no. Reply to is best left alone and empty according to the man pages, but my setup was keeping the from line as the actual sender, not the list, so I added the name of the list into that field. That way people at least have the easy option to reply publicly. The resend_host variable alters the $whoami of majordomo.cf. This is important should you wish to use several virtual domains.

The next variable, restrict_post is very important. It's referenced whenever someone sends a post to the list as well as all the access variables above and below. It is undefined by default, but it's common practice to set it to the name of the list. For more than one list, put their names one after another separated by a space or a colon. Sender should be left as the default owner-*yourlist*. It is the first part of the e-mail address with administrative information for the list. The resend_host variable is appended to it after an @ sign.

The yes/no value in strip decides whether just the raw e-mail address or the entire commented address is saved for subscribers of the list. I left it at no. You might want to disable set it as yes if the names of your list members should be kept anonymous, even to you. Subject_prefix is the word begging all resent mail from the list in the subject line of the message, like Webtoolkit:.

I set subscribe_policy to open+confirm, which means that anyone can subscribe only themselves to the list. Majordomo checks the from address and matches it against subscribe webtoolkit mayname@mayaddress.com. The confirm option, the same for all policies, sends a message back to the sender asking that they confirm their registration with a coded return e-mail. It's an extra step, but will prevent people from subscribing people to your list by mistake, thinking they were only sending a message. If I had chosen auto+confirm, it would allow anybody to subscribe anybody, which can be helpful if there is a department head who must subscribe new hires or a customer of yours who wants to subscribe her or his customers. Closed lists bounce all subscribe and unsubscribe requests to the list owner for approval.

I actually used taboo_body, showing my age and New Hampshire conservative tendencies. I don't want people saying the book stinks or using profanity, so, in /regular expression brackets/, I placed words some of my readers might find offensive. Keep each one on its own line, stacked on top of one another.

T I P Some lists have had problems with Microsoft's e-mail programs. A recent post by Peter Bostrom to Majordomo-users fixed this with the taboo_header variable in the list config like so:

```
taboo_headers       <<   END

/^content-transfer-encoding: quoted-printable/i

END
```

He also suggests advising Microsoft users to turn off Rich Text Formatting.

Taboo_headers is the same, but intended more to catch small binary viruses. You could test for mime type, or other potentially bad information in headers. Again, keep in mind that you, the list owner, will be getting messages for approval. The unsubscribe_policy is the same as subscribe. Be careful if you're worried that a competitor or hacker would want to unsubscribe your list.

The next two variables are again, access restrictions. I set which open; it merely queries which list a user belongs to. I closed the who command; it's nobody's business who is subscribed to my list.

One final note is that Majordomo sends back >>>> at the end of the config. Get rid of it. The line above it, last modified, is commented, and so is fine. If everything is configured properly, Majordomo should now work seamlessly.

User Commands to Majordomo

Now that you are up and running, try a few commands to test if your customization options worked. First, to majordomo@yourcompany.com, send a message with a blank subject (it doesn't have to be blank but Majordomo ignores it) and body of subscribe yourlistname, where the list is the actual name of your list. The other option is to send to yourlistname-request@yourcompany.com with just subscribe in the body.

If you chose the +confirm in the majordomo.cf, you'll get back two messages: one with the title Majordomo Results, which acknowledges your subscribe request and provides directions for the other message, and a second (you may get it first due to Internet unpredictability) called Confirmation for subscribe *listname* (Figure 8.3).

It is your authorization code. Use your reply function to respond and remove all lines but the one beginning with auth and send it back to majordomo@yourcompany.com. You'll then get a Welcome message. One warning: you may want to leave your list at open rather than auto. My mailer (Pine) couldn't subscribe to majordomo-users@greatcircle.com because I'm using a virtual as my From. Technically, my mail is paulh@tiac.net, but they forward all my mail @world-media.com into that account. For some reason, the Greatcircle Majordomo read in my name from the <> portion and didn't like it. After several attempts, by altering the authorization code, I was finally able to subscribe. These are the other commands users may send to Majordomo and their results.

unsubscribe mylist. It does as you might imagine, but surprisingly this command generates the most errors for users. They send it to listname@ instead of majordomo@, so it then gets bounced to the list owner.

which. It's how you ask Majordomo which lists you are subscribed to. If you optionally type an e-mail address after it on the same line, it will return the results for that user. This can be a good tool for IS managers who need to report on usage for your own internal lists. You can also send a partial e-mail address, like just yourcompany.com, to see which lists all members of your company are subscribed to.

who. We visited this in our configuration settings. If you left the who access open, anyone can send this command with the listname appended and get the e-mail addresses (and their names if you didn't strip them) for the entire list. Try sending e-mail to majordomo@greatcircle.com with the subject who majordomo-users. I should be on it, as will the list owner, Brent Chapman.

info. This works much the same way, but sends that .info file we created earlier.

index. Sometimes list owners archive back issues of the list, as well as additional help files and useful software. Sending this command to majordomo@ with the name of the list after it in the body of your message returns a complete file list. Figure 8.4 shows the top of the message returned.

get. This is how you retrieve those files. You would send e-mail to majordomo @greatcircle.com with get majordomo-users majordomo.users.9209 in the body of the message. It returns two messages. The first confirms your get request, the second is the actual file.

lists. As you can see (and we'll install), Majordomo can handle many lists at one time. Sending this command gives you a list of all on any one system.

help. Are these explanations confusing? If so, the help command will give you a more detailed explanation. It's very easy to understand and gives numerous examples. For users, who you'll support as the list owner, help is great because it automatically interpolates the $whoami variable from the majordomo.cf configuration file. The help file is also sent whenever someone sends a bad command to Majordomo.

end. If you've been testing these commands as we go, they are breaking if you include a signature line below the commands in body of your e-mail. Placing the word "end" on a line by itself makes Majordomo ignore all commands after it. This also works for multiple commands at once. Try putting info list-name, index listname, and who listname and end, each on a separate line and by itself, in the body of your e-mail message to majordomo@greatcircle.com. You'll get back a long message with all three responses.

List Administration Commands to Majordomo

Hidden in the original directory structure you got by untaring the Majordomo archive is a Doc directory. Go there now and check out the file list-owner-info. You'll distribute this to the owners and moderators of lists for the system, so you should understand it thoroughly. It begins by asking the list owner to send a newinfo command to the list and to make sure that the list owner is subscribed. Then it gives a brief overview of the public commands, and it explores the undocumented commands kept aside for list owners. Here's an overview.

Figure 8.3 Confirmation for subscribe *listname*.

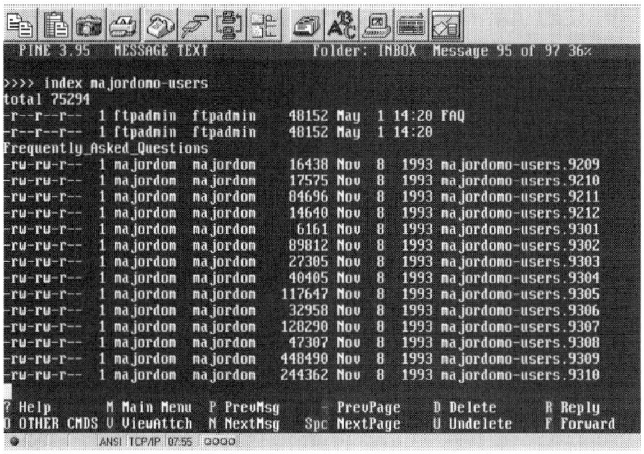

Figure 8.4 Index Command.

approve. This is how you approve subscriptions to closed lists. You'll also use it for people who subscribe from other than their own e-mail address (usually they have multiple addresses). In the body of your message to Majordomo type approve password subscribe listname email@address exactly in that syntax where password is the first password in your list config called admin-passwd, not approve_passwd. This works exactly the same for unsubscribe.

approve (who). If you set up your list with the who command as closed, the only way to access the names on your list is through a password system. It's much like the subscribe: approve password who listname with the same admin password as the last. It should return a list of all your subscribers' e-mail addresses, as well as the number of subscribers and their names if you did not strip them in your listname configuration file.

passwd. This is handy for list owners who might be using an employee to moderate the list. If that employee leaves, or you are using a different volunteer or intern every week, this command gives you the power to change the admin password remotely at any time. Send to Majordomo the message passwd list-name oldpassword newpassword where passwd is not your password, but the actual command and the old and new passwords are again the administrative.

newintro. When you subscribe to any list you automatically get back the file we created called listname.intro. It says "Hey, Welcome to the list, don't do anything nasty." This command lets you change the text to include new happenings and events if they are appropriate, as they come up from a remote location. Put newintro list password on a line by itself, then follow it with your new text.

Majordomo reads everything in after the newintro line until the end of your e-mail or the word EOF on a line by itself. If successful, Majordomo will send you back a results message. If it fails, it also sends a message to the Majordomo overseer. In my case, I had accidentally left the webtoolkit.intro file at 664, but had been root when I created it, so Majordomo couldn't rewrite it. The overseer message easily diagnosed the problem.

config. This retrieves the latest copy of the list config file. Its syntax is config listname password, where password is the admin as before. Send that in the body of your message to Majordomo and it will return a documented copy of your current configuration. We did this earlier when setting up the webtoolkit list.

newconfig. Again, we did this with the setup earlier. By editing the default config and sending it to majordomo@ with newconfig listname password as the first line, you will update the variables for the list. Keep in mind that you send the old password, not the new one, if you've changed it in the update you are sending.

writeconfig. I found this to be a strange command at first. It's mainly for updating your config for new versions of Majordomo. When you install a new version it will have new variables that become active with their instructions on how to set them up. The writeconfig reads in the old variables and places them in the new template. So if you've removed all the coaching instructions from your list config (like I have), writeconfig will put all that stuff back in, with the new stuff added.

approve. If you set up your list as closed, or even if it's open and you restricted who could post or what words were not allowed, you'll get messages with the word BOUNCE as the first word in the subject.

Configuring Digests

Just about any list you're on will have a few people complaining that there are too many posts and "when can we get a digest version?" I hate digests, but that's besides the point. If you create a Majordomo list you need them. Your customers will demand it.

What's a digest? Some of you are asking that I'm sure. It's a system you set up in Majordomo that sends multiple messages at one time, cutting down on the number of messages users receive and (supposedly) saving them the time of wading through them. The number of messages that digest cues before sending is dependent upon the length variables we set in the config. We'll make some modifications to the Majordomo alias file as we go, and in fact, create a whole new list, called webtoolkit-digest. We've already done a few of the steps needed by creating the digest and archive directories. I'll follow the same format with numbered steps and explain the process in detail. You'll find some basic install documentation beyond what's here in README.digest, which is located in the Doc directory off the original untar directory.

First we need to make a list like we did for the main webtoolkit. In the lists directory, create the file webtoolkit-digest with the same touch webtoolkit-digest command. Make sure you are logged in as user Majordomo or someone in the same group. Set the permissions with CHMOD 664 webtoolkit-digest. Check to make sure you have the digest and directory permissions set to 775 or 777. The README.digest says to create them here, but we already did. Now we make changes to the alias file. I followed the NEWLIST directions almost exactly and it worked fine. This is my sample configuration, but note that there may be some line wraps in the printed version.

```
webtoolkit:      "|/usr/local/majordomo/bin/wrapper resend -l webtoolkit
webtoolkit-outgoing"

webtoolkit-digest: webtoolkit

#webtoolkit-list:  :include:/usr/local/majordomo/bin/lists/webtoolkit

webtoolkit-outgoing: :include:/usr/local/majordomo/bin/lists/webtoolkit,

        "| /usr/local/majordomo/bin/wrapper digest -r -C -l webtoolkit-digest
webtoolkit-digest-outgoing",

                "| /usr/local/majordomo/bin/wrapper archive2.pl -a  -m

                -f /usr/local/majordomo/bin/lists/webtoolkit.archive"




owner-webtoolkit:    paulh@world-media.com

owner-webtoolkit-outgoing: owner-webtoolkit
```

```
webtoolkit-owner:    paulh@world-media.com

owner-webtoolkit-digest:owner-webtoolkit

owner-webtoolkit-digest-outgoing:owner-webtoolkit


webtoolkit-request: "|/usr/local/majordomo/bin/wrapper request-answer webtoolkit"

webtoolkit-digest-request: "|/usr/local/majordomo/bin/wrapper request-answer

webtoolkit-digest"


webtoolkit-approval: paulh@world-media.com

test-digest-approval: webtoolkit-approval
```

On the CD Look in the /sourcecode/UNIX/majordomo/tips directory for a sample file.

As you can see, we've eliminated the webtoolkit-list (by placing a # in front of it) and created several other aliases to assist us in generating a digest list. The first major one is test-outgoing. The webtoolkit alias is sent to it through resend in the first line. The first thing webtoolkit does is include the webtoolkit mail list for resend, then it sends the same text through digest, then through archive, with lots of information piped into archive2.pl. This means that any mail message sent to webtoolkit@curley.interwebb.com is sent to the list, digest, and archive. In NEWLIST, this is the suggestion, so that's what I did. The other aliases I added were to webtoolkit-request and digest-request. It seems the request-answer program handles them in a special way, so I used it as the NEWLIST suggests.

The flags to digest are -r, which means use the size and time elements in the configuration file to decide when to send digests, -C, which tells Majordomo to use the standard majordomo.cf and webtoolkit-digest.cf, and -l with the webtoolkit-digest list specified.

Next I cheated. The directions say to send the config command to Majordomo with the password webtoolkit-digest.admin, like we did for the main list, but all it really needs are the digest variables. Everything else is the same. In fact, it appears we didn't even need the digest variables in the original config after all, but I don't have the guts to disable them. I cheated by sending a config webtoolkit mypassword to Majordomo, receiving my config, then forwarding it back to Majordomo with the command newconfig webtoolkit-digest webtoolkit-digest.admin. Now I've got my settings and the same password and settings for both lists. Note also that I plan to redo this every time I update the webtookit config.

If you get a message back from Majordomo with the subject MAJORDOMO ABORT (mj_digest) with the body:

MAJORDOMO ABORT (mj_digest)!!

No messages.

Stopped

you've probably got a file-globbing problem with your shell. A patch is posted by Dave Wolfe, a frequenter of Majordomo-users at www.hpc.uh.edu/majordomo-workers/9703/msg00071.html. This was over my head so my sysadmin people handled it. I'd suggest the same unless you are comfortable with both Perl and advanced Unix-speak.

If all your settings are correct, a new digest should go out whenever the limits you specified in the listname-digest configuration are met. Send the command subscribe listname-digest to majordomo@ before trying it, then send a really big couple of messages to listname@yourdomain and see if it works. On my first try, I had messed up a few of the aliases, but if you've followed my format there should be no problems.

If this doesn't work for you, try looking in the file quick-digest-setup, which is a text file in the Doc directory where you originally installed Majordomo. It has a less complicated version that is not as comprehensive as the preceding one, but gets the job done.

SVList: NT (and Windows 95) Only

I didn't think something like Majordomo existed for NT until I ran across this little utility from Soft Ventures of Calgary, Canada. It gives you almost complete functionality from within an easy-to-use interface. All it requires is that you have a POP mail account at an ISP, so even the Unix devotees among you should give it a look if you use a Windows 95 box at all.

You probably won't want to use your standard e-mail account for this. Ask your ISP for a second mailbox, which most will give you for free and those who don't will charge only a few bucks. You can, technically, use only one box with one of SVList's options, which I'll cover, but for ease of use for both you and your users it's best to get a second box with a name like mylist@isp.net. The name should be intuitive as people will send all correspondence to the list.

SVList checks that new mailbox and downloads messages to your hard drive. Don't confuse it with your normal e-mail, even though it works the same. Think of the new box as just a second e-mail account that has nothing to do with the administration of the list. You'll have to subscribe just like everyone else, and you'll be subject to SVList's controls, so watch out. You don't want to have to ban yourself.

The file as of August 1997 is in the /software directory as the file SVList21.exe. You might want to get the latest from Soft Ventures at www.cadvision.com/ softventures/. It lists all their products and offers you two versions of SVList, one built for systems running remote access and one for those who aren't. Version 2.1 was released in May of 1997. I should note here that SVList has a strange key system to unlock the software when you register it. The key works for only two weeks, then is dead and you have to get a new one. It's meant to prevent people who post keys to newsgroups from distributing a particular version's key and giving away the program for free. It's only thirty bucks. Some people...

If you run the SVList.exe, you'll see that it's a standard Winzip self extractor. Click Setup and it will install Winzip in the directory you specify automatically (SVL21C is the default). Now if you run the program, you'll get a menu with a button that says Check Mail Now at the top. For now, ignore everything on this page and go into the File menu and Properties/Preferences.

You'll get a menu like that in Figure 8.5, which automatically pops up the Setup menu. Plug in the e-mail address of the second account I suggested you get or your single e-mail address if you chose to go that route.

Set the POP3, which should look something like granite.interwebb.com or some such mail server at the ISP you use. The SMTP server may be the same or may be different. It depends on your ISP, but make sure you don't assume that these are the

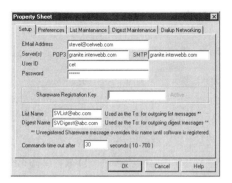

Figure 8.5 SVList menu options.

same. A wrong entry will break the functionality. Plug in your user ID and password. It should be the same one you use for your login.

The shareware copy you're using won't let you change the list name until you register it and pay the $30 license fee. The digest name is the same, so don't bother changing it until you register it. This is not a time limited copy, but it will say Unregistered on all list e-mail. You can leave the Commands time out after ## seconds. Unless you're on a modem under 14,400 baud, leave this at 30.

Next click the Preferences tab. The first box is Check mail on startup/Check every # minutes. This tells SVList whether to check your mailbox when the program starts up or to wait for you to click that Check Mail Now button we ignored before. They make it optional because not all of us are connected to the Internet all the time. The # minutes is the same. Only use it if you expect to be connected to the Internet when you launch SVList.

Moderated List means that you will be asked whether a message is OK when a new message comes into the list. If you expect a ton of messages from people who don't belong, you might want to check it. Keep in mind, though, that moderating a list is very time-consuming. The added feature that this gives you is that you can approve subscriptions to the list. This is the first of two ways, the second of which I'll get to soon. It also will control whether people can unsubscribe each other as you'll be approving every message that comes in.

The next tag is fairly important but may sound confusing on first look. When SVList creates a list, by default everyone subscribed to the list is able to post e-mail messages. If you check News Letter Mode, it turns that off. Only approved authors, which we'll set under the next tab, can post, so the list is more of a newsletter than a listserv-type mailing list. In this way SVList is almost as effective as Tickler, but does not provide a user-selection of different types of content.

Only Post Messages From Members is one lesser step of control for basic administration. It prevents people from spamming the list. Someone could still subscribe, spam, then unsubscribe, but they would at least be forced to give you their real e-mail address. We'll address this with the next tab as well.

The way people SUBSCRIBE, UNSUBSCRIBE, GET, and receive a DIRectory of files, and find out WHO participates in the list is by sending the keywords I just capitalized in the subject of messages to the list. Use Command Prefix is for lists that might have those administration words in normal subject matter, such as "Who does Bill Gates think he is?" or "What happens when I subscribe to the paper journal." By checking this option you force people to put some symbol before all commands to the list (% by default), so rather than send SUBSCRIBE in your subject, you'll instead send %SUBSCRIBE.

Use List Message Prefix is used only when you use your regular e-mail address for the mailing list. It forces people to put some character at the beginning of their subjects to tell SVList to extract and resend it. This symbol (I suggest a #) says "Hey, I'm for the list." Otherwise it's a standard e-mail to you and SVList ignores it.

Limit message size is there so you can prevent people from posting software or images to the list and eating your system resources. The default is set to 2500 characters, plenty for all but the lengthiest tombs of e-mail messages. You might want to jack this up if you intend to send a newsletter that is more than ten typed, double-spaced or five single-spaced pages.

The Set FROM and REPLY-TO addresses can be checked for either the list name or the sender's name. If you've ever been on a mailing list you'll understand the difference. If not, it might sound confusing, but isn't. When someone sends a message to the list, everyone on the list receives it. Then, preferably, they use the reply function in their e-mail program to reply, including >quoted lines to reference what the person said. The default for both of these is list address, not sender address, but I suggest you check Originator's Address in the FROM option. Most e-mail programs will send your reply to the list, but show you the message-author's e-mail address in case you want to reply privately. Pine, a Unix shell mail program (common on university systems) gives you a choice of who to send the reply to, but most don't. This configuration, with the list name as the REPLY-TO and author as the FROM, will be the most versatile for your users.

The disable commands menu is another way to control who can do what and when. The WHO command is the most sensitive of these. When someone sends it to your list they get back a complete message of everyone's e-mail address who's subscribed. This could be sensitive for fields ranging from politics and law to porn, so be sensitive to the needs of your list members when setting it. Most lists should disable it. It will prevent spammers from grabbing your list's address as well.

GET and DIR work together. If someone sends a DIR to the list, they get back a complete list of files from the /get directory under the main directory where you installed SVList. This can be digests, images, or software, but all binaries must be UUENCODED first as SVList does not encode. Disabling the GET command will allow people to find out what's there, but not allow them to grab it, so enable or disable both at the same time. Note, however, that the only directory it accesses is the /get directory, so your private files are not in danger.

The SUBSCRIBE disable is the other way I mentioned earlier to prevent people from subscribing themselves to and from the list for spamming or other activities they shouldn't do. If you check this, all subscribers will have to be added manually, which we'll cover on the next tab.

Next, we move to SUBSCRIBE requests and its options. Normal allows both digest and normal list. What they get depends on whether the word DIGEST is in their subject when they subscribe. Force List Only and Force Digest Only make SVList ignore the DIGEST command and subscribe everybody to whatever is checked.

The last checkbox is the logs. If you check it, it makes you a text file of all activity to the list. Click OK and we'll divert from the setup for a bit.

You can now test SVList by sending an e-mail to the e-mail you specified with the word subscribe in the subject. If you allowed it, you'll be subscribed automatically. If you send the subject subscribe digest, you'll get that instead whenever you manually delete a digest.

Now click Check Mail Now on the front screen. If you chose to moderate the list it will ask you to approve a message with the screen in Figure 8.6. You can click OK, which either processes a command (subscribe, unsubscribe, etc.) or posts a message to the board—delete, which does not post and deletes the message from the server; or ignore, which doesn't send or delete. Click OK to approve your subscriptions. You'll see the counter for list members and digest members jump accordingly.

Now send a few test messages to the list. If you signed up for the regular list, you'll get them back (and so will everyone else). If you subscribed only to the digest, you'll get nothing, but the digests counter will increment.

Once you have a few messages in the digest, try sending one. Click Compile and Send Digest. It will ask you if you wish to save it before sending, which will make it accessible to DIR and GET. Click Yes (or No) and save it as a digest filename in the /GET directory, which you'll have to create manually with the Windows or NT Explorer. Then see what you get at the mailbox you subscribed to digest from. If the digest sends, you're all set with the basic configuration. Try sending a DIR and GET if you enabled it. It should send back a file list and the file, respectively. The syntax for GET is GET filename.txt and will also work for uuencoded binary files.

Controlling a List

Figure 8.7 is a picture of the next tab, List Maintenance. It allows you to fully maintain the users on a list and to control the text that accompanies all messages. First, highlight the user name, then check the level of access they warrant. Full access allows them carte blanche for the list within the parameters you set under the preferences tab. Receive only will disable them from posting, but allow everything else. Post only is just the opposite; it disables your receipt of messages. Inactive lets you put someone on hold without removing them. Banned prevents any messages from hitting the list. Add new is to enter names into the database without making people subscribe. Delete gets rid of them permanently.

At the bottom of the screen are the three administrative text file options for the list. The welcome file is sent when someone subscribes. It should contain a brief

Figure 8.6 The approval screen.

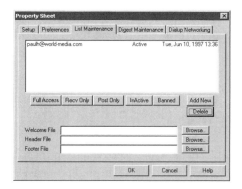

Figure 8.7 The List Maintenance tab.

introduction, mission statement, and list rules. It should also contain unsubscribe information and an explanation of the digest option, DIR and GET. The header and footer files are the text that wraps around all messages resent from the list. The header should read "This is a message from …" and the footer should include "To unsubscribe send e-mail with the word 'unsubscribe' as the subject to yourname@yourserver.com."

Digest Maintenance, the next tab, only has two other options. It lets you manually set (or reset after you've tested) the digest number. Disable subject list gets rid of the opening listing of message titles at the beginning of digest messages.

The last tab, Dialup Networking, selects the network connection SVList should use to log you onto the Internet when you click Check Mail Now from the main menu or when it automatically checks for incoming messages. This is meant for people who don't or can't leave their computer connected to the Internet all the time but need frequent list cycling. SVList will log you on, check and resend the list mail, then log off. Disable it if you plan to check the mail manually when you're online already. If you use it, plug in the appropriate values.

One thing to remember about SVList is that it only works when you check and resend the mail. It's not a server-based application, so unless you can regularly attend to it, set up as much automated as possible and don't moderate.

Setting Up a Web Virtual with SVList

Believe it or not, setting a list at listname@yourcompany.com is as easy as changing one field in SVList and phoning your ISP with the instruction to create a POP mailbox for that user. The field is in the File/Properties/Preferences menu. Click the Setup tab and change the e-mail address from yourname@yourISP.net to listname@yourcompany.com. That's it. Now send mail to the list and make sure the Reply To: field is set correctly and that mail is resent.

A Simple Mailing List with Pine

Though I don't think you could get a simpler and more cost-effective system than SVList (it was one of my "finds" while researching for the book), it might be easier for some of you just to use the addressbook feature in Pine to handle a simple mailing list. I wouldn't use this for more than ten users posting more than twenty messages a week. All it requires is a shell account on just about any Unix server. Most ISPs charge about $10 a month for this and should have pine installed on their system. If not, they'll put in for you. If you already have a PPP and have never seen a shell, it's like dealing with the old DOS text interface. You'll Telnet from your PPP to it with a terminal program. If you're on Windows 95 or NT, go to your Run menu and type "telnet." A window will pop up. Pull down the Connect menu and Remote System. There you'll type in the name the ISP assigns you and log in with your name and password. Once you get a prompt with either a % or $ in it, type "pine" (no quotes). Figure 8.8 is the main menu.

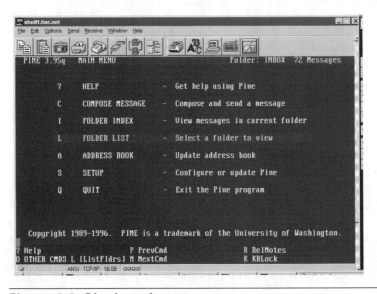

Figure 8.8 Pine's main menu.

On the CD In the software/ directory you'll find the 32-bit version of NetTerm, a great Telnet client. It's the file nt32420.exe. You'll also find the 16-bit version and more information at its homepage:

starbase.neosoft.com/~zkrr01/

You'll use the shell account as your e-mail box for the list and Telnet in to do your maintenance. All messages coming in will be forwarded to the list via Pine's forward command, but we'll get to that. First go to the address book window by typing "a" from the main menu. Then, once you are in the address book, type "n" for new entry. The entry screen will pop up and allow you to give the list a nickname and put in a comma-separated list of e-mail addresses in the last field. Press Control-X to save it.

Now any messages that come in to the list can be forwarded with only a few commands. First, send an e-mail or two to the "list." Then go into the shell and reopen Pine, typing "i" after it's running. This will take you to the inbox of the messages you just sent. Now type a semicolon (;). It will then ask you for a select criteria. Type "a" for all messages, then "a" again for apply command. Next type "f" for forward, and then in the To: e-mail field, type the name of the list entry you made in the address book. Press Control-X to send, and answer "y" for yes.

You'll now either want to delete or archive your messages. Type "a" again, which will let you apply another command. To delete them, just type "d" and then "x" for expunge. To save them, type "s," which will give you a field into which you can type a folder name. You, at present, have no folders, so name one. Pine will ask if you want to create it. Answer "y" for yes. The messages will be saved and marked with a "d." When you quit Pine you'll have the option to expunge them, and you should. Control-X will expunge them before you quit.

Before you make the folder name, think about your archive structure. Should the folder be named november-97-list or something else time-specific? That way you can make a new folder at given intervals. Pine saves its folders of mail in the /mail directory, so from your login prompt type cd mail and do an ls command. You'll see your folders, which are really just text files of the messages stacked on top of each other.

9

Tracking Visitors

This a difficult chapter to write because there are so many ambiguities in tracking visits to your website. Page views? Hits? Is this total hits? Does this include images? We've tried to cut through all of that with the first utility I'll cover. It's called Trakkit and it reads log files created by SiteWrapper as it wraps pages. Any page called with a ?pagename.html URL can be logged. As for what these are, we call them *hits*, because hitting <SHIFT> while clicking Reload will increment the logfile by one. It doesn't matter whether visitors have their images on or off, as those ridiculous little speedometers do, and it's not necessary to put any numbers on your homepage for the whole world to see. Trakkit's logs are completely private and password protected by default, though I'll explain how to disable it.

The second part of the chapter is for those of you who don't install SiteWrapper. Analog is meant for sites made up of static pages. It will work with FrontPage, Fusion, or any other flat file (.htm or .html) based system of creating pages, as well as Microsoft's Active Server Pages. Analog's results aren't quite as easy to use as Trakkit's but they work. The install is harder for NT than Unix and much less practical to use, so NT users might want to look for another utility we found in our travels, called HitList Standard, which we found on the Microsoft developer site but were unable to distribute with the book. The basic version is free and does a pretty good job.

As far as what logs mean, that's up to you. We've found it most helpful not to take the absolute number of hits as a real number of visitors, but instead to set a benchmark for a customer and analyze how different print advertisements, Internet advertising, and search engine manipulation helps their total. Logs are also great to examine the usability of your interface. If nobody is visiting freestuff.html, chances are that the navigation to that page needs to be more prominent. If everyone jumps to your sneakers section from your socks page, which you hoped they would find after sneakers, move your navigation until that occurs. Creative uses of log files are unlimited, and Trakkit is a powerful tool to make your task a reality.

Quick Start: Unix

1. There are three files in the zip archive at /sourcecode/UNIX/trakkit/: trakkit.cgi, cyan.gif, and red.gif. Upload them into the base directory of the webserver where index.cgi is running.

2. Then check the Perl location at the #! top of trakkit.cgi. If it's different than yours, change it to the right location. This should be Perl 5.003 or better. If you're unsure of your Perl version, type perl -v at the shell prompt. If you don't know where Perl 5 is (you should by now), type which perl from the shell.

3. Before you close that file, hold up. You also have to change the require statement at line 10 in trakkit.cgi to the filename you changed config.cfg to in the installation of SiteWrapper. Be sure not to erase the semicolon, then save trakkit.cgi to the server.

4. Set the permissions on trakkit.cgi to execute with CHMOD 755 trakkit.cgi.

5. Make a directory called logs/ off the main (it has to be called logs). Set its permissions to CHMOD 777, allowing the webserver to read, write, and execute.

6. Then open your configuration file, config.cfg, or whatever you renamed it, in the text editor and add the variable called @logs. Basic instructions are in the file already, so you may have already done this in the SiteWrapper chapter. If not, you need to set the array with every page you'd like to log. Set it as @logs = ("home-page.htm","otherpage.htm","ourinfo.htm","lotsOitems.htm", "etc.htm");, making sure to include homepage.htm in the array (that's your homepage) and to finish the line with a semicolon.

7. Then, if you have Perl installed on your local machine, run a perl -c on it once you're done. I explained how to do this in the Perl chapter. If you have shell access to the server do it there.

8. Now hit your homepage several times, preferably from several different accounts. Then verify that log files are writing by looking in the logs/ directory. If you view them as text files, they're pretty cryptic, but don't worry, that's what Trakkit is for.

9. Then hit trakkit.cgi. If it gives you a server error, chances are you've not done a perl -c on it and a quote or something is missing in the config. One other source might be required files. You must have a config.cfg, or whatever you changed it to, and cgi-lib.pl, the library by Steven E. Brenner.

10. If you're successful, you should get a screen like Figure 9.1. Plug in your password, the one you encrypted with Encrypt.cgi in the SiteWrapper chapter, and check off your display choices and log files. Then click OK, Trakkit!

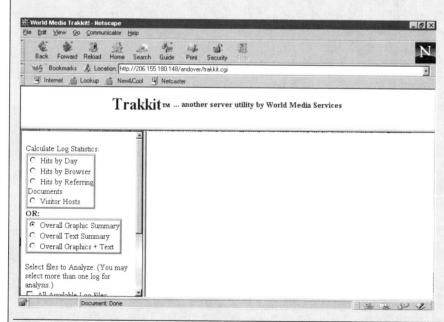

Figure 9.1 Trakkit's output screen.

Quick Start: NT

1. The zip archive is the /sourcecode/NT/trakkit directory. I've also put an unzipped in the unzipped directory one down from that one. There are only three files to Trakkit: trakkit.cgi, cyan.gif, and red.gif. You should already have config.cfg in your base directory, as well as cgi-lib.pl, both of which we installed back in the SiteWrapper chapter. Upload the three Trakkit files into your main directory, the same one that index.cgi runs in.

2. Make a directory called logs/ off the main (it has to be called logs). It will house your SiteWrapper log files. Note here that these are different from server log files. You'll set which pages log hits in the next step.

3. Open config.cfg, or whatever you renamed it for security reasons. You'll see instructions for creating a @logs array. We found it an overly burdensome task to use the data from every page on the site, but you can very easily set these if you like. Trakkit has several view options for multiple files at a time. Set it as @logs = ("homepage.htm","otherpage.htm","ourinfo.htm","lotsOitems.htm", "etc.htm");, making sure to include homepage.htm in the array (that's your homepage) and to finish the line with a semicolon. Then, if you have Perl installed on your local machine, run a perl -c on it once you're done. I explained how to do this in the Perl chapter.

4. Open the actual trakkit.cgi file. Change the require statement at line 10 in trakkit.cgi to the filename you changed config.cfg to in the installation of SiteWrapper. Be sure not to erase the semicolon, then save trakkit.cgi to the server.

5. Hit your homepage several times, preferably from several different accounts. Then verify that log files are writing by looking in the logs/ directory. If you view them as text files, they're pretty cryptic, but don't worry, that's what Trakkit is for. If they are not there, check with the system administrator to make sure that you can create server-readable directories. If you can't, have her or him re-create the logs directory, then retest it.

6. Hit trakkit.cgi from your web browser. You should get a screen like Figure 9.1. If you don't, such as a "document contains no data," there is an error in the config. Other errors could possibly be that you forgot to modify the require config line. Do a perl -c on trakkit.cgi just to make sure. Besides the config, you should also have Steven E. Brenner's cgi-lib.pl installed from the SiteWrapper chapter.

7. Plug in your password, the one you encrypted with Encrypt.cgi in the SiteWrapper chapter, select the data set you'd like and which page's logfile to munge, then OK, Trakkit!

Understanding Trakkit's Output

Try generating Overall Text and Graphics for your newly created logfile. At the top of the screen you'll see the number of your total hits with a cyan bar one pixel long for each hit. Figure 9.2 shows this for a log of index.htm, June of 97. It has 676 hits (note that I made one of the first modifications to the layout I'll explain later).

Scrolling down in that right frame, you'll hit IP address information. The top five will show you your most frequent visitors. The main purpose of this section is to eliminate hits from people within your organization from your real hit total. As you can see from our example in Figure 9.3, 185 of our hits came from one single address. From the following information we found out that this was a spider that hit the page 185 times in two days, but we'll get to that. What's important is that we can slice that number right off the top of our 676, bringing us down to 491. Then, in three of the next four you'll notice an asterisk at the end. That's because

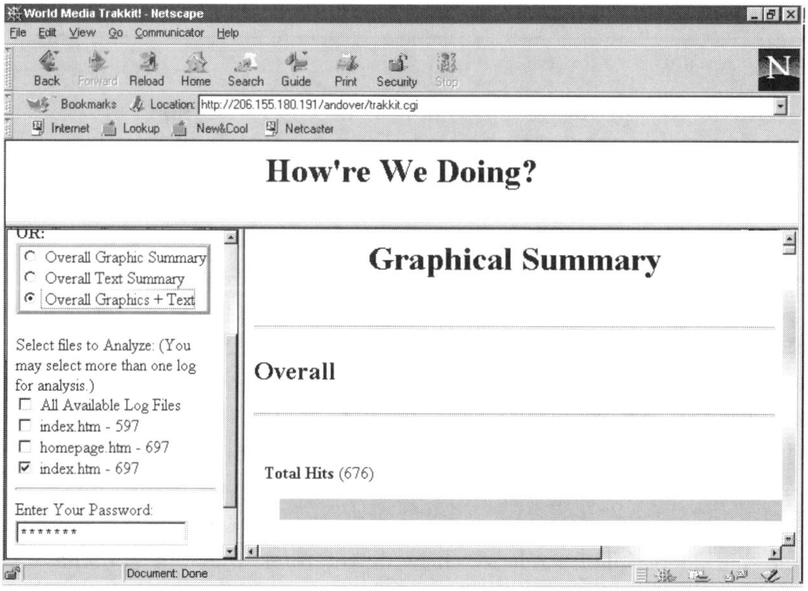

Figure 9.2 A homepage log file.

Five most frequent visitors: (Full text listings below)	
198.49.174.34	▓▓▓▓▓▓▓▓▓▓▓▓▓▓ - 185 (27% of total)
207.60.174.*	▓▓▓ - 31 (4% of total)
207.60.164.*	▓▓▓ - 23 (3% of total)
206.85.103.61	▓▓ - 17 (2% of total)
198.107.240.*	▓▓ - 16 (2% of total)

Figure 9.3 Eliminate hits by spiders and other automation programs.

three of my employees default their homepage in Netscape to our URL. We've munged several addresses into class C blocks because they dial in through accounts that assign dynamic IP, so their hits are divided into 255 possible addresses (one class C block). If we didn't munge the last three-digit number, their hits would not show up on the most frequent visitors, and we wouldn't know to reduce our number of hits. Unfortunately this isn't foolproof in our case—our ISP (tiac.net) has ten thousand customers, many of whom dial from that same pool of addresses. One other note before I go on is that this feature will also munge hits from behind a proxy server like many corporations and AOL use between users, their firewall, and the Internet. We were unable to tell from an nslookup, but that's probably what the 206.85.103.61 represents.

T I P At line 298 of Trakkit is the subroutine call for combining dynamic IP addresses into one class C. If you are on an intranet, this would prevent you from researching the machines on your system. Delete line 298 and your IP addresses will stay in tact.

The five highest referring documents are perhaps the most valuable statistic in Trakkit. It shows you what you're doing right. In Figure 9.4, the top three were all that would fit in the browser window. Of the hits, 521 had no referring document, which means that someone typed www.world-media.com into their browser's location window. From this figure we can extract most of the frequent visitor hits because the default pages in both MSIE and Netscape log as no referrer. Beyond that, we can see that 21 people hit reload, showing the referrer as our homepage. Then we get into real hits with 20 people from the Nashua web services section of

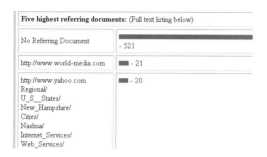

Figure 9.4 Referring document information.

Yahoo!. Also on our list were people jumping from my articles on the Webtechniques site.

The next section contains the five most common keywords used to find us on engines from where we could extract the data. We do this by breaking apart the garble you see in the URL when you're searching at Infoseek and others. On Infoseek I searched for Nashua, New Hampshire Web Services and got www.infoseek.com/Titles?qt=nashua+new+hampshire+web+services&col=WW&sv=IS&lk=ip-noframes&nh=10. Your query words travel with the URL. We dissect this string and look for keywords. You'll use this feature to analyze the thought process of your potential customers when they are searching in your industry. For instance, in Figure 9.5, the top words of our client, an employment firm (www.mas-jobs.com), shows that most people are searching for the word "jobs" when they find MAS. That means that we could probably enhance both their homepage and their search engine listings to include more of that word, and that we might want to plant the word career more often. Some people must have searched for career, and so they didn't find us.

If the next section, Search Engine Information, seems duplicative, it's probably not. Your top referrers will not likely be search engines but comarketing agreements and advertisements from other companies on the web in businesses complementary to yours. We included search engines specifically to help your ability to analyze which engines you are optimized for and which ones need more help. What works on one won't work on another. You can use SiteWrapper to manipulate this some, as I explained in Chapter 6, and this part of Trakkit will discern how your changes are working. Trakkit gives you the top five here and a complete list in the full text listing.

Ten Most Common Keywords:	
jobs	▬▬▬▬ - 55
boston jobs	▬▬▬▬ - 47
computer jobs	▬▬▬▬ - 42
jobs boston	▬▬ - 20
software jobs	▬▬ - 20
new hampshire jobs	▬▬ - 19
jobs.com	▬▬ - 17
mas	▬▬ - 16

Figure 9.5 Trakkit decodes keyword referrer information.

Browser information, the next section in Trakkit as we scroll down the right frame, should help in deciding how to optimize your site. The full text listing is more helpful than just the top five because both Netscape and Microsoft Internet Explorer send several user agent names depending upon operating system. For the top five we've munged several together, just to give a brief picture of what version numbers people are using. In Figure 9.6, you'll see that this was how we found the 185 hits from a spider. It called itself Java1.0.2. You can also see that the majority of our visitors could view Java.

Next we get to the full text listings, which starts with Hit Per Day. This is very useful if part of your advertising is in print publications or if you mail promotions to a database. If your hits go up when the advertising in question appears or arrives, you know it was successful. After a couple you should be able to benchmark a performance level, then measure the success of future ads against your past history on Trakkit.

Hits Per Day can also tell you if your server was down for any long periods of time. If you normally average fifteen hits on Mondays and twenty on Tuesdays,

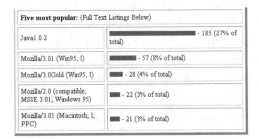

Five most popular: (Full Text Listings Below)	
Java1.0.2	▬▬▬▬▬▬▬ - 185 (27% of total)
Mozilla/3.01 (Win95; I)	▬▬▬ - 57 (8% of total)
Mozilla/3.0Gold (Win95; I)	▬▬ - 28 (4% of total)
Mozilla/2.0 (compatible; MSIE 3.01; Windows 95)	▬▬ - 22 (3% of total)
Mozilla/3.01 (Macintosh; I; PPC)	▬▬ - 21 (3% of total)

Figure 9.6 What software were they using?

then encounter a brown-out for one week, you should probably contact your Internet Service Provider to see what was up. If several brown-outs show over the course of a month or two, switch providers.

The rest is a complete analysis of these results with no munging, combining, or summarizing. If you get thousands of hits a month, Trakkit's output will be enormous—several hundred thousand bytes long. That's why we made the top listings as a general overview. That much data is too cumbersome, and the top several usually make up a strong majority of your hits, especially going forward from here as the web standardizes. A couple sections later, we'll look at customizing some of this output to the needs of your site.

An Extra Trakkit Password

As with the other utilities in the book that run in concert with SiteWrapper, we've set an optional password for Trakkit. It's called $trakkit_password and should be put in the config next to $password and like $password, should be the garble generated by Encrypt.cgi.

This password is optional thanks to the following code in Trakkit:

```
14: if ($trakkit_password ne "") {

15:     $password = $trakkit_password;

16: }
```

Line 14 starts a simple if statement. It says if $trakkit_password does not exist, use $password. I mention this little section of code because you're going to see other passwords in other programs we install as we go. At any time you could share a password between two or three, but not a fourth. An example is if you didn't want your employees to access log files, but needed them to post WebPost and Tickler pages.

Customizing the Look

I'm assuming that most readers of this book will be installing these utilities for multiple clients or departments if you're an in-house webmaster. In that case, you'll probably want to change the name at the top of your screen to My Company's Log Files or something similar. Nowhere in the code license are you required to keep our name on anything. For Trakkit, you'll start in the following code, which changes frame 1, the top bar:

```
140: sub frame_1 {

141:    print<<END;

142: <CENTER>

143: <TABLE CELLPADDING=2 BORDER=0>

144: <TR><TH><FONT SIZE=6>Trakkit</FONT><FONT

SIZE=1><SUP>TM</SUP></FONT></TH><TH><FONT SIZE=3>... another server utility by

World Media Services</FONT>

145: </TH></TR></TABLE>

146: </CENTER>

147: END

148: }
```

The whole frame_1 subroutine is nothing more than a here document spitting out a table. Replace it with your title, in whatever HTML you wish. And don't forget, because we're including config.cfg, you can reference any variables in it and manually add new ones if the header needs them (Like $trakkitadministrator= "youremail\@yourserver.com";, as in <H3>Send your e-mail to the <a href=mailto:$trakkitadministrator>the logs administrator</a></H3>.

Next we'll change the <TITLE> of the page. Before we changed frame one only, and it's where we begin to alter the nuts and bolts of Trakkit. Line 81 begins the here document that spits out the intro page:

```
81:    print<<END;

82: Content-type: text/html

83:

84: <HTML>

85: <HEAD>

86: <TITLE>World Media Trakkit!

87: </TITLE>
```

```
88: </HEAD>

89: <FRAMESET ROWS=20%,*>

90:     <FRAME SCROLLING="no" NORESIZE SRC=$ENV{'SCRIPT_NAME'}?frame_1>

91:     <FRAME NORESIZE SRC=$ENV{'SCRIPT_NAME'}?bottom NAME=bottom>

92: <NOFRAMES>

93: <BODY>

94: END

95:     &frame_1;

96:     &menu;

97:

98: print "</BODY></NOFRAMES></FRAMESET>";
```

I wouldn't mess with the frameset too much, but notice that at lines 95 and 96 we put the contents of frame 1 and the main menu into the <NOFRAMES> tag. If you want a total nonframes version, delete the <FRAMESET> entirely starting at line 89 and just leave the <BODY> at 93 and </BODY> in line 98. You'll also need to modify the <TITLE> at line 127.

Now we're going to work our way down through the code to customize more of the look and optimize Trakkit's output to the needs of your logs. We've not yet scaled SiteWrapper to millions of hits, but it has handled thousands. If your site gets more than 300 hits per month, you'll want to follow along here.

Our first concern is that Trakkit's logs (actually SiteWrapper's logs) will get too big. If so, you can customize how often a log file is restarted to make them more frequent. The default is once a month. We begin with this set of variable definitions at SiteWrapper line 31:

```
($sec,$min,$hour,$mday,$mon,$year,$wday,$yday,$isdst) = localtime(time);

$imnumb = $wday +1;

$mon++;      # mon goes from 0..11, so increment for human readability

$thisday= (Sunday,Monday,Tuesday,Wednesday,Thursday,Friday,Saturday)[(localtime)
[6]];
```

```
$thismonth=(January,February,March,April,May,June,July,August,September,October,

November,December)[(localtime)[4]];
```

This is a small library of date, time, and day variables from the localtime function in Perl. At the top, with a few modifications below it, the array delivers the corrected values for the current second, minute, hour, day of the month (1-31), month number, two-number year, weekday number (1-7), year day (1-366), and whether we are currently in daylight savings time. At the bottom we convert the numbers into words for day of the week and name of month.

At line 111 of SiteWrapper, we read some of those variables to create the file name of our log file. This line also controls the directory where the log file is printed:

```
$logFile = "./logs/$mon$year.$document_filename.log";
```

This prints a July 1997 log for homepage.htm of 797.homepage.log. We've used the $mon (month number) and $year (2 digit) to name our logs. To name the log something different, you'd use:

```
$logFile = "./logs/$thisday-$thismonth-$mday-19$year.$document_filename.log";
```

which would return a log like Wednesday-July-2-1997.homepage.log. In Trakkit, on the left frame, you'd have a checkbox of homepage.htm - Wednesday-July-2-1997 (it would overlap the frame). This would also mean that a new log file would be written every day.

Now we'll look at the rest of how the left frame is formatted. At line 152 is &menu subroutine that assembles the radio button form dynamically and grabs all the files in your logs directory:

```
152: sub menu {

153: print<<END;

154: <BR>

155: <FORM METHOD=POST TARGET="output" ACTION="$ENV{"SCRIPT_NAME"}">

156: <INPUT TYPE=HIDDEN NAME="log_analyze" VALUE="1">

157: Calculate Log Statistics:<BR>
```

```
158:  <TABLE BORDER=3 CELLPADDING=0 CELLSPACING=0>

159:  <TR><TD>

160:  <INPUT TYPE=RADIO NAME="method" VALUE="3"> Hits by Day<BR>

161:  <INPUT TYPE=RADIO NAME="method" VALUE="4"> Hits by Browser<BR>

162:  <INPUT TYPE=RADIO NAME="method" VALUE="5"> Hits by Referring Documents<BR>

163:  <INPUT TYPE=RADIO NAME="method" VALUE="6"> Visitor Hosts<BR>

164:  </TD></TR></TABLE><STRONG>OR:</STRONG><BR>

165:  <TABLE BORDER=3 CELLPADDING=0 CELLSPACING=0>

166:  <TR><TD>

167:  <INPUT TYPE=RADIO NAME="method" VALUE="1"> Overall Graphic Summary<BR>

168:  <INPUT TYPE=RADIO NAME="method" VALUE="2"> Overall Text Summary<BR>

169:  <INPUT TYPE=RADIO NAME="method" VALUE="0"> Overall Graphics + Text<BR>

170:  </TD></TABLE>

171:  <P>

172:  Select files to Analyze:

173:  (You may select more than one log for analysis.)<BR>

174:  <INPUT TYPE=checkbox NAME="files" VALUE="@files_in_logs"> All Available Log
Files

175:  END

176:

177:  foreach $file (@files_in_logs) {

178:      $file =~ /(.*)\.(.*)\.(.*)\.log/;

179:      $fname = "$2.$3";

180:      $myear = $1;
```

```
181:    print "<BR><INPUT TYPE=checkbox NAME=\"files\" VALUE=\"$file\"> $fname -

$myear";

182: }
```

It's crucial you don't lose any of the hidden variables or the names and value pairs of the radio buttons. But besides that, the HTML is yours to modify. This could even be a public area on your site if you disable the password, which you would do in the code starting at line 184:

```
184: print<<END;

185: <HR>

186: Enter Your Password: <BR><INPUT TYPE=PASSWORD NAME=password SIZE=20><BR>

187: <h2><INPUT TYPE=SUBMIT VALUE="OK, Trakkit!"></h2>

188: </FORM>

189:

190: </BODY>

191: </HTML>

192: END
```

Rather than go into Trakkit and actually remove the password like we'll do with other utilities in the book, it's easier—and easier to reverse—if you set a $trakkit-password, then change the input type of the field at line 186 to hidden, then add a VALUE="yourtrakkitpassword" attribute into the code. Get rid of the Enter Your Password and Trakkit will be accessible to all.

Moving down in the code to line 234, we begin to dissect the query string I just mentioned. Unless you're comfortable with Perl, I wouldn't mess with it, but if you can edit the code, it would do you well to go in and review the search engine query strings from time to time. At line 252, you'll see that we had to make a special consideration for ExCite. It differs in the way it stores its keywords. This is also where you'd add another engine, like HotBot or WebCrawler, duplicating the following elsif:

Preventing Log Snoopers

At line 111 of SiteColors, when we renamed the log file you saw that the default location is the logs directory. You should have made the directory in the Quick Start. Change line 111 to another directory name, make the directory on your server, CHMOD it 777, and your logs will be in a less public location (at least public to readers of this book). Line 221 in Trakkit is where the logs are read in from that directory:

```
221:        open(TEMPFILE, "logs/$file");
```

Modify both line 111 of SiteColors and 221 of Trakkit, and your logs will be in a different directory. You could also use this feature to change the log directory every year without losing the previous year's records. Make a thisyearlogs directory, CHMOD it 777 (Unix only), put a copy of Trakkit in the directory (755), and remove the logs/ from the path. Then you'll change only line 111 of SiteWrapper every year, but install a new Trakkit every year.

```
234:        if ($refer eq "") {

235:            $refer = "No Referring Document";

236:        } elsif ($refer =~ /\?/) {

237:            if ($refer =~ /(lycos|altavista|yahoo|infoseek|excite)/) {

238:                $refer .= "&";

239:                if ($refer =~ /lycos/) {

240:                    $refer =~ /query=(.+?)&/;

241:                    $term = $1;

242:                } elsif ($refer =~ /altavista/) {

243:                    $refer =~ /q=(.+?)&/;

244:                    $term = $1;

245:                } elsif ($refer =~ /yahoo/) {

246:                    $refer =~ /p=(.+?)&/;

247:                    $term = $1;
```

```
248:                    } elsif ($refer =~ /infoseek/) {
249:                        $refer =~ /qt=(.+?)&/;
250:                        $term = $1;
251:                    } elsif ($refer =~ /excite/) {
252:                        if ($refer =~ /searchType=Keyword/) {
253:                            $refer =~ /search=(.+?)&/;
254:                            $term = $1;
255:                        }
```

That's right, it's elsif with no second "e." While writing this I jumped over to HotBot. It sends its keywords as MT=keyword+keyword+keyword, so I added the following after line 255:

```
elsif ($refer =~ /hotbot/) {
                $refer =~ /MT=(.+?)&/;
                $term = $1;

        }
```

Don't worry about the decoding from there. The rest is hard coded into the HTTP draft specification as far as how the strings are sent. I mentioned this section so you could keep up with the changes in the engines.

All the Explained descriptions for the various results listings begin at line 380. What's there is meant for novices who have been given an overview of what these things mean but need a refresher once a month when they check their log files. You can, of course, change or remove these, but keep in mind that they are here documents. You will have to remove the whole thing down to the END. Rather than remove it I suggest you rename the variables:

```
380: sub graphic_summary {
381:     $browser_text =<<END;
382: <STRONG>Explained:</STRONG><BR><EM>Mozilla</EM> - Netscape<BR>
383: <EM>Mozilla (MSIE)</EM> - Microsoft Internet Explorer<BR>
```

384: <EM>(Proxy)</EM> - Visitor is behind a firewall (includes CIS,
AOL,

Prodigy,

385: etc)

386: <EM>Lynx</EM> - Text-only browser

387: <EM>SPRY</EM> - Old Mosaic/Compuserve Browser

388: <EM>WebExplorer</EM> - IBM OS/2 based browser

389: <EM>IWENG</EM> - Can be America Online

390: END

391:

392:     $refertext =<<END;

393: <STRONG>Explained:</STRONG>

394: <EM>No Referring Document</EM> - Visitor typed $server directly into the

browser

395: window.

396: <EM>$server/\?anypage.html</EM> - Visitor jumped directly to this page

while

397: reading anypage.html
<EM>http://www.searchengine.com</EM> - Visitor

jumped

398: here from a Web Referral Search Engine (Search Terms Listed Below)

399: <EM>http://www.anotherhomepage.com</EM> - Visitor jumped from a site that

400: had a hotlink to your site.
";

401: END

402:

403:     $visitor_text =<<END;

404: <STRONG>Explained:</STRONG>
These numerics are host Internet Protocol

(IP)

```
405: numbers.

406: <BR>A * indicates that a \"floating\" system, used by many Internet Service

407: Providers, was evident.

408: END

409:

410:     $keyword_text =<<END;

411: <STRONG>Explained:</STRONG><BR>When someone searches for a Web Page with a

412: search engine like Lycos or AltaVista, they use keywords, or queries, to
find

413: information. Your pages were found by the following keywords.<BR>

414: END
```

For instance, at line 381 you might switch $browser_text to $browser_txt, which would prevent it from being displayed in the browser output. Then repeat the same tactic at lines 392, 403, and 410. Then, if in a future copy you want to put the text back in, you can either switch the variables back (you might want to put a #comment line reminding you) or change the calling of them to the new name.

At line 416, we begin to print the right results frame. You won't change much more of this except possibly the relative size of the colored lines. The Trakkit distribution comes with two small images, red.gif and cyan.gif. Their width is given a pixel for each hit, perfect for sites with less than 300–400 hits, which is more than the average for most small to medium businesses. Many of you will have more, perhaps hundreds of times more, so you'll have to edit the image widths beginning with first print statement:

```
416:     print<<END;

417: <P><h1><CENTER>Graphical Summary</CENTER></h1></CENTER><P>

418: END

419:
```

```
420:    if (@files_form => 1 ) {

421:        print "<BR><HR><h2>Overall</h2><HR><P>\n";

422:        print<<END;

423: <TABLE CELLSPACING=5 CELLPADDING=5 BORDER=0 WIDTH=500>

424: <TR><TD COLSPAN=2><STRONG>Total Hits</STRONG> ($all_num_hits)<BR></TD></TR>

425: <TR><TD WIDTH=20></TD><TD><IMG SRC=cyan.gif WIDTH=$all_num_hits HEIGHT=20>

426: END
```

As you see in line 424, we print the total number of hits with $all_num_hits, then in 425 use $all_num_hits to define the width of cyan.gif. To reduce it by a tenth (700 hits will render 70 pixels wide), set a new variable as $width_of_allhits= $all_num_hits / 10; then replace $all_num_hits at line 425 with $width_of_allhits in the WIDTH of the HTML.

You'll add a similar line at the if statement starting at line 427:

```
427:        if (@files_form != 1) {

428:            foreach $file (@files_form) {

429:                $file =~ /(.*)\.(.*)\.(.*)\.log/;

430:                $fname = "$2.$3";

431:                $myear = $1;

432:                $temp = $number_hits{$file} / $all_num_hits;

433:                $temp = $temp * 100;

434:                $temp = int($temp);

435:                $percent = "$temp% of total";

436:                print "<TR><TD>$fname ($myear)</TD></TR><TR><TD
WIDTH=20></TD><TD><IMG SRC=red.gif WIDTH=$number_hits{$file} HEIGHT=10> - $num-
ber_hits{$file} ($percent)<BR>\n</TR>";

437:            }
```

Here you'll add a line after 435, another new variable as $printpercent = $number_hits{$file} / 10; and plug $printpercent into the HTML at line 436. That will control the look of the percentage displayed when you select multiple files for analysis at once, as in Figure 9.7.

You'll do this new variable definition every time you find a .gif in the code. Lines 450 to 455 are for frequent visitors, 481 to 488 is the top referrer section, 498 and 499 control the top keywords, 519 to 525 is the search engine section, and 535 to 544 is the most common browser code.

Analog: An Alternative to Trakkit

In keeping with this book's purpose, I don't want to lock you into using any one of our automation packages by requiring one to use others. Trakkit demands that you install SiteWrapper. For traditional Unix and NT logfiles it's useless (though we're changing this in the future). If you're not installing SiteWrapper, this might be an alternative. It requires that you have shell access on Unix, but not root, or full access to the MSDOS prompt on NT, but not necessarily its GUI.

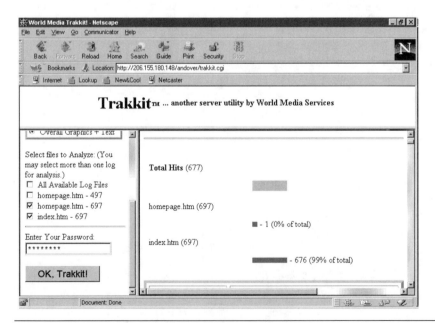

Figure 9.7 Customizing for lots of hits.

We found Analog by searching at Infoseek for log analysis tools. It was the best of scores that we looked at and the winner of several that we installed and reviewed. Though it is a compiled program not in Perl, we found it easy to install on Unix (Linux), and the Intel/NT binary worked flawlessly, albeit cryptically. It works with all standard common log files and also with the extended format that includes the referrer, agent, and other information like Trakkit. Analog is free to all according to its license, and you may redistribute it and charge for installing and running it.

Analog for Unix

On the CD, look in the /software/ directory look for the file analog.2.11.tar.gz (or download the latest from www.statslab.cam.ac.uk/~tret1/analog). Upload it to the server, in your www.yourcompany.com directory and type gunzip *.gz. Then type tar -xvf analog.2.11.tar to unroll the archive into its directory structure, starting with an analog2.11 directory. This assumes that you have shell access to the server. If you don't, ask the system administrator to install Analog for you.

Next we have to compile Analog for our server. First bring up analhead.h, the header file, bring it up in your editor, and change line 21 to reflect the directory where you just untared Analog from, not analog, which you'll see is tacked onto the next line automatically. The correct syntax for line 21 is define HTTPDIR "/path/to/analogtarfile/". Save the file.

Type make at the shell prompt. You'll get a whole bunch of gcc lines, then it will put you back at the prompt. The correct output should look like Figure 9.8. Analog is now successfully compiled. We had hoped to compile binaries for those who don't have shell access, but it appears from the code that you have to compile in the location. If you can't get the sysadmin to do it, use Trakkit. Now we have to configure it. Bring analog.cfg up in Multi-Edit or whatever editor you're comfortable with that can save files as plain text. Emacs and vi are fine.

Figure 9.9 should be a bit different than the default you get with the distribution. To start we've added an optional HOSTNAME to line 10 of the file. It's the default name displayed at the top of Analog's HTML file of your stats.

The next is HOSTURL. Here is where you'd put in the separate name of a virtual on the system if you have separate log files for each, but for our example it's the base URL of the webserver. That's why we do a separate config file for each virtual server.

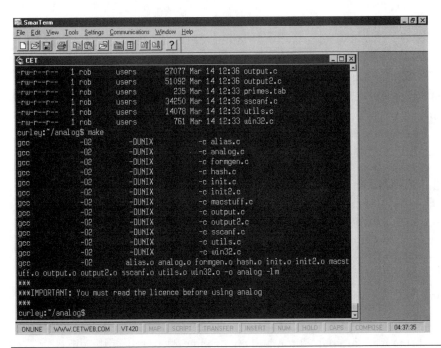

Figure 9.8 Analog's compiler messages.

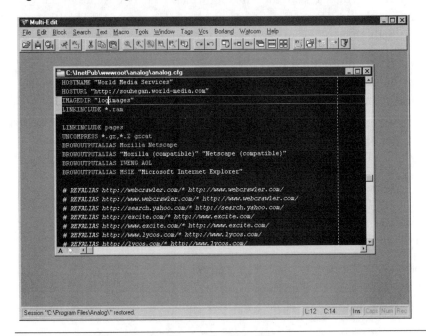

Figure 9.9 Edit the configuration settings.

Set it to your www.yourcompany.com. That will print your URL as a reference and hotlink it.

For IMAGEDIR, we're setting the place where you want Analog to look for its images in the HTML file it generates. This will be what's in the SRC of the images. Set it as relative to your webserver, we're calling it logimages, then copy the images from the install directory into your virtual directory/logimages. If you installed Analog off the wwwroot directory, you can set IMAGEDIR "/analog/images".

Once you see the log files that Analog generates you'll understand the next variable easily. As I said, it's an HTML file that shows reports for each of your pages, images, and multimedia files. Each file is listed in the HTML page, and if it's a .htm or .html page, Analog automatically hotlinks to that page. That's what LINKINCLUDE pages means. We added a second type for .ram, Real Audio Files.

There's a chance that your server automatically GZIPs your log files on the fly, drastically reducing their file size, but it's not common enough in these days of cheap hard drives to make it a default in Figure 9.9. This next variable, UNCOMPRESS, unzips them on the fly. Set it as UNCOMPRESS *.gz "gunzip -c" on that line if you need it.

The next four lines are all the same variable. It's called BROWOUTPUTALIAS and converts the word Mozilla to Netscape, IWENG to AOL, and MSIE to Microsoft Internet Explorer.

We now have to add a variable to tell Analog where to find its log file. Add the variable LOGFILE "/full/path/to/your/logfile". If you are running several virtual servers, each with their own log file, you'll want to install a copy of Analog for each. To run Analog month by month, you'll have to modify the file with the new log each time. Below that are a whole bunch of commented lines called REFALIAS. It's not as big a deal as it looks. By uncommenting the line you'll automatically link the HTML report, where it gives you referrer information, to the search engine it came from.

For Unix, Analog provides a premade form interface to configure it. Bring up the file analform.c in your editor. On line 22, put in the full path to the Analog program, including the file itself. The correct syntax is:

```
#define COMMAND "/full/path/to/analog/analog".
```

Save the file, then type make form. It makes analform.cgi and analform.html.

If you didn't untar Analog in your webserver's main directory or a directory where you are allowed to run CGI programs, move analform.cgi to that location and set its permissions to CHMOD 755. Then change the form action URL in anal-form.html to the correct path and move it to where you can hit it from a web browser. If you set the logfile path correctly, you should be able to hit Submit on the form and get back your overall results.

Analog for NT

We've put the latest version in the /software/ directory as the file an21w32.exe. It's a self-extracting archive. The install is through the normal Windows self-installation screens we're all used to. The default directory is /Program/Files/Analog. We put it in the wwwroot, which is under the InetPub directory, shown in Figure 9.8. That will make it more accessible when we're doing web tasks, and make the output file, and HTML file, able to be hit from a web browser. If we had left it as the default, that would not be so. As you can see from the tree listing, Analog is a Win32 command line program.

First we have to configure it. Bring analog.cfg up in Multi-Edit or whatever editor you're comfortable with that can save files as plain text—Notepad is fine. Here is where we're stuck by the limitations of Internet Information Server 3.0. We can't get it to spit a different log file for different virtual servers. If your server can, you'll make a separate config for every virtual server you intend to log. But for this one we're going to pretend only one web is running on this server.

Figure 9.9 should be a bit different than the default you get with the distribution. To start, we've added an optional HOSTNAME to line 10 of the file. It's the default name displayed at the top of Analog's HTML file of your stats.

The next is HOSTURL. Here is where you'd put in the separate name of a virtual on the system if you have separate log files for each, but for our example it's the base URL of the webserver. That's why we do a separate config file for each virtual server. Set it to your www.yourcompany.com. That will print your URL as a reference.

For IMAGEDIR, we're setting the place where you want Analog to look for its images in the HTML file it generates. This will be what's in the SRC of the images.

Set it as relative to your webserver, so we're calling it logimages, then copy the images from the install directory into your virtual directory/logimages. If you installed Analog off the wwwroot directory, you can set IMAGEDIR "/analog/images".

Once you see the log files that Analog generates, you'll understand the next variable easily. As I said, it's an HTML file that shows reports for each of your pages, images, and multimedia files. Each file is listed in the HTML page, and if it's a .htm or .html page, Analog automatically hotlinks to that page. That's what LINK-INCLUDE pages means. We added a second type, .ram, for RealAudio files.

We ignore the UNCOMPRESS variable for NT. It's for Unix servers that use gzip to compress their log files (from back in the old days when hard drives were expensive).

The next four lines are all the same variable. It's called BROWOUTPUTALIAS and converts the word Mozilla to Netscape, IWENG to AOL, and MSIE to Microsoft Internet Explorer.

Below that are a whole bunch of commented lines called REFALIAS. It's not as big a deal as it looks. By uncommenting the line you'll automatically link the HTML report, where it gives you referrer information, to the search engine it came from.

Now we have to find the file name of a logfile to feed to Analog. But first we have to convert the standard NT log files to NCSA compatible. This was originally a Unix application that has since been ported to NT. Don't worry, Microsoft thought of this. In the /Windows/System32/Inetsrv/ find the program convlog.exe (you won't see the .exe if extensions are disabled in your NT Explorer window). Open a DOS window, then from your NT Explorer, drag the convlog.exe file into the window. This will put the path name at your cursor. Optionally, just cd to the Inetsrv directory and type convlog.exe there, but don't press Enter yet. You have to type a flag and a filename, so the full command is convlog.exe -t ncsa logfile.name.log. See the following sidebar for the workaround for this.

You should still be at the command line after just converting the log files. If you made them NCSA by default with the sidebar example, go to the MSDOS

Setting NT Log Defaults

You can avoid the whole process of finding log files and converting them by using, from your Start menu, Programs/Microsoft Internet Server/Internet Service Manager. Double-click your webserver, labelled with a WWW, then the Logging Tab (Figure 9.10). Make sure Log to File is checked, then choose NCSA format as the default. Here you'll also choose the frequency of your logs (we chose monthly), and where NT should put your files. We chose to put them in the same directory as Analog to ease the number of steps required to generate a new report every month.

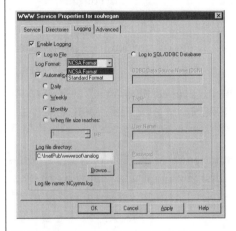

Figure 9.10 The Internet service manager.

prompt and into the wwwroot/analog directory. If you've set your logfiles to be placed in the analog directory, type the command analog your.logfile.log. If it's in another directory, type analog \path\to\your.logfile.log (C:\windows\system32\ logfiles\).

That should have made a file called analout.html, shown in Figure 9.11. Remember that these stats are for this log file only. To generate a report for another, you'll have to run Analog again from the command line. Month to month you'll be overwriting analout.html, so you might want to rename it before running a second report.

More on Analog

When you installed Analog by either running the executable on NT or untaring and compiling it on Unix, it made a file called Readme.html, which contains complete

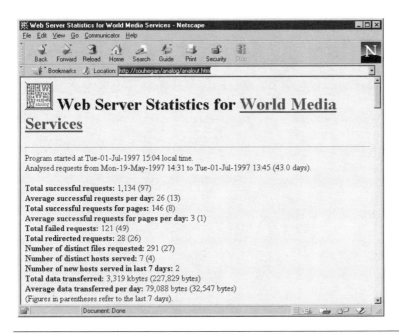

Figure 9.11 Analog's output file.

help files on how to understand the output and set parameters on how it's compiled and presented. Most of it is understandable, so I won't reiterate it here. If you are running mostly static files on your server, Analog is a good choice for a free and customizable solution.

Shopping Carts:
Saving State

In this chapter I won't waste a lot of time explaining how and why HTTP doesn't track state. In the Introduction, I asked that you know a bit about how the browser and server talk to each other. I assume you know this as part of that, but in short, when you hit a webserver, it doesn't know or care who you are. When you return it doesn't remember that you've been there before, so tracking what someone just ordered on the last page is impossible. Customization, based on a user's preferences is also a lost cause, but yet you've seen it done.

This chapter is about forcing the server to remember, mostly in the ordering context. We'll cover two parts: the part I recommend and the part I don't. First, we're going to look at a variation of Chapter 6's SiteWrapper that tracks and stores orders, then totals it and delivers the results. Then, in that second part, we'll look at cookies, a most maligned way to keep state on the web.

For the shopping cart, I suggest that you read and understand Chapter 6. SiteWrapper naturally saves state as every page is wrapped through a CGI. Within this context, I'm not addressing how to customize a page for someone, but Chapter 6 gives you a couple of examples as a place to start. More important, the SiteWrapper chapter talks about how wrapping pages works by using a central configuration file and tacked on headers and footers. There is one divergence in one variable in the configuration file between the index.cgi in that chapter and in this one. Otherwise they are the same. The customizations we'll do are to the wrapped HTML pages and their syntax for sending orders. This archive comes with three other order-processing Perl programs.

I'm not as strongly against cookies as it appears by my earlier comments. We've used them as an optional enhancement to wrapped pages, because the one thing SiteWrapper can't do is recognize who you are when you return to the site after leaving. You have to log back in. At www.expertsinternational.com we offered people a checkbox to log them in automatically with a cookie. All we send is their encrypted user ID. Cookies have their place on the web, but still may go away entirely due to an industry initiative to replace them with a new profiling standard. I won't get into the possible security violations of cookies or how they actually work. Again, I expect you to know it, at least in general. One note I will make is that the utility of cookies is extremely limited in the retail webspace in the foreseeable future. Cookies don't work well through firewalls, which precludes them from use on many online services. Some have made concessions, but as of this writing, America Online does not support them and though WebTV does, it is having difficulty with the caching system. Also, even if a cookie is accepted, there is no guarantee that your cookie will be there when the user returns. Browser limitations are 300 total cookies, 4 kilobytes per cookie, and 20 cookies per server.

SiteWrapper's Shopping Cart

After having read Chapter 6, you should understand how SiteWrapper grabs its variables dynamically as the page loads. This can work for not only your 800 number or the background color of the page, but also for an order number variable. Rather than grab it from the config, however, we're pitching and catching it from page to page. When you first hit index.cgi, you are assigned the variable $order_numb, set to whatever the site's log files have incremented to. More accurately, this variable could be called $visitor_number, but it's more impressive to your visitors if they think thousands of people have ordered. Of course, maybe they have.

We pitch and catch these variables in two ways. One is by including an <INPUT TYPE=HIDDEN NAME=order_numb VALUE=$order_numb> in every form on the site, and the other is by tacking a ?order_numb=$order_numb onto every internal URL. When the page wraps, the hidden fields and URL additions are evaluated by SiteWrapper, plugging in the correct value. When you first hit the homepage, you are assigned a unique order_numb automatically.

We've addressed two problems I've not seen on any other noncookies cart. One is passing the $order_numb variable through a server-side image map. For client maps you can just tack on the same URL additions, but a server mapfile isn't evaluated first. It's hit as an active program. We answered this by automatically writing a unique map file for every visitor. When you hit the homepage or any wrapped page without an order_numb assigned, the cart grabs a template map and makes one with your number. Then, as you traverse the site the number of your map file automatically is used for click-arounds, keeping your state secure.

The other problem is in the ordering structure. I've not found a system anywhere else that allows you to order different colors of different items in different sizes on one page with singles of items with no size or color. You'll see what I mean in a later example. First, though, let's get going.

Quick Start: Unix

1. Because this affects the base URL functionality of your site, you may want to try this first in a test directory. It comes with a complete demonstration in the distribution. That directory, for the test, will be the $server that we set in the config. Regardless of where this installation goes, you'll now go to your server and make three directories, mapfiles, orders, and logs, as spurs off of where index.cgi will be placed. SiteWrapper users may already have the logs directory created from the Trakkit chapter. Refer to it on the use of the log files.

2. Then CHMOD those three directories to 777. The server must write to all of them. If you made a temp directory make sure either the directory is 777 or tagfile.dat and wmsdb.error are 666. Those files sit in the base directory as SiteColors and the error file, respectively. Refer to the SiteWrapper chapter for the use of SiteColors.

3. Next, in the /sourcecode/UNIX/wrapcart/ directory you'll find wrap-cart.zip. There is also an unzipped directory of the entire archive. Open every CGI program, Encrypt.cgi, index.cgi, modify.cgi, sub_tot.cgi, and total.cgi, and check the Perl location at the top. The default is /usr/bin/perl5, which has become a bit of a standard, but we've seen systems with locations as strange as /usr/sbin/perl-5. Often an ISP will default different servers to different locations. Ask the system administrator if you are unsure, run "which perl" at the shell prompt or from the shell script I gave you in Chapter 4.

4. Upload all of the files to the directory where you'll be installing index.cgi. If this is a temp, you shouldn't keep it there if you decide to use it. The order number we're tracking will be lost if your visitors

go to any nonwrapped page. Note that SiteWrapper users will be replacing index.cgi, which will only break your %jumpnames variable. We'll reset that later.

5. Now CHMOD all the .cgi files to 755 so the server can execute them. If all is well with the Perl location and permissions, you should now be able to hit index.cgi and see a page like the one shown in Figure 10.3, our Jurassic Pets example homepage.

6. If you haven't installed SiteWrapper, bring up config.cfg in your editor. If you have installed SiteWrapper, bring up your config.cfg or whatever you renamed it. For security reasons, it's a good idea to rename your config file and then edit the "require config.cfg"; line in each of the CGI programs to the name you choose.

7. Now we'll edit some variables. Some will be duplicative for SiteWrapper users, but follow along because there is one you'll have to change. The first is $serveradmin = "wrapcart\@world-media.com";. Change it to the e-mail of the person in charge of the shopping cart. And don't forget to \escape the @ sign or the line will break Perl.

8. Next edit the $server = "http://www.yourdomain.com"; line to the location of your server where the shopping cart will run. I strongly suggest you run it as index.cgi on your base directory (www.yourdomain.com), as your users will lose their order numbers by not going to a wrapped page.

9. There is a program called Encrypt.cgi in the distribution. Hit that to generate a password, then change the $password = "luTDemOTOK09k"; to the garble it gives you. Don't ever plug the actual password into the variable definition. It has to be the garble.

10. The next variable is set with the pages of our example site as @logs = ("homepage.htm", "stego.htm", "wooly.htm", "tyranosr.htm", "thanks.htm");. You'll replace all but homepage.htm and possibly thanks.htm with the values for your project. This will hit the log file when each page is accessed for you to decode with Trakkit.

11. This version of SiteWrapper, as with the original, allows you to tack headers and footers for the whole site. They are loaded dynamically with each HTTP request. Our next two variables identify these files as $headerfile = "head.wms"; and $footerfile = "foot.wms";. An overview of how to edit them is a subheading in the SiteWrapper chapter.

12. This is where the setup diverges from SiteWrapper. We've used a standard array, not a hash, to define the @jumpnames variable. If

this is your first config, this is nothing new. Figure 10.1 shows the setup. If you have a hash from SiteWrapper, just convert it as the example shows. For each page you'll put a quote, the page's file-name, a colon, then the title you want to appear in the $JUMPLIST and $TEXTLIST elements on the page. Further discussion of their use is, again, in the SiteWrapper chapter. This array format of the $JUMPLIST allows you to order the list yourself rather than use Perl's default.

13. Then set your %titlenames array as an associative array, with each page name separated by a comma and surrounded by quotes.

14. The rest of the variables are specific mainly to this chapter. The first is %taxes = ("CT", .06);, which sets the sales tax for the state in which we're selling. In this example, the cart is in Connecticut, which has a six percent tax rate. In-state customers will pay this, others won't. Move to New Hampshire and it's a dead issue. We have no sales tax; set this value as ("").

15. The next section is shipping. Most of our clients offer free shipping over X dollars, which is the first variable, $free_ship_amt = 600000;. This sets the amount at $600,000. Dinosaurs are expensive to ship. The next variable, $shipping_amt = 10000;, is the dollar amount of shipping if they don't make the free amount. Don't put $ signs in either of these variables.

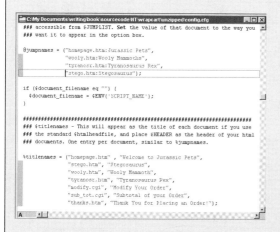

Figure 10.1 Changing the %jumpnames variable to a standard @jumpnames array.

```
# this is for Unix only
$sendmail_location = '/usr/bin/sendmail';
# this is for NT only
$smtpserver = "mailserver.yourdomain.com";

$recipient = 'orders\@world-media.com';
$from = "wrapcart\@world-media.com";
$thanks_url = "$server/index.cgi?thanks.htm";
```

Figure 10.2 Special variables you must add to your configuration.

16. The cart does three things with an order. First, it e-mails you a copy, then it writes a backup order file to the server, then it mails the customer a copy of his or her order. Here we'll work on the mail section. Set the $sendmail_location for your system, then set the $recipient = 'orders\@world-media.com'; e-mail to where orders should be sent. Then edit the $from = "wrapcart\@world-media.com"; variable, which is where people will send their reply should the order be broken. Then set the $thanks_url = "$server/index.cgi?thanks.htm"; variable, which is the thanks page after they place an order. Figure 10.2 shows the correct variable configurations in a Multi-Edit window.

Quick Start: NT

1. If you already have a site, it's probably a good idea to test this briefly in a separate directory. We're installing index.cgi, so this will effect your homepage. If you already have SiteWrapper installed, this isn't a big deal. It will only break your %jumpnames variable, which we'll reset later.

2. Now, as spurs off of where ever you installed index.cgi, make three directories called logs, mapfiles, and orders. The server will write to them. See the Trakkit chapter on the use of your log files.

3. In the /sourcecode/NT/wrapcart/ directory, you'll find wrapcart.zip. There is also an unzipped directory of the entire archive. If you haven't installed SiteWrapper, bring up config.cfg in your editor. If you have installed SiteWrapper, bring up your config.cfg or whatever you renamed it. For security reasons it's a good idea to rename your config file then edit the "require config.cfg"; line in each of the CGI programs to the name you choose.

4. Now we'll edit some variables. Some will be duplicative for SiteWrapper users, but follow along because there is one you'll have to change. The first is $serveradmin = "wrapcart\@world-media.com";. Change it to the e-mail of the person in charge of the

shopping cart. Don't forget to \escape the @ sign or the line will break Perl.

5. Next edit the $server = "http://www.yourdomain.com"; line to the location of your server where the shopping cart will run. I strongly suggest you run it as index.cgi on your base directory (www.yourdomain.com), as your users will lose their order numbers by not going to a wrapped page.

6. There is a program called Encrypt.cgi in the distribution. Hit that to generate a password, then change the $password = "luTDemOTOK09k"; to the garble it gives you. Don't ever plug the actual password into to variable definition; it has to be the garble.

7. The next variable is set with the pages of our example site as @logs = ("homepage.htm", "stego.htm", "wooly.htm", "tyranosr.htm", "thanks.htm");. You'll replace all but homepage.htm and possibly thanks.htm with the values for your project. This will hit the log file when each page is accessed for you to decode with Trakkit.

8. This version of SiteWrapper, as with the original, allows you to tack headers and footers for the whole site. They are loaded dynamically with each HTTP request. Our next two variables identify these files as $headerfile = "head.wms"; and $footerfile = "foot.wms";. An overview of how to edit them is a subheading in the SiteWrapper chapter.

9. This is where the setup diverges from SiteWrapper. We've used a standard array, not a hash, to define the @jumpnames variable. If this is your first config, this is nothing new. Figure 10.1 shows the setup. If you have a hash from SiteWrapper, just convert it as the example shows. For each page you'll put a quote, the page's file-name, a colon, then the title you want to appear in the $JUMPLIST and $TEXTLIST elements on the page. Further discussion of their use is, again, in the SiteWrapper chapter.

10. Then set your %titlenames array as an associative array, with each page name separated by a comma and surrounded by quotes.

11. The rest of the variables are specific mainly to this chapter. The first is %taxes = ("CT", .06);, which sets the sales tax for the state in which we're selling. In this example, the cart is in Connecticut, which has a six percent tax rate. In-state customers will pay this, others won't. Move to New Hampshire and it's a dead issue. We have no sales tax; set this value as ("").

12. The next section is shipping. Most of our clients offer free shipping over X dollars, which is the first variable, $free_ship_amt = 600000;.

> This sets the amount at $600,000. Dinosaurs are expensive to ship. The next variable, $shipping_amt = 10000;, is the dollar amount of shipping if they don't make the free amount. Don't put $ signs in either of these variables.
>
> 13. The cart does three things with an order. First it e-mails you a copy, then it writes a backup order file to the server, then it mails the customer a copy of his or her order. Here we'll work on the mail section. Set the $smtpserver for your system, then set the $recipient = 'orders\@world-media.com'; e-mail to where orders should be sent. Edit the $from = "wrapcart\@world-media.com"; variable, which is where people will send their reply should the order be broken, then set the $thanks_url = "$server/index.cgi?thanks.htm"; variable, which is the thanks page after they place an order.

Placing an Order

Before we get into customizing this thing, it's important that you understand the logic of what happens when someone hits the homepage and then traverses through the ordering process. You hit index.cgi once, in Figure 10.3. When you did, you were given the order number 1001 automatically. Look in the mapfiles directory now. You should have a file there called 1001.map, shown in the top of Figure 10.4. As you can see, it's different from the map file in the bottom half, which is the tempmap.map included in the distribution. The top says order_numb=1001, and the bottom says order_numb=$order_numb. When index.cgi runs, it automatically writes a map file for you after assigning you a unique order number. If you look in the logs directory, there should be an order-number.dat file with 1001 in it. It will increment when someone else hits the site. Click on a dinosaur. It will take you to the page where the map file is referenced. Figure 10.5 is the Wooly page. In the Location bar of your browser, you'll see that same order number. View the source. The map file is referenced as 1001.map in the mapfiles directory. If you return to the homepage, hover your mouse over one of the dinosaur images. You'll see how it's passed. You'll tack that same &order_numb=$order_numb onto every URL in the site.

Now we'll place an order. Scroll down the dinosaur page and choose which size you want, then Add these to my order. You'll be bounced back to the page you just came from. Scroll down to its bottom. It should say Your order so far; list the quantity, name, and size of dinosaur just ordered, then subtotal your order with shipping. Let's now modify our order.

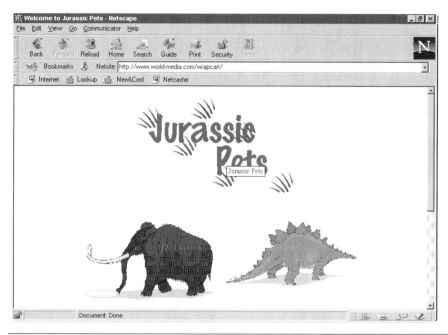

Figure 10.3 The Jurassic Pets homepage.

By clicking Modify order number 1001 you just wiped out your order file. It peeled it up into modify.cgi and deleted it from the orders directory, where it was named 1001.tmp. To keep your order, click the Update/Remove/Re-submit button. You'll go back to the homepage where you can continue to shop. Your order, as you can again see by hovering the mouse, has been retained. At the bottom of the homepage is again your order total. Let's finish.

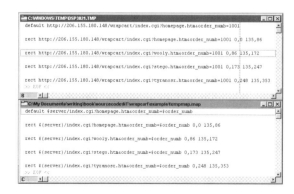

Figure 10.4 SiteWrapper automatically assigns your customer/order number to your own personal map file.

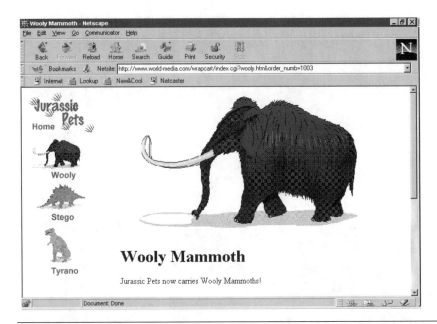

Figure 10.5 The individual dinosaur page. Note that it can contain any number and type of item.

Hopefully you're at Figure 10.6. Complete the personal information, plug in the credit card number, then click the Submit button. In a few minutes you should get two e-mails, one that was sent to you as the business owner, one as the customer. The business owner one will contain credit card information. The customer one, confirming the order, will not. Look in the orders directory; there should be a file named with today's date.orders. It is an exact duplicate of all of today's orders, sans credit card information. We'll look at all this later when we edit the actual CGI programs, but first let's see how the items HTML works.

Setting Up Product Pages

For each item in SiteWrapper there is a set of variables, both visible and invisible, required to process the order. They affect item name, price, and size. Bring up the tyranosr.htm page in your editor. It should contain the following:

$HEADER

<CENTER>

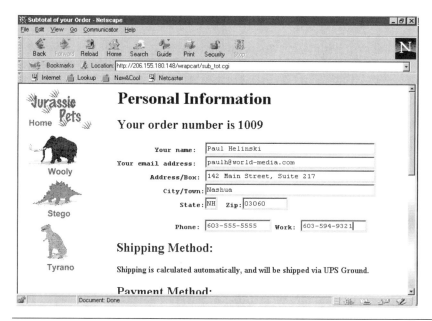

Figure 10.6 Completing your order.

```
<IMG SRC=tyranosr.gif BORDER=0 HEIGHT=308 WIDTH=450>

</CENTER><BR><h1>King of the Dinosaurs<BR>

Tyranosaurus Rex</h1>


Jurassic Pets now carries Tyranosaurus Rexii!<BR>

<h2>Only \$99,990 each!</h2>(plus shipping and handling)<BR>
```

Up to here it's standard header information. If you haven't installed SiteWrapper, you'll want to review it for how these middle pages grab dynamic elements from the config. Note that in the <h2> tag is an escaped dollar sign. If you don't put the backslash before it, Perl will treat the price as a potential variable and wipe it out on the finished HTML page.

```
<FORM METHOD=POST ACTION=index.cgi>

<INPUT TYPE=HIDDEN NAME=order_numb VALUE="$order_numb">

<INPUT TYPE=HIDDEN NAME=sub_total VALUE=1>
```

```
<INPUT TYPE=HIDDEN NAME=sender VALUE="tyranosr.htm">
```

Then we start the form with index.cgi as our processor. It calls the needed subroutines from cart.pl, which is required at the top of the code. The first hidden variable is our order number, which is read in and reassigned in $order_numb. Next we tell the index to use the subtotal.cgi program in processing our order, the third is the referring page that it should bounce us back to after processing the item.

```
<INPUT TYPE=HIDDEN NAME=itemname_0003 VALUE="Tyranosaurus Rex">
```

```
<INPUT TYPE=HIDDEN NAME=price_0003 VALUE="99990.00">
```

Each item must have these two identifiers to initiate itself on the system. The first is itemname_0003, which is item number 0003. You can change that number to anything you like, even itemname_tyrano or itemname_bigbruiser. What's crucial is that you don't break the syntax of the itemname_ with the underscore, then the item's reference name or number. The value for the itemname variable should be the full name of the item as it should appear in the order. In the NAME field, we store stock number/identifier; in the VALUE, its actual name.

The next hidden field is much the same. You must keep the price_0003 or price_tyrano format, and the NAME should be exactly the same as the itemname variable. There also must be an underscore between the word price and its stock number/identifier. The VALUE should not include a dollar sign and must include the decimal point with the cents after, even if, like here, it's a whole dollar amount.

```
Enter the Number of Small Tyranosaurus Rexii: <INPUT TYPE=TEXT NAME=size_0003_S
SIZE=10><BR>
```

```
Enter the Number of Medium Tyranosaurus Rexii: <INPUT TYPE=TEXT NAME=size_0003_M

SIZE=10><BR>
```

```
Enter the Number of Large Tyranosaurus Rexii:

<INPUT TYPE=TEXT NAME=size_0003_L SIZE=10><BR>
```

```
Enter the Number of Extra-Large Tyranosaurus Rexii:

<INPUT TYPE=TEXT NAME=size_0003_XL SIZE=10><BR>
```

Now we've put four choices of Tyranosaurus in four sizes, each sending a NAME=size_0003_S or other size variable. Note that the SIZE attribute has nothing to do with the size of the item. That's the size of the INPUT box. What's mandatory here is that every item must send a size, underscore, stocknumber/identifier, underscore, size of item variable. What if your item has no size? We'll get to that.

```
<INPUT TYPE=SUBMIT VALUE="Add These To My Order"><BR>

</FORM>

</BLOCKQUOTE>

$FOOTER
```

At the end, we close the form and then the document with the $FOOTER variable, and here we've also closed the </BLOCKQUOTE>, which we could've just as easily done within the footer.

What you're not seeing here is where we got our image map. That's in the head.wms file along with the beginning of that <BLOCKQUOTE>.

```
<HTML>

<HEAD>

<TITLE>

$titlenames{"$document_filename"}

</TITLE>

</HEAD>

$bodytag


<A HREF="$server/mapfiles/$order_numb.map">

<IMG ISMAP ALIGN=LEFT VALIGN=TOP BORDER=0 HEIGHT=360 WIDTH=137 SRC=buttbar.gif>

</A>

<BLOCKQUOTE>
```

As with standard SiteWrapper, the %titlenames variable gives us our <TITLE>, then after the $bodytag is the image mapped button bar. The map points to mapfiles/$order_numb.map, which is evaluated in dynamically and called by 1001.map according to the current mapfile.

Let's go back and add an item. Open stego.htm in your editor. You'll find a commented out item called kibble:

```
<h2>SPECIAL THIS WEEK!</h2>

<h3>Stego Kibble: \$1485.00</h3>

<INPUT TYPE=HIDDEN NAME=itemname_kibble VALUE="StegoKibble">

<INPUT TYPE=HIDDEN NAME=price_kibble VALUE="1485.00">

Number of Boxes: <INPUT TYPE=TEXT NAME=size_kibble_# SIZE=10>  -->
```

In the Number of Boxes INPUT box, we've still used the size_kibble_ format but tacked on a # sign at the end. This signals index.cgi and cart.pl that the item has no size. We still set up itemname_kibble the same with its associated VALUE, as well as the price_kibble with its price. Only the size variable changes, and the syntax must be exact, as size, underscore, item, underscore, number sign.

For multiple colors of an item I've added a sweater to the Stego page as follows:

```
<h2>Stego Sweaters in Three Colors \$1995</h2>

<table border=2 cellpadding=5 cellspacing=5 bgcolor=tan>

<tr><td><strong>Blue</strong><br>

<INPUT TYPE=HIDDEN NAME=itemname_stegsweatblue VALUE="Blue Stego Sweater">

<INPUT TYPE=HIDDEN NAME=price_stegsweatblue VALUE="1995.00">

Small:<INPUT TYPE=TEXT NAME=size_stegsweatblue_S SIZE=3> Medium:<INPUT

TYPE=TEXT NAME=size_stegsweatblue_M SIZE=3> <br>Large:<INPUT TYPE=TEXT

NAME=size_stegsweatblue_L SIZE=3> Extra-Large:<INPUT TYPE=TEXT

NAME=size_stegsweatblue_XL SIZE=3> <br> </td>



<td><strong>Green</strong><br>

<INPUT TYPE=HIDDEN NAME=itemname_stegsweatgreen VALUE="Green Stego Sweater">
```

```
<INPUT TYPE=HIDDEN NAME=price_stegsweatgreen VALUE="1995.00">

Small:<INPUT TYPE=TEXT NAME=size_stegsweatgreen_S SIZE=3> Medium:<INPUT

TYPE=TEXT NAME=size_stegsweatgreen_M SIZE=3> <br>Large:<INPUT TYPE=TEXT

NAME=size_stegsweatgreen_L SIZE=3> Extra-Large:<INPUT TYPE=TEXT

NAME=size_stegsweatgreen_XL SIZE=3>  <br></td></tr>

<tr>

<td><strong>Yellow</strong><br>

<INPUT TYPE=HIDDEN NAME=itemname_stegsweatyellow VALUE="Yellow Stego Sweater">

<INPUT TYPE=HIDDEN NAME=price_stegsweatyellow VALUE="1995.00">

Small:<INPUT TYPE=TEXT NAME=size_stegsweatyellow_S SIZE=3> Medium:<INPUT

TYPE=TEXT NAME=size_stegsweatyellow_M SIZE=3><br> Large:<INPUT TYPE=TEXT

NAME=size_stegsweatyellow_L SIZE=3> Extra-Large:<INPUT TYPE=TEXT

NAME=size_stegsweatyellow_XL SIZE=3>  <br> </td>


<td><strong>Red</strong><br>

<INPUT TYPE=HIDDEN NAME=itemname_stegsweatred VALUE="Red Stego Sweater">

<INPUT TYPE=HIDDEN NAME=price_stegsweatred VALUE="1995.00">

Small:<INPUT TYPE=TEXT NAME=size_stegsweatred_S SIZE=3> Medium:<INPUT

TYPE=TEXT NAME=size_stegsweatred_M SIZE=3> <br>Large:<INPUT TYPE=TEXT

NAME=size_stegsweatred_L SIZE=3> Extra-Large:<INPUT TYPE=TEXT

NAME=size_stegsweatred_XL SIZE=3>    </td>  </tr></table>
```

Each color of sweater has its own itemname/price set of hidden variables, then small input fields for its sizes. This is the only way you can order multiples of a colored and sized item. The finished page is in Figure 10.7. It's a lot of code, but as I explained, not many carts allow this.

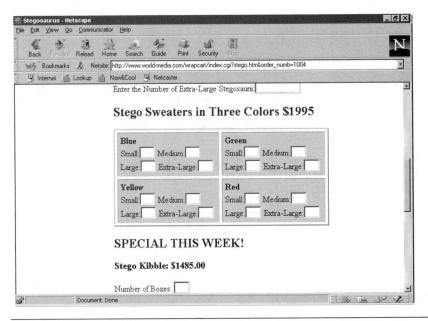

Figure 10.7 Multiple items, colors, and sizes can go anywhere.

On the Web At www.world-media.com/wrapcart, we've put up this demo Jurassic Pets site. By hitting stego.htm and the other pages without the ? mark, you'll be able to download them and see how they work. Also, there is config.cfg. They are, of course, in the example directories as well.

Working with Image Map Files

Back in Figure 10.4, we looked at the default mapfile tempmap.map. It may not work on your system. Most servers automatically parse map files these days, but some use the CERN and some use the NCSA format. Trial and error will work, or if worse comes to worst, ask your ISP. I prefer the former, so I use the preferences menu in MapThis and try them both. Figure 10.8 is how we set our variables in the map editing program. I've set the hotspot as the full URL to the example site I'm putting in. Note that I could also set it as $server/index.cgi?order_number=$order_numb as the entire string is evaluated through the config. If you're tracking other variable sets, you'll tack them onto the string just as normal, with &variablename=value for each. MapThis will also make client-side image maps, which you'll edit the same way, adding ?order_numb=$order_numb and the USEMAP attribute to your image tag. If you go this route, you might want to disable the following code. Every mapped imaged on the site should have its own map file, and you need not name it tempmap.map.

 O n   t h e   C D Guess what? MapThis is free! It is no longer supported, but still has the award winning interface many of us have used over the past year. On the CD, it is in the software/ directory as mpths131.exe for Windows 95. The commercial version, presumably better but untested by me, is at www.mediatec.com/ and has won this year's PC Magazine shareware award.

Once your map files are created, go into cart.pl at line 79. Here is where we identify the name of the file to be evaluated and written to the mapfiles directory. I'm going to change the name of our map file to buttons.map:

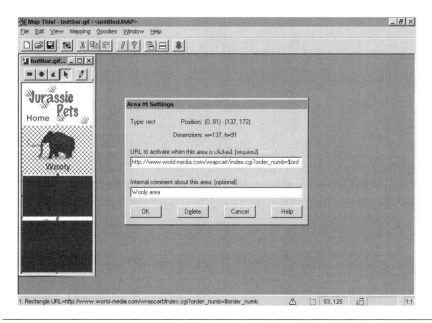

Figure 10.8 Variables in the map editing program.

```
if (!(-e "mapfiles/$order_numb.map")) {

    open(NEW, "> mapfiles/$order_numb.map");

      ## Change tempmap.map here

    $tempstring = &file_to_string("button.map");

    print(NEW "$tempstring");

    close(NEW);

  }
```

In the $tempstring variable I've changed the name to button.map. The cart.pl routine will evaluate that file automatically and store it in $order_numb.map in the mapfiles directory. You'll call the file as we did in the head.wms file earlier. To make two maps for two different images, you must replicate this entire routine of code as I've done here:

```
if (!(-e "mapfiles/$order_numb2.map")) {

    open(NEW, "> mapfiles/$order_numb2.map");

      ## Change tempmap.map here

    $tempstring = &file_to_string("image2.map");

    print(NEW "$tempstring");

    close(NEW);

  }
```

Not only have I changed the file we read in to image2.map, I've also added a 2 after the $order_numb in the first two lines. I'll call this second map as <ahref="$order_number2.map"><img src="image2.gif" ismap></a> in the header, footer, or page middle.

Ensuring Order Security

I bet you're cringing at the thought that everyone reading this book will know where to look for your orders based on the format you saw in the orders/directory. You can edit this format at line 66 of the total.cgi program:

```
65:

66: open(ORDERFILE, ">> ./orders/$mday.$mon.$year.orders");

67:
```

You can add security in two ways here. In the first, you'll just change the orders/ directory to another, like completed/ or something, then on Unix only, CHMOD the directory 777. Your temp orders will still be in orders/ which doesn't matter because there is no contact information saved in the .tmp files. But the finished orders generated by total.cgi will go into a directory unknown to the readers of this book. The second way is to rename the extension .orders at the end of the line. Call it .finished, .txt, or something else. Then put a dummy index.html file in the orders/ or your renamed directory so that a directory listing will be impossible. You could also make your orders directory not readable by the webserver.

On another security note, your customers reading this book are probably wondering why on earth you would ever e-mail their credit card information to yourself from the webserver. What about SET, where supposedly their card number is never saved? Chances are you've put total.cgi on a secure SSL server. They think they are safe, then you go off and mail their credit card information. Unfortunately, mailing card information is the most common way to handle Internet orders. Real-time credit card validation is expensive. We use a piece of software called STOMP API from Outreach Communications (www.outreach.com) for our clients who can afford it, but for many this ultra-secure method is out of reach (pun intended, wince).

The cart, however, can offer a more secure means than the default of mailing. First you'll rename that orders/ directory as I suggested and put it somewhere not readable by the webserver. Then change the code at line 44:

```
44: if ($open eq "MAIL") {

45:     $orderstring .= <<ENDORDER;

46: Card Number: $card1

47: Card Verify: $card2

48: Expires: $expiration

49: ENDORDER
```

```
50: }
```

Change the $open eq "MAIL" to $open eq "ORDERFILE" then go to line 81:

```
81:

82: foreach $open ("MAIL", "ORDERFILE", "MAILBACK") {

83: $totalstring = &printtotal;
```

Remove "MAIL" from the three choices. That will kill the confirm mail altogether, which is useless to you without a credit card number.

Storing a Relational Database of Orders

If you have Access or another relational database installed, it would be a waste of time to sift through the orders stored in the current ORDERFILE file. They are stacked on top of each other formatted exactly like the e-mail. This was designed as a backup system only, counting on fulfillment through the e-mailed system. But if you're going the security route or just want to make your life easier, it's more efficient to save a daily file of tab delimited files that are linked to each other through the $order_number variable. You would import them with a macro and run daily queries for fulfillment. Here is some sample code to create two files, one with the extension .personal and one with the extension .data. I'm grabbing the personal information from the top of total.cgi and the data from the temp file in the orders/ directory. Note that the files have to be flocked and CHMODed on Unix. Otherwise they'll overwrite. You'll want to get rid of the flock and CHMOD lines on NT. I don't know how NT handles the overwrite situation, but I assume the requests are cued automatically.

```
if (open(ORDER, "./orders/$order_numb.tmp")) {


open (PERSONAL, ">>/usr/local/orders/$mday.$mon.$year.personal");

flock(PERSONAL, 2);

print PERSONAL "

$order_numb\t$name\t$address\t$city\t$state\t$zip\t$email\t$homephone\t$work-

phone\t$paytype\t$card1\t$card2\t$expiration\t$order_numb\t$hour:$min,

$mon/$mday/$year";
```

```
close(PERSONAL);

chmod(0666, "/usr/local/orders/$mday.$mon.$year.personal");



open (DATA, ">>/usr/local/orders/$mday.$mon.$year.data");

flock(DATA, 2);

while (<ORDER>) {                                    #while loop open

        chop;

        local($itemnumber, $name, $size, $price, $quantity)  = split (/\t/,$_);

print DATA "$order_numb\t$itemnumber\t$name\t$size\t$price\t$quantity";

close(DATA);

chmod (0666, "/usr/local/orders/$mday.$mon.$year.personal");


        }


               }
```

Taking Out the Trash

By default, the cart leaves the files accumulated in orders/ and mapfiles/ alone.
Nothing old gets deleted. But over time these can build, especially the maps. If
you're limited in drive space, you might want to enable the remold subroutine at
line 15 in cart.pl. First go to line 22 and set the number of days to wait before
removing a file. In the distribution it's set to two:

```
15: sub remold {

.


.


19:     local($secsinday) = 86400;

20:     local($time) = time();

21:     ## Set this next variable to the number of days to remove files.

22:     local($dieinxdays) = 2;
```

Then you have to enable it in index.cgi. It's commented out at the very end:

```
#&remold("./mapfiles/", "map");

#&remold("./orders/", "tmp");
```

Get rid of the #comments. Then, if you've changed the location of either the map files or temp files, change that, along with the file extension. Note that there is no dot on the file extension.

Using and Setting Cookies: The Other Option

The most misunderstood aspect of using cookies is that they cannot be called from a static document. You can set one through a META tag in Netscape only, but you cannot read one in and track state with one without the use of JavaScript. JavaScript can both set and get a cookie on an otherwise static document. Most cookie action on the web is handled through CGI.

On the Web If for some reason, you can't do CGI on your server, change servers. If you can't, check out www.sna.com/mmatteo/Java/jscookies.html for a demo of how to track state with client persistent JavaScript Cookies. All the code you need is there with a demo that keeps track of how many times you've visited the page.

We've written a utility called the Cookie Jar that allows you to run a simple subroutine, passing cookie variables back and forth between the server and the cookies.txt file of the browser. You'll find it in the /sourcecode/UNIX/cookiejar and /sourcecode/NT/cookiejar directories as cookiejar.pl. I'm going to add the functionality to index.cgi of the shopping cart we just installed. First I add the following to the top of index.cgi:

```
require "cookiejar.pl";

%cookies = &get_cookie;

$cookieonename= "userid";
```

```
$cookieonevalue="USRNUMB$sec$min$hour$mday$mon$year";

$cookieoneexpire=" Thursday, 17-July-1997 00:00:00 EDT;";
```

The last three lines are the variables that the cookie jar sends by default. For each cookie you send, required fields are name and value, with expire as an option. If expire isn't set, cookiejar.pl automatically sends January 31, 2000. If you do set a date as I have, make sure to keep it in the exact same format as this example or it will not be read. Note here that I didn't name these variables just $name and $value, because we can set more than one cookie at a time. To actually set the cookies, we'll go down to line 64 of index.cgi where I'm setting a cookie for all .htm, .html, and .cgi files we evaluate in through SiteWrapper. By setting the following together with the variable definitions, you should have Figure 10.9 sent to your browser if you set the approve option in Netscape:

```
if ($document_filename =~ /htm/i) {

        &set_cookie($cookieonename, $cookieonevalue, $cookieoneexpire);

        &Content_type("text/html");

    if (-e "$document_filename") {

        &print_file("$document_filename");

    } else {

        &print_file("error.htm");

    }

    } elsif ($document_filename =~ /\.cgi/i) {

    if (-e "$document_filename") {

        &set_cookie($cookieonename, $cookieonevalue, $cookieoneexpire);

        &Location("$server/$document_filename");
```

In the second line and second-to-last line I've called the &set_cookie subroutine located in cookiejar.pl and sent it the three values I just set. I've put the set cookie before the content-type, which is required, in both cases. Now I can call my cookie back by putting the $cookies{userid} variable in any wrapped page. I set the preceding %cookies = &get_cookie; line, the %cookies array is available to me at any

Figure 10.9 Set Netscape to approve all cookies, and this will pop up if you are configured correctly.

time. If you are using the cookies library in another CGI program, you'll want to put in both the require line and &get_cookie line at the top of your code, generating the %cookies array. I've called the $cookies{userid} variable in the HTML of homepage.htm in Figure 10.10.

 On the CD In the same example directories you'll find index.cookies and homepage.cookies, which contain the examples here.

Figure 10.10 Check if the cookie is set with SiteWrapper.

Extra Crumbs

By default, your cookie is served only to your domain, so if a program on www.yourcompany.com sets a cookie, the &get_cookie will work on any server under the yourcompany.com domain. To limit it to just shopping.yourdomain.com you'll put that in the cookie set reference at line 51 of cookiejar.pl:

```
print(STDOUT "Set-Cookie: $name=$value; domain=shopping.yourdomain.com
path=/products; $expire\n");
```

Now your www address won't be sent the cookie. Notice also that I've set a path variable as /products, which means that the shopping.yourdomain.com home-page won't get the cookie either. Only when you click into a product page will it be sent. Beyond shopping, this could be used for intranet tracking and access for different departments.

The other attribute you can put in the code is the word "secure." That limits the sending of cookies by only SSL encrypted servers. I don't know that many users want their profile stored in a cookie, which I addressed in the opening, but if you do, use the secure option.

11

Unlimited Growth
with WebPost

This utility was the one that sparked the whole book. WebPost started with a client of ours, a law firm, who needed to post weekly articles to their website. Real Estate Law, Intellectual Property–their firm was very large and covered over fifteen specialties. These articles would be split evenly among all of them, and they would love to be able to archive old articles on the web so that people could search them. That's where the problem came in. Even with conversion programs from MS Word to HTML, someone would have to devote full-time to the management of the site, updating the links with new articles.

So that was our first task. We needed a program on the server that would automatically update the links on the node documents when a new page was uploaded to the web. Main pages like Intellectual Property Articles automatically would notice that a new file existed and add the new link to it. Perl could do this by reading directory listings, so each category of law had to have its own directory.

Then we thought about the Next Article and Previous Article options we had seen on other sites. Did they hand-code all those links? Yes, they did. And if they changed their minds and wanted to reorder the articles, they had to go back and manually re-edit the links. We had already developed the idea of a central configuration file, which many of you have already experienced with SiteWrapper, to keep track of links as they come and go, but to take this one step further, we decided that the configuration file should contain the order of the pages. That was when WebPost began. It became evident that we needed more than just a system that read directories. We needed an engine but there was more, and it is still evolving.

Today WebPost starts you from an administrative menu as you'll see later. This is just a webform with radio buttons for Add a New Document, Edit, Delete, and Upload a File. Each choice connects you to another form, from which you make changes to the site in the form fields, then click Submit to record the changes to the site. There is no local editor, but WebPost autocodes the HTML of lists, hotlinks, images, and subheaders with a simple bracketing system. It automatically updates the main link pages, changes the next and previous in each document, and keeps track of who has changed what. But rather than continue expounding, let's install it and see how the features actually work.

Because we have so much to cover, I'm going to minimize the separation of Unix and NT to the first basic steps. Once it's ready to run, we'll continue with the Quick Start a bit, then divert into the actual demonstration of the features. I'm going to assume that you have not installed SiteWrapper, which means that you do not already have a central configuration file. If you have installed SiteWrapper already, don't overwrite your index.cgi with WebPost's. I'll explain later how to bring WebPost's functionality into your homepage. As we edit webpost.cfg, ignore the variables you've already set and add the ones you haven't. In some places I'll mention line numbers and show them in the code. In some places I won't. If I don't, it's code that you can cut and paste into the file to try it. Line numbers at the beginning will break Perl, so I'd rather not confuse you. Here we go!

Quick Start: Unix

1. In the /sourcecode/UNIX/webpost/ directory, you'll find webpost.zip. Unzip it and install it into a local directory so you can work on the files. There is also an unzipped directory in case you're one of the two people who own a computer who have not installed Winzip.

2. Now you have to decide how you'll be running WebPost. If it is to run as index.cgi from your homepage, install it in your base directory at www.yourcompany.com. If it is to run as a spur off the main, like inventory/, make that directory and install it there. Unless you've already installed SiteWrapper, upload all the files to the web-

server. If you've installed SiteWrapper, again, don't overwrite index.cgi. Read ahead as we cover WebPost's special homepage variables. You'll be able to continue with the Quick Start, but only if you delete the variables we cover from webpost.cfg and add the line require "webpost.cfg"; to your index.cgi. You won't yet be able to view your homepage titles of new WebPost documents automatically until we get to the customization section later. CHMOD the index.cgi file to 755.

3. Make a directory under where you just installed WebPost called logs/. CHMOD it 777.

4. If you did just upload index.cgi, hit it with your web browser. You should get Figure 11.1. Don't click around from there. There are a few steps to follow before WebPost will be fully functional.

5. Next bring up webpost.cfg in your editor. At line 10 is the $server variable. Set it as $server="http://www.yourserver.com"; with no trailing slash. If you've just installed WebPost into a spur directory or your home directory, set $server="http://www.yourprovider.com/~yourname"; again, with no trailing slash. If you've installed SiteWrapper, edit the require lines on every CGI program on the site. You're renaming webpost.cfg with yourconfig.cfg. All of them

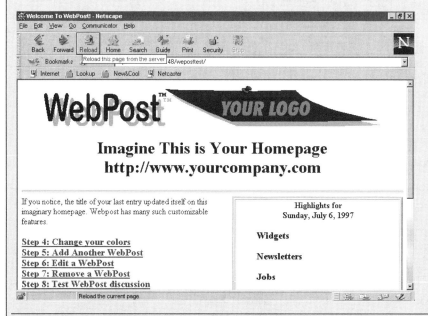

Figure 11.1 WebPost's sample homepage.

should be tickler.cgi, admin.cgi, bodytag.cgi, delete.cgi, edit.cgi, Encrypt.cgi, parser.cgi, submit.cgi, upload.cgi, vc.cgi, and wmsdb.cgi. Multi-Edit allows you to do this automatically with its multiple file search and replace, shown in Figure 11.2.

6. You'll also want to check the Perl location on all of them as well. If it's wrong, use the same search and replace from Multi-Edit.

7. Go into the main directory where you installed WebPost and CHMOD all the CGI files to 755.

8. Then hit the file Encrypt.cgi with your browser. It will generate the value to plug into the next variable in our webpost.cfg at line 16, $password. The default in the config is luTDemOTOK09k, which is the encrypted word "password" on most systems. You can leave it alone for now if you like, but verify that it matches for your system by using the Encrypt program anyway. Don't ever, no matter what, plug a real word into the $password variable. The password you submit from the form is encrypted and matched by WebPost. And no, there is no way to decrypt a password without an advanced hacker algorithm (that's not a challenge, we're all friends here).

9. Make a directory called "upload" and one called "data." You'll change the name of the latter later, but for now data is fine. Then CHMOD both directories to 777.

10. Next, cd (change directory) to the data/ directory and make five new directories called 1,2,3,4, and 5, the actual numbers. That is where WebPost will store your files. Then CHMOD all the directories 777.

11. Hit admin.cgi with your browser now. You should get Figure 11.3. Leave Submit New Documents checked, plug in the password you just encrypted (the actual word, not the garble), and hit I'm Ready To Move On.

Figure 11.2 Multi-Edit's search and replace.

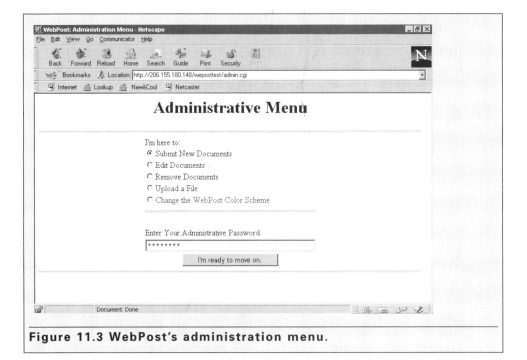

Figure 11.3 WebPost's administration menu.

Quick Start: NT

1. In the /sourcecode/UNIX/webpost/ directory you'll find webost.zip. Unzip it and install it into a local directory so you can work on the files. There is also an unzipped directory in case you're one of the two people who own a computer who have not installed Winzip.

2. Now you have to decide how you'll be running WebPost. If it is to run as index.cgi from your homepage, install it in your base directory at www.yourcompany.com. If it is to run as a spur off the main, like inventory/, make that directory and install it there. Unless you've already installed SiteWrapper, upload all the files to the webserver. If you've installed SiteWrapper, don't overwrite index.cgi. Read ahead into the customization as we cover WebPost's configuration options and special homepage variables. You'll be able to continue with the Quick Start, but only if you delete the variables we cover from web-post.cfg and add the line require "webpost.cfg"; to your index.cgi. You won't yet be able to view your homepage titles of new WebPost documents automatically until we get to the customization section later.

3. Make a logs/ directory under where you just installed WebPost.

4. If you did upload index.cgi, hit it with your web browser. You should get Figure 11.1. Don't click around from there. There are a few steps to follow before WebPost will be fully functional.

5. Next bring up webpost.cfg in your editor. At line 10 is the $server variable. Set it as $server="http://www.yourserver.com"; with no trailing slash. If you've just installed WebPost into a spur directory or your home directory, set $server="http://www.yourprovider.com/~yourname"; again, with no trailing slash. If you've installed SiteWrapper, edit the require lines that call webpost.cfg with your-config.cfg on all the CGI programs on the site. All of them should be tickler.cgi, admin.cgi, bodytag.cgi, delete.cgi, edit.cgi, Encrypt.cgi, parser.cgi, submit.cgi, upload.cgi, vc.cgi, and wmsdb.cgi. Multi-Edit allows you to do this automatically with its multiple file search and replace, shown in Figure 11.2.

6. Then hit the file Encrypt.cgi with your browser. It will generate the value to plug into the next variable in our webpost.cfg at line 16, $password. The default in the config is luTDemOTOK09k, which is the encrypted word "password" on most systems. You can leave it alone for now if you like, but verify that it matches for your system by using the Encrypt program anyway. Don't ever, no matter what, plug a real word into the $password variable. The password you submit from the form is encrypted and matched by WebPost. And no, there is no way to decrypt a password without an advanced hacker algorithm (that's not a challenge, we're all friends here).

7. Make a directory called "upload" and one called "data." You'll change the name of the latter later, but for now data is fine. One note is that if you're working from a remote location through FTP, some installations of NT Server won't allow you to rename directories. You can just delete it later instead and start fresh with whatever you're going to rename data.

8. Next, cd (change directory) to the data/ directory and make five new directories called 1,2,3,4, and 5, the actual numbers. That is where WebPost will store your files.

9. Hit admin.cgi with your browser. You should get Figure 11.3. Leave Submit New Documents checked, plug in the password you just encrypted (the actual word, not the garble), and hit I'm ready to move on.

Continuing the Quick Start for All Platforms

1. Everyone should now be at submit.cgi. You didn't really have to use the admin.cgi menu to get here, but it's a convenient way to centralize all the administration for the actual users of the system. The first choice you'll have at the top is the date that the document was actually published. The default will be today's date, but we included the option to change the date so old documents could be archived in the correct order. For each of WebPost's categories, the dates control the order in which these pages appear on the main link page.

2. Now we'll insert a dummy title for the document. Call it "1972 Plymouth Duster," following our car dealership example, next, or "Earnings Up This Quarter" if one of your WebPost categories potentially could be press releases.

3. Next is author. The dummy config for the Quick Start has two, neither checked by default. Make sure to check one. You'll see how this affects the document in a bit.

4. Then check a category. The dummy examples really aren't representative of the way you'd use WebPost's category structure, but they work for our purposes. More likely you'd be splitting topics below one of those, as I explained previously with our law firm. The Articles would be split to Real Estate Law, Intellectual Property. The Cars would split to Two Door, Four Door, etc. We'll be setting categories after the Quick Start.

5. Do you want to e-mail an update to members? That's one of WebPost's features I neglected to mention. It has a copy of Tickler built into it (Chapter 7). Visitors to the site will be able to sign up by the categories you specify, so if you get a Chevy Lumina, they won't get a message if they've signed up only for Sport Utilities. You can check the box for now, but unless you check the sendmail location in webpost.cfg (Unix only) and sign up your e-mail at tickler.cgi, it won't do anything. Also, NT users should see the warning in the Tickler chapter regarding the lack of sockets support in Perl for Win32. If the bug in Perl is fixed, you'll have to specify the SMTP host, which we'll get to later.

6. The next section is for images. We'll use it later, but for now just put in the URL of a graphic that you know is on the web into the Where? field. Give its full URL with http://. Height, Width, and Alternate text are optional, but Caption is a neat feature you can try. If you put in a caption, WebPost puts a table around the image with your caption

below it. The next input field is Hotlink. It will make your image click-able, BORDER=0. The final field, Image Alignment, puts either the image or the table with the image in it where you want it on the page. You can repeat this process for Image 2 and 3. I've filled out some values from the recent Mars landing. They don't match our title, but do you know how hard it is to find good 72 Duster pictures? Figure 11.4 is the set of input boxes.

7. Next you'll see a box that says Turn Off WebPost Autocoding. As I mentioned, WebPost automatically codes certain pieces of HTML, shown in Figure 11.5. This checkbox turns that coding off so you can paste precoded HTML into the form box without the worry of WebPost breaking it by trying to autocode it. Leave that unchecked for now.

8. To turn autocoding off, below the checkbox is a quick reference card of the autocoding features. Table 11.1 shows this a bit clearer, with the resulting HTML. Fill the <TEXTAREA> with some sample text, and try inserting the autocodes. Put a plus sign at the beginning of a line, followed by space, followed by your bullet text, then another plus on the next line, WebPost will make you a bulleted list. Make a [[Subhead]H] anywhere in the text, or [[hotlink your text to a URL]http://www .yourserver.com] with the simple bracket system. Images are the toughest to understand. You identified what and where they are in the preceding section, so now you have to tell WebPost where to put them in the document. For the first image, put $$$1 in the text wherever you want it, then $$$2 for image two and $$$3 for image 3. They will size, align, and hotlink as you specified

Paragraphs	Subheaders
text blank line text	[[subhead text]H]
Images	**Hotlinking**
Text next to image $$$imagenumber (e.g. $$$1)	[[text to be hotlinked]http://www.hotlink.com]
Bullet List	**Numbered List**

+ bullet1 (space after + sign)
+ bullet2
 	
will look like:
 	
   • bullet1
   • bullet2
	- Name of chapter (space after - sign)
	- Name of next chapter
	
	will look like:
	
	   1. Name of chapter
	   2. Name of next chapter

Figure 11.4 There are six more of these image input boxes at the bottom of the submit and edit menus.

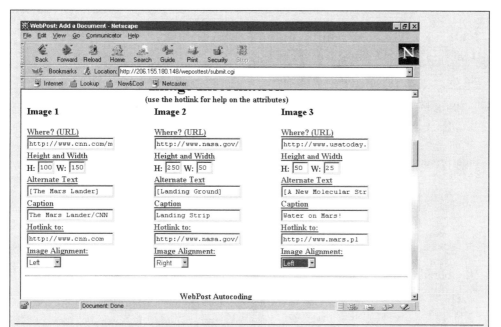

Figure 11.5 Web Post's autocode features on the submit (and edit) screens act as a cheat sheet for your users.

them in the image section. The rest of the text automatically will <P>aragraph where you do and line
eak where you do. Netscape and Microsoft Internet Explorer limit the total size of the document you can paste into a <TEXTAREA> to just over 24,000 characters, which is about 5,000 words.

9. Then enter your password and Click Here When Finished. WebPost will give you the options to go see your new page or revisit your homepage. Click View Your WebPost, then return to the homepage. As you'll see if you're following along, index.cgi automatically grabbed the newest listing in Cars and inserted it into the homepage (Figure 11.6).

10. Go back to admin.cgi and select the edit option, which will take you to edit.cgi. You could, again, go directly to edit.cgi. Once you're there, you should have a menu of your categories, in bold black, followed by one optional hotlink and radio button for whatever you named your document (mine is 72 Plymouth Duster), to view it before editing to the hotlink. To edit it, select the radio button and plug in your password.

Table 11.1 WebPost's Autocoding Features Make It Easy for Your Users to Keep Their Sites Fresh

Name	WebPost Markup	Resulting HTML
Paragraphs	Paragraph one blank line Paragraph two	Paragraph one \<P> Paragraph two
Line Breaks	Line one Line two	Line one\ Line two\
Bullet List	+ Bullet one + Bullet two	\<UL> \<LI> Bullet one \<LI> Bullet two \</UL>
Numbered List	- Item one - Item two	\<OL> \<LI> Item one \<LI> Item two
Hotlinking	[[text to be hotlinked]http://www.hotlink.com]	\<A HREF="http://www.hotlink.com">text to be hotlinked\</A>
Subheaders Image Insertion	[[Subhead text]H] This is text with images in it. Where ever you $$$1 like just put in an image $$$2 tag with three dollar signs and the number of the image $$$3 you've plugged in above.	\<H2>Subhead text\</H2> This is text with images in it. Where ever you \<IMG SRC="http://www.images.com/yourimage1.gif"> like just put in an image \<IMG SRC="http://www.images.com/yourimage2.gif"> tag with three dollar signs and the number of the image \<IMG SRC="http://www.images.com/yourimage3.gif"> you've plugged in above.

11. The edit screen is much like the submit, but with a couple of differences. One is that the author in this version isn't checked automatically. Make

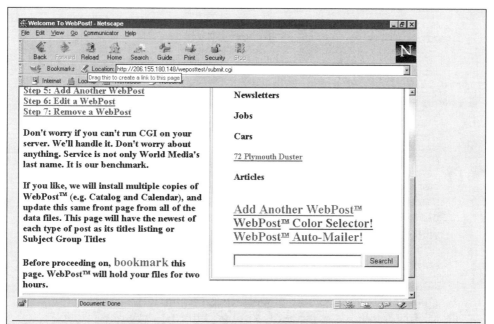

Figure 11.6 The homepage automatically inserts new page names.

sure to recheck it. The other is that your image information is not plugged in to the Where and other fields automatically. We left it coded, within the text, as HTML. If you have captions, this can get cumbersome as you navigate around the original text, but we did it for a reason. The submit menu has only nine fields for images. There are six more at the bottom I didn't tell you about before. But $$$9 might not be enough for some sites. This gives you the freedom to include up to nine more from every edit screen you bring up with $$$1 to $$$9 again. The old ones stay hard coded into the document from where they were. WebPost won't break the HTML.

12. The other note I should mention about the edit is that it automatically saves the URL of the document you are editing if you keep it in the same category. This will protect you from the dead link problems most people go through by editing and renaming documents. Altavista doesn't care that you changed the content of a URL. It looks for ExactDocumentName.html and that's it. Though WebPost's URLs are a bit more complicated (parser.cgi?FILE=data/4/data.4), you won't have to worry. The one exception is when you change a category of an entry. The file location changes, but it doesn't mess up other files on the site. Once a URL is used, it's gone from the available list.

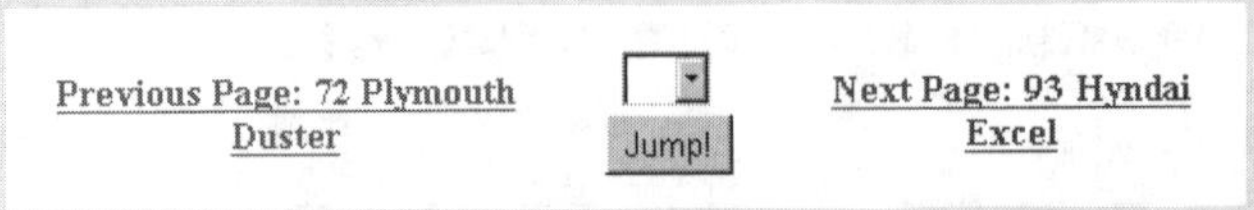

| Previous Page: 72 Plymouth Duster | [ ] [▾] Jump! | Next Page: 93 Hyndai Excel |

Figure 11.7 WebPost automatically re-indexes, creating dynamic Next and Previous links.

13. Go back the submit screen and put in a couple more dummy entries. Then scroll to the bottom of one of the entries. There should be a Previous Page: and Next Page:, as in Figure 11.7.

14. You should have several entries now, so let's delete one. Go to delete.cgi and select a checkbox from the menu, then plug in your password and click I'm Ready to Delete Those Articles. Again, as with the edit, you can preview them first, making sure you have the right document to delete. Note that there isn't any Windows-like confirm screen asking if you're sure. Be very careful when deleting.

15. Another feature you should test before we move on is the HTTP file upload. It will only work on newer versions of Netscape and Microsoft Internet Explorer that support the 1.1 draft of HTTP and JavaScript. You'll find it from the main admin.cgi or directly at upload.html. Name the file on the server (yourimage.gif or .jpg), then Browse for the file on your computer (that's the JavaScript). When you've found it, plug in your password and click the Send File button. You should be greeted with a Thanks page and a URL to the image. Notice that it points automatically to the upload directory, which is also where WebPost looks by default if you include no http://... in the Where? of the image information.

16. We've also used the file upload for clients who need to reference images and other types of documents from their body text, WebPost's autocoding feature will create a hotlink in the following formatwww.yourserver.com/upload/yourfile.movthis is particularly useful when a document is too long to fit within the 24,000 or so character limit of the <TEXTAREA> field. Our experts at www.expertsinternational.com slice tables and other linkable objects out of their commentary and upload them as small HTML files (after saving them as HTML in Word). Then when they refer to the table, they merely hotlink it from the text. You'll use this for sound files, multimedia, and other downloadable file types as well.

17. Lastly, we'll look at bodytag.cgi, which is the color changer for the whole site. If you installed SiteWrapper, you've already seen this as SiteColors, but we include it in the distribution of WebPost in

case you haven't. It's simple to use. Just plug in your password and select the color you want to change. More on this in Chapter 7.

 On the CD As I promised earlier, the nifty homepage tricks in WebPost aren't limited to WebPost's index.cgi. The variables we're using from within it can be called from SiteWrapper as well. In the zip-file and unzipped directories you'll find WebPost.pl. At the top of your SiteWrapper index.cgi, add the line require "WebPost.pl";.

Customizing WebPost

You've just installed the WebPost demo, which doesn't do you much good if you're selling cars. Don't worry, you haven't wasted much effort. As we continue, you'll use the same program base you already installed. On Unix, you will rename the data/ directory. On NT, if you can't rename it, you'll just create a new one with the same numbered spurs you just created. WebPost is easy, both to install and use. Before we go on, it's important that you and the people for whom you are installing it understand that. I've had people walk out of lectures at Mecklermedia's web conferences because they thought WebPost was some proprietary system we were selling. It's not. And customizing it and maintaining is equally as easy.

First we'll go back into webpost.cfg and edit more of the variables that we ignored for the Quick Start. If you've installed SiteWrapper already, you'll be adding these to your config.cfg or whatever you renamed it.

The first variable you'll encounter after $password, which we set earlier, is $sendmail_location = "/usr/bin/sendmail";. Find it on your system or contact your sysadmin. The next variable should be $htmlheadfile. This is going to be the header that you want for the entire site. Most likely it will contain an image in the upper-left corner with a button bar either at the top or along the side. The default head.wms that comes with the distribution contains the following:

```
<HTML>

<HEAD>

<TITLE>
```

```
$name_of_org: $thispagetitle
```

```
</TITLE>
```

```
</HEAD>
```

```
$BODYTAG
```

We'll set the $name_of_org variable later. It's a good idea to have the name of your company in every URL, so if someone prints the page they'll know where it came from. The other variable in the <TITLE> field is $thispagetitle. It is grabbed dynamically for some pages; we'll set it for others. Below $BODYTAG, which grabs the information from SiteColors, you'll put your logo and button bar HTML. We've found it useful to keep this information in one place because logos and button bars can change for the whole site as often as once a year.

When changing a header graphic, you could just name it the same name as the old file. The new picture would be displayed automatically. But if the size changed, your HEIGHT and WIDTH attributes would mess it up. So how do you compensate? Leave off the HEIGHT and WIDTH in the first place, which makes your pages appear to load much slower. One hung image can hang a whole page. By using head.wms, you can keep in the attributes and change the whole site by editing one file. If you installed SiteWrapper already, you've already seen the benefits.

The $htmltailfile is the same, except for your contact information and copyright notice. The HTML you begin with in foot.wms is even simpler:

```
<P>
```

```
$JUMPLIST
```

```
<BR>
```

```
$TEXTLIST
```

```
</BODY>
```

```
</HTML>
```

You already saw the look of what $JUMPLIST gives you on the resulting WebPost page and in Figure 11.6, except that its values were empty. Once we set the variables that control them, both $JUMPLIST and $TEXTLIST will contain all the major areas of your site, including WebPost's categories. $JUMPLIST is a drop-down list, $TEXTLIST is each page name in text, separated by a pipe (|). You could, of course, manually insert the HTML into the header and footer, but sometimes you'll need them in the middles of documents. That's why they're in variables. This is useful on loooooong documents where the reader might decide they've had enough half way in. Giving them a periodic $JUMPLIST to save them having to scroll all the way to the top or bottom will be appreciated.

The next variable outputs a file of all the items you'll post in WebPost. Rarely will it be that you'll make this file available to visitors because it can be really huge, but if you want to hotlink to all the cars we have, name it $outfname = "all_of_our_cars.html";, which is what I'm using for this demo.

I mentioned earlier that we would be changing the name of the data/ directory to something more intuitive for your site. This next variable, $dbfname = "data";, is the first place we see "data" used. It's the output file name put in that database directory. I'm renaming it "cars."

Now we alter that data/ directory. First edit the name to whatever you want to call the directory/ off of your main. I'm calling mine cars, then making a cars/ directory. Rename the $dbdir = "data"; variable to your "yourstuff," and don't include the slash in the variable naming. Just change the word "data" to "yourstuff."

Don't forget to go to the server and either change the name of that directory or make a new one called whatever is in $dbdir. It should be CHMOD 777 on Unix.

The next variable controls what your visitors will get when there are no items in a category. Figure 11.8 (www.golftoo.com—great discounts!) shows something close to the default included in $none_yet = "none.wms";. Note that their header and footer are dynamically tacked on. What's in the actual HTML of none.yet is simple:

```
<CENTER><h1>We're Sorry!</h1></CENTER><P>

There are no data files at the present time.
```

Now we go to a variable that controls a word used on static pages generated by WebPost that contains every listing on the site. I noted the "all the cars" page earlier, which lists cars by category. The other two are all the cars by title alphabetically and all the cars by author, which we'll disable for this example later. Replace the $type_of_doc = "Posting"; to Cars or whatever you are posting. It's printed on the page, not in a URL, so capitalize it.

In $name_of_org, I switched it to Henry's Used Cars, our example business. It's crucial that this title be descriptive because, as you saw from head.wms, it's printed

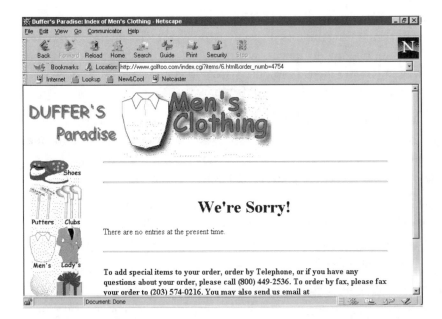

Figure 11.8 The sample none.wms file. Hopefully you'll have lots of stuff so nobody will ever see it.

in the <TITLE> field of every WebPost page. Many search engines spidering your site will rely on your <TITLE> as their sole descriptor.

The next section governs the copy of Tickler that's included with the WebPost distribution. The first variable is $emaildbfile = "emails";. In the Tickler installation we called this emails.db. If you've already installed Tickler, change it to whatever you renamed it back then. I'll show you later how to integrate the two. Tickler's other variables are $adminemail = "webpost\@world-media.com"; set to yours with the @ sign escaped with a backslash, and $emailheadfile = "update.wms";, which is the text that WebPost grabs for the top of its tickle messages. If you've installed Tickler, you know this file as update.txt. Change it, or use a separate one for WebPost categories than for the rest of the site. Non-Tickler installers should go to Chapter 7 for instructions on how to edit both that and confirm.txt.

NT users must, as with Tickler, add another variable here, as explained in the actual configuration file. It's $smtpserver = "yourmachine.yourhost.com"; and is crucial for Tickler to send its messages. Look in the Tickler chapter and on our website at www .world-media.com/webtoolkit for the latest on Perl for Win32. There was a bug preventing the reliable sending of messages as of this writing, but it should be fixed soon.

Now we get into the heart of WebPost's configuration. The next variable is $numgroups = 5;, which you should recognize from the Quick Start as the number of groups we created under the data/ directory. I'm leaving it at five because I've got five categories of information, which we'll set in the next variable. When you set this number, make sure you create a directory under the $dbdir directory for each number up to and including this number, then on Unix, CHMOD each one to 777.

You'll see %groupnames set as our defaults from the demo:

```
%groupnames = (1, "Widgets", 2, "Newsletters", 3, "Jobs", 4,

    "Cars", 5, "Articles");
```

As you can see, each directory is associated with a category of information. My categories will be set as:

```
%groupnames = (1, "2 Doors", 2, "4 Doors", 3, "Sport Utilities", 4,

    "Mini-Vans", 5, "Info About Henry's");
```

The next variable you'll see is %titlenames. For SiteWrapper installers with Tickler, you already have a %ticklerpages variable in your config. Don't worry, WebPost knows how to look in both it and %groupnames for tickle messages. You'll leave the static information on your site alone wrapped through SiteWrapper and tickled through Tickler. Non-Tickler users need to put in the variable $response = "$server/yourThankspage.html";, two down from %groupnames, so when people sign up for tickles you thank them properly. Note that for SiteWrapper users this will be $server?yourThankspage.html.

Next you'll come to the section that controls the $JUMPLIST and $TEXTLIST lists of pages:

```
@jumpnames = ("$dbdir/1.html:$groupnames{'1'}",

                "$dbdir/2.html:$groupnames{'2'}",

                "$dbdir/3.html:$groupnames{'3'}",

                "$dbdir/4.html:$groupnames{'4'}",

                "$dbdir/5.html:$groupnames{'5'}"

                );
```

The default is formatted so that you will get the main category listings as your choices automatically, with 2 Door first and About Henry's last. You'll reorder them by moving the listing up and down in the array. To add a new WebPost category to the list, you'll follow the same format, changing only the key number. To add an eternal page, a static one, you'll add "yourpage.html:Page Name" onto the array. The one exception is the homepage, in which case you'll add "?:Henry's Homepage" to the top of the list. WebPost uses SiteWrapper's redirect routine:

```
@jumpnames = ( "?:Henry's Homepage",

              "$dbdir/1.html:$groupnames{'1'}",

              "$dbdir/2.html:$groupnames{'2'}",

              "$dbdir/3.html:$groupnames{'3'}",

              "$dbdir/4.html:$groupnames{'4'}",

              "$dbdir/5.html:$groupnames{'5'}"

              );
```

The next set of variables controls the author options for the site:

```
$authors_yes = 1;

$authorfname = "authorindex.html";

$authordir = "authors/";

%authorDB = ("John Doe", "doe.html","Jane Doe",

"http://www.anonymouse.com/jane.html");
```

If $authors_yes is set to 1, that static HTML page I wrote about earlier will be written every time you insert or edit a WebPost document. The filename is controlled by $authorfname. The next variable, $authordir, is where the author home-pages are located. You'll see what this means in the default for the next variable, %authorDB. It's a hash of your authors and their homepage locations. The first entry is John Doe. His homepage is in the authors/ directory on our site as the document doe.html. The parser that grabs this variable automatically tacks $authordir before the document name if it sees no http:// in the hash value. As you'll see from postings, authors are included automatically by default, linked to their homepage.

Note that these can also be mailto: addresses; just make sure $authordir is unde-
fined (empty as "";).

The third full index I mentioned earlier is controlled by the next set of variables:

```
$titles_yes = 0;

$title_head_fname = "titleind.wms";

$titlefname = "titleindex.html";
```

I've set $titles_yes to 1 because some people might want a list of all the cars I have
for sale. The next is a little file that prints at the top of the title index. It's only one line
in the distribution that says "This is an index by title of every post.<P>." We needed it
for a client so we included it in this version. Neither the category nor the author index
have this option. The third variable is the filename you'll call as the URL.

Next is an option we very rarely use on WebPost. It limits what IP address editors to the site can come from. The first variable is $check_ips = 0;, which you'll set
to 1 to activate it. The second, @ip_number = ("192.80.84.1");, is the list of actual
IP numbers. Note that this won't work for people on the dynamic IP addressing
system used by most ISPs. You would have to list every IP in the pool, and then you
would be open to other people from the ISP editing the site. It's quite useful from
firewalls, which always use the same address, and on an intranet it's perfect to limit
access to a few machines regardless of who has the password.

If you set the next variable, $dovc = 0;, to 1, make a vc/ directory off the main
directory, not off the renamed data/ directory, and on Unix, CHMOD it to 777. It's
a simple version control system that tracks and prints versions of WebPost documents that people edit and delete. There is no restore written, but to make one
would be easy.

The rest of the code in webpost.cfg shouldn't need to be touched. If you're using
SiteWrapper you'll recognize it from config.cfg. It reads in the SiteColors data file.

Put Your Homepage Here!

When you installed index.cgi as the default homepage, the layout in Figure 11.1
greeted you. From my best guess, you probably don't want to leave it as that layout.
Now we're going to edit it. Bring up index.cgi in our editor and go to line 37 where
the subroutine printhomepage begins:

```
37: sub printhomepage
38: ##########################################################################
39:
40: {
41:   &Content_type("text/html");
42: print <<ENDHTML;
43: <!-- DOCTYPE HTML PUBLIC "-//IETF//DTD HTML 3.0//EN" "html.dtd"        -->
44: <!-- HTML Code (C) 1996, World Media Services                          -->
45: <!-- WWW:   http://www.world-media.com                                 -->
46: <!-- Phone: (603) 594-9321      Tel/FAX                                -->
47: <!-- Email: webmaster\@world-media.com                                 -->
48: <!--                                      -->
49: <!-- This document was automatically generated by the WMS WebPost (R),  -->
50: <!-- and is (C) 1996 World Media Services.                 -->
51:
52: <HTML>
53: <HEAD>
54: <META HTTP-EQUIV=REFRESH CONTENT=\"180; URL=$server\">
55: <TITLE>
56: Welcome To WebPost!
57: </TITLE>
58: </HEAD>
59: $bodytag
60: <CENTER><IMG SRC=webpost.gif ALT="WebPost System"></CENTER><P>
61: <h1 align=center>Imagine This is Your Homepage<BR>
```

```
62: http://www.yourcompany.com</h1>

63: <center>$blah_tags

64: </CENTER><P>

65: <HR>

66: <TABLE BORDER=3 VALIGN=TOP ALIGN=RIGHT>      <!-- Beginning of Left Table -->

67: <TR><TD><CENTER><h4>Highlights for<BR>${thisday}, ${thismonth} ${mday},

19${year}</h4></CENTER><P>

68: <A NAME=1>

69: <UL>

70: <H2>

71: $article_tags

72: <BR><A HREF=submit.cgi>Add Another WebPost<SUP><FONT

SIZE=1>TM</FONT></SUP></A>

73: <BR><A HREF=bodytag.cgi>WebPost<SUP><font size=1>TM</font></SUP> Color

Selector!</A>

74: <BR><A HREF=tickler.cgi>WebPost<SUP><FONT SIZE=1>TM</FONT></SUP> Auto-

Mailer!</A>

75: <BR>$wpostlink

76: <H2>

77: $art_tags

78: $title_tags

79: $author_tags

80: </h2>

81: </UL><P>

82: </h3>
```

```
83: </TR>

84: </TABLE>                    <!-- End of Left Table -->

85:

86: If you notice, the title of your last entry updated itself on this

87: imaginary homepage.  Webpost has many such customizable features.<P>

88: <h3><A HREF="bodytag.cgi">Step 4: Change your colors</A><br>

89: <A HREF="admin.cgi">Step 5: Add Another WebPost</A><BR>

90: <A HREF="admin.cgi">Step 6: Edit a WebPost</A><BR>

91: <A HREF="admin.cgi">Step 7: Remove a WebPost</A><BR>

92: <p>  Don't worry if you <strong>can't run CGI on your server</strong>.

We'll handle it.  Don't worry about anything. <strong> Service</strong> is not

only World Media's last name.  It is our benchmark.

93: <P>If you like, we will install multiple copies of WebPost<SUP><FONT

SIZE=1>TM</FONT></SUP> (e.g. Catalog  and  Calendar), and update this same front

page from all of the data files.  This page will have the newest of each type

of post as its titles listing or Subject Group Titles

94: <P>Before proceeding on, <strong><font size=+2

color=red>bookmark</font></strong> this page.

95: WebPost<FONT SIZE=1><SUP>TM</SUP></FONT> will hold your files for two hours.

96: </TABLE>

97: <HR></CENTER>

98: ENDHTML

99: &print_file($htmltailfile);

100: }    ##printhomepage
```

As you can see, this is the default HTML index.cgi spits out by calling the &printhomepage subroutine at line 101. For those of you using SiteWrapper, you've got the best of both worlds. Your homepage.htm is called by default by SiteWrapper. You can wrap other, non-WebPost pages, and your homepage can include the same dynamic variables by calling require WebPost.pl in your index.cgi. This is actually the preferred way to run index.cgi, but we put this subroutine in to demonstrate WebPost's homepage variables. If you think it's too dangerous to edit the actual CGI every time you make an HTML change to your homepage, install SiteWrapper first.

Most of the HTML in the printhomepage subroutine is standard. I've not put $HEADER at the top because the layout of my homepage looks nothing like the other pages on the site. On the homepage my logo isn't small; it's in the left-hand corner and is a central building block of the page. I do, however, want to use the SiteColors data to load my colors dynamically. The first variable you find addresses this at line 59. The $bodytag gives me the <BODY BGCOLOR=#... I need.

The next variable is at line 63. It's $blah_tags, which is actually nothing. We included it only to demonstrate that the variables listed here are the automated ones in WebPost. You can name any variable anything in the config and call it from within your homepage here or on any WebPost configuration or input page. So if $800number was in the config, you'd put it in foot.wms to grab automatically. You could also use it in text you input into WebPost's submit and edit menus. So if somewhere in our About Henry's pages we say "If you want to know more about the car call us at $800number," it automatically would be peeled from the config.

At line 67 is the date line. It shows the variables ${thisday}, ${thismonth} ${mday}, 19${year}. Those aren't associative arrays—those braces are optional. They tell a here document not to confuse the variables with the rest of the text. You'll find a complete set of date and time variables at the top of sitewrapper.pl.

Figure 11.9 shows what we've got now. There is a <TABLE> on the right with the latest car in each of WebPost's categories. There is a lot of information in that table, but at line 71 you'll see only $article_tags . That's it—one variable prints it all. To control the look of $article_tags, we go up to the for statement at line 12 in index.cgi where we iterate through the number of groups you set in $numgroups. For each group, open the $dbdir file and see if anything exists:

```
12: for ($x = 1; $x <= $numgroups; $x++) {

13:     if (-s "$dbdir/$x/num$dbfname") {
```

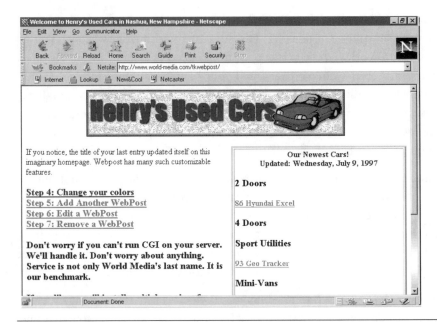

Figure 11.9 The car section of the homepage before we change it.

```
14:        open(DB, "$dbdir/$x/num$dbfname");

15:        $/ = "\n";

16:        @data = <DB>;

17:                ($date, $fname, $subject, $author) = split(/``/,$data[0]);

18:        close(DB);

19:        $article{"$x"} = "<A HREF=parser.cgi?FILE=$fname>$subject</A><BR>\n";

20:        } else {

21:        $article{"$x"} = "";

22:        }

23:        undef(@data);

24:        $article_tags .= "<H3>$groupnames{$x}</h3><h4>$article{$x}</h4>";

25: }
```

Then at lines 16 and 17, we eat that file's newest article title (in our case it's a car). At line 19 we've given $article{"x"} an HTML value pointing to the parser if an article exists. Note that $subject is all we're printing here, but you have the $date the article was posted, its file name, and the $author as well. Then, if no file exists in that group we set it blank just in case. At line 24 we define the actual $article_tags variable by putting the $groupnames{$x} in a <H3> tag, the actual $article name in a <H4> below it. I'm turning the whole banana into a definition list:

```
$article{"$x"} = "<A HREF=parser.cgi?FILE=$fname>$subject</A>\n";

    } else {

    $article{"$x"} = "";

    }

    undef(@data);



  $article_tags .= "<strong><DT><A HREF=\"$server/$dbdir/$x.html\">$group-

names{$x}</A></strong></DT><dd>$article{$x}</dd>";
```

I've not only changed the layout here. If you look in the new HREF for $group-names{$x}, I've also hotlinked the group names to their actual link node (all the sport utilities). Then I'm going to remove the lines 72–74, but not 75. The $wpostlink variable is an optional search box that activates only when there are things to search. We put it in because the demo on our site is empty when you first hit it. You can replace the variable $wpostlink with the actual HTML of:

```
<FORM METHOD=POST ACTION=\"search.cgi\">

<INPUT TYPE=HIDDEN NAME=\"valid_search\" VALUE=\"true\">

<INPUT TYPE=HIDDEN NAME=\"extended\" VALUE=\"yes\">

<INPUT TYPE=HIDDEN NAME=\"boolean\" VALUE=\"AND\">

<INPUT TYPE=HIDDEN NAME=\"case\" VALUE=\"Insensitive\">

<INPUT NAME=\"terms\" SIZE=30>

<INPUT TYPE=SUBMIT VALUE=\"Search!\"></FORM>
```

Right now it's pointing to a nonexistent program called search.cgi, which we'll get to in the search chapter. Then you can get rid of lines 77–82; they are old deprecated features from a previous version.

All my changes resulted in Figure 11.10. I've seeded all my keywords into the pages introduction, duplicating my location on purpose (the car business is mostly local). To duplicate this in SiteWrapper you'll include the previous variables in with your homepage.htm. That will keep you mostly out of index.cgi, which is easy to break. The one thing we can't take out is the formatting of $article_tags. Be careful when you change it; presumably this index.cgi will shut down your site if it's broken.

Modifying "All the 2 Doors": Link Node

Now we'll move from the homepage to an area of the site I've only touched on, the link node. Its layout is controlled by two files, the first of which is template.wms. It is what wraps around the individual names of the pages:

$HEADER

<P>

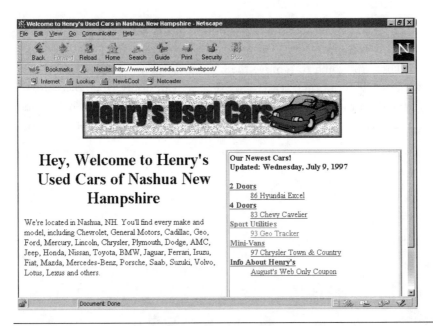

Figure 11.10 The homepage after we've modified it.

```
<CENTER><h1>$titlestring</h1></CENTER><P>

<ul>

$datastring

</ul>

$FOOTER
```

 On the Web You'll see this demo at www.world-media.com/ tkwebpost. I've left the config as webpost.cfg, which you can hit with your browser and save if you like. I've duplicated a copy of my index.cgi as index2.txt so you can see how I used the variables and modified the $article_tags at the top. SiteWrapper users will modify WebPost.pl with the same modifications, then insert the same variables into homepage.htm.

The $titlestring variable holds the name value in %groupnames for this group. The number of the group from %groupnames is in $numgroup, so I'm replacing the <H1> tag with <img src="$server/$groupnum.gif" alt="$titlestring">, then renaming my 2door.gif, 1.gif. then 4door.gif will become 2.gif, and so on, following the %groupnames hash. This automatically will peel the correct image for the group, as in Figure 11.11.

From the screen capture, you'll see that I had already included <IMG SRC="$server/ buttbar.gif" align=left width=350 height=75> in head.wms, so every page after the homepage displayed the button bar. The two blank buttons are for future use.

The $datastring variable is made from the other file I mentioned, format.wms. It's composed of only one line in the demo, <LI><A HREF="$server/parser.cgi?FILE =$fname">$subject</A>, with $subject listed as the only variable. You also have available $author and $date. In Figure 11.11, I substitute the <LI> for an image button and included it in the HREF because some people click it. I've done it by wrapping a <TABLE> around $datastring in template.wms. This is what format.wms looks like in Figure 11.12:

```
<tr><td><A HREF="$server/parser.cgi?FILE=$fname"><img
src=$server/button.gif></a></td><td>
```

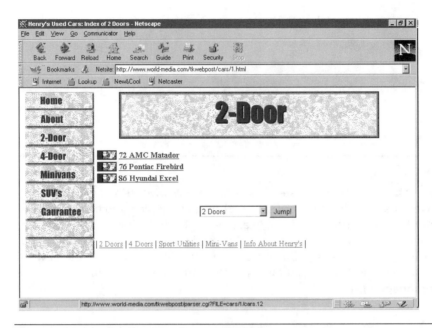

Figure 11.11 Adding an image for every group.

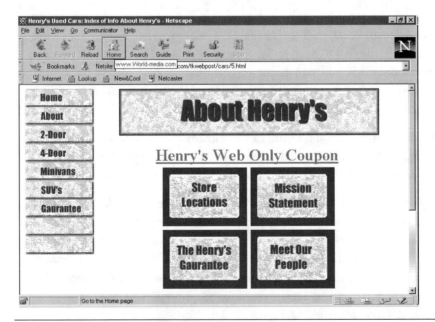

Figure 11.12 Sometimes you'll completely eliminate the automatic functions of format.wms.

```
<A HREF="$server/parser.cgi?FILE=$fname">

<strong>$subject</strong></A></td></tr>
```

There is one trick to WebPost that we very rarely use. If a file called templ1.wms exists in the base $server directory, it will grab that instead of template.wms. So if one category, like About Henry's, is more suited to a customized page of links, that one category can be customized without affecting the others.

I did this with Henry's by making a templ5.wms file composed of the following:

```
$HEADER

<P>

<CENTER><h1><img src="$server/$groupnum.gif" alt="$titlestring"></h1></CENTER><P>

<h1 align=center><a href="$server/parser.cgi?FILE=cars/5/cars.1">Henry's Web

Only Coupon</a>

<CENTER><TABLE CELLSPACING=5 CELLPADDING=10 COLS=2 width=300 BGCOLOR="#000099"

><TR>

<TD><A HREF="$server/parser.cgi?FILE=cars/5/cars.2">

<IMG SRC="$server/storelocbox.GIF" BORDER=0 HEIGHT=91 WIDTH=142 ALIGN=ABSCEN-

TER></A></TD>

<TD><A HREF="$server/parser.cgi?FILE=cars/5/cars.4">

<IMG SRC="$server/missionbox.GIF" BORDER=0 HEIGHT=91

WIDTH=142></A></TD></TR><TR>

<TD><A HREF="$server/parser.cgi?FILE=cars/5/cars.0">

<IMG SRC="$server/gauranteebox.GIF" BORDER=0 HEIGHT=91 WIDTH=142></A></TD>

<TD><A HREF="$server/parser.cgi?FILE=cars/5/cars.3">

<IMG SRC="$server/meetpeoplebox.GIF" BORDER=0 HEIGHT=91 WIDTH=142></A></TD></TR>

</TABLE></CENTER>

$FOOTER
```

I got rid of $datastring entirely, which meant that I had to look up the URLs for each of Henry's "About Henry's" category manually and insert their parser file into the HTML. The easiest way to do this is from the edit menu, which lists all the files. And while we're on the subject, the edit menu is how I'll control the hotlinks for the whole About Henry's area. Remember, as long as you don't switch categories with edit, the URL won't change. That means that rather than put in a new web coupon for September, I'll edit August.

Formatting the 76 Firebird

Up till now, we've worked on every part of WebPost except the final leaf nodes, the pages WebPost actually makes. Here we'll be working with three files: submit.cgi, edit.cgi, and parser.cgi. All three work together to format those final pages. The examples I'll use won't be inclusive for all your needs. It's meant more as a vehicle to familiarize you with the code, with what's printed where, and what sections are key to making WebPost work for you and the administrative users you're installing it for.

Before we get into the creative stuff we'll take a look at how the parser makes the page. It starts at line 20:

```
&print_file($htmlheadfile);

&print_data;

&print_jump;
```

First we print the evaluated contents of head.wms, then the middle of the document, then the Next/Previous listings with the $JUMPLIST in the middle. Note that there is no &print_file($htmltailfile) after the &print_jump statement. That's because it looks ugly printing another $JUMPLIST after just printing it between the Next and Previous documents. But $JUMPLIST is an integral part of the footer. We can't leave it out. This snippet can be included to fix that. It removes the $JUMPLIST from the text of foot.wms or whatever you've put in $htmlfooterfile in the config, before it evaluates it: Insert the following at line 65 of the parser between the print statement that ends the </TABLE> and the one that ends the </BODY> and </HTML>:

```
$/ = "\n";

 open (FILE, "$htmltailfile");

while (<FILE>) {
```

```
$newfooter .= $_;

}

close (FILE);

$newfooter =~ s/\$JUMPLIST//;

print eval qq/"$newfooter"/;
```

Then remove $TEXTLIST before the end of the table at line 63 of the parser. Your footer will then tack onto all WebPost documents without reprinting the $JUMPLIST.

As we continue into customization, more often than not we've found that you'll be eliminating things from WebPost, not adding, because not everyone needs to have the capability to alter the date of the entry. You will use authors only on publications, and unless the organization uses a scanner or digital camera, photos can be disabled as well.

As I explained in the opening, it's easy to get rid of the things you don't need from WebPost. We've found it easier just to comment out HTML than to find workarounds for the parser. Most of the variables are required anyway, so eliminating them would be a chore. Just leave them as the default and follow my instructions as we move down both the submit and edit. I'm giving you the actual code to look for as well as the line number because line numbers can change through the versions, but this code shouldn't.

To take away the ability to set the date on a WebPost page as different from today, put an HTML comment tag at the end of line 27 of submit.cgi. The default is today, so that's what submit.cgi will log:

```
print("</TD><TD><!-- ");
```

End the comment at line 55:

```
print(" --> <BR>\n");
```

This will hide the menu but not disable the passing of the date. And don't forget, you have to disable the edit as well. Start your comment in edit.cgi at line 96:

```
print("<TD><!-- ");
```

and then end the comment at line 119:

```
print " --> </td></tr>
```

For authors on the submit, it's lines 59:

```
<TR><TD><!-- Select the Author of the Document:</TD><TD>
```

then again at 66:

```
print("<BR>--> </TD></TR><TR><TD>Select the Category of the Job:</TD><TH>\n");
```

For the edit, it's line 121:

```
print "<TR><TD><!-- Author of Document:<TD>";
```

Close it at 128:

```
print " --> </td></tr>";
```

Don't worry about a default author on documents. The default is none, and that's what the parser prints. So if there's no author, there will be nothing in the <H2> tag of author.

If you're not using the Tickler built into WebPost, you'll want to wipe out the option on both the submit and the edit. Here it is commented out at line 79 and 80 of the submit and 161 of the edit:

```
<!-- <TR><TH ALIGN=LEFT>Do you want to e-mail an update to Members?</TH>

<TD><INPUT TYPE=radio NAME="mailit" VALUE="yes" CHECKED>Yes <INPUT TYPE=radio

NAME="mailit" VALUE="no">No</TD></TR> -->
```

The most commonly disabled feature on WebPost is the ability to include images. As with everything else, you don't really disable it, you just don't show them the image menu. Here it is commented out in the submit at line 83 in the middle of a here document:

```
<HR><BR>

<!-- <TABLE BORDER=4  CELLSPACING=0  CELLPADDING=0>
```

Then you'll finish the comments at line 151:

```
</TABLE>

<HR> -->

<P>
```

In the edit it's a bit different. The images begin at the end of a here document at line 158. Then there is a for statement below. You'll put the comment in the here document and ignore the other.

```
<!-- <TABLE WIDTH=100% BORDER=0 COLUMNS=3>

<TR><TH COLSPAN=3>Image Information<BR> (use the hotlink for help on the attrib-

utes)</tr><TR>

ENDHTML
```

Pick it back up at line 195 by ending the comment in the last print statement of the table.

```
print "</tr></table> -->";
```

At line 155 of the submit, you'll find the quick reference card for WebPost's autocoding. To disable it you'll start at 155, as I have in the first line. To disable just the option to turn off autocoding, you'll just surround the <h3> tag as I have in line 157:

```
<!-- <CENTER>

<caption><STRONG>WebPost Autocoding<BR>Quick Reference Card</STRONG></caption>

<!-- <h3><INPUT TYPE=CHECKBOX NAME=Noauto VALUE="1"> Turn Off Webpost

Autocoding</h3> -->

<table border=1 cellpadding=2 cellspacing=2 width=80%>
```

It ends at line 167, commented here:

```
</TR>

</table></CENTER> -->
```

In the edit they are separated more. First, at line 199, you'll find the little check-box that turns off WebPost's autocoding. Comment it out as follows:

```
print("<BR CLEAR=LEFT>\nNow you may edit the text of your Commentary as much as
you like. <P>");

    if ( $addl_vars{"Noauto"} == 1 ) {
```

```
        $noauto = "<!-- <h3><INPUT TYPE=CHECKBOX NAME=Noauto VALUE=\"1\"

CHECKED> Turn Off Webpost Autocoding</h3> -->";

    } else {

        $noauto = "<!-- <h3><INPUT TYPE=CHECKBOX NAME=Noauto VALUE=\"1\"> Turn

Off Webpost Autocoding</h3> -->";

    }
```

The quick reference card begins at line 207:

```
<!-- <CENTER>

<caption><STRONG>WebPost Autocoding<BR>Quick Reference Card</STRONG></caption>
```

Go to the end of it at line 224 and finish the comment:

```
</TABLE>

<P><HR> -->

END
```

That's it for turning things off; now we'll add and specially format a couple additional variables. The submit, edit, and parser can pitch and catch such things as price, location, and mileage, which we'll add to Henry's. Start by opening submit.cgi and adding the following at line 170:

```
<table border=2 bgcolor=yellow>
<tr><td>Price:<input type=text size=20 name=price></td><td>

Location: <input type=text  size=20 name=location></td><td>

Mileage: <input type=text  size=20 name=mileage></td></tr></table>
```

That should give you the input boxes I've inputted values for in Figure 11.13. For the edit, we have to grab the variables when the form loads, so I'll add a here document with everything we need:

```
print<<END;

    <table border=2 bgcolor=yellow>

<tr><td>Price:<input type=text value ="$addl_vars{price}" size=20
```

Type, or "cut" and "paste", your text into this box. Hit [RETURN] once at the end of lines if not having line-wrap annoys you (not needed with Netscape 2.0).

Figure 11.13 Adding input boxes to the submit menu.

```
name=price></td><td>

Location: <input type=text  value="$addl_vars{location}"size=20 name=loca-

tion></td><td>

Mileage: <input type=text  value="$addl_vars{mileage}" size=20

name=mileage></td></tr></table>

END
```

The edit peels each variable from the file with the value attribute of the form input and places it in value so it will show as the default when someone edits a document. This should render on the edit just as it does on the submit in Figure 11.13.

But before submitting anything, open wmsstorer.cgi and edit the array at line 194:

```
@list_of_vars = ("Noauto", "new_var_2", "new_var_3", "expires");
```

That's the default that comes with the distribution. The only one really in use is Noauto, which you must make sure not to delete. That's the one that turns off the autocode. For Henry's, our code will look like:

```
@list_of_vars = ("Noauto", "price", "location", "mileage");
```

This will parse the variables we're sending from the submit into the resulting WebPost stored document that the parser reads.

We move into parser.cgi at line 223 where we grab the variables stored by wmsstorer.cgi and parse them into a finished document:

```
223:    $date = $data[0];

224:    $title = $data[1];

225:    $authorname = $data[2];
```

```
226:      $authorURL = $data[3];

227:

228:      $authorname =~ s/(\s+)$//g;

229:

230:      if ( $authorDB{"$authorname"} ne "" ) {

231:          $authorname = "<A HREF=$authorDB{\"$authorname\"}>$authorname</A>";

232:      }

233:

234:      print<<ENDHTML;

235: <h1><STRONG>\n$title\n</STRONG></H1>

236: <h2>$authorname</h2><P>

237: ENDHTML

238:    for ($num_field = 4; $num_field <= $end; $num_field++) {

239:        if ( $addl_vars{'Noauto'} eq "1" ) {

240:            print eval qq/"$data[$num_field]<P>\n"/;

241:        } else {

242:            $temptext = &webpost_parse($data[$num_field]);

243:            $temptext =~ s/"/\\"/g;

244:            $temptext = eval qq/"$temptext"/;

245:            print "$temptext";

246:            undef($temptext);
```

Lines 223 to 226 are the variables that WebPost automatically supplies. We can use not only $title and $authorname, which you've seen in the default configuration, but also $date and $authorURL, which can also be accessed by $authorDB{"$authorname"} as we did in line 231. Note that we've re-stored the $authorname variable with that URL, so any time you include $authorname, the name will hotlink to the author's homepage automatically. To use just them, either comment out line 231 or use $data[2], from where we've taken the author's name originally, in line 225.

These things are printed within the here document at line 234. In the default you see title and author, then the body text is below at line 245. For Henry's, I'm going to do a bit of customizing:

```
print<<ENDHTML;

<table border=0 bgcolor=yellow cellpadding=5 cellspacing=5>

<tr><td valign=top>

<h1>$title</H1></td><td><font size=6><b>Harry's Discount Price</b><br>

$addl_vars{price}</font>

</td></tr>

<tr><td>Location: $addl_vars{location}</td><td>Mileage:

$addl_vars{mileage}</td></tr>

<tr><td colspan=2><table bgcolor=white><tr><td>
ENDHTML

    for ($num_field = 4; $num_field <= $end; $num_field++) {

        if ( $addl_vars{'Noauto'} eq "1" ) {

            print eval qq/"$data[$num_field]<P>\n"/;

        } else {

            $temptext = &webpost_parse($data[$num_field]);

            $temptext =~ s/"/\\"/g;

            $temptext = eval qq/"$temptext"/;

            print "$temptext</td></tr></table></td></tr> </table>

";
```

This results in a page like Figure 11.14 (with some text stolen from this chapter as a placeholder). I've nested two tables within the here document, calling those

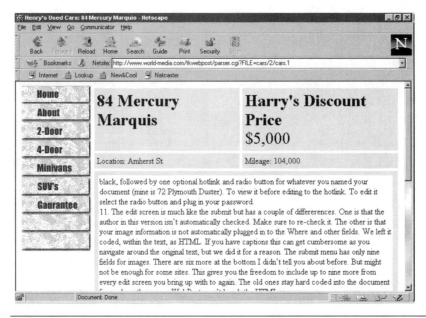

Figure 11.14 The resulting page.

same $addl_vars variables we called in the edit.cgi changes, then closed the two tables after my $temptext. Who says automation is inflexible?

Logging Hits to the Homepage

Including index.cgi as part of WebPost was more a way to demonstrate its variables than anything else. Ideally you'll want to install SiteWrapper and include WebPost.pl instead, then add WebPost's additional variables to your config.cfg. But if you do want to keep index.cgi running, as I have on Henry's, you'll want to add a hit logging section from SiteWrapper's capabilities that we've required into index.cgi with sitewrapper.pl.

To add hits to index.cgi, you'll first go into webpost.cfg and add a @logs="index.cgi"; line. Then go into index.cgi and add the line &LogHit("index.cgi");. This will index your hits every time someone hits the homepage. See the chapter on tracking visitors and install Trakkit to decode these logs.

Logging Hits to All the 2 Doors

The first thing you're probably asking is whether you can log hits to the 76 Firebird. No, this release can't. A future version will, though, so stay tuned. But I will tell you how to log category hits. At line 84 of sitewrapper.pl you'll cut and paste the following at line 114 of parser.cgi:

```
$logFile = "./logs/$mon$year.$document_filename.log";

        $date = sprintf("%02d/%02d/%02d

%02d:%02d:%02d",$year,$mon,$mday,$hour,$min,$sec);

        open(LOG,">> $logFile") || die "$0: can\'t open $logFile: $!\n";

        print (LOG   "$date\t",$ENV{'REMOTE_HOST'},"\t",

        $ENV{'HTTP_REFERER'},"\t",$ENV{'HTTP_USER_AGENT'},"\t","\n");

        close(LOG);
```

Replace $document_filename to "Postgroup.$groupnum" and you're good to go. Now, every time someone visits a 2 Door, a log file is made that can be decoded by Trakkit. See the statistics chapter for more.

On the CD The entire Henry's website, including my modifications to the layout, logging, and usability, are in the example/ directory of both the /sourcecode/UNIX/webpost/ and /sourcecode/NT/webpost/ directories. They should drag and drop right into your site. Check the book's website for updates on NT and the sockets problem with sending mail. It should be fixed by the time you read this and we'll have a new download to replace the version of Perl on the CD.

Adapting Tickler

On both the submit and edit, you saw a "do you want to e-mail an update to members" option. The program this activates is called tickler.cgi and is in the WebPost distribution. For those of you who installed Tickler in Chapter 7, you'll want to upgrade your version to this one. It parses both %ticklerpages from the SiteWrapper.cfg and %groupnames from webpost.cfg. If you added WebPost's functionality to SiteWrapper, change the require webpost.cfg to the name of your config. Then all of your old ?page.htm enabled pages will still be active along with WebPost's groups.

If this is your first encounter with Tickler, you'll see that it's pretty plain right now. Customizing it is easy, with full instructions in its chapter. The line numbers will be a bit different, but there's not much code to wade through. Be sure to customize not only Tickler, but its e-mail files as well. This could be the single most productive addition to your website.

Version Tracking and Accountability

By modern accountability standards, this version of vc.cgi is an infant. It tells you who did what, but does not save the documents that are edited or deleted. A future version will, and we'll even make a restore function, so stay tuned at the book's website as you use the utilities in the book.

To use version control, just hit it with your browser. On Unix make sure the Perl location is pointing to Perl5 and that the file is CHMOD 755. On NT it should run with no modification. You'll get a screen like Figure 11.15, sorted by group.

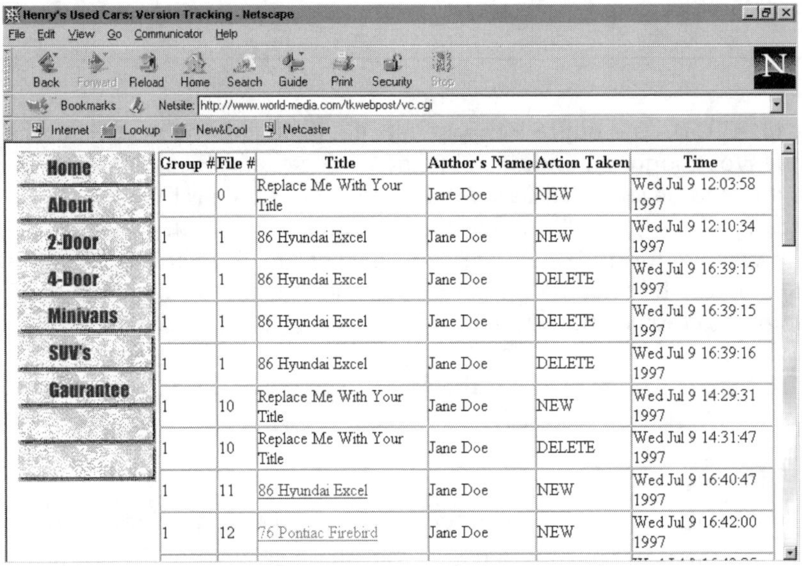

Figure 11.15 The version tracking screen.

12

Searching Your Website

There are two types of people in the world—patient and impatient. If you go to Yahoo! and search through the hierarchical categories until you find the page of what you're looking for, you are patient. If you hit the homepage, type in a keyword, and pluck through the results, you are impatient. This chapter is about giving us impatient souls an outlet for finding what we need on your website.

We started the utilities in this chapter with the methodology from search at Matt Wright's script archive located at worldwidemart.com/scripts/. Since then, they expanded in their capabilities and choices of layout, but you should still check Matt's site for some great stuff.

These aren't search engine searches. When you click Search on Altavista, you don't really search the pages of HTML for matches; you search a subset of them in an indexed database. Each engine has its own indexing scheme, but none search full text. It would be impossible within the time constraints of a web search (especially for those extra-impatient of us impatient souls).

The utilities in this chapter are different. They search the actual text of the pages. If your site is enormous this might not be a viable alternative. You might have to buy a real engine and properly index your site. Many of them even allow you to include SQL database queries.

But for most of us, there aren't more than a couple hundred documents on our site. And most of the documents are fairly short. Under these specifications, plain text search shouldn't be more than fifteen seconds, considered the absolute max in web-time. Time yours after the Quick Start.

I've divided the chapter into three sections and three Quick Starts. The first is for those of you using Fusion or some other client system that outputs static HTML files. It requires no installation of SiteWrapper, WebPost, or other utility in the book. The second is for those of you who have installed SiteWrapper but not WebPost. It requires your standard config file with the %titlenames variable as its reference for which documents to search. The third is for WebPost users. It grabs from your categories and composes links to the documents.

Static Sites

Most of you reading this book already have a site up and running as static HTML files. If you're just flipping through the chapters for something quick to install, this is where to start. With a few simple variable definitions you'll have a search up and running for your site in no time.

Quick Start: Unix

1. In the /sourcecode/UNIX/searches/simple directory, you'll find stat-search.cgi. Open it in your editor and check the Perl location for a match on your system to Perl 5. If you don't know where it is, type which perl at the shell prompt. If it gives you a location, type perl -v and verify that it's at least Perl 5.003. If it comes back as version 4.036, try the same with which perl5. If that fails or you don't have shell access to the server, ask your system administrator.

2. At line six is the variable $server. Replace the value with one for your server, and make sure to leave off the trailing slash. Some of you might be limited to a cgi-bin, in which you'd put $server/cgi-bin. This is where the actual statsearch.cgi is located.

3. At line seven you see the variable definition $baseurl = "$server";. If statsearch.cgi is to be run from the same directory as the documents it finds, or as the base directory under the directories (as www.your-domain.com/startsearch.cgi), leave it as $server. Otherwise set it as your document root. Again, don't put a slash at the end.

4. Next down you'll find @files. Set it as an array with (".htm",".asp",".shtml") and any other file types you want to search on the system. Note that .htm catches both .htm and .html.

5. Set the directories you want to search. The default, @directories_to_search = (".", './products');, is set to show you the way you would do a directory off the main. I've set ./products instead of just "products" alone. There should be additional path information in relation to where statsearch.cgi is being run.

6. You should be able to leave the next variable, $search_url = "$server/$ENV{'SCRIPT_NAME'}";, alone. It automatically points to the program you are running.

7. Change line 17 to the name of your organization in $name_of_org ="Our Site";.

8. Move down the &print_header subroutine at line 32 (Figure 12.1). Fill that in and the print_footer below it with the material from your site that you want to put at the top and bottom of the document. Both the search screen and the results screen will sandwich their contents between them.

9. Now upload the file and CHMOD it 755, then try hitting it with your browser. It should give you a screen with your header and footer, a box for your keywords, and choices for AND/OR and case insensitive/sensitive. Try typing in keywords and search. You should get output similar to Figure 12.2.

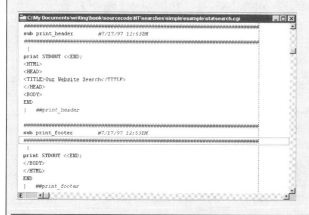

Figure 12.1 Customizing the top of the search screen.

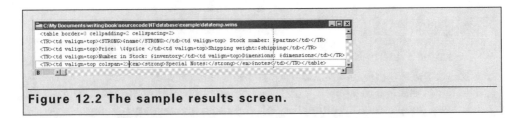

Figure 12.2 The sample results screen.

Quick Start: NT

1. In the /sourcecode/NT/searches/simple directory, you'll find stat-search.cgi. Open it in your editor.

2. At line six is the variable $server. Replace the value with one for your server and make sure to leave off the trailing slash. Some of you might be limited to a cgi-bin, in which you'd put $server/cgi-bin. This is where the actual statsearch.cgi is located.

3. At line seven you see the variable definition $baseurl = "$server";. If statsearch.cgi is to be run from the same directory as the documents it finds or as the base directory under the directories (as www.your-domain.com/startsearch.cgi), leave it as $server. Otherwise set it as your document root. Again, don't put a slash at the end.

4. Next down you'll find @files. Set it as an array with (".htm",".asp",".shtml") and any other file types you want to search on the system. Note that .htm catches both .htm and .html.

5. Then set the directories you want to search. The default, @directories_to_search = (".", './products');, is set to show you the way you would do a directory off the main. I've set ./products instead of just "products" alone. There should be additional path information in relation to where statsearch.cgi is being run.

6. You should be able to leave the next variable, $search_url = "$server/$ENV{'SCRIPT_NAME'}";, alone. It automatically points to the program you are running.

7. Then change line 17 to the name of your organization in $name_of_org ="Our Site";.

8. Move down the &print_header subroutine at line 32 (Figure 12.1). Fill that in and the print_footer below it with the material from your site that you want to put at the top and bottom of the document. Both the search screen and the results screen will sandwich their contents between them.

9. Upload the file and try hitting it with your browser. It should give you a screen with your header and footer, a box for your keywords, and choices for AND/OR and case insensitive/sensitive. Try typing in keywords and search. You should get output similar to Figure 12.2.

Customizing Static Search

Earlier, you saw how to alter the top and bottom of your search and results pages. Now we'll modify the code in between and separate some out for other pages to use. First let's look at the page from which visitors conduct their searches. It's in a here document at line 65:

```
65:     print <<ENDHTML;

66: <hr><p>

67: <form method=POST action="$ENV{'SCRIPT_NAME'}">

68: <input type=hidden name="valid_search" value="true">

69: <center><table border=0>

70: <tr>

71: <th>Your Text to Search For:<BR>

72: <th><input type=text name="terms" size=40><BR>

73: <tr>

74: <th>Boolean: <select name="boolean">

75: <option>AND

76: <option>OR

77: </select><BR>

78: <th>Case Sensitivity:<select name="case">

79: <option>Insensitive

80: <option>Sensitive

81: </select><br>
```

```
82: <TR><TH>Display Results As:<BR><TD><INPUT TYPE=Radio NAME=extended

VALUE="no">Titles Only <BR><INPUT TYPE=Radio NAME=extended VALUE="yes" CHECKED>

<STRONG>Extended Form</STRONG> (Default)<BR>

83: <tr>

84: <th><h2><input type=submit value="Begin Search"></h2><TH><h2><input

type=reset VALUE="Reset Search"></h2>

85: </table>

86: </form>

87: </center>

88: <HR><p>

89: ENDHTML
```

At line 68 is the hidden variable valid_search; make sure it stays. Then at 72 is terms variable. You'll need to keep that the same as well, but you may increase or decrease the box size and add a VALUE attribute if you like. At 74 is a select list for the variable name boolean. Its two options are "and" and "or." If you want to default all searches to this one or the other, get rid of the select list and use an <INPUT TYPE=HIDDEN NAME=boolean VALUE=AND> tag in its place. You must send the boolean operator but you needn't show it to them; likewise with the case and extended variables. You may replace them both with hiddens as <INPUT TYPE=HIDDEN NAME=case VALUE=Insensitive><INPUT TYPE=HIDDEN NAME=extended VALUE=yes>.

Now we're left with just a box and a Submit button, which you can now transplant onto other pages of your site, but rather than use the action="$ENV {'SCRIPT_NAME'}" in your <FORM> tag, you'll have to rename it as the actual script name that you rename it. The complete HTML would be as follows:

```
<form method=POST action="statsearch.cgi">

<input type=hidden name="valid_search" value="true">

<input type=text name="terms" size=40>

<INPUT TYPE=HIDDEN NAME=boolean VALUE=AND>
```

```
<INPUT TYPE=HIDDEN NAME=case VALUE=Insensitive>

<INPUT TYPE=HIDDEN NAME=extended VALUE=yes>

<input type=submit value="Begin Search"></form>
```

I've inserted it into the NHDivorce site in Figure 12.3.

The Results Middle

All three of these programs have a section of code that controls the look of the <ul> list of results. In this version, it starts at line 251 where we open the list:

```
251:    print "<ul>\n";

252:    foreach $key (keys(%include)) {

253:        if ($include{$key} eq 'yes') {

254:          print "<li><FONT SIZE=+1><a
href=\"$baseurl/$key\">$titles{$key}</a></FONT>\n<BR>";

255:          if ($FORM{extended} eq "yes") {

256:            print "<STRONG>Abstract:</STRONG><DD> . . . $abstracts{$key} . . .
<BR>\n";
```

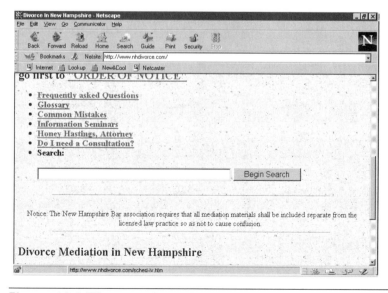

Figure 12.3 The search on NHDivorce.com.

```
257:          print "<DD><A HREF=\"$key\">$baseurl/$key</A> - $date{$key}<P>\n";

258:          }

259:          }

260:      }

261:    print "</ul>\n";

262:    print "<hr>\n";

263:    print "<ul>\n<li><a href=\"$search_url\">Back to Search Page</a>\n";

264:    print "</ul>\n";
```

This spits out the default, shown in Figure 12.4. At line 254 is the hotlink to the URL and <TITLE>, then at 256 and 257 are the abstract and printed URL you get by sending an extended=yes variable. For NHDivorce.com I'm not going to customize it, but a full example is in the following SiteWrapper version. The only difference between it and this version is that there is a ? in the wrapped document URLs. It should be plain to see should you adapt the modifications yourself.

One final area I'll show you is the code before this that prints the top of the middle, right after the header. It tells you if and how your search resulted. We begin at line 241:

```
241:    print "<CENTER>\n  <h1>Results of Search in $name_of_org</h1>\n
</center><P>\n";

242:    if ($results == "0") {

243:        print "<h2>We're very sorry, but your search did not yield any
results.</h2> You may want to broaden the parameters of your search.<BR>";

244:    } else {

245:        if ($results != 1) {

246:        print("Your search yielded $results results.<BR>\n");

247:        } else {
```

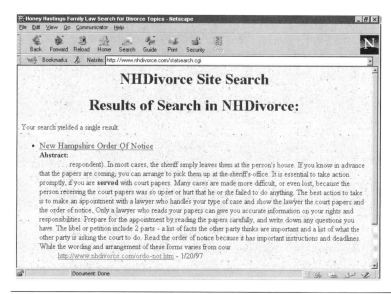

Figure 12.4 The results page.

```
248:        print("Your search yielded a single result.<BR>\n");

249:        }
```

The code you'll modify is at lines 241, 243, 246, and 248. The only mandatory variable is at 246 with $results. That's the number of matches.

 On the CD In the example directory, you'll find the sample home-page and statsearch.cgi program from www.nhdivorce.com. Note that the homepage is in index.cgi. The site was created in the days before SiteWrapper but after Trakkit, so is set up to log hits from an otherwise static homepage.

SiteWrapper Search

By now you've gotten used to SiteWrapper's central configuration file and its associated %titlenames variable. That's where this version of the search gets its pages to check for your visitor's keywords. This was intentional for security. Many of the free search scripts I've found out there make it very hard to isolate certain documents from a search, especially if they are in the same directory as all the other files. Sample searches I've done have turned up CGI programs and secret files on the sites to which I shouldn't have had access. Here, no %titlenames name, no search.

Quick Start: Unix

1. In the /sourcecode/searches/wrapper/ directory, you'll find wrapsearch.cgi. Open it in your editor and rename the require "config.cfg" line to the name and location of your configuration file. Also check the Perl location for Perl5 as in the first step, earlier.

2. Then move down to line 8 and edit the $baseurl = "$server";. This is the http://www... that wrapsearch.cgi will tack on to the file name of the document it finds. In Figure 12.5, it's the URL line before the ?pagename.htm that's printed on the page, helpful to those who print their search results and refer to them later. If your document root is a spur of the $server location, add the /directory name to the variable.

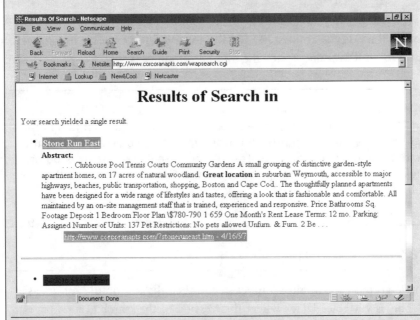

Figure 12.5 Make sure to add the $server variable for the results page.

3. Next you'll move down to line 16 and edit @directories_to_search = ("."); If your files located in %titlenames are in more than one directory, set it to (".",",","./other","/other2").

4. Upload wrapsearch.cgi and sitewrapper.pl to the webserver, then CHMOD wrapsearch.cgi to 755. When you run it you'll get a boolean box of choices and a box to plug your search term into. Your standard $HEADER and $FOOTER should be tacked on automatically.

Quick Start: NT

1. In the /sourcecode/NT/searches/wrapper/ directory, you'll find wrapsearch.cgi. Open it in your editor and rename the require "config.cfg" line to the name and location of your configuration file.

2. Then move down to line 8 and edit the $baseurl = "$server"; This is the http://www... that wrapsearch.cgi will tack on to the filename of the document it finds. In Figure 12.5, it's the URL line before the ?pagename.htm that's printed on the page, helpful to those who print their search results and refer to them later. If your document root is a spur of the $server location, add the /directory name to the variable.

3. Move down to line 16 and edit @directories_to_search = ("."); If your files located in %titlenames are in more than one directory, set it to (".",",","./other","/other2").

4. Upload wrapsearch.cgi and sitewrapper.pl to the webserver. When you run it you'll get a boolean box of choices and a box to plug your search term into. Your standard $HEADER and $FOOTER should be tacked on automatically.

Customizing Wrapsearch

Rather than duplicate the same instructions, read the customization instruction from the static search to modify the search page and to replicate its input box on other pages than the one generated by wrapsearch.cgi. The same here document begins at line 42 in this version.

This wrapper version, however, can do something the other can't. You already have $headerfile, called with &print_file($headerfile); at lines 41 and 321, and $footerfile, called with &print_file($footerfile); at lines 67 and 259. You can add an additional search header and footer, or even an alternate one just for the search pages by adding new variables in the config, then calling them with the same subroutine. An example would be creating $searchtop = "searchtop.wms"; in the config, then calling it below line 41 with &print_file($searchtop);. Then you'd have not only the header at the top of the page, but additional header-only information at the top of all your results pages. I'd see this as a "Don't find what you're looking for?" button leading to a separate webform or, on the results pages, possibly an order form completion at the bottom. To accomplish the latter you'd have to create a special page/product array in the config as well.

The Results Middle

This version wraps the ? into the URL of documents it finds, then puts together the results in a bulleted list, returning just the title if the expanded variable is set to no, or the title, abstract, and printed URL if the expanded variable is set to yes. To alter the look of the expanded version, we start at line 243 with the beginning of the <ul>:

```
243:     print "<ul>\n";

244:

245:

246:     foreach $key (keys(%include)) {

247:         if ($include{$key} eq 'yes') {

248:             print "<li><FONT SIZE=+1><a
href=\"$baseurl/?$key\">$titles{$key}</a></FONT>\n<BR>";

249:             if ($FORM{extended} eq "yes") {

250:                 print "<STRONG>Abstract:</STRONG><DD> . . . $abstracts{$key} . . .
<BR>\n";

251:                 print "<DD><A HREF=\"?$key\">$baseurl/?$key</A> - $date{$key}<P>\n";

252:

253:             }

254:         }

255:     }

256:     print "</ul>\n";
```

```
257:    print "<hr>\n";

258:    print "<ul>\n<li><table border=0><TR><TD bgcolor=$tablebgcolor><a

href=\"$search_url\">Back to Search Page</a></td></tr></table>\n";

259:    print "</ul>\n";
```

At 248 begins the <li> for each search result. This lines prints whether the
extended variable is selected or not. You can alter its format any way you like, even
by getting rid of the <ul> list altogether. I've modified the code that produces Figure
12.5 because Corcoran Management's (www.CorcoranApts.com) site has a light
LINK color in their <BODY> tag. For each search result, I print two little tables
with the background color grabbed from the $tablebgcolor in the config we use for
the rest of the site:

```
foreach $key (keys(%include)) {

    if ($include{$key} eq 'yes') {

    print "<li><table border=0><TR><TD bgcolor=$tablebgcolor><FONT SIZE=+1><a

href=\"$baseurl/?$key\">$titles{$key}</a></FONT></td></tr></table>\n";

        if ($FORM{extended} eq "yes") {

    print "<STRONG>Abstract:</STRONG><DD> . . . $abstracts{$key} . . .

<BR>\n";

        print "<DD><table border=0><TR><TD bgcolor=$tablebgcolor><A

HREF=\"?$key\">$baseurl/?$key</A><font color=white> -

$date{$key}</font></td></tr></table>\n";

        }
```

I haven't modified the bottom at all, but you can pick that up at line 257. The
crucial code is in the $baseurl/?key variable, which is the full http://... to the docu-
ment, the $titles{key} variable, which is the actual <TITLE> of the document, the
$abstracts{key} variable, which is the abstract text with the bold in it, and the
$date{key} variable, the date of the document. The last you may want to get rid of
if you have really old stuff.

The only other thing you might want to modify is at the top of the middle section that tells you the results of your search. Here it is at line 233:

```
233:    print "<CENTER>\n  <h1>Results of Search in $name_of_org</h1>\n </center><P>\n";

234:    if ($results == "0") {

235:        print "<h2>We're very sorry, but your search did not yield any results.</h2> You may want to broaden the parameters of your search.<BR>";

236:    } else {

237:        if ($results != 1) {

238:        print("Your search yielded $results results.<BR>\n");

239:        } else {

240:        print("Your search yielded a single result.<BR>\n");

241:        }
```

The lines you'll want to look at are 233, 235, 238, and 240. Be careful of $name_of_org at 233 and $results at 238. But besides that you may modify the whole message.

 On the CD In the example directory, you'll find the code for the modifications I made. It should cut and paste from theirs into yours with no problem. I have modified the require config line for security.

WebPost Search

When we set up Henry's in Chapter 11, I promised that we'd eventually add a search. In this chapter we'll not only add one but customize it to meet Henry's needs. That can even include a search box on every page, giving people easy access to find more of what they need.

Quick Start: Unix

1. This version of the search is in the /sourcecode/UNIX/searches/web-post directory as webpostsearch.cgi. Open it in your editor and check the Perl location according to the instructions in the first step of the static search.

2. Make sure the require "webpost.cfg"; line is changed to the name of your actual config. As I explained in the WebPost chapter, it's best to rename it for security reasons.

3. The only other modification is at line 9, $baseurl = "$server";. If your document root is different than the $server variable in the config, tack on the extra $server/directory information to the variable definition. This location is what is put before "found" documents to show people the entire path. It's important to get this right as many people print search results and refer to them later.

4. Once you've checked and set the preceding variable, upload web-postsearch.cgi to the webserver and CHMOD it to 755, readable and executable by the server. You should then be able to hit it with your browser and get Figure 12.6.

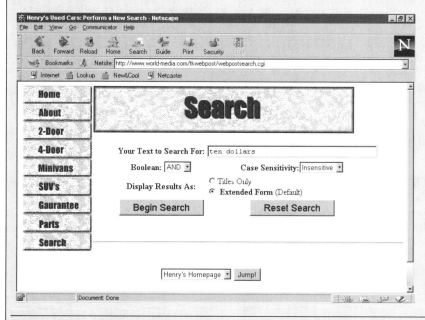

Figure 12.6 The starting screen.

Quick Start: NT

1. Open webpostsearch.cgi in your editor. It's located in the /source-code/NT/searches/webpost directory. Change line 3, require "web-post.cfg";, to the name of the config you changed it to on your system. In the WebPost chapter, I suggested that you change its name for password and other security.

2. At line 9 you'll change $baseurl = "$server"; if your document root is different from the location on your system. Tack on the extra $server/directory information to the variable definition. This location is what is put before "found" documents to show people the entire path. It's important to get this right as many people print search results and refer to them later. Most will leave this as $server.

3. Upload webpostsearch.cgi to the server. You should be able to hit it with your browser and get Figure 12.6.

Customizing WebPost Search

As with the static and wrapped versions of the search, you can modify the search page generated by webpostsearch.cgi. Follow the instructions in the static section starting at line 39. You can also add the box for searching, as I explained earlier, and that may be added to any and all pages, but we'll cover that next. Most of your top and bottom customization can be done from your standard $headerfile and $footerfile, but take a look at my example in the wrapped section for adding a special search-only top and bottom. You'll just add new variables to the config and call the &print_file subroutine.

The Results Middle

This version of the search is as easily customizable as the code I modified for the SiteWrapper version. The top, starting at line 228, begins the same then changes, but picks back up in a similar fashion at line 237:

```
228:    print "<ul>\n";

229:    foreach $key (keys(%include)) {

230:       if ($include{$key} eq 'yes') {

231:       push(@temptitles, "$titles{$key}");

232:       $titlehash{"$titles{$key}"} = $key;
```

```
233:         }

234:     }

235:     foreach $title (sort keys(%titlehash)) {

236:         $key = $titlehash{$title};

237:         print "<li><FONT SIZE=+1><a

href=\"$baseurl/parser.cgi?FILE=$key\">$titles{$key}</a></FONT>\n<BR>";

238:         if ($FORM{extended} eq "yes") {

239:         print "<STRONG>Abstract:</STRONG><DD> . . . $abstracts{$key} . . .

<BR>\n";

240:         # this changes

241:         print "<DD><A

HREF=\"$baseurl/parser.cgi?FILE=$key\">$baseurl/parser.cgi?FILE=$key</A> -

$date{$key}<P>\n";

242:         }

243:     }

244:     print "</ul>\n";

245:     print "<hr>\n";

246:     print "<ul>\n<li><a href=\"$search_url\">Back to Search Page</a>\n";

247:     print "</ul>\n";

248:     print "<hr>\n";
```

The variables to be careful of start at line 237 with $baseurl/parser.cgi?FILE= $key and $titles{$key}. They are the full URL to the page and page <TITLE>, respectively. Next is $abstracts{$key} at line 239. That's the characters around the search term with the search terms bolded. Line 241 is the $date{$key} variable that prints the date the file was last modified. You might want to ax this if you have mostly old stuff.

More Search Boxes

The first thing I'd like to do with Henry's is put search boxes all over the site. First I'll make the subroutine in Figure 12.7 and add it to sitewrapper.pl, which is required by all the CGI programs including the search. Now we can call &print_box anywhere in the code and it will execute, printing a search box with up to the first four keywords we are searching on. First I'll put it in webpostsearch.cgi with a &print_box; right after the require lines, then at line 218 I'll add the following:

```
print "Content-type: text/html\n\n";

&print_file($htmlheadfile);

print $printbox;

print "<CENTER>\n  <h1>Results of Search in $title</h1>\n </center><P>\n";
```

This puts a new search box on my results page, aligned in the upper-right corner in Figure 12.8. Right now they're stuck with my choices for results, without extended, and set to boolean "and." But you could very well extend this to include more options. I'm just very conscious of screen real estate.

Now I'll put it on my main index pages by adding my subroutine at the top of wmsdb.cgi. It's the program that makes the "All the two doors" pages:

```
require "sitewrapper.pl";

require "webpost.cfg";

&print_box;

open(STDERR, ">> wmsdb.error");
```

Figure 12.7 We'll reuse this code for each box we print.

Figure 12.8 Search from the results page.

Then I'll change template.wms as follows:

$HEADER

<P>

<CENTER><h1><img src="$server/$groupnum.gif" alt="$titlestring"></h1></CENTER><P>

$boxhtml

<table border=0>

$datastring

</table>

$FOOTER

Now it has $boxhtml hard-coded into my pages. Again, one note that I mentioned in the initial setup—changes to format.wms and template.wms don't take until you either submit a new document or manually run wmsdb.cgi. Figure 12.9 is the result.

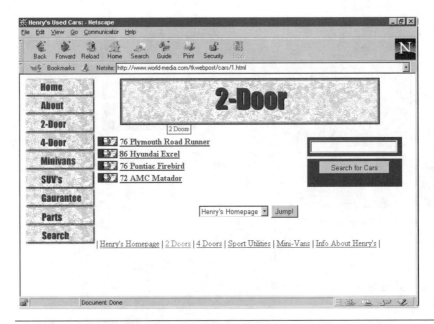

Figure 12.9 Search from the link node.

The last thing I'll do is add the box into my footer. For that I have to add the same &print_box; statement at the end of my require statements in parser.cgi just as I did for wmsdb.cgi. Then I'll go down into parser.cgi at line 50, the print_jump subroutine, and add the line print ("<tr><th colspan=3>$boxhtml</th></tr><tr>"); into the code as follows:

```
sub print_jump {

    &JumpGate;

    print("<P><TABLE BORDER=0 CELLSPACING=0 CELLPADDING=2 WIDTH=480><TR>");

    print("<tr><th colspan=3>$boxhtml</th></tr><tr>");

    if (-e $prevfname) {

        print("<TH ROWSPAN=2><A HREF=parser.cgi?FILE=$prevfname>Previous Page:

$prevsubj</A><BR>\n");

    } else {

        print("<TH ROWSPAN=2> </TH>");
```

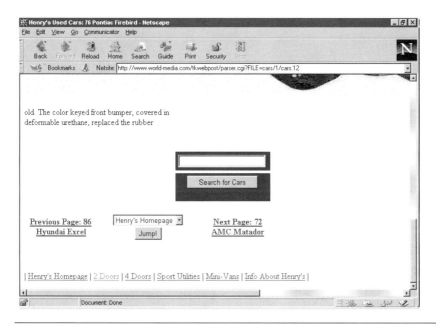

Figure 12.10 The search box on Henry's footer.

 On the CD In the example directory of the WebPost search, you'll find the modified code, and back in the WebPost/example directory, you'll find the addition in SiteWrapper.pl as well as the additions to parser.cgi, wmsdb.cgi, template.wms, and footer.wms.

That gives me Figure 12.10 at the bottom of every Henry's page. By changing the box in sitewrapper.pl I will change the properties for the whole site.

Adding a Directory
of Hotlinks

U ntil recently I would never advise a client to provide a jump-off on their website. Whether it was the client's trade organization, CEO's college, or even our World Media homepage, I didn't see justification to give someone a reason to leave the site. It was hard enough to get them there in the first place. Why give them an easy out?

But in this era of information glut and hundreds of thousands of useless pages of Web, perhaps it is the only "killer app" that has emerged in the authoritative clearinghouse of links. It's the single biggest attractor to the most popular websites. If you act as what some would call an intelligent agent, searching for links, checking them for relevance and accuracy, your site will become information central for your industry. I still strongly warn against jump-offs as a replacement for brief and compelling content, but as an integral piece of your site, you can't go wrong with a comprehensive hotlink section.

Installing AddaLink

This chapter contains only one utility, but it's extremely useful for keeping up links on your site. This will be a section of your site, similar to the user-interface of a Yahoo! type search engine. There are both categories of information to pluck through and the ability to plug in a keyword and have delivered back a rack of relevant pages. All of the administration is through a webform. And you control not only links, but the addition and removal of entire categories. In the following instructions, I'll take you through the basic install for all platforms, then cover the extensive customization options in the code for look and feel as well as function and password protection.

Quick Start: Unix

1. The sourcecode for AddaLink is in /sourcecode/UNIX/addalink; there you'll find addalink.zip and an upzipped directory with all the files, links.cgi, linkadmin.cgi, and links.wms. There is also a sample entire config included in the distribution in case you did not install SiteWrapper and another include file called sitewrapper.pl.

2. Open links.cgi and linkadmin.cgi in your text editor or Multi-Edit. Change the require config.cfg lines to whatever you renamed them back in the SiteWrapper chapter. If this is your first automation tool, you'll want to rename config.cfg when you install it, then change the require lines accordingly.

3. Make sure that in both files the #! line at the top matches Perl on your system. If you have shell access to the server, you'll find this with which perl or which perl5. Many systems leave /usr/bin/perl for Perl 4.036 so old CGI programs don't break. You need the location of Perl 5.003 or better.

4. Bring your config file (or config.cfg if this is your first one) in your editor and add three variables at the end: $linkdbfile = "links.db";, $linkcatsfile = "linkcats.db";, $errorfname = "error.htm";, or change the values to file names of your choice. The sample config that comes with AddaLink has these built in with the previous values as the defaults.

5. Save or upload all the files to the webserver in the same directory that you've installed index.cgi. You can use another directory, but make sure the require lines point to the right place with relative or full path names (for full path names be sure to rename the config for security).

6. Change the permissions of links.cgi with CHMOD 755 links.cgi. Do the same for linkadmin.cgi. This will make them executable from the web.

7. Figure 13.1 should be what you get by hitting linkadmin.cgi from your browser. As you can see, there is no menu option to add a link yet. First we have to install a category. Click Add a Bookmark category and I'm Ready to Move On.

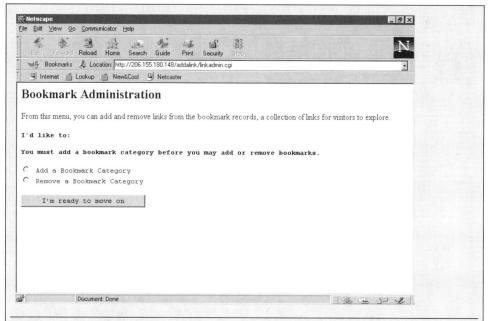

Figure 13.1 First add a category to put your links in.

8. The screen you get should be asking you for the name of a new category. If your site is an Arts site, you might put Opera. If it's a company intranet you'd put Human Resources. I'm going to make one for the book called Free/Shareware CGI Resources. Now enter your password from the $password variable in the config. Later I'll show you how to either disable this or set a separate one just for AddaLink. Then click I'd Like to Add this Bookmark category.

9. You now should have a category set up. Go back to linkadmin.cgi and hit SHIFT, RELOAD in your browser. This will refresh the page, adding the ability to insert a bookmark. Click Add a Bookmark and I'm Ready to Move On.

10. Figure 13.2 shows the next screen with the values for the client for whom AddaLink was written. Notice that I've added a few categories, including AddaLink examples, which I'm checking in this example. Add your link in and click I'd Like to Add this Link. Note that you have to use the full http:// for web resources. Many of your links could be FTP, so defaulting to HTTP isn't a good idea.

11. Now, if you hit links.cgi it should give you a list of your categories. By clicking on them, you'll get the URL you just added. If you plug in

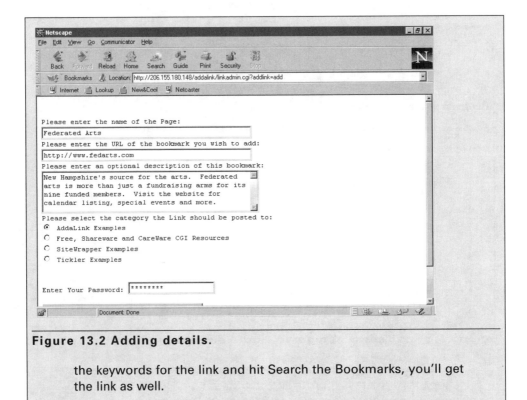

Figure 13.2 Adding details.

the keywords for the link and hit Search the Bookmarks, you'll get
the link as well.

Quick Start: NT

1. The sourcecode for AddaLink is in /sourcecode/NT/addalink; there
   you'll find addalink.zip and an upzipped directory with all the files,
   links.cgi, linkadmin.cgi, and links.wms. There is also a sample entire
   config included in the distribution in case you did not install
   SiteWrapper and another include file called sitewrapper.pl.

2. Open links.cgi and linkadmin.cgi in your text editor or Multi-Edit.
   Change the require config.cfg lines to whatever you renamed them
   back in the SiteWrapper chapter. If this is your first automation tool,
   you'll want to rename config.cfg when you install it, then change the
   require lines accordingly.

3. Bring your config file (or config.cfg if this is your first one) in your editor and add three variables at the end: $linkdbfile = "links.db";,
   $linkcatsfile = "linkcats.db";, $errorfname = "error.htm";, or change the
   values to file names of your choice. The sample config that comes with
   AddaLink has these built in with the previous values as the defaults.

4. Save or upload all the files to the webserver in the same directory that you've installed index.cgi. Make sure your system administrator has not set that directory write protected.

5. You should get Figure 13.1 by hitting linkadmin.cgi from your browser. As you can see, there is no menu option to add a link yet. First we have to install a category. Click Add a Bookmark category and I'm Ready to Move On.

6. The screen you get should be asking you for the name of a new category. If your site is an Arts site, you might put Opera. If it's a company intranet you'd put Human Resources. I'm going to make one for the book called Free/Shareware CGI Resources. Now enter your password from the $password variable in the config. Later I'll show you how to either disable this or set a separate one just for AddaLink. Then click I'd Like to Add this Bookmark category.

7. If you got a "Document Contains No Data" from Internet Information Server, you have to change the subroutine at line 444 of linkadmin.cgi. Some versions of Perl for Win32 don't support, or only partially support, the printing of Location back to the script that it just came from (it seems to work in some places but not in others). This is the subroutine as it comes on the CD (keep in mind that your copy doesn't and should not include line numbers):

```
444: sub print_location

445: #

446: #   This subroutine redirects the browser back to the main admin form.

447: #

448: ############################################################################

449: {

450:     if ( $ENV{'PERLXS'} eq "PerlIS" ) {

451:         print(STDOUT "HTTP/1.0 302 OK\n");

452:     }

453:

454:     print(STDOUT "Location: $ENV{'SCRIPT_NAME'}\n\n");
```

```
455:

456:     return 1;

457: }    ##print_location
```

8. In line 454, you'll change Location: to http://www.yourcompany.com/ links.cgi from the environment variable. It will bounce you to the links page so you can check your work. If you're adding several at a time, just hit your back button.

9. You now should have a category set up. Go back to linkadmin.cgi and hit SHIFT, RELOAD in your browser. This will refresh the page, adding the ability to insert a bookmark. Click Add a Bookmark and I'm Ready to Move On. Note that you have to use the full http:// for web resources. Many of your links could be FTP, so defaulting to HTTP isn't a good idea.

10. Figure 13.2 shows the next screen with the values for the client for whom AddaLink was written. Notice that I've added a few categories, including AddaLink examples, which I'm checking in this example. Add your link in and click I'd Like to Add this Link. Note that you have to use the full http:// for web resources. Many of your links could be FTP, so defaulting to HTTP isn't a good idea.

11. Now, if you hit links.cgi, it should give you a list of your categories. By clicking on them, you'll get the URL you just added. If you plug in the keywords for the link and hit Search the Bookmarks, you'll get the link as well.

Changing the Look of the Links: All Platforms

There are three screens in link.cgi. The first is the one that lists the categories. It also has a form input box for the search. The second is the screen of links you get by clicking on a category, and the third is the list you get from searching the links database.

In the first, I'll call it stage 1 of AddaLink, the categories are displayed with the search box at the bottom starting at line 115 of links.cgi:

```
115: sub give_menu

    .

    .

122:    {
```

```
123:    $thispagetitle = "$name_of_org: Bookmarks";

.

.

127:    foreach $category (@link_category_list) {

128:        $link_category = $category;

129:        $link_category =~ s/\s/\+/g;

130:        $filestring .= "<LI><STRONG><A
HREF=$ENV{'SCRIPT_NAME'}?category=$link_category>$category</A></STRONG><BR>\n";

131:    }

.

.

137:    print<<END;

138: Content-type: text/html

139:

140: $HEADER

141:

142: $bbar

143:

144: <BLOCKQUOTE>

145: <UL>

146: $filestring

147: </UL>

148: <P>

149: <FORM METHOD=POST ACTION=$ENV{'SCRIPT_NAME'}>

150: Keywords: <INPUT TYPE=TEXT NAME=keywords SIZE=20><BR>
```

```
151: <INPUT TYPE=RADIO NAME=boolean VALUE="AND" checked>AND / <INPUT TYPE=RADIO

NAME=boolean VALUE="OR">OR<P>

152:

153: <INPUT TYPE=SUBMIT VALUE="Search the Bookmarks">

154: </FORM>

155:

156: </BLOCKQUOTE>

157:

158: $FOOTER

159: END

160:

161:

162: }    ##give_menu
```

At line 123, we'll first change the title to $name_of_org: Wild World of Hotlinks (I've set $name_of_org as a config variable). That's just the title of the main link page, not a <H1> at the top or anything. That comes at line 143 after $HEADER and $bbar (we put $bbar in just to show you how you'd import it from an existing site). I'm going to put in the same as I did with the title but within <H1> tags. We've put a <BLOCKQUOTE> in to break up the page a bit. Microsoft Internet Explorer doesn't seem to do well with the tag so you may want to delete it.

The look of how the categories stack on top of each other is defined as a combination between line 130 and the <UL> at line 145, closed at line 147. In my example, I'm changing it to a definition list and setting each category as a <dd>. Then I'm going to move the search form to the upper right by putting it in a table that is slightly gray. Figure 13.3 is the result. Now click on a link and we'll go to stage 2.

Here links are displayed for this category starting at line 166:

```
166: sub display_links
```

.

.

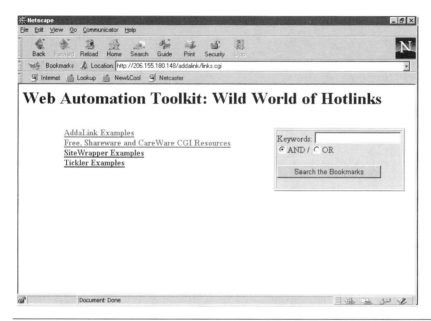

Figure 13.3 Customizing the catgories view.

```
172:  {

173:

174:     $thispagetitle = "$name_of_org: Bookmarks";

    .

    .

189:     foreach $category ($in{'category'}) {

190:         $filestring .= "<UL><h2>$category</h2>\n";

191:         foreach $url (sort byname keys(%links)) {

192:             if ( $cat_of{"$url"} eq $category ) {

193:                 $filestring .= &file_to_string("links.wms");

194:             }

195:         }
```

```
196:      $filestring .= "</UL>\n";

197:

198:    }

199:

200:    $filestring .= "\n";

201:

.

.

205:

206:    print<<END;

207: Content-type: text/html

208:

209: $HEADER

210:

211: $bbar

212:

213: <BLOCKQUOTE>

214: $filestring

215: </BLOCKQUOTE>

216:

217: $FOOTER

218: END

219:

220: }    ##display_links
```

At line 174, we again change the name of the page in its <TITLE> field. $this-pagetitle is used to plug the title into your $headerfile document specified in the config. I'm using the same $name_of_org: Wild World Of Hotlinks.

You'll see a second <UL> at line 190, followed by the category name in <H2> tags. The <LI> tags we'll change later, but first I'm again switching this to a <DL>. I'll leave the <H2> alone. I like it indented within the list, but I'll put it in a <DT> for correct HMTL. Note that in the $filestring definition there is a \n newline character at the end of the <H2> tag. It's only for readable HTML.

Then I have to modify $filestring at 196 to finish my <DL> and remove line 199 because <DD> tags automatically include a <BR>. Next we jump down into 206 where the here document that prints the actual page begins.

Did you catch line 193 where we read in links.wms? You uploaded it at the beginning of the Quick Start. It changes the way the middle of this page appears. Each URL peels through its contents: <LI><A HREF=$url>$links{"$url"}</A>
$descript{"$url"}. You can't modify the actual variables used, but I'm switching the <LI> to a <DD>. Bring it up in your editor and see how it works, even if you don't modify it.

The last thing I'll do is pick up at line 206 to add my title and table again. Keep in mind that I could put this in my $headerfile, but that I'm not because I only want this at the top of these pages, not every other one on the site. Figure 13.4 is my result. Now, when I click on a category link, I don't have to hit my back button to be able to search.

But what about the search? That's our third screen of AddaLink. Its modifiable code starts at line 43:

```
43:     $thispagetitle = "$name_of_org: Bookmarks";

  .


  .

79:     foreach $category (@link_category_list) {

80:         if ( $links_in{"$category"} != 0 ) {

81:             $filestring .= "<UL><STRONG>$category</STRONG><BR>\n";
```

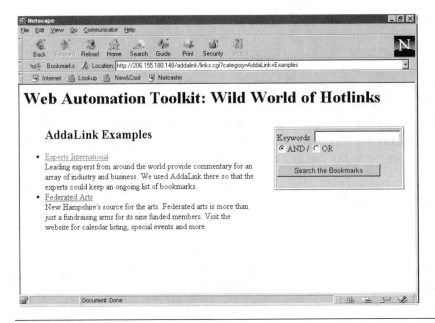

Figure 13.4 Adding a search box.

```
82:         foreach $url (sort byname keys(%links)) {

83:             if ( $cat_of{"$url"} eq $category ) {

84:                 $filestring .= &file_to_string("links.wms");

85:             }

86:         }

87:         $filestring .= "</UL>\n";

88:     }

89:

90:  }

91:

92:  $filestring .= "<BR>\n";

93:
```

.

.

```
98:     print<<END;

99:  Content-type: text/html

100:

101: $HEADER

102:

103: $bbar

104:

105: <BLOCKQUOTE>

106: $filestring

107: </BLOCKQUOTE>

108:

109: $FOOTER

110: END

111:

112: }    ##search_links
```

And again it's the same. Change $thispagetitle, then move down to lines 81 through 92 to modify the way the list of URLs looks. At line 84, it peels links.wms and plugs in its format. I should note here that if you want the search page and the standard link page to look different, you should identify a different file than links.wms, like searchlinks.wms, which I'll do here. In my searchlinks.wms, I'm printing the variable $url after the title, so in case people print the document they'll have it on the page. I'm also putting in the table with the search box again, but changing the Submit button to say "Search Again?" And the last thing I'm adding is into the input field on the little form for the search. On these result pages I want it not only to say "Search Again?", but also to have their previous search automatically entered into the box as a VALUE= "in{keywords} tag. I'm grabbing the keywords variable from the form as it submits to links.cgi. You'll see the changes in Figure 13.5. Compare it to Figure 13.4 and you'll see what I've done.

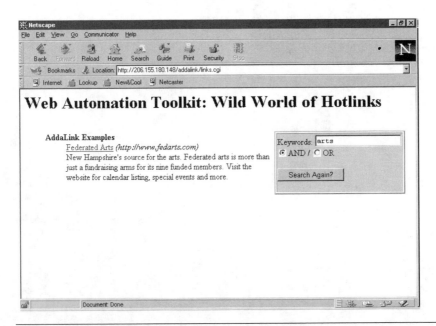

Figure 13.5 Grab the $in{keywords} variable to allow people to modify their search.

On the CD The examples I've just made are in the /sourcecode/NT/addalink/example/ and /sourcecode/UNIX/example directories. This program is cross platform except for that possible little NT edit of the Location line. Drag and drop them from server to server. You'll also find lineadmin.cgi and linelinks.cgi, which SHOULD NOT BE USED, but which are each programs with line numbers specified for reference if your editor doesn't show line numbers. Whatever you do, don't install the line examples.

Link Administration Options

We've defaulted the administration of links to a password protected system. You can't, without providing a password, allow people to post new or remove unwanted links. But what if you do? What if you'd like a free-for-all link page on your site?

It's easy to change. At line 322 is the code that encrypts and returns the password field. I'm going to comment it out with # signs before the three lines:

```
322:    # if ( crypt($in{'admin_password'}, substr($password, 0, 2)) ne $pass-
word ) {

323:    #    return 0;

324:    #}
```

Duplicate this exactly at line 398. That's where the categories are added.

I'm also putting comment tags around the password field in the HTML at line 244, as <!-- Enter Your Password: <INPUT TYPE=PASSWORD NAME=admin_password SIZE=20><P> -->. Then 152 is the add category field. That will completely eliminate all references to passwords. Don't bother with the delete forms, we'll get to those next.

Many of you are noticing the danger in including a remove option within a free-for-all link page. There are lots of nasty people on the web (and nice ones too) that will remove hours of research and inputting of resources for their simple pleasure of making you do it over again.

So at line 85, we comment out the <!--<INPUT TYPE=RADIO NAME=addlink VALUE="del"> Remove a Bookmark --> line, then do the same for the <!--<INPUT TYPE=RADIO NAME=addlink VALUE=delcat> Remove a Bookmark Category --> line at 108. That should leave you with Figure 13.6.

But that's not all, is it? What's to prevent someone from running linkadmin.cgi from their site and submitting a remove manually to your server? Ha! At lines 366 and 420, we've left in the password to remove. So that means when you, the administrator,

On the Web Take a look at 206.155.180.148/addalink/links.cgi and linkadmin.cgi. It's a no-password example of the code we're editing here. And just like our last example, I've included the source on the CD in /sourcecode/NT/addalink/nopassword/ and /sourcecode/UNIX/addalink/nopassword/.

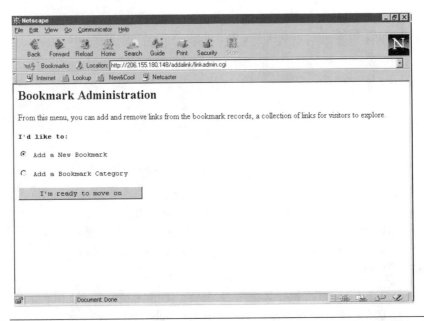

Figure 13.6 In some cases you'll want to remove the ability to delete.

want to remove links, you can manually type the URL www.yourserver.com/linkadmin
.cgi?addlink=del and remove a link. To remove a category, it will be www.yourserver
.com/linkadmin.cgi:addlink=delcat.

To alter the look of this new linking section we have three screens: the main
administration, the Add a Bookmark, and the Add a Category. First let's look at the
main; line 72 begins the subroutine:

```
72: sub admin_form
```

```
73: # This subroutine provides the base administration form.
```

.

.

```
78:    $thispagetitle = "Administrate Links for $name_of_org";
```

.

.

349

Adding a Directory of Hotlinks

```
83: $booktext=<<END;

84: <INPUT TYPE=RADIO NAME=addlink VALUE="add"> Add a New Bookmark

85: <!-- <INPUT TYPE=RADIO NAME=addlink VALUE="del"> Remove a Bookmark -->

86: END

87:    } else {

88:        $booktext = "<STRONG>You must add a bookmark category before you
may add or remove bookmarks.</STRONG>\n";

89:    }

90:

91:    print<<END;

92: Content-type: text/html

93:

94: $HEADER

95:

96: <FORM METHOD=GET NAME=verifyInput ACTION=$ENV{'SCRIPT_NAME'}>

97:

98: <h2>Bookmark Administration</h2>

99:

100: From this menu, you can add and remove links from the bookmark records,

101: a collection of links for visitors to explore.<P>

102:

103: <PRE>

104: <STRONG>I'd like to:</STRONG>

105:

106: $booktext
```

```
107: <INPUT TYPE=RADIO NAME=addlink VALUE=addcat> Add a Bookmark Category

108: <!-- <INPUT TYPE=RADIO NAME=addlink VALUE=delcat> Remove a Bookmark

Category -->

109:

110: <INPUT TYPE=SUBMIT VALUE="I'm ready to move on">

111: </FORM>

112:

113: $FOOTER

114: END

115:

116: }    ##admin_form
```

By now $thispagetitle at line 78 must be familiar. Plug in whatever matches your other edits to links.cgi that you already made. Then edit the beginning of the main body at line 84. It's the HTML to add a new bookmark. The category option follows.

Multiple Passwords

You should see four places in linkadmin.cgi where the code "if (crypt($in{'admin_password'}, substr($password, 0, 2)) ne $password) { return 0; }" occurs, spanning three lines at 322, 366, 398, and 420 in the line numbering of the original source before edits. In any of those four, you can replace the variable $password with another, like $linksubmit-password or $linkremovepassword, which you'll put in the config using the same encrypted format that you set $password with back in the SiteWrapper chapter. This gives you the freedom not only to distribute separate AddaLink only passwords, but the ability to assign different ones for different functions. This is particularly useful with categories. If your site has a scope of what you will support and cover, you may want to limit category submissions to the administrators, while opening up link submissions to your clients.

Line 88 should be left alone. You only get it the first time you run linkadmin.cgi without any categories specified. Then from 98 to 113 is the look of the page. As long as you don't mess with the END tag at 114, everything is just standard

HTML. You'll see $booktext in there. It's what you modified at line 84. Make sure to include it. The only other thing is to be careful not to delete any form variables, but move them around however you like.

The next screen, add a link, starts at line 206, with the same $thispagetitle at 212:

```
206: sub give_form

207: # This subroutine provides a form to add a new bookmark.

    .

    .

212:     $thispagetitle = "Add a Bookmark to $name_of_org";

    .

    .

216:     $categories = <<END;

217: Please select the category the Link should be posted to:

218: END

219:     foreach $category (@link_category_list) {

220:         $category =~ s/\n//g;

221:         if ($category eq $link_category_list[0])  {

222:             $categories .= "<INPUT TYPE=RADIO NAME=category VALUE=\"$cate-
gory\" checked> $category\n";

223:         } else {

224:             $categories .= "<INPUT TYPE=RADIO NAME=category VALUE=\"$cate-
gory\"> $category\n";

225:         }

226:     }

227:
```

```
228:    print<<END;

229: Content-type: text/html

230:

231: $HEADER

232:

233: <PRE>

234: <FORM METHOD=POST NAME=verifyInput ACTION=$ENV{'SCRIPT_NAME'}>

235:

236: Please enter the name of the Page:

237: <INPUT TYPE=TEXT NAME=link_name SIZE=50 MAXSIZE=80>

238: Please enter the URL of the bookmark you wish to add:

239: <INPUT TYPE=TEXT NAME=page_url SIZE=50 MAXSIZE=80>

240: Please enter an optional description of this bookmark:

241: <TEXTAREA NAME=description COLS=50 ROWS=4 WRAP=PHYSICAL></textarea>

242: $categories

243:

244: <!-- Enter Your Password: <INPUT TYPE=PASSWORD NAME=admin_password
SIZE=20><P> -->

245: <INPUT TYPE=SUBMIT VALUE="I'd like to add this link.">

246: </FORM>

247:

248: $FOOTER

249: END

250:

251:

252: }    ##give_form
```

I wouldn't mess with the category stuff much beyond line 211. Change that, then move on to line 227 and get rid of the <PRE> tag. The form will look good with some customization. At line 242 is the $categories variable that was configured after 211. Leave that in, then at line 243 is that END tag you must be careful of. Adding invisible characters, spaces, tabs, and newlines after it is one of the most frustrating mistakes to find in Perl (even though I've warned you twenty times).

The last screen to modify is the add categories page. Its code starts with the subroutine at line 119, then picking up at $thispagetitle at 124:

```
119: sub addcat_form

 .

 .

124:    $thispagetitle = "Add a Bookmark Category to $name_of_org";

 .

128:    $categories = <<END;

129: <strong>Here is a list of currently available categories:</strong><P>

130: END

131:    foreach $category (@link_category_list) {

132:        $category =~ s/\n//g;

133:        $categories .= "$category<BR>";

134:    }

135:

136:

137:    print<<END;

138: Content-type: text/html

139:

140: $HEADER

141:

142: <FORM METHOD=POST NAME=verifyInput ACTION=$ENV{'SCRIPT_NAME'}>
```

```
143: <input type=hidden

name=addcat VALUE="YES">

144:

145: $categories

146:

147: <BR>

148: <STRONG>Enter the new category name:<BR></STRONG>

149: <INPUT TYPE=TEXT NAME=newcat SIZE=60>

150: <P>

151:

152: Enter Your Password: <INPUT TYPE=PASSWORD NAME=admin_password SIZE=20><P>

153: <INPUT TYPE=SUBMIT VALUE="I'd like to add this Bookmark Category">

154:

155: </FORM>

156:

157: $FOOTER

158: END

159:

160:

161: }    ##addcat_form
```

Again at 129 is the intro to the category listings, except this isn't a list of radio buttons. From 131 to 133, the program iterates through the existing categories. If you don't want to print them, get rid of 129 to 133. It's just informational. The other way to do this is to leave the $category variable out of the HTML and text between lines 137 and 158. Again, as before, feel free to alter the HTML without fear of breaking something, just as long as you keep the form variables intact.

A Free Web
Database

The easiest way to keep your site current is through a database. Most utilities in the book use one, but they are very specific and only customizable within a small margin. They do what they do. This chapter is about adapting your data into a searchable, customizable engine. Whether it's products, customer accounts, client lists, or help topics, you'll be able to track and store information and update it dynamically.

With our first utility, QuickDB, you'll update your information through the web. This is geared for organizations with lots of data but no in-house database. We've run into this a lot with catalog sales. Many companies produce a printed product but keep no internal database of its contents. Even phone order representatives refer to the catalog. That's what it's been at Henry's, the example car dealership from the WebPost chapter. They've always kept an inventory of common parts on hand, but never kept track of what's in stock and what isn't. The shelves are labeled by part number, so they just look up the number in the book and find the part. Sound familiar? Don't worry. With hundreds of hours of data entry, Henry's will soon be able to sell those '63 Corvette original tail lights that have been on the shelf since 1963, as well as the 1996 Lexus nose they got stuck with last week when the customer changed his mind about totaling the car.

In the second part of the chapter, we'll look at adapting existing databases on your native system to the web from a cost-control perspective. The hubbub of the industry will tell you that in order to search your simple product database on the web you have to license a thousand dollar rapid application development environment and learn the full spectrum of SQL. My solution is a halfway for those of us who have the time and money for neither.

QuickDB

We first developed this utility for the National Standards Authority of Ireland (www.nsaicert.com). They had a printed directory of their ISO 9000 certifications and C Marked products (both quality standards) but no database from which to grab the information. To bring it to the site, we would have to make them a web-administrateable engine from which to add, edit, and delete entries.

At first we started to look at commercial vendors. Binary formats are fastest, especially with the advanced query sets of SQL, but then we realized that SQL was overkill for this client. Why ask them to license a database when their records would never grow larger than a few thousand? Plain text was the answer, and this utility was the result. From a standard web browser you can add, edit, and delete database entries, and customizing its fields and look is as simple as installing it.

First we'll run through the Quick Starts as usual, then I'll show you the basic functionality and menus. After that we'll try adapting your existing data to the same format with the sample database that comes with Access. Unless your database has over five thousand records, this should work fine for you. Above that, will be slower, but still a viable option with a brief warning on the search page.

Quick Start: Unix

1. First we'll open the archive. In the /sourcecode/UNIX/database directory is the db.zip archive. There is also an unzipped directory. If you've not installed SiteWrapper or WebPost and have no config file, open db.cfg in your editor. If you do have a config already, add the variables you don't recognize to your config, then change the require "idb.cfg"; in adddb.cgi, browsedb.cgi, deletedb.cgi, editdb.cgi, and searchdb.cgi to the name of your config.

2. Check the Perl location in each of the CGI programs. It should point to the right location for Perl 5.003 or newer. I know I say this in

every chapter, but the way the book is constructed we require no previous chapters to start from here. If you're unsure of Perl's location, either type which perl or which perl5 at your shell prompt, or, if you don't have shell access, ask your system administrator.

3. Now, back in db.cfg, the first variable you'll edit or add is $db_server= "http://www.yourcompany.com";. This should reflect the directory where the database will be running. If it's in your base document directory and you're using SiteWrapper, set $db_server=$server;. If you are putting it in a spur off the main, set it as http://www .yourcomany.com/db if you're in db.cfg, or as $db_server= "$server/db"; if you're in a SiteWrapper config. Whatever directory you install QuickDB into, make sure its permissions are set to CHMOD 777, readable and writeable by the server. Also, if you're calling ../config.cfg or similar with SiteWrapper, make sure your $headerfile and $footerfile are full path names from the root of the server, not the document root.

4. Set your password in db.cfg by first generating the garble you'll need with the Encrypt.cgi program in the distribution. Hit it with your browser, plug in your real word, like the word "password," then click Submit. You'll be given back a bunch of nonsense. Plug that into the password variable. SiteWrapper users can skip this.

5. Set the $headerfile and $footerfile variables with the names of your files. The header should contain <HTML><HEAD><TITLE>, etc., and the footer </BODY> and </HTML>. The HTML of these files will be tacked onto the top and bottom of every database generated page. Take a look at the SiteWrapper chapter if you haven't, because $JUMPLIST and $TEXTLIST are available as well.

6. At the bottom of the file, you'll pick up with the rest of the variables, shown in Figure 14.1. Before we start editing you have to decide on your data. What fields do you want to keep track of? I'm setting up a parts database for Henry's, from the WebPost chapter, so my fields are part number, part name, dimensions, price, shipping weight, current inventory, category, and a notes field. In @datatemplate you'll set a variable name for each field. These are the NAME attributes in the <FORM> we'll be setting up, so keep them as one word, preferably all lowercase or other standard you've used in the past.

7. Then for each you'll set a formal name in %description, which you'll see is an associative array. In the figure, partno goes with Part Number, name with Name, right though notes and Special Notes. The second name for each variable, the capitalized one, will be used

Figure 14.1 Data specific to QuickDB.

on the input screens to describe what you're putting in. So if partno should be SKU number, set the formal description to that. If your normal system is Catalog/Part, then set its descriptor to that.

8. In $var_to_index_by, choose the variable by which to index the results of database searches. I'm choosing name rather than part number because people will most likely be searching for names, not numbers. This will decide how items are displayed from the top to bottom of page.

9. The next variable you can leave as $datatemplatefile = 'datatemp.wms';, but then you'll have to make a datatemp.wms in your HTML editor. I've made a simple table in Figure 14.2 to match my data. I'm calling each variable by its value in the @datatemplate array. Both the search and browse programs will iterate through the data and write a foreach on this file. So if my query from the web page returns three parts from the database, the page will contain three tables. Note, before we move on, that I had to \$ escape the price dollar sign. That's so it won't be interpreted by Perl as the start of a variable definition.

10. But what about the top and bottom of the results pages? That's where the $browsefile = 'browse.wms'; variable comes in. If you open browse.wms in your editor you'll see that it's very simple, only $HEADER, $FOOTER, and a variable called $stringdata in between. This is the top and bottom above and below those three tables I just referred to. The $stringdata variable is the HTML of the three tables.

Figure 14.2 Working with the data variables.

Besides $HEADER and $FOOTER, you can add "Results of your Parts Search:" or "We have the following:" at the top and maybe a "Don't see what you're looking for..." line at the bottom. Between datatemp.wms, browse.wms, and your standard headers and footers, you should have all the creative freedom you need.

11. Upload all the files to the server and CHMOD them all to 755, readable and executable by the webserver. You should then be able to hit adddb.cgi and get Figure 14.3. If you can't, recheck the Perl location for Perl5 and the location of the config in the require lines of adddb.cgi and the other CGI programs. If no data file appears, called dbase.db, you probably forgot to set the directory permissions to 777.

12. As you can see, I've kept my data entry pretty simple. Don't put a dollar sign in the price because we've already done that in the HTML. I'm also doing that for the shipping weight. This will help us later when we plug the shopping cart into the project in the website-only chapter. The other thing I'd notice here before we move on is that I've written the category name in all lowercase. I'm not printing it to the screen ever. We'll use it next.

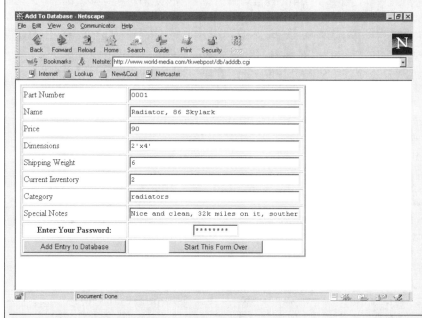

Figure 14.3 Adding to the database.

Quick Start: NT

1. In the /sourcecode/NT/database directory is the db.zip archive. There is also an unzipped directory. If you've not installed SiteWrapper or WebPost and have no config file, open db.cfg in your editor. If you do have a config already, add the variables you don't recognize to your config, then change the require "idb.cfg"; in adddb.cgi, browsedb.cgi, deletedb.cgi, editdb.cgi, and searchdb.cgi to the name of your config.

2. The first variable you'll edit or add is $db_server = "http://www .yourcompany.com";. This should reflect the directory where the database will be running. If it's in your base document directory and you're using SiteWrapper, set $db_server=$server;. If you are putting it in a spur off the main, set it as http://www.yourcomany.com/db if you're in db.cfg, or as $db_server="$server/db"; if you're in a SiteWrapper config. Whatever directory you install QuickDB into, make sure it's accessible and writeable. Also, if you're calling ../config.cfg or similar with SiteWrapper, make sure your $headerfile and $footerfile are full path names from the root of the server, not the document root.

3. Set your password in db.cfg by first generating the garble you'll need with the Encrypt.cgi program in the distribution. Hit it with your browser, plug in your real word, like the word "password," then click Submit. You'll be given back a bunch of nonsense. Plug that into the password variable. SiteWrapper users can skip this.

4. Now set the $headerfile and $footerfile variables with the names of your files. The header should contain <HTML><HEAD><TITLE>, etc., and the footer </BODY> and </HTML>. The HTML of these files will be tacked onto the top and bottom of every database generated page. Take a look at the SiteWrapper chapter if you haven't, because $JUMPLIST and $TEXTLIST are available as well.

5. At the bottom of the file, you'll pick up with the rest of the variables, shown in Figure 14.1. Before we start editing, you have to decide on your data. What fields do you want to keep track of? I'm setting up a parts database for Henry's from the WebPost chapter, so my fields are part number, part name, dimensions, price, shipping weight, current inventory, category, and a notes field. In @datatemplate, you'll set a variable name for each field. These are the NAME attribute in the <FORM> we'll be setting up, so keep them as one word, preferably all lowercase or other standard you've used in the past.

6. For each, you'll set a formal name in %description, which you'll see is an associative array. In the figure, partno goes with Part Number,

name with Name, right though notes and Special Notes. The second name for each variable, the capitalized one, will be used on the input screens to describe what you're putting in. So if partno should be SKU number, set the formal description to that. If your normal system is Catalog/Part, then set its descriptor to that.

7. In $var_to_index_by, choose the variable by which to index the results of database searches. I'm choosing name rather than part number because people will most likely be searching for names, not numbers. This will decide how items are displayed from the top to bottom of page.

8. The next variable you can leave as $datatemplatefile = 'datatemp.wms';, but then you'll have to make a datatemp.wms in your HTML editor. I've made a simple table in Figure 14.2 to match my data. I'm calling each variable by its value in the @datatemplate array. Both the search and browse programs will iterate through the data and write a foreach on this file. So if my query from the web page returns three parts from the database, the page will contain three tables. Note, before we move on, that I had to \$ escape the price dollar sign. That's so it won't be interpreted by Perl as the start of a variable definition.

9. But what about the top and bottom of the results pages? That's where the $browsefile = 'browse.wms'; variable comes in. If you open browse.wms in your editor, you'll see that it's very simple, only $HEADER, $FOOTER, and a variable called $stringdata in between. This is the top and bottom above and below those three tables I just referred to. The $stringdata variable is the HTML of the three tables. Besides $HEADER and $FOOTER, you can add "Results of your Parts Search:" or "We have the following:" at the top, and maybe a "Don't see what you're looking for…" line at the bottom. Between datatemp.wms, browse.wms, and your standard headers and footers, you should have all the creative freedom you need.

10. Now upload all the files to the server. You should then be able to hit adddb.cgi and get Figure 14.3. As you can see, I've kept my data entry pretty simple. Don't put a dollar sign in the price because we've already done that in the HTML. I'm also doing that for the shipping weight. This will help us later when we plug the shopping cart into the project in the website-only chapter. The other thing I'd notice here before we move on is that I've written the category name in all lowercase. I'm not printing it to the screen ever. We'll use it next.

The Administration Menus

You've seen how we add an entry to the database. Edit works much the same, but you select which one you want first. In Figure 14.4, you'll see the selection page. The entries are listed alphabetically according to the $var_to_index_by you set in the config. Here Automatic Transmission is first and Water Pump is last, based on the Perl sort function. If your database is huge, this page can be burgeoning. If you're a hacker, modify the edit to search on a name. We might provide a version that does this on the book website, so make sure to check. If it's very difficult with $var_to_index_by as your sort variable, try resetting it to stock number or category.

The delete menu works much the same. You get a screen like Figure 14.4 by hitting deletedb.cgi. Click on a part name; you'll be asked for your password and a yes and no Submit button to verify that you really want to delete the entry. The double verification system can be time consuming, but if the purpose of the resources in this book is to allow nontechnical personal access to your website's administration, an extra check can't hurt.

The Search Choices

Most people will cite the reason for Yahoo!'s early success as their dual interface. If you're a keyword person, plug in your words and sort through the results. If you hate

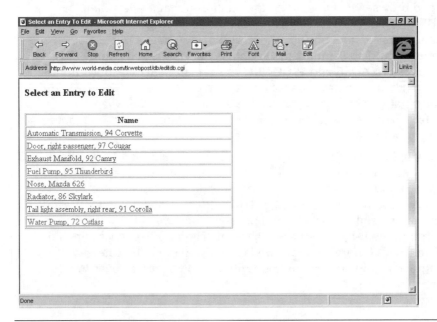

Figure 14.4 The edit screen.

sorting thousands of relevant hits of nonsense, try plucking through their directory structure. It will lead you to a whole page of the exact thing for which you are looking. We've tried to replicate that functionality in QuickDB's search options. With a little customization and a lot of creativity, you can replicate that dual structure.

Put a few more entries into your database, then hit searchdb.cgi. It gives you nothing. That's because searchdb.cgi needs a variable called searchterm sent to it. In your distribution should be an index.html that looks like Figure 14.5. It leads to all the interconnected programs on the site. The search box is an input form that leads to the search. From there you can plug in the search terms and get back a results page. The default for keywords is "or." So if someone plugs in 72 and Monte Carlo, they'll still get the 72 Cutlass parts. Hackers can make minor changes at line 50 by changing the foreach on the search terms to:

```
foreach $searchterm (@searchterms) {

        if ($line =~ /$searchterm/i) {

        $match = 1;

        }
```

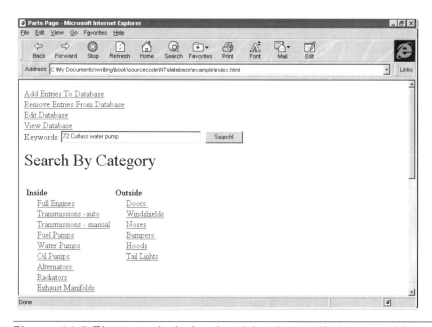

Figure 14.5 The sample index.html leads to all the searching options.

```
        else {$match = 0 ;

            last;
```

This will make the match an "and," so that every term to match on has to be in the database entry. So if I misspelled 72 Citless by mistake, I'd get nothing.

The browsedb.cgi is a bit different. It grabs the data file, sorts it according to $var_to_index_by, then spits every item in the file. Again, if your data is huge this can be cumbersome, but otherwise it's useful. As I mentioned, some people just take a printout of everything you offer. Whether your database houses real estate listings or luncheon specials, offering a full print feature will be of use to many of your visitors.

Special Searches

But what about the rest of the page in Figure14.4? I've listed several categories of parts at the top. That's where the category that we set up in @datatemplate comes in. Every part I enter into the database logs one of a preselected set of category names into the text of the actual entry. These are engines; transmissions_auto, transmissions_manual, fuel_pumps, water_pumps, oil_pumps, alternators, radiators, exhaust_manifolds, intake_manifolds, and valve_covers in the Inside selections; and doors, windshields, noses, bumpers, hoods, and tail_lights in the Outside selections. The HTML of that index.html screen looks like Figure 14.6. By clicking the category links, they are sent to the searchdb.cgi?searchterm=transmissions_auto, the search program with the category keyword plugged into the URL.

I've done the same for model names. If one of my visitors owns only a Monte Carlo, she might go right to the keyword and search for it. If, however, she came to

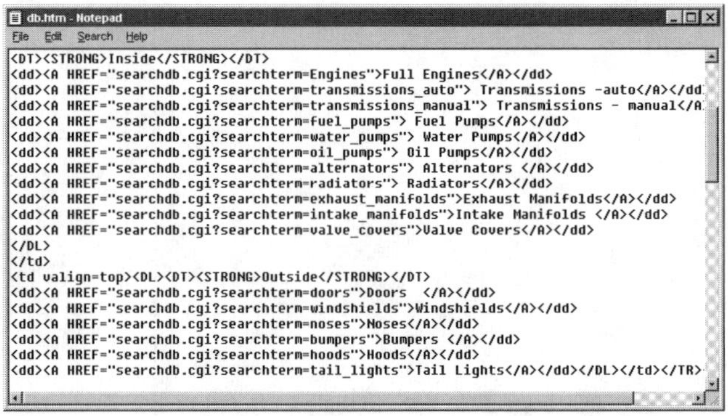


```
<DT><STRONG>Inside</STRONG></DT>
<dd><A HREF="searchdb.cgi?searchterm=Engines">Full Engines</A></dd>
<dd><A HREF="searchdb.cgi?searchterm=transmissions_auto"> Transmissions -auto</A></dd
<dd><A HREF="searchdb.cgi?searchterm=transmissions_manual"> Transmissions - manual</A
<dd><A HREF="searchdb.cgi?searchterm=fuel_pumps"> Fuel Pumps</A></dd>
<dd><A HREF="searchdb.cgi?searchterm=water_pumps"> Water Pumps</A></dd>
<dd><A HREF="searchdb.cgi?searchterm=oil_pumps"> Oil Pumps</A></dd>
<dd><A HREF="searchdb.cgi?searchterm=alternators"> Alternators </A></dd>
<dd><A HREF="searchdb.cgi?searchterm=radiators"> Radiators</A></dd>
<dd><A HREF="searchdb.cgi?searchterm=exhaust_manifolds">Exhaust Manifolds</A></dd>
<dd><A HREF="searchdb.cgi?searchterm=intake_manifolds">Intake Manifolds </A></dd>
<dd><A HREF="searchdb.cgi?searchterm=valve_covers">Valve Covers</A></dd>
</DL>
</td>
<td valign=top><DL><DT><STRONG>Outside</STRONG></DT>
<dd><A HREF="searchdb.cgi?searchterm=doors">Doors  </A></dd>
<dd><A HREF="searchdb.cgi?searchterm=windshields">Windshields</A></dd>
<dd><A HREF="searchdb.cgi?searchterm=noses">Noses</A></dd>
<dd><A HREF="searchdb.cgi?searchterm=bumpers">Bumpers </A></dd>
<dd><A HREF="searchdb.cgi?searchterm=hoods">Hoods</A></dd>
<dd><A HREF="searchdb.cgi?searchterm=tail_lights">Tail Lights</A></dd></DL></td></TR>
```

Figure 14.6 Making an indexed listing from your database categories.

the site looking for a side mirror for her boyfriend's Toyota Corolla, she might not think to look for special Monte Carlo parts. That's why on my main parts page I offer more of these special searches by model. In the Chevy section is <A HREF="searchdb.cgi?searchterm=Monte+Carlo">Monte Carlo</A>, which searches the database on the two words in the model. Note how I had to include a + to reflect the whitespace. In Figure 14.7 I've replicated this for several models, and if you look at the bottom in the status box you'll see that I refined a few of the Acura models by setting <A HREF="searchdb.cgi?searchterm=RL+acura"> RL</A>. The RL alone would catch several modern every-day words, so I added the word Acura. Now I have to remember to include that word in my item title.

 O n t h e C D I've provided the modified index.html and Henry's configuration files in the example directory under the main database directory. You'll find that I modified all the CGI programs to include a require "../webpost.cfg" line. This is so the search and browse know where to get their color information from through the $HEADER and $FOOTER. You can avoid this by replacing those variables in the browse.wms file with standard tops and bottoms of HTML. My searchdb.cgi in this example has also been modified as I explained to the "and" boolean query.

Adapting Your Data to QuickDB

When I first approached this chapter, my goal was to give webmasters on a budget a third alternative to either writing a custom CGI/API program for their database or learning and implementing SQL. For an extremely large data set, those are your best two options, with the custom program the preferred, but most of us are only dealing with a few thousand records. And usually these records are in a desktop database like Access, Fox Pro, or Paradox database. In this example, I've taken the sample file that comes with Microsoft Access for Windows 95 for a company called Northwind. In the small box of Figure 14.8, I've brought up the eight tables in the database. We're interested in the Products, so I selected it.

In the backset of the figure is the products listing in view mode. The records are black because I've selected the Select All Records option of the Edit menu, then copied them into my clipboard. By pasting them into Notepad I get Figure 14.9,

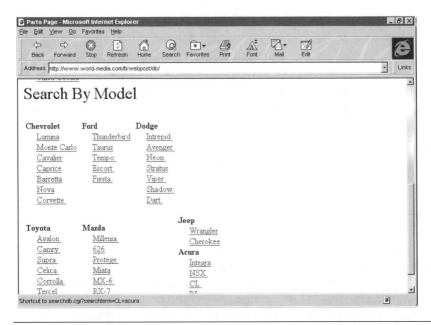

Figure 14.7 Special searches by model.

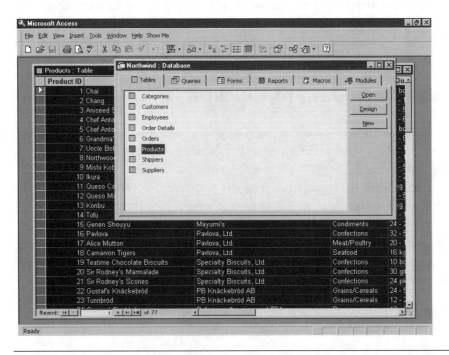

Figure 14.8 The sample tables in Microsoft's Access for Windows 95.

which is a tab-delimited list of the entire database with the column headings at the top. If your data is too big for Notepad, try another editor that doesn't line wrap and can save as plain text. Beware of Multi-Edit, though. I tried that first and had problems accessing the first line of data.

Some of you are asking why I didn't just Export the table as text and tabs. We tried that, but unless you Save as HTML in Access (which spits out one huge ugly table), it wouldn't resolve the Categories and Suppliers names from the associated tables. It saved the category not as Beverages, but as 1, which is the corresponding number for Beverages in the Categories table. We could have exported all the tables and made a custom CGI that queried and matched them all, but that's the option we're trying to avoid. If your database is nonassociative, just one table, the Export should work fine. I included this example because this will be the most difficult system you should encounter.

Now, at the top of your text file, you most likely have the names of your fields. Cut that and paste it into the db.cfg or your config file, then modify both the @datatemplate and %description as I have in Figure 14.10. Then choose a variable to index by.

Next you'll have to make a new datatemp.wms file matching your fields. I kept the same table format from before, but included this table's extra information about ordered items and whether an item was discontinued:

```
<table border=0 cellpadding=2 cellspacing=2>

<TR><td valign=top><STRONG><font color=orange>$Name by

$Supplier</font></STRONG></td>
```

Figure 14.9 The tab delimited list that we exported.

Figure 14.10 Add the field names to db.cfg.

```
<td valign=top> Stock number: $ID</td></TR>

<TR><td valign=top>Price: $Unit_Price </td>

<td valign=top>Supplier:$Supplier</td></TR>

<TR><td valign=top>Number in Stock: $Units_In_Stock</td>

<td valign=top>Units On Order $Units_On_Order</td></TR>

<TR><td valign=top>Minimum Order $Quantity_Per_Unit</td>

<td valign=top><em><strong>Is this Discontinued?:</strong></em>

$Discontinued</td></TR></table>
```

I deduced also that Quantity Per Unit was how many items were in a case, so I set that as my minimum order. By searching on the supplier Exotic Liquids, I now get a screen like Figure 14.11. As you can see, I kept the configuration files the same from the last example. If you use this for your database, you'll adapt it either with headers and footers called from db.cfg or with your config.cfg from SiteWrapper or WebPost.

For security, you might want to change the name of the file from dbase.db to another name. That way all the readers of this book won't know where to download your entire database. This is particularly sensitive if some of those fields contain proprietary knowledge or customer contact information. If your database can export out a query, leaving off the sensitive information, adapt the @datatemplate and $descriptions variables to that subset. And after you select a filename to save it as, do a multifile search and replace for dbase.db in all of the CGI programs with Multi-Edit or your editor.

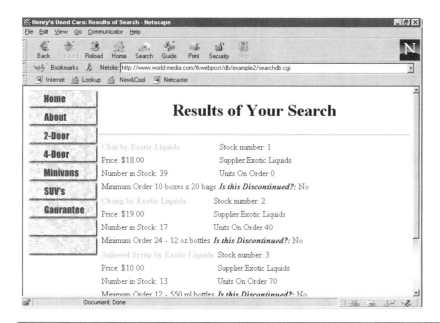

Figure 14.11 You've got it right when a full listing by category comes up.

One last issue is that you should save a new set of your data, cut off the first row of descriptions, and re-upload the file whenever your local records change. By using adddb.cgi, editdb.cgi, or deletedb.cgi, you'll only change the web copy, which in our Access example doesn't even resemble a real table in our database. Re-uploading is your best bet no matter what the case.

 O n t h e C D Off that /database directory should be an example2 directory. The files you'll need to replicate this example are db.cfg and dbase.db (I didn't change the file name). The original Access database is in the Fusion directory from our example in Chapter 2.

Discussions, Forums,
Bulletin Boards

From *Wired* to *Business Week*, the media is alive with talk of virtual communities. What started with USENET and CompuServe/AOL has grown into destinations on the web, usable and administrateable through any web browser. Big players in the industry have capitalized on the trend for intranet use, calling basic BBS utilities *groupware*. Computers are a cold realm of logic. Without a cohesive human bond on your website, its chances for a dedicated group of users is questionable. In this chapter, we'll add a powerful online community to your web or intranet site with very little budget, costing just your time to learn the install.

First we'll look at our rendition of an old web hack (I mean that in a complimentary way) that many of you have seen on some very popular sites. We've cleaned up a couple of the usability bugs and added some capabilities not in the original, plus wrapped it into SiteWrapper's and WebPost's config files if you have either installed. Both of the Quick Starts are easy. You should be set up in ten minutes.

Then we'll take a look at the FrontPage board. Since I covered FrontPage back in Chapter 3, I thought it appropriate to include it here. It's not as useful if the person running FrontPage is not the one administrating the board, but if you are installing your own site or administrating many areas for different clients, it's a great system.

TIP As you should have noticed in the WebPost chapter, webpost.cfg calls different head and foot files than SiteWrapper. This utility looks for the SiteWrapper version, so to adapt it to WebPost's config you'll add $headerfile and $footerfile as follows. I'm setting them as the same file here, but you can keep them separate by using the syntax for the normal $htmlheadfile and $htmltailfile.

```
############################################################################

# $htmlheadfile - this variable contains the filename of the default HTML

# header for your entire installation of WebPost(tm).


$htmlheadfile = "/full/path/to/head.wms";          # Filename for HTML Head

$headerfile=$htmlheadfile;

############################################################################

# $htmltailfile - this variable contains the filename of the default HTML

# 'footer' for your entire installation of WebPost(tm).


$htmltailfile = "/ful/path/to/foot.wms";           # Filename for HTML Tail

$footerfile=$htmltailfile;



############################################################################
```

discussion.web

This board was originally called WWWBoard by Matt Wright at worldwidemart/scripts. Since we adopted it, the code has gone through several changes. First, we made it so that you could use standard $HEADER and $FOOTER files with SiteWrapper, but ran into a problem down the road. Matt's version rewrote the index.html page and each message.htm as a static file. As you know from previous chapters, this is taboo for us because we prefer that all pages on the system be able to listen for everything from the page's colors to shopping cart variables.

So we made every page wrap, which meant changing the code entirely. It still prints static HTML files, but they are like SiteWrapper middles more than completed pages. It's also customizable as to which config you grab the page variables from, so if one department has its look and feel and another has another, each can graft its look onto the board.

Also, the original utility required a jump between posting your message as well. We eliminated this step with the standard print Location: you've seen elsewhere leading you straight to your message. After you post, you see the same message that the rest of the world sees. You then can even reply to yourself if that is fun to you. As you can see in the following figures, especially Figure 15.4, I do.

But besides my fun, the most useful feature we added was the ability to both post and mail your reply at the same time. We've found this useful for exceptionally slow boards with not much activity, but very important activity when it occurs. This way you can post a message and not return until you get an e-mail inviting you back. The actual reply is mailed with its subject as the message Subject: field. We'll run through the setup, including the e-mail addition, then customize the look and feel.

Quick Start: Unix

1. We're going to install only one copy here, but make a special directory for each copy of the board you wish to install called discussion/ or another name of your choosing. This will house one entire discussion area. It's crucial that you do not use your main directory if you intend to install several boards. Name the directories whatever you want (discussion1, discussion2, etc.), but they have to be separate from the main. Then CHMOD them each to 777.

2. In the /sourcecode/UNIX/discussion directory, you'll find discweb.zip. There is also an unzipped directory of the four files, index.cgi, discadmin.cgi, discboard.cfg, and discboard.cgi. Open each and check the Perl location to make sure it points to Perl on your system. By now you probably know it, but if not, ask your sysadmin or type which perl at your shell prompt.

---

3. The file discboard.cfg is in your editor. You should have a set of variables like those in Figure 15.1. If you named the directory something other than discussion, you'll want to change the values in $baseurl and $cgi_url, substituting the word discussion for the name of your directory. For subsequent copies you'll name it that directory as well.

4. Then make a directory under discussion called messages or whatever you want to rename it. CHMOD the messages directory to 777. If you do rename it, change the $mesgdir variable as well. The rest of discboard.cfg can stay unchanged. Those are pretty much leftovers from Matt's version. Make sure to leave $mesgfile = "index.cgi";. That's what enables you to use SiteWrapper's variables. If you haven't installed SiteWrapper, grab a copy of config.cfg and sitewrapper.pl and upload them into the directory. You'll need to set the $server variable in your config.cfg, as well as the $sendmail_location.

5. Go into the three CGI programs and change the require lines that look for ../config.cfg to whatever you renamed your config. If you've just uploaded sitewrapper.pl and config.cfg, set the require lines to the directory where you put them, which will most likely mean getting rid of the ../ before the file name.

6. Upload the four files to the discussion directory. Then CHMOD discboard.cgi and discadmin.cgi to 755.

7. This next step might seem weird but you really have to do it. Make sure you save a backup copy of index.cgi, then go into your discussion directory and CHMOD 777 index.cgi. The discussion board actually rewrites it on the fly. Originally Matt had it writing a static HTML file, but we made it a CGI so everything could wrap.

8. Hit index.cgi. You should get results like that in Figure 15.2. Try posting a message. If either step breaks, you probably have the require lines pointing to the wrong place or forgot to CHMOD either the main discussion or the messages directory.

Figure 15.1 The discussion.web variables.

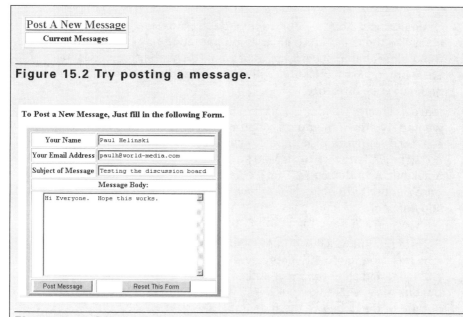

Post A New Message
Current Messages

Figure 15.2 Try posting a message.

To Post a New Message, Just fill in the following Form.

Your Name	Paul Helinski
Your Email Address	paulh@world-media.com
Subject of Message	Testing the discussion board

Message Body:

Hi Everyone. Hope this works.

[Post Message]   [Reset This Form]

Figure 15.3 Compose your message.

9. Once it's running, the interface is fairly intuitive. You should get a screen like Figure 15.3 to post, then once you post you will be shown your message, with invitations at the top of the screen to reply, view replies (of which there will be none), or return to the discussion main page. If you go to the discussion main page, you'll see a link to the message you just viewed. If you click Reply, you'll be jumped down in the page where the original message will be quoted. From there you have the choice to just post your reply or post and e-mail if the original poster supplied a valid e-mail address.

Quick Start: NT

1. Make a special directory for each copy of the board you wish to install called discussion/ or another name of your choosing. This will house one entire discussion area. It's crucial that you do not install this in your main directory if you use several boards. Name the directories whatever you want (discussion1, discussion2, etc.), but they have to be separate from the main. We're only going to set one up here.

2. In the /sourcecode/NT/discussion directory, you'll find discweb.zip. There is also an unzipped directory of the four files, index.cgi, discadmin.cgi, discboard.cfg, and discboard.cgi.

3. Open discboard.cfg in your editor. You should have a set of variables like those in Figure 15.1. If you named the directory something other than discussion, you'll want to change the values in $baseurl and $cgi_url, substituting the word discussion for the name of your directory.

4. Make a directory under discussion called messages or whatever you want to rename it. If you do rename it, change the $mesgdir variable as well. The rest of discboard.cfg can stay unchanged. Those are pretty much leftovers from Matt's version. Make sure to leave $mesgfile = "index.cgi";. That's what enables you to use SiteWrapper's variables. If you haven't installed SiteWrapper, grab a copy of config.cfg and sitewrapper.pl and upload them into the directory. You'll need to set the $server variable in your config.cfg.

5. Go into the three CGI programs and change the require lines that look for ../config.cfg to whatever you renamed your config. If you've just uploaded sitewrapper.pl and config.cfg, set the require lines to the directory where you put them, which will most likely mean getting rid of the ../ before the filename.

6. Now you be able to upload the files and hit index.cgi, getting back Figure 15.2. If you don't, you've probably not pointed the require lines to the right places. Make sure they match.

7. Once it's going, try posting a message. The interface is fairly intuitive. You should get a screen like that in Figure 15.3. Once you post you will be shown your message, with invitations at the top of the screen to reply, view replies (of which there will be none), or return to the discussion main page. If you go to the discussion main page, you'll see a link to the message you just viewed. If you click Reply, you'll jump down in the page where the original message will be quoted. From there you have the choice to just post your reply or post and e-mail if the original poster supplied a valid e-mail address. The e-mail might not work on NT with the version of Perl on the CD. Check the book website for news of the bug fix.

Customizing the Look

By now you're probably blinded by the <TABLE> layout of the formatted messages. We designed that because we thought it would stand out as different. It's different all right, but tiring to use. But rather than give you the finished, <TABLE>-free version, we'll work the look out together so you can get a feel for how discussion.web formats its messages. Look at the original code at line 207; I've changed the usability and function as follows:

```
207: \$HEADER

208:    <blockquote>

209:      <h2>$subject</h2>

210: <P>
```

I've kept the $HEADER the same. It has to be backslashed because it is evaluated not here, but as the document loads in the browser. I've gotten rid of the <CENTER> tag that was around the title. Left alignment is best for usability.

```
211: <A HREF="#reply">Reply To This Message</A> || <A HREF="$baseurl/$mesg-
file?\$variable_string">Discussion Main Page</A> || <A HREF="#followups">View
Replies</A><BR>

212:      <P><BR><P>
```

It's crucial to put the Reply buttons as close to the message as possible. You could move it above the title, which might be better, and you could, of course, substitute button images for the hotlinks. The <P>
<P> is to keep Netscape from collapsing whitespace before the message. I want to make it as readable as possible, hence the <blockquote> at the beginning, slimming down the width of the text lines. The more whitespace the better.

```
213: <b>Posted by: </b>

214: ENDTXT

215:    if ($email) {

216:      print NEWFILE " $name (<a href=\"mailto:$email\">$email</a>) <BR>\n";

217:    } else {

218:      print NEWFILE " $name<br>\n";

219:    }

220:    print NEWFILE "<b>Posted On: </b>$long_date <BR>\n";

221:    if ($followup == 1) {
```

```
222:        print NEWFILE "<b> In Reply to: </b> <a

href=\"$baseurl/$mesgfile?/msg=$last_message\.$ext&\$variable_string\">$origsub-

ject</a></STRONG><BR> By: <STRONG>";

223:        if ($origemail) {

224:        print NEWFILE "<a href=\"$origemail\">$origname</a></STRONG> on $orig-

date<BR>\n";

225:        } else {

226:        print NEWFILE "$origname</STRONG> on $origdate<BR>\n";

227:        }

228:     }

229:      print<<ENDTXT;

230: <P><b>Message:</b> <br>

231:       $body

232: <P>
```

This used to be the meat of the <TABLE>. I've removed all the table references and substituted bold tags and simple line breaks. Be careful not to break the Perl code. There are several nested braces of statements. Note that the if statements at 221 and 223 force you to duplicate the same line with HTML. That's why the table might not have made sense at first look.

```
233:    <b><a name="followups">Replies To This Message:</a></b><p>

234: <ul><!--insert: $num-->

235: </ul><!--end: $num-->   </blockquote>

236: <HR><P><BR><P><BR><P>
```

I've ended the blockquote after the original message and its listings of follow ups. The <ul> at 234 is a hidden tag that the board looks for when inserting its list of replies. Don't change its formatting at all. Figure 15.4 shows the layout as I've just configured. At 237, I've changed the reply section a bit as well. The table stays this time, but I've added the actual $subject of the message to the top of the reply.

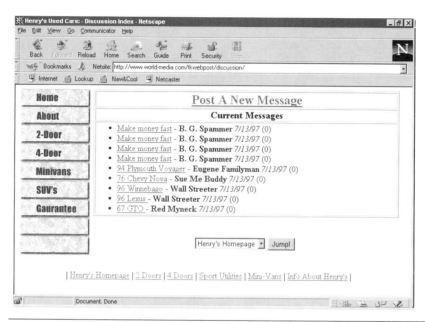

Figure 15.4 A sample custom layout.

```
237: <h2><a name="reply">Reply to:<br> <font
color=red>[$subject]</font></a></h2><p>

238: <form method=POST action="$cgi_url">

239: <input type=hidden name="valid_form" value="1">

240: ENDTXT

241:

242:    print "<input type=hidden name=\"followup\" value=\"";

243:    if ($followup == 1) {

244:        foreach $followup_num (@followup_num) {

245:            print "$followup_num,";

246:        }

247:    }

248:    print NEWFILE "$num\">\n";
```

```
249:    print NEWFILE "<input type=hidden name=\"origname\" value=\"$name\">\n";

250:    if ($email) {

251:        print NEWFILE "<input type=hidden name=\"origemail\"
value=\"$email\">\n";

252:    }

253:  print NEWFILE <<END;

254: <input type=hidden name="origsubject" value="$subject">

255: <input type=hidden name="origdate" value="$long_date">

256: <CENTER><TABLE BORDER=1 width=80%>
```

This is where the actual table begins. I've cleaned up a lot of the missing </td> and </th> tags at the ends of lines. Again, next we're duplicating some table information for if statements. One key area I've changed is at 262 and 265. The default copy doesn't let people change the title to replies. It prints a hidden variable, sending the reply title to the new message, then in text it printed the title for you to view, not change. I commented out the hidden variables and changed the subject line to an input box with the old title as the value attribute.

```
257: <TR><TH>Your Name:<BR></th><TD><INPUT TYPE=TEXT NAME=name size=30><BR></td>

258: <TR><TH>E-Mail Address:<BR></th><TD><INPUT TYPE=TEXT NAME=email size=30>
<BR>

259: END

260:    if ($subject_line == 1) {

261:        if ($subject_line =~ /^Re:/) {

262:            # print NEWFILE "<input type=hidden name=\"subject\" value=\"$sub-
ject\"></td>\n";

263:            print NEWFILE "<TR><TH>Subject of Message:<BR><TD><input
type=text name=\"subject\" value=\"$subject\"><BR></td> \n";

264:        } else {
```

```
265:        # print NEWFILE "<input type=hidden name=\"subject\" value=\"Re:
$subject\"></td>\n";

266:        print NEWFILE "<TR><TH>Subject of Message:<BR><TD><input
type=text name=\"subject\" value=\"Re: $subject\"></td>\n";

267:        }

268:    } elsif ($subject_line == 2) {

269:      print NEWFILE "<TR><TH>Subject of Message: <BR></th><TD><input
type=text name=\"subject\" size=30></td>\n";

270:    } else {

271:        if ($subject =~ /^Re:/) {

272:        print NEWFILE "<TR><TH>Subject of Message: <BR></th><TD><input
type=text name=\"subject\"value=\"$subject\" size=30><BR></td>\n";

273:        } else {

274:        print NEWFILE "<TR><TH>Subject of Message: <BR></th><TD><input
type=text name=\"subject\" value=\"Re: $subject\" size=30><BR></td>\n";

275:        }

276:    }

277:    print NEWFILE "<TR><TD ALIGN=LEFT COLSPAN=2><br>\n";

278:    print NEWFILE "<TR><Td COLSPAN=2><textarea name=\"body\" WRAP=PHYSICAL
COLS=65 ROWS=10>\n";
```

I've also opened up the width of the input box and changed the pipe (|) to a greater than symbol at line 285. You have to use the > sign rather than the actual character.

```
279:    print NEWFILE "$name ($email) was quoted as saying:\n";

280:  if ($quote_text == 1) {

281:    @chunks_of_body = split(/\&lt\;p\&gt\;/,$hidden_body);
```

```
282:     foreach $chunk_of_body (@chunks_of_body) {

283:          @lines_of_body = split(/\&lt\;br\&gt\;/,$chunk_of_body);

284:          foreach $line_of_body (@lines_of_body) {

285:          print NEWFILE "&gt; $line_of_body\n";

286:          }

287:          print NEWFILE "\n";

288:     }

289: }

290: print<<END;

291: </textarea></td></tr>

292: <TR><TH><input type=submit NAME=submit_type value="Post This

Reply"></th><th> <INPUT TYPE=submit NAME=submit_type value="Post and Mail

Reply"></th></tr></TABLE>

293: \$FOOTER

294: END

295:     select(STDOUT);

296:     close(NEWFILE);
```

And at the end I've again left the backslash before the footer. I'm going to insert this into Henry's used cars, so we'll grab his information. Figure 15.5 is the result.

Administration

Now we move from discboard.cgi to discadmin.cgi. You won't want to modify it much, except to change its title. I'll go through the functionality first, then we'll hack a bit of the code just to get a feel for what happens where.

If you go to discadmin.cgi with your browser now, you'll get four choices, the first of which is Remove Messages. Click and you'll be presented with a list of all the board's messages, by message, newest to oldest, but with one twist. Replies are inserted before their original messages. In Figure 15.6, message 11, Voyager for 69

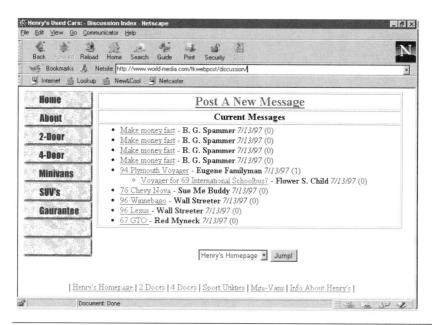

Figure 15.5 The result on Henry's.

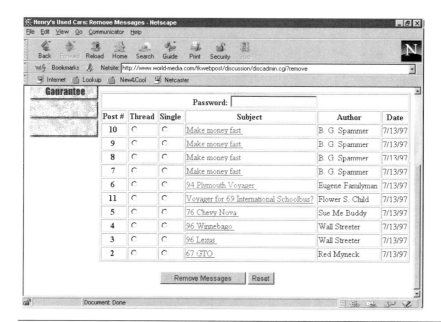

Figure 15.6 Deleting messages.

International Schoolbus?, is in reply to the 94 Voyager. By checking the radio button for messages on it, but not thread on the Voyager, will erase that message only. The thread for the Voyager will get rid of them both.

The next choice is to remove by message number. This is much like the last but messages are stacked by number, oldest to newest, with no exceptions for replies. This can give you a flexible alternative to clearing out messages by date, wiping a whole date's worth at one time. If one message from two months ago has had activity but the rest have been dead, you'll manually remove the dead ones, leaving the active ones alive. Note that if you inadvertently check a radio button there is no way to uncheck it.

FrontPage Discussion

We're going to use the wizard for this. From the Create a New FrontPage Web section of the Getting Started menu, select From a Wizard or Template.

Use the Discussion Web Wizard. Then under the Web Server or File Location drop box, select the www or IP number of the server on which you want the discussion board. Name it discussion or something intuitive for your forum. Click OK. FrontPage will ask for your user name and password. Click OK again.

FrontPage will munge for a bit, then pop up the second part of the wizard. It's a picture of a guy handing out paper. Click Next. It will then ask you if you want, besides the submission form, a table of contents, search form, threaded replies, and a confirmation page. We selected All and clicked Next.

Then you'll put in the title of the discussion, which we'll call Using FrontPage Discussion. It also asks you for a hidden directory for your data files. Call it whatever you like and click Next.

This next section is a bit confusing. It asks you what fields you want people to input when discussing different topics. The first choice, subject, comments, is just that. The second adds the capability to allow the user to select a category, which is different from having multiple boards. That we'll add with bot, later. The third is like category, but for products, if yours is a catalog site like the Chapter 3 demo. Set your choice and click Next.

Decide who will have access to the discussion. Answer yes on the next tab if only registered users can view the group, no if the board is open to all. The administration of the access will be through the FrontPage explorer. We're going to select yes, then click Next.

On the next screen we chose Newest to Oldest as the way the table of contents publishes discussion topics. Then click Next, then yes, on the next tab. That sets the homepage of /discussion as the table of contents.

Select the search options if you chose to include a search of the discussion. We selected the bottom, subject, size, date, and score. Then click Next, which will lead you to the next page to choose your colors. Choose them and click Next again.

Next you select whether you want frames and the format with which to display them. We chose the Dual interface, which sets the <NOFRAMES> tag. Click Next, then Finish. FrontPage will again munge for a bit, then you'll have a ready-made discussion like Figure 15.7.

If you checked the yes earlier, FrontPage will give you a self add form to save you the administrative hassles of adding new people. You can, as it explains, upload it to your server in the root web. A bot processes the form. Under the Tools/Permissions tab, you'll have to Use Unique Permissions for This Web, then

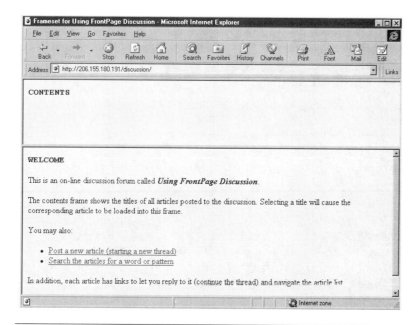

Figure 15.7 A standard FrontPage discussion.

Apply, then select Only Users have Browse Access, then OK. If you intend to save that registration file to the root web, hit your File/Open FrontPage Web, open the web below the discussion board you just installed and, after waiting for it to come up, go back to the FrontPage editor with the Self Registration Form and do a Save As from the File menu. Then hit the file name you gave it on the server and register a user. It should look something like Figure 15.8.

Adding a Second Discussion

Now we're going to use the manual bot creation menu rather than the wizard to create another discussion board on the same site. But instead of putting it in through the discussion web we just created, I'm going to tack it into our root web that we created back in Chapter 3. Open the root web and go to the FrontPage editor. Start a new page with the extreme left page icon.

On the bottom of the button bar in the right-hand corner are the form tools. We'll use these to make our submission form. First click the text box and then double-click on the box for the field's name and properties. We're setting up a customer service board, so we're requiring that they fill all the fields for product, date purchased, and

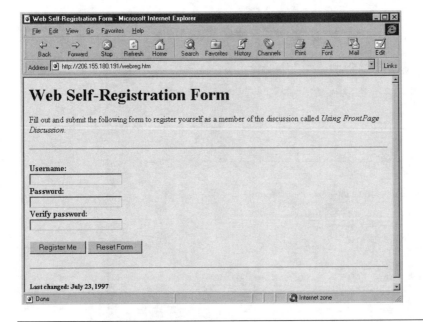

Figure 15.8 Registering a user.

quantity purchased, as well as their e-mail. If you are unfamiliar with the FrontPage editor, refer to the documentation. It's very simple to create a form.

Now we write a custom CGI to process the form? No, that's what the discussion bot handles. Right-click inside the form and select Form Properties. Then, under the Form Handler select the WebBot Discussion Component. The Settings... tab will lead you to a Discussion tab with title and directory like before and will allow you to save the time, date, user name (if it was password protected), and user machine. Select what you like and the Order newest to oldest if you so choose. Also pick your colors.

Under the Article tab, you can pick your header and footer and additional information if you'd like it. Then the Confirm page allows you to set the confirmation page, a page saying "Thanks for submitting" that you'll have to make, and the validation page saying "Sorry, you forgot a required field" if you set the form properties to validate. Click OK twice, then Save As from the file menu. It will ask you to name both the title and file name of the form you just created.

After doing all this, we realized that the form we just created had no link to find the discussion board. In the directory you created this board, find toc.html. That's the table of contents. To make a fancy frames/noframes interface like the wizard, you'll have to make a <FRAMESET> page manually. If you want a search you'll have to do that yourself as well. In short, use the wizard for more boards, just select the Add to the Current Web checkbox from your root web, then don't set the discussion main as the homepage.

Removing Messages

Because the first utility in this chapter makes it very easy to administrate messages remotely, I thought it appropriate to walk you through the process on FrontPage. First, under the Tools//Web Settings, select the Advanced tab and Show documents in Hidden Directories. Then, in the FrontPage Explorer, go to the directory on the server where you created the board you want to edit. Each of the articles is labeled as 0000001.htm, 000002.htm, and so on with the subject of the posting. If there are several of the same title, with the RE: FrontPage automatically puts on the reply, go to the actual board and find the file name. You can delete them manually by highlighting the file and pressing your Delete button. When you're done, select Tool/Manually Re-Calculate Hyperlinks. The offending message will be removed from the table of contents.

16

Live Web
Chat Rooms

Sometimes threaded discussion doesn't cut it in a community. It's too controlled, focused, and topic related. Sometimes people just want to talk. Chat messages blast in, one after another, and go away after a given time, so it's more a live thought process than an organized forum. Chat can be very exciting, even addictive.

The most publicized chat rooms are those on America Online, CompuServe, and Prodigy, which all use proprietary systems. But most chats use a system called Internet Relay Chat through one of five major networks, the biggest of which is EFNet, serving 23,000 users at any one time. It requires that you use a proprietary client application installed on your local machine or Telnet to a chat server from a Unix shell account.

On websites, most of the big chats use a Java client downloaded to your web browser (HotWired, as an example). It connects to one of these IRC servers and allows you to pick from one of the site's rooms. For high-profile sites this might be your best choice, but proprietary Java clients that run on only 32-bit systems are the focus of this book. A 486/33 with eight megabytes of RAM won't run that applet. Chat is enormously useful for business purposes, and many business users are on those old 486 machines running Windows 3.1. The following two utilities run in a browser

Figure 16.1 IRC chat isn't the place for business.

through a standard HTML interface. Both use frames, but the first gives users a <NOFRAMES> choice.

But why do you need a chat room on your site in the first place? Most I've seen are cluttered with garbage like Figure 16.1. On IRC that's the case. I don't know where they come from, but somebody has the time to waste (certainly no one who works with me) and apparently lots of nothing to share with the world. That's why I suggest, as you'll see in the following Quick Start, that you be as specific as you can in naming your rooms. Chat can be a useful business tool and a fun addition to any site with a targeted audience. Just be careful where you market it as a few bad apples can destroy an otherwise productive area.

We've successfully ported both of the following applications from Unix to NT and ASAPI. They run like lightning. On all platforms, the first is slightly more involved to configure but more versatile and easier to administrate in the long run. The second is quick and easy but requires that you manually remove a file to start a new chat.

Dynamic.chat

This is an adaptation of Gunther Birzniek's BBS script located at selena.mcp.com/ Scripts/bbs.html. We've made some modifications to the interface and ported the parts of the code that wouldn't run on Perl/ISAPI for NT. But in general, all copyright and redistribution rights are his. You are free to use the copy on the CD or upgrade to his latest at the URL on Selena Sol's site, though if you do download the latest, I can't guarantee its function on NT. For full-function, cross-platform access, you can't beat this one for ease of installation and use.

Quick Start: Unix

1. In the /sourcecode/UNIX/dynamicchat/ directory, you'll find the zipfile dynchat.zip. There is also an unzipped directory of the four files. Make a separate chat directory on your server, called whatever you wish, and CHMOD the directory 777 and upload the files into it.

2. Bring up index.cgi in your editor and check the Perl location so that it matches your system. As I've explained before but will repeat for every chapter, either type which perl at the prompt or ask your system administrator. Then type perl -v to make sure the Perl version is 5.003 or above. If you get 4.036, type which perl5 or ask your sysadmin for the location of Perl5.

3. Re-upload index.cgi to the server and hit it with your web browser. You should get a screen like Figure 16.2. I've filled in my values. Don't go on to the next screen yet, you'll get an error.

4. Open chat.setup in your editor and scroll down to the variable @chat_rooms. You'll see the instructions to reset it with the actual

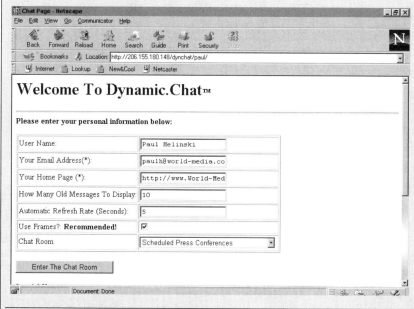

Figure 16.2 Logging on to Dynamic.chat.

names of your chat rooms. In Figure 16.3, I'm using "Scheduled Press Conferences" and "Customer Support 8 AM –10 PM EST" to illustrate that it's very important to be as specific as you can with chat rooms. As you saw from Figure 16.1, a lot of nonsense can show up in chat rooms. Other, very specific rooms might be "Last Wednesday's Canoe Trip" or "3 PM Staff Meeting July 12 1997." You can't be too specific on time or topic, because the demise of rooms are usually a lack of one or both. Either no one shows up at the scheduled time or there is a constant noise floor of nonsense around the clock.

5. The next variable is @chat_room_directories, which I set as "press" and "support." We'll create these later.

6. The @chat_room_variable variable is hard to understand unless you're familiar with way CGI works. These are the ?room=support variables that will be sent over HTTP. I just used the same as the directory names so as to be intuitive to the users.

7. The way we're configuring the program, you'll want to leave the next variable, $chat_script = "index.cgi"; alone. That way people can just hit your chat directory instead of chat.cgi, which is tricky on NT anyway.

8. Both $no_html and $no_html_images are your call. If you set them to on, they will prevent people from <H1>Posting Their Chat in Headers and Other HTML</H1> and <IMG SRC="http://www.myaw-fulserver.com/expletive.gif> images that could be annoying to users who are there to conduct otherwise serious discussion. If you're using the rooms for business, it might be useful for users to post fig-ures they've uploaded to the web previously.

9. I left the $chat_session_dir = "Sessions"; alone because the word is in-tuitive to someone who might administrate the program at a later date.

10. The $chat_session_length = 1; means that one day after the last message the current session within the room will stay active. If, after

Figure 16.3 Be specific about chat rooms.

one day, you hit the room, it will show no messages. This variable and several others must be in the percentage or multiple of one day formats. The example they give is in the next variable.

11. In $chat_who_length, you set how long the program should wait before completely refreshing the list of who is participating in the chat room. Set it at multiples of one hour, or 1/24/12 as their example suggests, which uses standard Perl division of one day, divided by 24 hours, divided by 12, which is one twelfth of one hour or five minutes. If set to that, my name goes dead from the View Occupants list five minutes after my last activity.

12. In Figure 16.4, you'll see what $chat_announce_entry = "on"; controls. If you turn if off, the Please Welcome messages will go away. It's nice to know who's there without having to click the View Occupants button.

13. Next is $prune_how_many_days, which by default is set to one quarter of a day or six hours. That means that any message older than six hours will be deleted no matter how many messages are in the current room.

14. As you could see from the first screen of the interface where I logged in, each user can choose how many old messages to display.

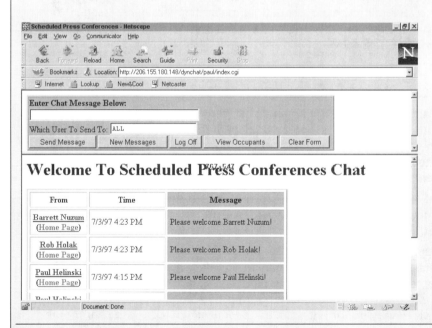

Figure 16.4 Controlling the welcome messages.

The next variable, $prune_how_many_sequences, automatically keeps the number of available messages lower than the number you set, so even if I've set a hundred past messages in my preferences I'll get only the value here. One note is that if you intend to build a search of old archives, set this high into the thousands. This is true for the previous variable as well.

15. We added the last variable to control the color of the table background color in the message part of the bottom frame. The default is a basic gray. Don't forget to leave the 1; at the end, and make sure all the variables have a value or the program will break.

16. Now we have to go make the directories I specified in the @chat_room_directories and $chat_session_dir variables. For me, that's support, press, and Sessions. After they are created, CHMOD each of them to 777.

17. Go ahead and log in. You should be greeted with a Please Welcome message if you set that option on. If you set it off, click View Occupants. You should be there. To add another room, alter the @chat_rooms, @chat_room_directories and @chat_room_variable entries, keeping the order of each in relation to each other, and add a new directory. To remove a room, just edit the three variables. The old directory will be an archive of the time and how many messages you put in the $prune_how_many_days and $prune_how_many_sequences variables, respectively.

Quick Start: NT

1. In the /sourcecode/NT/dynamicchat/ directory, you'll find the zipfile dynchat.zip. There is also an unzipped directory of the four files. Make a separate chat directory on your server and upload the files. Don't call the directory "chat" though. NT and Internet Information Server seem to make it automatically password protected.

2. Hit that directory with your browser. You should get a screen like Figure 16.2. I've filled in my values. Don't go on to the next screen yet; you'll get an error.

3. Open chat.setup in your editor and scroll down to the variable @chat_rooms. You'll see the instructions to reset it with the actual names of your chat rooms. In Figure 16.3, I'm using "Scheduled Press Conferences" and "Customer Support 8 AM–10 PM EST" to illustrate that it's very important to be as specific as you can with chat rooms. As you saw from Figure 16.1, a lot of nonsense can show up in chat

rooms. Other, very specific rooms might be "Last Wednesday's Canoe Trip" or "3 PM Staff Meeting July 12 1997." You can't be too specific on time or topic, because the demise of rooms are usually a lack of one or both. Either no one shows up at the scheduled time or there is a constant noise floor of nonsense around the clock.

4. The next variable is @chat_room_directories, which I set as "press" and "support." We'll create these later.

5. The @chat_room_variable variable is hard to understand unless you're familiar with way CGI works. These are the ?room=support variables that will be sent over HTTP. I just used the same as the directory names so as to be intuitive to the users.

6. The way we're configuring the program you'll want to leave the next variable, $chat_script = "index.cgi"; alone. That way people can just hit your chat directory instead of chat.cgi, which is tricky on NT anyway.

7. Both $no_html and $no_html_images are your call. If you set them to on, they will prevent people from <H1>Posting Their Chat in Headers and Other HTML</H1> and <IMG SRC="http://www.myawefulserver.com/expletive.gif> images that could be annoying to users who are there to conduct otherwise serious discussion. If you're using the rooms for business, it might be useful for users to post figures they've uploaded to the web previously.

8. I left the $chat_session_dir = "Sessions"; alone because the word is intuitive to someone who might administrate the program at a later date.

9. The $chat_session_length = 1; means that one day after the last message the current session within the room will stay active. If, after one day, you hit the room, it will show no messages. This variable and several others must be in the percentage or multiple of one day formats. The example they give is in the next variable.

10. In $chat_who_length, you set how long the program should wait before completely refreshing the list of who is participating in the chat room. Set it at multiples of one hour, or 1/24/12 as their example suggests, which uses standard Perl division of one day, divided by 24 hours, divided by 12, which is one twelfth of one hour or five minutes. If set to that, my name goes dead from the View Occupants list five minutes after my last activity.

11. In Figure 16.4, you'll see what $chat_announce_entry = "on"; controls. If you turn it off, the Please Welcome messages will go away. It's nice to know who's there without having to click the View Occupants button.

12. Next is $prune_how_many_days, which by default is set to one quarter of a day or six hours. That means that any message older than

> six hours will be deleted no matter how many messages are in the
> current room.
>
> 13. As you could see from the first screen of the interface where I
>   logged in, each user can choose how many old messages to display.
>   The next variable, $prune_how_many_sequences, automatically
>   keeps the number of available messages lower than the number you
>   set, so even if I've set a hundred past messages in my preferences,
>   I'll get only the value here. One note is that if you intend to build a
>   search of old archives, set this high into the thousands. This is true
>   for the previous variable as well.
>
> 14. We added the last variable to control the color of the table back-
>   ground color in the message part of the bottom frame. The default is
>   a basic gray. Don't forget to leave the 1; at the end, and make sure
>   all the variables have a value or the program will break.
>
> 15. Now we have to go make the directories I specified in the
>   @chat_room_directories and $chat_session_dir variables. For me,
>   that's support, press, and Sessions.
>
> 16. Go ahead and log in. You should be greeted with a Please Welcome
>   message if you set that option on. If you set it off, click View
>   Occupants. You should be there. To add another room, alter the
>   @chat_rooms, @chat_room_directories, and @chat_room_variable
>   entries, keeping the order of each in relation to each other, and add
>   a new directory. To remove a room, just edit the three variables. The
>   old directory will be an archive of the time and how many messages
>   you put in the $prune_how_many_days and
> $prune_how_many_sequences variables, respectively.

Customizing the Look

There's not much to dynamic.chat that you'd want to change, but what there is you
must change to make it look and feel like your site. We'll start with the first menu
you get hitting index.cgi. It says Welcome To Dynamic.Chat at the top, which is our
name for this adaptation of Gunther's original program. The code to change this
page is in chat-html.pl, and the include file begins at line 54 with the here document for the page.

```
54: print <<__END_OF_ENTRANCE__;

55: <HTML>

56: <HEAD>
```

```
57: <TITLE>Chat Page</TITLE>

58: </HEAD>

59: <BODY BGCOLOR="#FFFFFF">

60: <H1>Welcome To Dynamic.Chat<FONT SIZE=1><SUP>TM</SUP></FONT></H1>

61: <H2>$chat_error</H2>

62: <FORM METHOD=POST ACTION=index.cgi>

63: <INPUT TYPE=HIDDEN NAME=setup VALUE=$setup>.

64: <HR>

65: <STRONG>Please enter your personal informationbelow:</STRONG><p>

66:

67: <TABLE BORDER=1>

68: <TR>

69: <TD ALIGHT=RIGHT>User Name:</TD>

70: <TD><INPUT NAME=chat_username></TD>

71: </TR>

72: <TR>

73: <TD ALIGHT=RIGHT>Your Email Address(*):</TD>

74: <TD><INPUT NAME=chat_email></TD>

75: </TR>

76: <TR>

77: <TD ALIGHT=RIGHT>Your Home Page (*):</TD>

78: <TD><INPUT NAME=chat_http></TD>

79: </TR>

80: <TR>

81: <TD ALIGHT=RIGHT>How Many Old Messages To Display:</TD>
```

```
82: <TD><INPUT NAME=how_many_old VALUE="10"></TD>

83: </TR>

84: <TR>

85: <TD ALIGHT=RIGHT>Automatic Refresh Rate (Seconds):</TD>

86: <TD><INPUT NAME=refresh_rate VALUE="0"></TD>

87: </TR>

88: <TR>

89: <TD ALIGHT=RIGHT>Use Frames?:<STRONG>Recommended!</strong></TD>

90: <TD><INPUT TYPE=checkbox NAME=frames></TD>

91: </TR>

92: <TR>

93: <TD ALIGHT=RIGHT>Chat Room</TD>

94: <TD><SELECT NAME=chat_room>

95: $chat_room_options

96: </SELECT>

97: </TD>

98: </TR>

99: </TABLE>

100: <P>

101: <INPUT TYPE=SUBMIT NAME=enter_chat VALUE="Enter The ChatRoom">

102:

103: <P>

104: <STRONG>Special Notes:</STRONG><P>

105: (*) Indicates Optional Information<P>

106: Choose <STRONG>how many old messages</STRONG> to display if you want to
```

```
107: display some older messages along with the new ones whenever you fresh

108: the chat message list.

109: <P>

110: Additionally, if you use Netscape 2.0 or another browser that supports

111: the HTML <STRONG>Refresh</STRONG> tag, then you can state the number of

112: seconds you want to pass before the chat message list is automatically

113: refreshed for you. This lets you display new messages automatically.

114: <P>

115: If you are using Netscape 2.0 or another browser that supports

116: <STRONG>Frames</STRONG>, it is highly suggested that you turn frames ON.

117: This allows the messages to be displayed in one frame, while you submit

118: your own chat messages in another one on the same screen.

119:

120:   <HR>

121: </FORM><BR>

122: </BODY>

123: </HTML>

124: __END_OF_ENTRANCE__
```

At line 57, I changed the <TITLE> of the page, followed by the <H1> in line 60. The <H2> below it you should leave alone. That's where the error message comes back if the program experiences a problem. I also used the $tablebackcolor variable from the chat.setup we configured to get people used to the color scheme. Be careful not to lose any form variables or the $chat_room_options variable at line 95. Figure 16.5 is the result of my changes, and it also shows what the $chat_error variable returns if you forget a field.

Moving on, let's click Enter the Chat Room. At the top of the bottom frame, you'll see Welcome to *nameofchatroom* Chat. It's derived at line 244 from the $chat_room_name variable. To get rid of the whole message, delete that line. If you

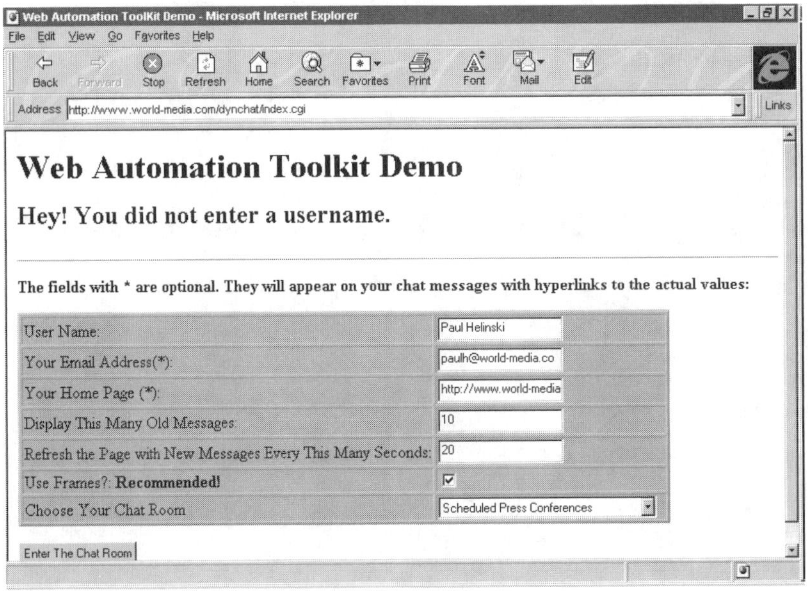

Figure 16.5 A customized look with colored tables.

want to keep its title, but get rid of the "Welcome to" and "Chat" before it, just leave the variable name at line 244.

You can, however, put a welcome message in the top frame very easily. The code that prints it is at line 273 with another here document :

```
273:    print <<__END_OF_CHAT_SUBMIT__;

274: $form_header

275:

276: <INPUT TYPE=HIDDEN NAME=session VALUE=$session>

277: <INPUT TYPE=HIDDEN NAME=chat_room VALUE=$chat_room>

278: $more_hidden

279: <TABLE BORDER=3 BGCOLOR="$tablebackcolor" CELLPADDING=1CELLSPACING=0>

280: <TR><TD>

281: <STRONG>Enter Chat Message Below:</STRONG>
```

```
282: <BR>

283: <INPUT TYPE=TEXT SIZE=40 NAME=chat_message>

284: <BR>

285: Which User To Send To:

286: <INPUT TYPE=TEXT NAME=chat_to_user VALUE="ALL">

287: <BR>

288: <INPUT TYPE=SUBMIT NAME=submit_message VALUE="Send Message">

289: <INPUT TYPE=SUBMIT NAME=refresh_chat VALUE="New Messages">

290: <INPUT TYPE=SUBMIT NAME=logoff VALUE="Log Off">

291: <INPUT TYPE=SUBMIT NAME=occupants VALUE="View Occupants">292: <INPUT

TYPE=RESET VALUE="Clear Form">

293:

294: </TD></TR></TABLE>

295: </FORM>

296: __END_OF_CHAT_SUBMIT__
```

I put a table in after line 294 aligned right with no border and the same $tableback-color variable to regulate its color. Besides that modification, You are free to change the layout, but again, be careful of the form variable names. And at line 274 make sure to leave the header in there or the browser won't be able to decode the output.

I'm not going to get into drastically changing the bottom frame with the messages, but one thing that would be nice to change is the section where it prints the date and time of the messages, along with (NEW) for messages you haven't yet seen. First we go to line 378 where it stores the value to be printed for new messages:

```
376:         $chat_buffer .= "\n<TD>";

377:         if ($x > $user_last_read) {

378:             $chat_buffer .= " (New) "

379:         }
```

```
380:          if ($msg_to_user =~ /^$user_name$/i ||381:

($msg_from_user =~ /^$user_name$/i &&

382:              $msg_to_user ne "ALL")) {

383:          if ($msg_from_user =~ /^$user_name$/i) {

384:              $temp = " to (Private $msg_to_user)";

385:          }

386:

387:              $chat_buffer .= "<STRONG>$temp</STRONG><BR>\n ";

388:          $temp = "";

389:            }

390:          $chat_buffer .= " $msg_date_time</TD>";

391:          $chat_buffer .= "\n";
```

I switched it to $chat_buffer .= " <IMG SRC=\"new.gif\"> "; making sure to backslash the the double quotes. You'll see the results in Figure 16.6. Then I decided I wanted the time and date before the new image I just put in, so I went into the code and moved some stuff around:

```
375:          $chat_buffer .= "</TD>\n";

376:          $chat_buffer .= "\n<TD>";

376.5:        $chat_buffer .= " $msg_date_time";

377:          if ($x > $user_last_read) {

378:              $chat_buffer .= "<IMG SRC=\"new.gif\">   "

379:            }

380:          if ($msg_to_user =~ /^$user_name$/i ||

381:              ($msg_from_user =~ /^$user_name$/i &&

382:              $msg_to_user ne "ALL")) {

383:          if ($msg_from_user =~ /^$user_name$/i) {
```

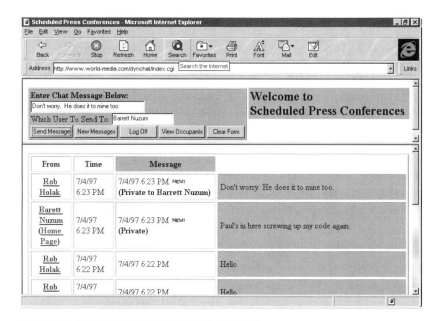

Figure 16.6   Adding an image for new messages.

```
384:              $temp = " to (Private $msg_to_user)";

385:          }

386:

387:              $chat_buffer .= "<STRONG>$temp</STRONG><BR>\n ";

388:          $temp = "";

389:          }

390:          $chat_buffer .= "</TD>";

391:          $chat_buffer .= "\n";
```

You can see that at line 378 I've already added in the image to replace the (NEW) sign. Then at 390, I've gotten rid of $msg_date_time. At 376.5, you'll see that I added a line back in with it, before the if statement that prints the .gif I added.

If you're an experienced Perl hacker, you'll be able to experiment with more of the layout in the bottom frame. I only have moderate experience and I'm rusty.

On the CD The example I just created is both at www.world-media.com/dynchat/ and on the CD in the /sourcecode/UNIX/dynamic-chat/example/ and /sourcecode/NT/dynamicchat/example/ directories. I've also left in the numbered line files using the linenumber.pl program we used back in the server side include section of Chapter 3.

When I tried to modify the location of the (Private to) message at line 384, I messed it up and had to start over again. It's a pretty good interface the way it is. The only problem with dynamic.chat, and Gunther's original, is its size. For hundreds or thousands of users, you would need a multiple processor server for Unix. I don't think it will scale well otherwise. On NT it might, the ISAPI filter is really fast, but I wouldn't try more than one hundred users on anything short of a Pentium Pro 200 with 64 megabytes of RAM. Take a look at the next program; its scalability is a concern.

QuikChat: A Quick Alternative

As I mentioned in the introduction to the chapter, this is about the easiest chat software you'll find. Edit one file, upload it to the server, change the permissions if you're on Unix, and run it. It took me about a half hour to figure it out and install the first room, then a second with a different title.

QuikChat is also ultra-sensitive to system resources, which might be your biggest concern if you're installing this for a huge event with hundreds of participants. That's the biggest weakness of web-based chat. It'll kill your processor if too many people use it at the same time. This one doesn't have the features that dynamic.chat offers, but your processor will thank you. It's a much simpler and smaller program to run three times a second, especially for Unix, which has to start a new incidence of Perl for every process. QuikChat's only problem is that it has no way to expire messages after a time, so a long, hundred-user chat would make for heavy load times as the middle frame is one huge file of every chat message. For scheduled chats that's OK. You could call a break and manually remove the file, but for an ongoing, round-the-clock international forum I don't see QuikChat of much use without minor modifications that would make the main index run as a CGI, which would make the program more resource intensive. Like most things in computing, it's give and take.

Matt Hahnfield wrote QuickChat and was kind enough to let us use it for the book. There might be a new version out at www.cs.hope.edu/~hahnfld/, so you might want to check there before loading this one. Matt's e-mail is at the end of the chapter. Thank him; it's a dandy piece of work.

Quick Start: Unix

1. In the /sourcecode/UNIX/quikchat/ directory, you'll find the zipfile quikchat.zip and an unzipped directory of the seven files. Open quikchat.cgi and check the Perl location. See the previous Quick Start if you are unsure as to how to do this.

2. While you still have quikchat.cgi in your editor, scroll down to where Matt lists the $filepath variable. If quikchat.cgi will be in a different directory than your .htm files, you'll want to put the full path from the webservers root here. Make sure to follow it with a slash like Matt's example of $filepath='/home/hahnfld/public_html/';.

3. The next variable is how you want your default room documents to be referenced. The default is .htm, but if the rest of your site is .html, you'll want to change this. In the customization, we'll make a new HTML file for each room.

4. I tested the next variable, and it's actually a crucial component to cross-platform access to QuikChat. It determines whether users on Microsoft Internet Explorer can see new messages as they are entered into QuikChat. New messages will appear at the top of the screen if you set $iecompatable=1;. This is because IE doesn't appear to recognize the #END in assigning a <FRAMESET>. Leave this variable as 0, and IE users will not think your room works. The top of the middle frame never changes.

5. If you do set the IE option to 1, go into index.htm and remove the #END from the frame target or new messages won't show on Netscape. Figure 16.7 will be the result.

6. Make a directory of the main on your webserver. Name it whatever you wish.

7. Change the directory's permissions to CHMOD 777 and upload all the files into it.

8. Make quickchat.cgi executable with CHMOD 755 quikchat.cgi.

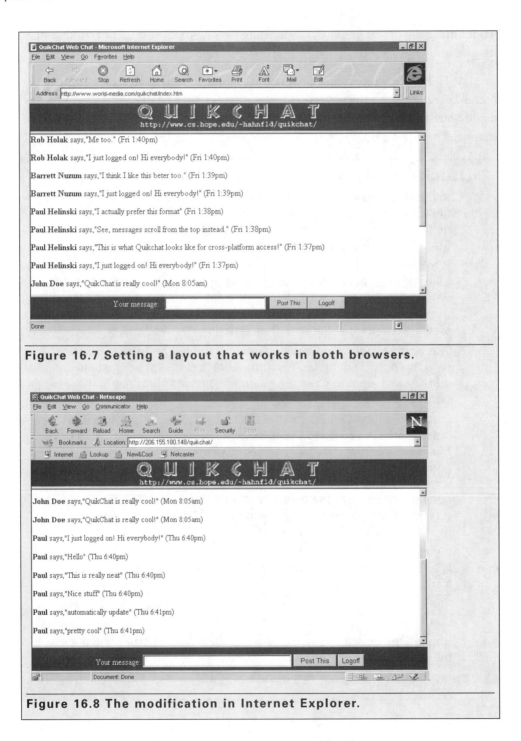

Figure 16.7 Setting a layout that works in both browsers.

Figure 16.8 The modification in Internet Explorer.

9. Then enable messages.htm to be written as the webserver with CHMOD 666 message.htm.

10. Hit index.htm with your web browser. You should get a screen like Figure 16.7, except you will be asked to log in from the bottom frame, and the screen will be all "John Doe says…" lines. Try posting some chat messages and see how quick QuikChat really is. Figure 16.8 is how it will look with the IE option set to 0.

Quick Start: NT

1. The first thing you'll do is create a directory under your main called something other than "chat." As I explained, either Internet Information Server or NT defaults them as password protected, at least in our tests.

2. You'll find the zipfile in /sourcecode/NT/quickchat/ on the CD called quikchat.zip. Unzip it and upload it to the directory you just created.

3. Open quikchat.cgi in your editor. Scroll down to where Matt lists the $filepath variable. If quikchat.cgi will be in a different directory than your .htm files, you'll want to put the full path from the webserver's root here. Make sure to follow it with a slash like Matt's example of $filepath='/home/hahnfld/public_html/';.

4. The next variable is how you want your default room documents to be referenced. The default is .htm, but if the rest of your site is .html, you'll want to change this. In the customization we'll make a new HTML file for each room.

5. I tested the next variable, and it's actually a crucial component to cross-platform access to QuikChat. It determines whether users on Microsoft Internet Explorer can see new messages as they are entered into QuikChat. New messages will appear at the top of the screen if you set $iecompatable=1;. This is because IE doesn't appear to recognize the #END in assigning a <FRAMESET>. Leave this variable as 0, and IE users will not think your room works. The top of the middle frame never changes.

6. If you do set the IE option to 1, go into index.htm and remove the #END from the frame target or new messages won't show on Netscape. Figure 16.7 will be the result.

7. Hit index.htm with your web browser. You should get a screen like Figure 16.8, except you will be asked to log in from the bottom frame, and the screen will be all "John Doe says…" lines. Try posting some chat messages and see how quick QuikChat really is. Figure 16.8 is how it will look with the IE option set to 0.

Multiple Rooms

If you open form.htm in your editor, you'll see the hidden variable "rooms" shown in the top of Figure 16.9 The default name is messages, as in messages.htm, the dummy chat room file you uploaded in the distribution. The first step to adding a room is copying messages.htm to another file called *yourroom*.htm, then change the hidden room variable to *yourroom*, exactly as you called the file. If your chat is about CGI programming, call the file cgi.htm and change the variable to cgi. Then save the form file as formcgi.htm or something similar. If you're on Unix you'll need to CHMOD the cgi.htm file to 666.

Open index.htm in your editor, shown in the bottom of Figure 16.9, and change the middle frame target to *yourroom*.htm. Note that the #END is still in there. You'll remove that as I explained previously. Then change the bottom frame target to formcgi.htm or whatever you called it. If you want a new header file for each room, open top.htm in your editor, change it and save it as topcgi.htm, then set the top frame target in index.htm to topcgi.htm.

Then you'll save index.htm as indexcgi.htm or something similar. What you've done with all of this is create a new room, accessible from the URL indexcgi.htm, that still uses the same quikchat.cgi program for its processing as the original messages.htm room. Do this for each of your boards, then make an interim link page listing each index*topic*.htm as the homepage for each room. You'll have to decide, however, whether to set the IE option to 1 or 0 for all rooms.

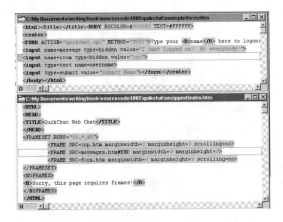

Figure 16.9 Adding extra rooms.

On the Web Take a look at www.world-media.com/quikchat/ indexcgi.htm for the files we just worked on. You'll be able to view source on each frame by right clicking in the frame from Netscape 2.x and above and Microsoft Internet Explorer 3.0 and above. I can't promise that anyone will be in the room, but feel free to copy the files and use them. Remember, quikchat.cgi is never changed for multiple rooms, so everything you need will be there.

Customizing the Look

You're probably wondering what's with the John Doe says... lines. We were told by the author Matt Hahnfield, that certain versions of Netscape break with less than fourteen lines of content in that middle frame, called messages.htm. We couldn't create the bug with our versions (3.0+), so it must affect some of the 2.x releases that had a few bugs with refreshing screens. Matt also asks that we not distribute any improved versions as he is the official support for QuikChat and it's impossible for him to keep track of other people's code. He did allow us to insert some modifications for cross-platform access on Internet Information Server and its ISAPI Perl interface. QuikChat was developed on NT, but using the old perl.exe method of invoking the program through batch files.

Changing the look and feel of QuikChat is pretty easy. Just modify the top, *yourname*.htm, and form.htm with standard HTML, including colors. Note that Matt keeps a copyright notice on the messages.htm file that prints the same white as the page in the distribution copy. As far as I know, you are required to keep all his notices intact, so I'd leave that in, as well as the ones in quikchat.cgi. And please don't redistribute the original or any modified copy. We had to get special permission for the book.

Could you modify QuikChat to be wrapped with SiteWrapper, so you didn't have to change the header, button-bar, and colors manually every time your site changed? Yes, just include sitewrapper.pl with a require line and add in the print-header functions as you've seen in so many of our other utilities. I'll respect Matt's wishes and not distribute one with the modifications already done. He was very nice to allow me to share his neat little utility with you. Please drop him a line if you find it useful and install it on your site. He's at sysop@cyberservices.com.

Search Engine
Agents

Every time a potential client asks how we can guarantee their place in a search engine, I wince. They are the most unpredictable arena of the Internet. Some are great; you give them a URL, they spider it and extract your key words from either the body text or a META tag. Others, like Yahoo!, are equally as effective, but take more work because you manually have to specify your keywords, a brief description, and the categories in which you belong. But others, I won't mention Webcrawler in particular (oops), have taken up to five repeated submissions before registering a page. Then, for all of them, guaranteeing placement is impossible unless you pay.

This chapter is devoted to making some sense of the mess. First we'll look at the niftiest piece of shareware I've ever come across (that's why I put it first). It's called the Web Promotion Spider by Millennium Software. You put in all the information about your URL, and it submits you to hundreds of engines and directories automatically.

Next we'll continue on the engine path with a program in Perl we built called Whereami?. It spiders the search engines for your keywords and reports back to you in e-mail that you're on "page 2 of Altavista, page 3 of Excite" etc. Whereami? won't run on NT as of this writing, but should with the next release of Perl for Win32, due out from Activewear about the same time as this book.

After Whereami? is yet another search engine checker that is not server-based. It's a Windows 95/NT custom client that spiders the engines and reports back to you in detailed HTML reports. The trial version was a bit buggy on my machine, but it's worth a look at their website for the newest version. For an IT manager who needs solid accountability, the registration price is well worth it.

Web Promotion Spider: Windows 95/NT

As I said in the opening, this piece of shareware was too good not to include in the book. At present they are submitting you to over 300 engines, and though I discourage this for the major ten engines or so, it never hurts to get some exposure where the stray visitor might find you. It also includes some international options, which I found useful as some of our clients have a large international following and client base.

As with any shareware program, you might want to download pages at beherenow.com/spider/download.htm for a new version. They release an upgrade every two or three weeks to keep up with the changes in the search engines. The file is usually only about 450k, a worthy download. Installing and running the Spider was flawless. The website offers several methods of payment for the $49.95 registration fee. My install instructions might differ from your interface as I'm going to download the newest one just before my deadline for the CD contents, but the functionality should be the same and the menus shouldn't differ too much.

> ## Quick Start: Unix/NT
>
> 1. The current release as I write this is 3.8.29. You should be able to install from the file in the /sourcecode/ directory. The file is wps3829.exe and just over 2.2 megabytes. It will guide you through the setup, then run the program.
> 2. You'll be presented with a screen of tab markers with Description as the checked tab. If it's not, check it, then fill in the required fields. As you'll see in the next step (and in Figure 17.1), we've put the site mas-jobs.com into the informational fields (an early client).
> 3. Click the keywords tab. As you can see, it asks you to provide the name of your organization and six key words. Duplicate the name of your business for the first one or two (you are allowed two word phrases in the six), and use the rest to provide words under which people might search for you.

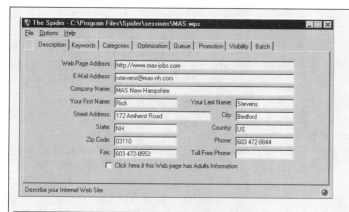

Figure 17.1 Starting with the Spider.

4. In the website description box, put a small blurb about your site. It limits the number of characters you can use, so be concise. Keep in mind that your task is to include as many keywords as possible. You can see from Figure 17.2 that it should read more like a classified ad than a true site description.

5. Your next tab is Categories. This is for the several search engines that require submissions into specific areas of their list. Go through each one and see what fits. Sometimes you'll have to compromise and pick a category that doesn't quite fit you. That's why they almost all default to "business," because just about everyone is that.

6. The top half of the next tab is pretty sneaky. It allows you to make several copies of your homepage, like index1.htm, index2.htm and so on, then it registers each one so you have several chances to be found on all the engines. I don't recommend this, but to use it you must first download a copy of your homepage, load it, make the

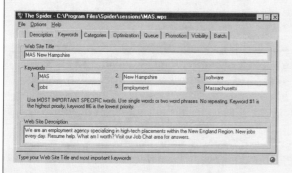

Figure 17.2 Your site description.

duplicates, and upload them. The spider takes care of the rest if you check the Generated Pages under the promotion tab.

TIP Don't rely on the spider for Yahoo!. As I write this there are 20,000 categories in the directory and the number is growing every day. You'll need to list in several of your industry pages as well as state and local directories. The best way I found is to go to Yahoo! and search, first under the keywords for your industry, then for your town, state, and any organization you belong to. Record every category where you find a related link and "Add URL" for that category. Yahoo! lets you submit more than one, but misspelling them is easy as they use underscores, caps, and lowercase in all the URLs. I keep a notepad window up and cut and paste all the categories I find into it, then copy and paste that list, stacked one on top of another, into the Yahoo! form field.

---

7. The bottom half is more legitimate. It's called Deep Promotion and allows you to register more than one page on your site at a time. To build the list first click the red plus sign on the left. That will pop up a box that says Add links for Deep promotion. It gives you three options. The first is blah. You manually specify pages on the web. The second is probably best when the spider is running on the server itself. You browse directories and link up every page. The third is the granddaddy of the three. It allows you to specify a homepage and extract links from it for deep promotion of every page. You can specify levels as well, so every link from the homepage can also be scanned for, then spidered for its own links, then every page hence. Neat stuff. You can then go back and remove them with the arrows and paint brush on the right-hand side.

8. For the next tab, Queue, I clicked the Select All button then unselected those that didn't fit. It automatically doesn't select adult sites (unless you checked that box) and some others that you will manually want to check if you are an educational, arts, or other special interest site. In Figure 17.3, you'll see the hidden function of the Select button. It allows you to pick by type of directory or to select all those you have not registered to yet. This is helpful when you upgrade the software, which occurs every two weeks or so. As new engines are added, you can select only the new ones.

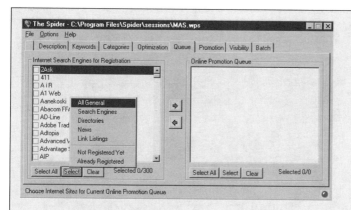

Figure 17.3 The select button's hidden features.

9. After you check all those that apply, make sure you click the right button in the middle to send them into the actual queue window. Checking them is only the first step. In the right-hand box are the same controls to select by category or those you have or haven't done yet. Left-click on the Select button to bring them up.

10. The promotion tab is your final step for registering one individual site. If you did the Generated Pages or Deep Promotion, check their boxes. After the process runs, you'll use the Show Registration Report button. When you upgrade the engines and run a second insertion into new engines, you'll use Erase Online Registration Data. Click the Run Online Registration and you're off. As you can see, it keeps you apprised of its progress, showing successes and failures. One point I should mention is that the top Total Search Engines for Registration is not the number of engines you selected. It's the total number available. You selected the total number in queue.

11. The next tab is not as useful as the utility we'll cover later. It's used to check the spider's work and pops up a mini window of the search engine you are checking. In Figure 17.4, you can see the Yahoo! window within the spider. It is an active browser window, so the "next 10" and other navigation works within it.

12. If you have to register multiple clients at a time, the tab will allow you to batch several jobs and let them run overnight. To use it, don't click the Run Online Registration button under the promotion tab. Instead go to the File menu and Save As whatever that clientsnameis.wps. Then under the batch tab, click the plus button for each file, then Run Session Batch. Left overnight, this will register them all at once.

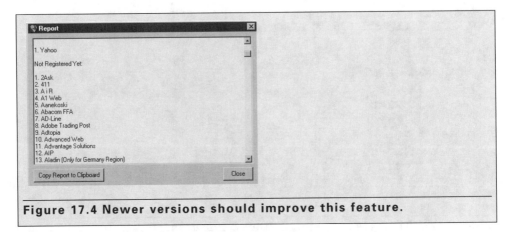

Figure 17.4 Newer versions should improve this feature.

Whereami? Unix Only (maybe)

Though the Spider includes a view function to check your status on the search engines, using it is as exciting as watching paint fade. Check URLs for search engine status a month after is a waste of time, so we automated it with a server-based CGI utility called Whereami?, shown in Figure 17.5.

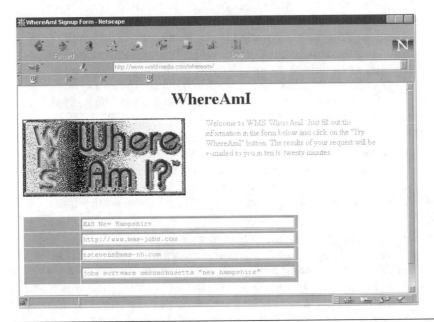

Figure 17.5 The Whereami? screen.

Whereami? started with a column by Randall Schwartz in *Webtechniques* magazine. He offered a way to hit a search engine and extract several of the results pages in succession, not just the first. In a browser, you're forced to click Next, Next, Next, looking through pages of nonsense for that one document that might actually match your query (heaven forbid). We took his idea one step further and parsed the output, searching the pages for the URL specified in Whereami?'s keywords field.

At first we tried popping this into a browser once the search completed, but it didn't work. The browser and server would both time out. E-mail seemed the answer, and that's how the results are sent today. Whereami? uses two programs, one to initiate the request and bounce back a thanks page, the other to spider the engines and send the e-mail. I'll take you through the basic setup, then look through some of the code to help you understand how it works. That way you'll be able to embrace and extend Whereami? to your needs. We plan to include a feature that resubmits you to the engines in the next release if it doesn't find you.

Unfortunately, as of the writing of this chapter, Whereami? will work only on Unix due to the sockets problem with NT described in the Tickler chapter. A fix is due out about the same time as this book, so be sure to check the book website for an update. The NT Quick Start would follow the Unix except for the CHMOD of files.

Quick Start: Unix

1. Unzip the archive in /sourcecode/UNIX/whereami on the CD. There is also an unzipped directory.

2. Bring up whereami.cgi and spider.cgi in your editor and check the Perl location. Make sure it matches your system. If you're unsure of the location for your system, ask your system administrator or type which perl at your shell prompt.

3. In spider.cgi, change the $sendmail_location variable to the location on your system.

4. Make a directory on your webserver called whereami/. Change its permissions to readable, writeable, and executable with CHMOD 777.

5. Then upload all the files in the Whereami? distribution to the webserver. If you have shell access to the server, include in your upload the file wwwmods.tgz. It's the entire library of Perl modules in the World Wide Web distribution. Type gunzip wwwmods.tgz then tar -xvf wwwmods.tgz at the prompt, untarring the archive into its directory structure.

6. If you have only FTP access, not shell, you'll have to go into the www-library on the CD. Into your main Whereami? directory, upload the two files you'll see there called LWP.pm and lwpcook.pod. Then make directories on the webserver for all of the directories you see there, beginning with auto, File, Font, etc. Change directories to auto in your FTP program on both the sides of your machine and the remote server. On your side, you'll see two new directories, LWP and URI. Make those on the server, then change directories on both sides to LWP. Again, you'll see two directories on your side, IO and UserAgent. Again, make those on the server side, then change directories on both sides to IO, where you'll see three files. Upload them to the webserver, then change your directories on both machines back down to LWP, from which you'll again see IO and UserAgent. Change directories on both sides to User-Agent and upload all its nine files to the webserver. Then change directories back down to LWP on both machines, and back down to auto. Everything in LWP is up there in the correct directory structure. Change to URI, from which you'll see one directory called URL. Make that on the server, then change directories to URL on both sides. On your side, you'll see three directories under URL called _generic, file, and http. Make directories for the three on the server, then change directories on both sides to _generic. Upload its files, then change directories back down to URL. Change directories to both file and http on both sides and upload their contents, then change directories back down to URI, then back down to auto, then back down to the main. Repeat what we just did for the remaining File, Font, HTML, and all the others. It's time consuming but there is no other choice if you only are allowed FTP.

Figure 17.6 E-mail from Whereami?

7. Whew! Now make the CGIs executable with CHMOD 755 whereami.cgi and CHMOD 755 spider.cgi. Then hit the directory with your browser, plug your information in, and click the Submit button. You should get an e-mail like Figure 17.6, but probably not with as good results. We're pretty good at using SiteWrapper to customize homepages for the various search engines.

T I P ActiveWare has posted a new copy of Perl to their website at www.activeware.com. We haven't had the time to test it, but Whereami? should work fine on NT with this latest patch. Use the sendmail.pl instructions from the Tickler chapter and replace the send-mail line with the sendmail subroutine in Whereami?'s code.

Customizing Whereami?

Besides the obvious alterations you'll want to make to index.html, thanks.html, and busy.html (which is used only when two people use Whereami? at the same time), the rest of Whereami? is highly customizable. We begin at line 14 with the HTTP_USER_AGENT sent to the engines:

```
14: $ua->agent("whereami/$VERSION (World Media Services)");
```

If you remember the Trakkit chapter, every piece of software that hits a website sends a user agent variable. The default here is whereami/0.9b (World Media Services). Yours can be 'Hello Mr. Search Engine' if you like. Just put it between the quotes.

At line 40, you'll find where we begin the e-mail message:

```
40:     print <<END;

41: From: whereami\@world-media.com

42: Subject: Search Engine Verification

43: To: $email

44: \n

45: END

46:     print "Here is a list of which search engines\n";
```

```
47:      print "contain references to your site and what\n";

48:      print "page it is listed on when looking for the\n";

49:      print "following keywords: ";

50:      $query =~ s/\+/ /g;

51:      print "$query\n\n";

52:      print @finds;

53:      close(MAIL);

54:      select(STDOUT);

55: }
```

The From: and Subject: should be changed to match your name and location.
Otherwise we'll be getting replies from all these things, which is bad. From 46 to
49 is a whole bunch of small print lines. You could replace them all with a here
document, just make sure to keep the variable query in at line 50.

Whereami?'s Log File

We've saved only the company, e-mail, and domain name in Whereami?'s log files.
The code to modify this is in whereami.cgi at line 39:

```
39: format LOGFILE =

40: @<<<<<<< @<<<<    @<<<<<<<<<<<<<<<<<<<<<<<<<<

@<<<<<<<<<<<<<<<<<<<<<<<<<<

41: $date,   $time,  $company,                          $email

42:

@<<<<<<<<<<<<<<<<<<<<<<<<<<<<<<<<<<<<<<<<<<<<<<<<<<<<<<<<

43:              $sitename
```

After learning a bit about Perl's format routines, you can alter it to print as you
wish. The other variable you may access besides $date, $time, $company, $email,
and $sitename is $query if you want to store their keywords.

A Windows Alternative to Whereami?

I found this piece of software right before the book deadline but, like the spider earlier, it was too useful to pass up. It's like Whereami? in that it searches the search engines for you, but beyond Whereami? it also allows you to track and update sessions, then save the results as HTML. If you have no access to a Unix machine, this program will give the benefits of Whereami? with an interface and results you will probably prefer. For those of us servicing clients and trying to lead people to our little tents in the desert, it's a useful tool. It's called WebPosition Agent by Innovative Solutions and Technologies at www.webposition.com.

   The demo you'll find on the CD is time limited and allows you only to check on three engines. I would go to their site and get the newest version as this one had a couple of bugs as I'll describe later. To register, there's a $99 personal version that gives you one domain name and only a few of the several analysis functions, plus it limits you to six keywords. Then there's a standard edition for $189. It gives you two domain names and unlimited keywords, plus all the pro features. The $289 pro allows up to ten domains. I tested the pro and it ran flawlessly, even checking their website automatically for updates to the software. All three offer free maintenance updates and lifetime support. There is also a 15 percent referral program if you want to point people there from your site (no, I didn't sign up!).

Quick Start: Windows 95/NT

1. This, again, is a Windows-based client, so installing it only takes using your Run from the Start menu and executing it from the CD. It's in the /software directory as wpsetup.exe. The auto-installer will guide you through setup.

2. Run the program and select New, which will pop up a five-tabbed mission box. Under tab 1, name your Mission and give it a URL. The URL manager will be useful only for the pro as the personal edition allows only one domain name.

3. Hit the Search tab. On the left, you'll find a box for your keywords. I thought at first that you had to type one on each line. This, I found, returned no results for my client's page. What the instructions don't tell you is that you can put multiple words on one line, as someone might search at the engines. In Figure 17.7, I included only one search with several terms. And though it looks like I have the quoted words "New Hampshire" on two lines, I did not press my ENTER

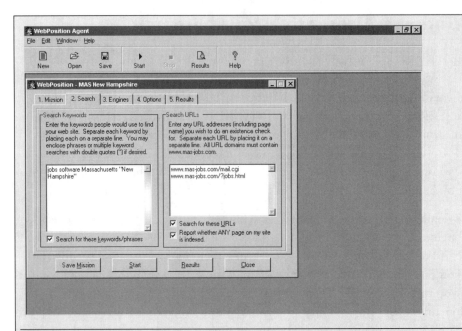

Figure 17.7 Here I've done one search with several terms.

button, so it included it all in one query in my results. Note that you do have to put quotes (á la Altavista's advanced query) around words that should be together. The right box is a bit like the spider's deep promotion. It allows you to check leaf pages on your site at the same time as the main one.

4. Click the Engines tab. The top three will be highlighted. That's all you're allowed for the trial. Ours had the top ten included. I selected only the top two in my demo.

5. The next tab is Options. As you can see from Figure 17.8, I upped the first value to 100. It's the number of search engine result URLs to scan. So when we go to Altavista, it will keep going through the Next pages until we get to the first 100 matches. If my URL isn't there by then, it will give up. The default is 30, which I thought was low. I often scroll through up to ten pages when I go to a search engine. I upped the Search engine time out—a minute isn't uncommon. And because I left this to munge overnight, I upped the simultaneous searches from 5 to 10. Bandwidth isn't a consideration, even at 28.8, when I'm sleeping. This didn't work great as I was warned by the program that I might not want to up the number from 5 due to system constraints. Unless you're on a P166+ and 56K, you might

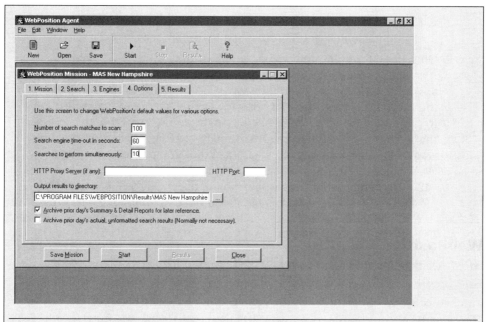

Figure 17.8 The Options tab.

want to leave it at 5, even while sleeping or doing something else at midnight that might distract you from browsing the web. The rest of the Options tab can pretty much stay the same unless you're on a proxy. Then you'll want to get the machine's name and port.

6. I should have remembered what the Results tab let you do before unlocking the trial version, but my registered pro version gives me all four summaries at the bottom. We'll look at them all, so even if yours doesn't you'll see the results. The other boxes, right below the results menu, are important. They ask you how many times to try an engine that's not responding and how often.

7. When I hit Start, I hit a bug. The program wouldn't let me put in URLs with a question mark in them. But I found a way around it by eliminating the http from the front. If you want to check other pages at your site at the same time as the homepage, start their URLs with a plain www or whatever yours starts with. You might want to check the WebPosition site for a newer version that corrects this before installing the one on the CD, especially if you're using SiteWrapper.

8. Once you are through these quirks, the start menu pops up a box asking if you'd like to create the results directory you just named (or left as the default like I did). Then it will ask you if you'd like to save

the mission settings before starting. Then it will run, automatically updating its search engine database in the process.

9. On second thought, don't up the number of simultaneous searches—it crashed it. I moved it back to 5 and it worked fine. My search only took about 40 minutes, but then when I came back to the computer the program had all kinds of error messages for me to wade through to get my results. The WebPosition analyzed my error log and found that I had too many applications running at once. My virtual memory was used up. For this reason I suggest that you do not run WebPosition with Microsoft Binder, Multi-Edit, Paint Shop Pro, WS_FTP, WinZip, and Netscape running, especially while you're playing a CD on your notebook, even if you have 32 megabytes of RAM.

WebPosition Results

After the spidering process, you'll be asked if you'd like to view the results in your browser. Click yes and Netscape, Microsoft Internet Explorer will launch automatically. Scroll down; with the pro version you'll get Figure 17.9. The first choice is the concise summary shown in Figure 17.10, which is for only Altavista. I changed my search words for this mission so my rank from the last time is not

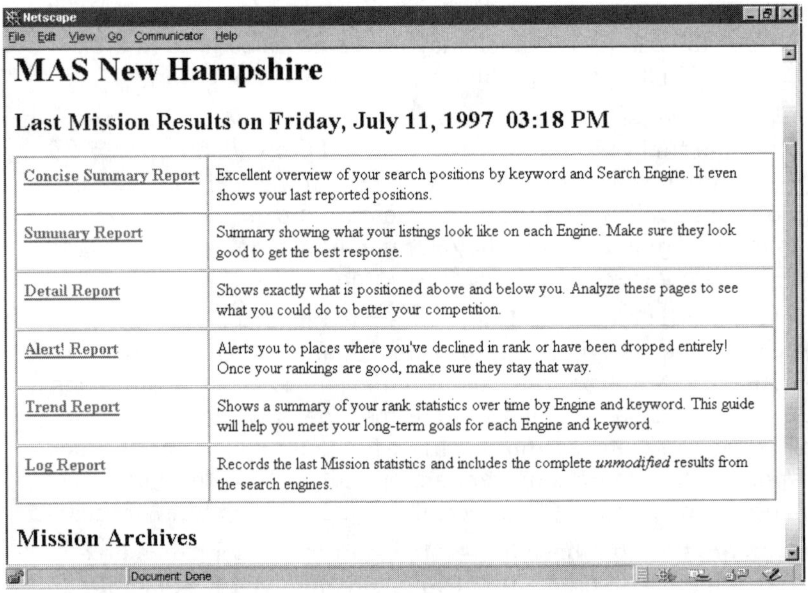

Figure 17.9 The pro results screen.

AltaVista					
jobs software Massachusetts "New Hampshire"	9	1	NA	NA	www.mas-jobs.com/homepag2.htm

Figure 17.10 Concise is one option of summary data.

shown. Notice that it was one of the Web Promotion Spider's alternate homepages that it found, not the MAS real homepage.

The second report is a summary of all the pages you have indexed on each of your search engines. WebPosition feeds each search engine your URL and reports back for how many pages each engine has you deep promoted and shows you the actual entries extracted from their pages. This feature actually seemed a bit buggy. It reported that MAS was found 19 times on Altavista but only showed me two of the pages.

The detail report is really neat. It exactly duplicates the pages from the search engines with all the listings before and below you for the entire number you selected on Options tab, 100 in my case. It marked my listing with a red Position 9, Page 1, and gave me links to everyone else. Now I can analyze and see what they did to beat us.

Because I changed my keywords my alert report was blank, but presumably it will give you a delta of only where you dropped in rank since the last time you ran the program. I'd like to see this expanded to include a quick delta of positive changes since last week as well. It's set up just like Figure 17.9.

The trend report is much the same, but in a macro-analysis. It stacks a list of date, position, page, and URL one on top of the other for each query on each engine. Over the course of a year, this could be useful to create a graph of your enhancements in comparison to the search results.

In the log report I found another bug. It gives you a record of the mission particulars along with the raw data from each engine; for me, the top 100 hits. WebPosition failed to report anything from Excite in my other reports. I had figured that the search engine request had failed. We had experienced difficulties with Whereami? that day. But in the raw data were the actual results from MAS, and they were listed first. Again, go to the site and get the newest version. I'm going to include the latest on the CD, of which I'm told a new one is coming in this week, but you might want to check anyway. WebPosition will update itself automatically when you run a mission, but I don't know if it will update patches.

Tracking
Banner Ads

Whittingham the first advertisements appeared, we all wondered if the Internet was dead. It was in fact, as we knew it, but most have perceived the change as good. Money has flown into the industry like no one ever imagined it could. The Internet has transformed from a geeky virtualsphere to an international information revolution.

The hard truth, as most of us old web geeks have to admit, is that quality content takes a budget. Whether from government grants and educational institutions like the old days or with revenue from the banner ads of today, writers, editors, and site administration staff have to get paid. And crucial to that payment is the ability to bill for either *page views* or *click-throughs*. In this chapter we'll log and track both.

We've narrowed page views down a bit to favor the advertisers. The utility we'll install here is called BannerLog. It tracks not the page view itself, but the actual image view, not incrementing for visitors with their images off, those using Lynx, the text-only browser, and those using a banner ad filtering software. The strength of this utility is in its ability to track the same banner over multiple pages, then give you a breakdown of not only total hits, but from which pages people most loaded the image.

Click-throughs are a bit simpler. You've seen utilities like our second utility, ClickThru, all over the web. It's a simple redirect that logs the hits and referring pages just as BannerLog. Each banner has its own click-through log file, so you can bill by www address. It assumes, of course, that the same banner always points to the same URL. Many companies, Proctor & Gamble the biggest, are refusing to pay for page views. They demand click-throughs. This utility gives them a complete rundown on the total numbers, hits by day, and page referrers. They'll be able to tell what's working and what's not, and you'll be able to bill them for your screen real estate.

This chapter is very short, but I thought it a crime not to include it. The utilities are easy, the saving of company administration great, and the income potential through the roof. After the Quick Starts, we'll cover one customization feature meant for the security of your logs.

BannerLog and ClickThru

This is about as simple as you can get in the world of CGI programs. It's only 53 lines. First it listens for the referring page, puts its attributes in a log file, and prints the HTTP header, then the image. You do have to modify the HTML, but that's part of the Quick Start.

Quick Start: Unix

1. From the files in the /sourcecode/UNIX/adtrakkit directory, open bannerlog.cgi in your editor and check the Perl location. If you don't know the location, type which perl at the shell prompt. If it returns a location, type perl -v to verify that it's Perl 5.003 or better. If it returns version 4.036, type which perl5 and the same -v. If all that fails or if you don't have shell access to begin with, ask your system administrator. Open clickthru.cgi and check the location in that, then upload both to the server.

2. CHMOD the permissions to 755 on both bannerlog.cgi and clickthru.cgi to make them executable by the web server.

3. In Figure 18.1, I've put a banner ad for this book on the Henry's homepage. The HTML for the image tag is <A HREF="clickthru.cgi? page=index.cgi&image=banner2.gif&redir=http://www.world-media.com/webtoolkit"><IMG BORDER=0 SRC="bannerlog.cgi? banner2.gif"></A>. The first part is the HREF, pointed to clickthru.cgi, with the variable page sent with the page name, the variable image sent with the image name, and the redir sent with the full URL of the redirect location. Make sure to keep the syntax exactly like it is, with no spaces and the ampersand character separating the form variables. The second part is the actual image SRC tag. Rather than it pointing to the actual image, it is set to bannerlog.cgi?imagename.gif. This can as easily be a .jpg, but again, keep the syntax the same.

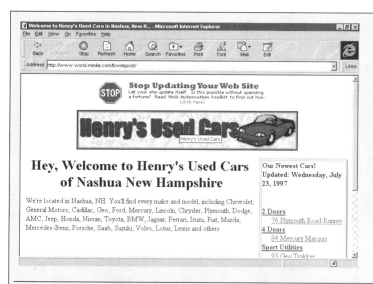

Figure 18.1 A sample banner ad on Henry's.

4. Then, before loading the page, make a directory called adlogs on your server. Set its permissions to 777, writeable by the server, then load the page. A file called monthyear.imagename.gif.log should increment. Click on it and a monthyear.clickthru-imagename.gif.log should increment. Now we'll install the analysis program.

Quick Start: NT

1. From the files in the /sourcecode/NT/adtrakkit directory, upload the files bannerlog.cgi and clickthru.cgi to the webserver.

2. In Figure 18.1, I've put a banner ad for this book on the Henry's homepage. The HTML for the image tag is <A HREF="clickthru.cgi ?page=index.cgi&image=banner2.gif&redir=http://www.world-media.com/webtoolkit"><IMG BORDER=0 SRC="bannerlog.cgi?banner2.gif"></A>. The first part is the HREF, pointed to clickthru.cgi, with the variable page sent with the page name, the variable image sent with the image name, and the redir sent with the full URL of the redirect location. Make sure to keep the syntax exactly like it is, with no spaces and the ampersand character separating the form variables. The second part is the actual image SRC tag. Rather than it pointing to the actual image, it is set to bannerlog.cgi?imagename .gif. This can as easily be a .jpg, but again, keep the syntax the same.

3. Then, before loading the page, make a directory called adlogs on your server, and load the page with the image. A file called monthyear.imagename.gif.log should increment. Click on it and a monthyear.clickthru-imagename.gif.log should increment. Now we'll install the analysis program.

AdTrakkit

If you set up Trakkit in Chapter 9, this should be mostly repetitive. This is a customized version for billing ad banners, so we've eliminated all of the IP and browser information. If you need quick reports, as well as a percentage of hits to click-though, AdTrakkit is a nicely streamlined version. The full Trakkit, FYI, does work as well.

Quick Start: Unix

1. In that same /adtrakkit directory is the file adtrakkit.cgi. Open that in your editor and check the Perl location as you did previously.

2. Point the require "webpost.cfg" line to the name of your SiteWrapper or WebPost config file. If you're using neither, make a file called webpost.cfg or whatever you put in the require line with three lines, the first is #!/usr/bin/perl5 or wherever your Perl location, the second will say $adtrakkitpassword="asgdjhcv.z.ce48";, where the garble generated by Encrypt.cgi is what's between the parenthesis. And the third line should be two characters—1;—and that's it. If you have a config, add the $adtrakkitpassword line, generating new code with Encrypt or just set it equal to $password. If you don't have an Encrypt password, put Encrypt.cgi on the server, set it to CHMOD 755, then hit it with your web browser. Plug in your password, and it will generate the garble you need between the parenthesis. Don't ever put a real word as $adtrakkitpassword. Only the garble works.

3. Then upload adtrakkit.cgi and CHMOD it to 755 making it executable. Hit it with your web browser, plug in your password, and select your

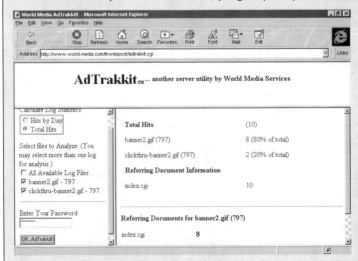

Figure 18.2 The banner version of trakkit.

files like in Figure 18.2. I've selected total hits and both the banner and click-through logs. The Total isn't useful here, but it would have been if I had selected two banners belonging to the same billing party. Below Total is a breakdown for each, which shows me that for every eight people who loaded the page, two clicked my banner. Below that is a total breakout of referring page, again for multiple banners attributed to one billing party, then a page-by-page breakout for each file.

Quick Start: NT

1. In that same /adtrakkit directory is the file adtrakkit.cgi. Change the require "webpost.cfg" line to the name of your SiteWrapper or WebPost config file. If you're using neither, make a file called web-post.cfg or whatever you put in the require line with three lines, the first is #!/usr/bin/perl5 or wherever your Perl location, the second will say $adtrakkitpassword="asgdjhcv.z.ce48";, where the garble generated by Encrypt.cgi is what's between the parenthesis. And the third line should be two characters—1;—and that's it. If you have a config, add the $adtrakkitpassword line, generating new code with Encrypt, or just set it equal to $password. If you don't have an Encrypt password, put Encrypt.cgi on the server and hit it with your web browser. Plug in your password and it will generate the garble you need between the parenthesis. Don't ever put a real word as $adtrakkitpassword. Only the garble works.

2. Upload adtrakkit.cgi and hit it with your web browser, plug in your password, and select your files like in Figure 18.2. I've selected total hits and both the banner and click-through logs. The Total isn't useful here, but it would have been if I had selected two banners belonging to the same billing party. Below Total is a breakdown for each, which shows me that for every eight people who loaded the page, two clicked my banner. Below that is a total breakout of referring page, again for multiple banners attributed to one billing party, then a page-by-page breakout for each file.

More Secure Log Files

There's not much about AdTrakkit that you'll need to change, but one is that you might not want to store your logs in such a public place as the adlogs directory. Anyone reading this book could hit the directory and download your files, then run their own AdTrakkit to decode your numbers. To change the location we'll first go into bannerlog.cgi at line 35 where we open the file:

```
35: open(LOGFILE, ">> adlogs/$tempmon$year.$true_img.log");
```

```
36: print (LOGFILE
```

```
"$date\t$ENV{'REMOTE_HOST'}\t$in{'page'}\t$ENV{'HTTP_USER_AGENT'}\n");
```

```
37: close(LOGFILE);
```

Change just the directory name on line 35, not the $tempmon... format. One thing we've found useful is to make a directory for each client and call separate copies of bannerlog.cgi and clickthru.cgi, with both of them pointed to that client's directory. In ClickThru it's at line 25:

```
25:       open(LOGFILE, ">> adlogs/$tempmon$year.clickthru-$in{'image'}.log");
```

```
26:       print (LOGFILE
```

```
"$date\t$ENV{'REMOTE_HOST'}\t$in{'page'}\t$ENV{'HTTP_USER_AGENT'}\n");
```

```
27:       close(LOGFILE);
```

Again you'll change the same code. Make sure that you make the directory stated on 35 and 25, and on Unix, CHMOD it 777. The last is in AdTrakkit itself at lines 14 and 225:

```
14: opendir(LOGDIR, "adlogs");
```

```
15: @files_in_logs = sort grep(/(.*)\.(.*)\.(.*)\.log/, readdir(LOGDIR));
```

```
16: closedir(LOGDIR);
```

```
   .


   .
```

```
225:          open(TEMPFILE, "adlogs/$file");
```

```
226:          $/ = "\n";
```

```
227:          @temp_array_of_records = <TEMPFILE>;
```

```
228:          $records{$file} = [ @temp_array_of_records ];
```

```
229:          close(TEMPFILE);
```

Change both of the lines to your directory. In the case I mentioned earlier, where you've made separate copies of the two logging CGIs for each client logging to their separate directories, you'll want to install a separate copy of adtrakkit.cgi for each of them. Put it in the log directory itself and change 14 and 225 to ".", the current directory.

CareWare
Causes

In some articles I wrote for *WebTechniques* magazine, we experimented with the idea of replacing freeware with *CareWare*. It met with some enthusiasm so I decided to take it forward into this book. Officially, the software license with all of the utilities we've written is included with the purchase of the book. You may use them yourself as many times and for as many projects or clients as you wish. World Media Service holds the full copyright to the sourcecode and we are the sole owners. I am the owner. I state this because for the magazines, an MIS manager thought the whole CareWare concept ambiguous and refused his webmaster permission to use SiteWrapper (costing his company thousands in the process). Again, officially, the software license is included with the purchase of this book. Donating to the causes below is voluntary. Our thanks if you do, and please let us know if you can.

> **Nobody's Children** provides shelter and medical support to both U.S. and international orphans. This past year they have supported several refugee camps in Bosnia and flown several Bosnian children to Boston for medical treatment.

Nobody's Children

P.O. Box 1076

Windham, NH 03087

603.893.0925

Circle of Children services the Pine Ridge Reservation in South Dakota. They match American sponsors with Indian children in need of support. Unlike many sponsor programs, however, Circle of Children allows direct contact with the families themselves. You send packages to the family, not to Circle of Children. Sponsors pay only a nominal administrative fee. Your donations will also help cover administrative expenses and allow expansion of their winter blanket drive and Christmas visit.

Circle of Children

809 South Street

Roslindale, MA 02131

As you've no-doubt noticed elsewhere in the book, I live in New Hampshire. If you do (or don't) and would like to help out the people who do, there are quite a few who could use your help. There are poor and hungry in every state, so feel free to choose the one in which you live. These types of organizations are everywhere if you look for them.

New Hampshire Fuel Assistance

P.O. Box 3804

Manchester, NH 03105-3804

Nashua Soup Kitchen & Shelter

42 Chestnut Street

Nashua, NH 03060

Index